HEIDEGGER'S CONFESSIONS

RELIGION AND POSTMODERNISM
A series edited by Thomas A. Carlson

RECENT BOOKS IN THE SERIES

Arts of Wonder: Enchanting Secularity—Walter De Maria, Diller + Scofidio, James Turrell, Andy Goldsworthy, by Jeffrey L. Kosky (2012)

God without Being: Hors-Texte, Second Edition, by Jean-Luc Marion (2012)

Secularism in Antebellum America, by John Lardas Modern (2011)

The Figural Jew: Politics and Identity in Postwar French Thought, by Sarah Hammerschlag (2010)

The Indiscrete Image: Infinitude and Creation of the Human, by Thomas A. Carlson (2008)

HEIDEGGER'S CONFESSIONS

The Remains of Saint Augustine in
Being and Time and Beyond

RYAN COYNE

THE UNIVERSITY OF CHICAGO PRESS
CHICAGO AND LONDON

The University of Chicago Press, Chicago 60637
The University of Chicago Press, Ltd., London
© 2015 by The University of Chicago
All rights reserved. Published 2015.
Paperback edition 2016
Printed in the United States of America

25 24 23 22 21 20 19 18 17 16   2 3 4 5 6

ISBN-13: 978-0-226-20930-2 (cloth)
ISBN-13: 978-0-226-41907-7 (paper)
ISBN-13: 978-0-226-20944-9 (e-book)
DOI: 10.7208/chicago/9780226209449.001.0001

Library of Congress Cataloging-in-Publication Data
Coyne, Ryan, author.
    Heidegger's confessions : the remains of Saint Augustine in Being and Time and beyond / Ryan Coyne.
        pages cm — (Religion and postmodernism)
    Includes bibliographical references and index.
    ISBN 978-0-226-20930-2 (cloth : alkaline paper) — ISBN 0-226-20930-x (cloth : alkaline paper) — ISBN 978-0-226-20944-9 (e-book) — ISBN 0-226-20944-x (e-book)   1. Heidegger, Martin, 1889–1976. 2. Augustine, Saint, Bishop of Hippo. 3. Philosophy and religion. I. Title. II. Series: Religion and postmodernism.
    B3279.H49C696 2015
    193—dc23
                                                            2014031387

♾ This paper meets the requirements of ANSI/NISO Z39.48-1992 (Permanence of Paper).

FOR SARAH AND LILA

CONTENTS

	Acknowledgments	ix
	Introduction	1
1.	Heidegger's Paul	17
2.	The *Cogito* Out-of-Reach	53
3.	The Remains of Christian Theology	87
4.	Testimony and the Irretrievable in *Being and Time*	124
5.	Temporality and Transformation, or Augustine through the Turn	157
6.	On Retraction	194
	Conclusion: Difference and De-Theologization	229
	Notes	243
	Selected Bibliography	279
	Index	297

ACKNOWLEDGMENTS

"What do you have that you have not received?" Augustine often quoted 1 Corinthians 4:7 as a reminder that while his faults were his own, what he accomplished he owed to the grace of others. Writing this book I have felt similarly about those who have sustained me along the way.

A fateful conversation with Jean-Luc Marion, on the corner of Dorchester and 59th Street in Chicago's Hyde Park, gave rise to this project. From that moment he has affirmed its development in countless ways. David Tracy's incomparable wisdom and openness continue to inspire me. He teaches by word and deed. For the better part of a decade, in two different institutional settings, I had the honor to study with Amy Hollywood, an exemplary scholar and a tireless champion of her students. I count myself lucky to call her a mentor and a friend.

Without the encouragement of my colleagues at the University of Chicago I could not have completed this project. I am grateful to Arnold Davidson for his guidance and generosity in reading this manuscript. My fascination with modern German philosophy I owe in part to Françoise Meltzer, whose lectures gave me a new perspective on Kant. Special thanks are due as well to Richard Rosengarten, for his faith in this project and for his support at every step along the way; Margaret Mitchell, for steadying me at key moments; and Paul Mendes-Flohr for his encouragement. It is a privilege to work at Swift Hall alongside so many admirable individuals. I am grateful to Dan Arnold, Jeff Stackert, and Catherine Brekus for their friendship and insight over the years. My ongoing conversations with Simeon Chavel, Franklin I. Gamwell, Clark Gilpin, Kevin Hector, Willemien Otten, Jim Robinson, Susan Schreiner, and Christian Wedemeyer have invigorated me. Over the years I have profited greatly from the mentorship of Bernard McGinn and Kathryn Tanner. Thanks as well to my students at the University of Chicago, with whom I have explored many of the ideas in this book.

The Georges Lurcy Charitable and Educational Trust supported this project, allowing me to study at the University of Paris IV, Sorbonne, and the Institut d'Études Augustiniennes. I also wish to thank the Woodrow Wilson National Fellowship Foundation and the Charlotte W. Newcombe Foundation for their support of this project. During the 2005–2006 academic year, the University of Chicago Center in Paris provided a home away from home. For this I am grateful to Robert Morrissey. Conversations with the following individuals helped me to clarify the stakes of my argument: Sophie-Jan Arrien, Bobby Baird, Charles Fox, Michael Kessler, Karla Pollmann, Kenneth Reinhard, Claude Romano, Eric Santner, Christoph Schmidt, and Christian Sommer. I am particularly grateful to Thomas Meyer for our conversations during the 2011–2012 academic year, and to many wonderful colleagues at Williams College, including Denise Buell, Edan Dekel, Alexandra Garbarini, Jason Josephson, Keith McPartland, Bernie Rhie, and Christian Thorne. Thanks as well to my teachers at Dartmouth College: Susan Ackerman, Nancy Frankenberry, Ronald Green, Kevin Reinhart, and the late Charles Stinson.

An earlier version of chapter 2 appeared as "A Difficult Proximity: The Figure of Augustine in Heidegger's Path," *Journal of Religion* 91, no. 3 (July 2011): 365–96. Thanks to Sylvain Camilleri for reading and discussing the material in this chapter. I am grateful to Kathryn Lofton for inviting me to present a version of chapter 5 in the Yale Religious Studies workshop, and to Linn Tonstad and Noreen Khawaja for their valuable feedback.

In preparing the manuscript for publication I often looked to my editor, Elizabeth Branch Dyson. She has my gratitude for her patience and wise counsel as she saw this project through to completion. Thanks as well to Kathryn Krug for her expert editorial assistance. The publication of this book in the Religion and Postmodernism series affords me the opportunity to thank the series editor Tom Carlson, whose work I have admired since I first began my graduate studies. I would also like to thank the anonymous readers on the manuscript for their feedback.

In the solitude of writing I have reflected often upon my father's passion for inquiry and my mother's generosity of spirit. They have encouraged me at every step, even when I gave full voice to the frustrations that accompany writing a book. I am grateful to my sister for her love. My heartfelt thanks are due to Mary Tabor and Del Persinger, and Alan and Bonnie Hammerschlag for their unfailing support and patience over the years. The same holds true for my extended family and for my friends: Sarabinh Levy-Brightman, Charles Stang, Jeffrey Israel, and Dina A.-R. Israel. In the years that I've devoted to this book my daughter has grown effortlessly in grace and loveliness, reminding me each day of the passage of time and the promise of the future. Finally, my deepest gratitude is reserved for the woman whose insight and philosophical acumen, whose sympathies and steadfast love have seen me through the daily travails of this work: Sarah, you are the joy of my mornings.

INTRODUCTION

On October 26, 1930, Martin Heidegger delivered a lecture at the Benedictine Archabbey in Beuron, Germany, entitled "Saint Augustine's Meditation on Time."[1] Transcripts of this work indicate that it was part of a conference for monks, clerics, and novitiates, and thus meant to be heard by them alone. Throughout the 1920s Heidegger had stayed at the monastery for short retreats, and he now intended to repay the community for its hospitality. Though written with a devout audience in mind, the lecture at Beuron anticipated the results of the seminar on Augustine that Heidegger conducted at the University of Freiburg during the fall semester of 1930.[2] Together these two events, the lecture and the seminar, marked the first time Heidegger revisited Augustine in a sustained manner since he had spent the summer of 1921 scrutinizing *Confessions*, Book 10.[3] And as the 1930 lecture and seminar would both consist of line-by-line commentaries on *Confessions*, Book 11, Augustine's famous treatise on time and eternity, it was as if Heidegger had picked up exactly where he left off almost a decade earlier, as if the two glosses on this classic Christian text were parts of some larger enigmatic whole.

An unexpected return. But does it matter, or is it just a curiosity? Certainly the choice to resume the commentary was a curious one, especially if we reflect upon the disparity between the two moments in Heidegger's career: the first belongs to the young Privatdozent in 1921, the instructor Edmund Husserl once described as "religiously oriented,"[4] the author of a work on Scotian grammar with a long-standing interest in phenomenology and a budding one in Aristotle, well on his way to abandoning the Catholicism of his youth—all traits that would make him strangely adept at showing how modern philosophy, as he put it, "came out of theology."[5] The second belongs to Husserl's newly minted successor at Freiburg, the author of *Being and Time* (1927), who in 1929 delivered a celebrated yet perplexing inaugural lecture as chair of philosophy entitled "What Is Metaphysics?"[6]—a thinker whom some now proclaimed to be the world's greatest living philosopher. Though we can easily imagine the first Heidegger grappling with Augustine, it is puzzling to think that the second paid him any mind. Had not *this* Heidegger lamented in *Being and Time* that certain residues or remainders of Christian theology "had not as yet been radically expunged"[7] from philosophy? Had he not faulted others for conflating reason with revelation? What could the author of "Phenomenology and Theology," a 1927 lecture which argues in part that Christian faith is the "mortal enemy"[8] of philosophy, have to gain by re-examining the *Confessions*?

It is tempting to view the 1930 texts on Augustine as disconnected from Heidegger's serious philosophical undertakings at the time—his work on German Idealism, for example, or his writings on Plato, Aristotle, and the Pre-Socratics; his growing sense that Nietzsche was waiting in the wings. In such a lineup, Augustine seems to be out of place. But what the Beuron lecture as well as the 1930–1931 Freiburg seminar course manuscript make clear is that this second pass through the *Confessions*, though brief, went right to the heart of matters at a critical juncture in Heidegger's thinking. Both 1930–1931 texts treat Book 11 as the climax of the *Confessions*. More importantly, the 1930 Beuron lecture asserts that in Book 11 Augustine turns toward the "deepest depth"[9] of confession, its "metaphysical ground,"[10] and that this turn propels Augustine into an entirely new kind of questioning.

The timing of this argument is no mere curiosity: sixteen years later, in the "Letter on Humanism" (1946), Heidegger would date the first inklings of his own attempt to overhaul the question of Being, or what is often called the "Turn" in his thinking, to 1930.[11] In other words, at the very moment Heidegger first began that "deep inquiry concerning man"[12] which would preoccupy him for the rest of his life, he saw its silhouette reflected, darkly, in the pages of the *Confessions*.

The argument of the 1930 Beuron lecture, discussed in detail below, is emblematic of the complex and often conflicted ways in which Heidegger sought to define himself against Christian theological sources throughout his career. The present study is a sustained attempt to isolate a single though crucial part of this story by concentrating on the figure of Augustine in Heidegger's path. Its goal is not to compare in depth the works of Heidegger and Augustine, but rather to analyze Heidegger's own portrayals of Augustinian concepts—what they contributed to his philosophical formation; the tensions they generated in his work; how they resurfaced over time; the often inapparent ways in which Heidegger dealt with their recurrence; and finally, what these recurrences reveal about Heidegger's critique of modern metaphysics.

The full justification for conducting such a tightly focused study can be given only at its end, once the textual evidence is spelled out in its entirety. However, it should be stated at the outset that in setting out to reconstitute the intricate and often serpentine paths by which concepts deemed to be "Augustinian" by Heidegger himself made their way into Heidegger's texts, this study is guided by the presupposition that these conceptual transpositions inform some of the major themes of Heidegger's philosophy from start to finish, and that retracing these paths can help us to better understand how this philosophy developed over the course of Heidegger's career. It is well known that this philosophy is indebted to Heidegger's extensive training in the history of Christian thought, as his contemporaries certainly recognized[13] and as he acknowledged.[14] While admitting that "a confrontation with Christianity reticently accompanied [his] entire path,"[15] Heidegger also maintained that his very reticence about this confrontation was a way of preserving, and simultaneously separating himself from, his theological provenance.[16] In recent years our appreciation of this confrontation and its complexity has grown considerably, thanks to the publication of Heidegger's early writings on Paul and Augustine and to the substantial body of sophisticated research to which it has given rise.[17] Because of this research, it is no longer controversial or novel to suggest that Heidegger appropriated certain concepts or structures from texts that are thoroughly embedded within the Christian theological tradition, placing them in the service of ends that were completely his own and that were by no means Christian or even recognizably theological. And yet because we are now better informed than ever regarding a theological archive that, as most readers would readily admit, provides in part the conditions of possibility for a philosophy such as Heidegger's, the question concerning the meaning of this archive and its subtler effects upon his thinking, and on our own, has grown in importance.

One of the central wagers of the present study is that this question can be posed only by examining in detail how certain discursive formations that take shape in Heidegger's early writings are rearticulated over time. Thus, the study as a whole begins by tracking the early Heidegger's confrontation with Augustine in 1921 as it reverberates throughout the period leading up to and including *Being and Time*, charting the creation and recurrence of structures and concepts in Heidegger's work that come out of Augustinian thought. It focuses as well on showing how these reverberations were carried forward, in non-obvious ways, by works Heidegger penned between 1930 and the early 1960s. The first step in spelling out this narrative is to show that some but not all of the categories Heidegger used in *Being and Time* to sketch the structure of human "being-there," or Dasein, were derived from his own interpretations of Augustine's theological anthropology. For many readers the evidence documenting these derivations will be relatively uncontroversial as they are established on firm textual grounds. However, the task of specifying exactly what role these derivations play in Heidegger's analysis of existence is a much thornier issue. Undoubtedly one could approach it from a variety of perspectives. The perspective adopted here is based on the claim that by taking on board certain Augustinian terms and altering their meanings, Heidegger counterintuitively sought to eradicate the last vestiges of Christian theology from what he called "first" philosophy or the science of Being. This is by no means to say that Heidegger neglected his theological heritage. On the contrary, his deep familiarity with the history of Christian thought and with its complex relation to modern German and French philosophical sources instilled in Heidegger a firm sense that philosophy could freely pursue the meaning of Being only if it first separated itself from the Christian tradition by means of the most painstaking exegeses of theological as well as non-theological texts.

The first three chapters make this case while suggesting that Heidegger's conceptual indebtedness to Augustine and to the Pauline epistles generated a hidden tension in his early writings that eventually influenced the composition and execution of *Being and Time*.[18] This tension results from the fact that Heidegger's way of trying to eradicate the vestiges, residues, or remains of Christian theology was counterintuitve in at least two senses. First, if it can be shown that Heidegger did knowingly introduce into his own philosophical vocabulary terms that are laden with theological meaning, it is difficult to understand how this could possibly accomplish his stated goal, reiterated throughout the 1920s, of disentangling ontology from revealed theology. Second, this general concern can be supplemented by a more specific one. In 1923 Heidegger leveled a criticism against Descartes that set the tone as well as the parameters for each of his subsequent repudiations of modern metaphysics—namely, that Descartes borrowed concepts "previously established in believing consciousness"[19] and secularized or de-theologized them, using them to designate universal structures of human freedom and intellection. Was not Heidegger already guilty of this same crime by 1923? How, then, could a second act of de-theologization cancel the one Heidegger attributed to Descartes?

The 1930 Beuron lecture was not the first time Heidegger saw his own descriptions of human "being-there" prefigured in a seminal Christian theological text. As I show in chapter 1, this also happened in his 1920–1921 reading of the Pauline epistles. In this earlier context, Heidegger was convinced that he could glean from Paul some indication of the genuinely phenomenological meaning of temporality as historical becoming, and he sought to extract this meaning from Paul by articulating an almost imperceptibly Christ-centered reading of 1 and 2 Thessalonians. This reading, in which Christ is hardly mentioned, is designed to show that the primordially Christian experience of time resembles an ongoing spiritual form of crucifixion. In its Christ-centeredness this reading is maximally "theological" in spite of Heidegger's protestations to the contrary, even as it is meant to yield a universally applicable concept of lived temporality. Moreover, on multiple occasions Heidegger admitted that it was by reading Augustine that he first came to define human "being-there" or existence as "care" (*Sorge*).[20] Is there not a manifest contradiction, then, in faulting Descartes for de-theologizing certain concepts when Heidegger was willing to utilize Paul and Augustine in this manner? Can we avoid suspecting that Heidegger's short-lived "phenomenology of religious life" suffices to gainsay his criticism of Cartesian metaphysics?

The question of "de-theologization" (*Enttheologisierung*) in Heidegger, which includes the dynamic of secularization Heidegger attributed to others, Descartes above all, as well as the related yet distinct issue of Heidegger's own indebtedness to theological sources, is part and parcel of the narrative recounted here. This question can be posed in a meaningful way only if we first briefly examine the peculiar ways of configuring philosophy, theology, and religion that allowed Heidegger to fault others for secularizing concepts while believing that, without contradicting himself, he could forge new concepts out of theological works in order to undo the adverse effects of secularization.

As a term *de-theologization* does not enjoy pride of place in the Heideggerian vocabulary. It makes the first of its two most prominent appearances during the 1920s in the above-mentioned 1923 criticism of Descartes. That criticism takes up the bulk of Heidegger's first lecture course at the University of Marburg in winter 1923–1924, which introduces students to phenomenological research by focusing in part on the ways in which Descartes surreptitiously rearticulated Thomistic concepts in his *Meditations on First Philosophy*. The finer details of this analysis are discussed in chapter 2, below. They matter less here than its conclusion, which states that the rational concept of human freedom in Cartesian metaphysics disguises certain key formulations in Thomas's soteriology: "Descartes transposes what is theologically designated as the working of God's grace to the relation of the intellect working on the will."[21] This conclusion, reached the year after Carl Schmitt first argued that "all significant concepts of the modern theory of the state are secularized theological concepts,"[22] led Heidegger to offer an observation worthy of Schmitt: "today secularized sentences are at work everywhere in philosophy, and as soon as one examines the claim of these sentences, one sees that the basis on which they alone have evidence has nothing to do with a purely rational knowledge."[23] Here the apparently harmless transfer of a conceptual relation from one domain of thought to another is said to have untold consequences on the configuration of rational inquiry in the modern European context. At Marburg in 1923–1924 Heidegger narrated the "development of the history of our mentality"[24] in such a way as to show that the meaning of truth had devolved over time, losing its primary meaning as disclosure, while becoming increasingly synonymous in modernity with certainty, correctness, and value. Descartes's use of Thomistic sentences, Heidegger claimed, was symptomatic of a larger set of historical forces that have effectively deprived modern philosophers of all access to the genuine meaning of truth and Being. Moreover, this forgetting of truth and Being is the precondition for modern metaphysics, which ascribes meaning to entities solely in terms of their usefulness for scientific technology.

The rudiments of the later Heidegger's influential critique of metaphysics are thus present in 1923. They are taken for granted in the 1926–1927 analysis of Descartes appearing in Heidegger's *The History of Philosophy from Thomas Aquinas to Kant*, in which Descartes is said to enact a decisive "transposition (*Umstellung*) of the question"[25] of Being toward the question of the subject. However, it would take another fifteen years before Heidegger could fit together all of its pieces. When he did, he argued that the form of subjective certitude evident in Descartes, undergirded by secularized sentences, found its ultimate expression in Hegel and Nietzsche. This led him in turn to suspect that European philosophy would eventually have to confront a nihilism the likes of which Nietzsche could scarcely fathom. The word *de-theologization* is absent from the 1938 essay "The Age of the World Picture," yet its argument elaborates the 1923 history of mentality in the direction of radical nihilism. The unquestioned preference granted in the modern era to an unconditional form of subjectivity, Heidegger here contended, "springs from the liberation of humanity from the bonds of the truth of Christian revelation and the doctrines of the Church, a liberation which frees itself for a self-legislation that is grounded in itself."[26] Like Simmel before him, Heidegger argued in 1938 that this self-legislation is a false liberation that tightens the bonds it is meant to break: "this liberation *from* the certainty of salvation discussed by revelation has to be, in itself, a liberation *to* a certainty in which man secures for himself the true as that which is known through his knowing."[27] Even Nietzsche's word that God is dead can be made to conform to the narrative according to which the historical dissolution of revealed theology actually bolsters the function of divine sovereignty while displacing it onto subjective self-certainty. On this model de-theologization as the vehicle of secularization is the secret accomplice of metaphysics. During the modern era it contributes to the formation of an all-encompassing worldview in which entities matter only insofar as they have value for a subject whose primary concern is to secure its own Being and to master its material surroundings. But if these are the defining features of modern metaphysics—the determination of beingness as utility, of truth as certainty, and of Being as will—they are hardly ones that spring fully formed from the hand of Descartes. Consolidated over time they correspond to impulses prevalent throughout the history of philosophy and theology that are ultimately traceable to the works of Plato and Aristotle, if not the Pre-Socratics.

In light of this argument Heidegger's second prominent use of the term *de-theologization* during the 1920s explains why he thought that by returning to theological sources he could undo the effects of Descartes's secularizing de-theologization: "In modern times," he writes in *Being and Time*, "the Christian definition [of man's Being] has been de-theologized [*enttheologisiert*]. But the idea of transcendence—that man is something that reaches beyond himself—is rooted in Christian dogmatics."[28] The remark is part of an effort to explain why modern philosophers have constantly ignored the fact that their inquiries into "man's Being"[29] are built upon inadequate ontological foundations. But it also says something about the nature of Christian theology, as it implies that Christian theological investigations of man's Being have been woefully inadequate. They too have relied upon precedents set by ancient ontology to such a degree that in the modern era they altogether lose their theological character. This criticism, Heidegger might have added, can and should be leveled against pre-modern Christian sources as well: when Descartes is said in 1923 to borrow from Thomas—a charge repeated and confirmed in 1926–1927[30]— the implication is that he adopts from the believing consciousness concepts which are more or less de-theologized *already* in the scholastic context— the effect, arguably, of myriad attempts on the part of theologians during the High Middle Ages to synthesize biblical and Greek sources. Descartes, in other words, borrows from the context of revealed theology concepts that do not truly belong there, but which appear in that realm as the result of overarching historical processes of conceptual deracination.

The early Heidegger, in short, used the term *de-theologization* equivocally. For him it signified the movement by which a term or a relation is stripped of its theological reference (which can take place *within* Christian theology) as well as the transpositions by which theological terms are removed from their primordially Christian theological domains and resituated elsewhere (which cannot). Although they are inextricably linked, neither of these two movements is reducible to the other. This equivocation is lodged in Heidegger's use of the term *theology* itself, which sometimes referred to the empirical body of literature that comprises the Christian theological tradition, and sometimes to an ideal set of discursive practices conducted within a highly specified domain of experience set apart from philosophy proper and made possible by the "event" of Christian revelation. That the equivocation affecting de-theologization was never resolved in the early works is perhaps due to the fact that the historical and conceptual origins of its twofold movement remained more or less obscure to Heidegger. However, at the end of the present study we will see that the later Heidegger could not resist hazarding an ontological explanation for de-theologization, laying its cause at the altar of Being itself and inadvertently revealing his own complicity in its dynamic.

Early on the term *religion* and its related forms suffer less from equivocal usage. Prior to *Being and Time*, the terms *religion*, *religious*, and *religiosity* (*Religiosität*) were all frequently aligned with the so-called event of Christian revelation, such that in 1922 Heidegger supported his assertion that philosophy is necessarily atheistic—in the sense that it must do without the biblical God—by suggesting that "the very idea of a philosophy of religion . . . is a pure illogicality [*ein purer Widersinn*]."[31] What justifies such a stark repudiation of the philosophy of religion? The purity of its illogical character is not difficult to grasp: "the object of philosophical research," he wrote in 1922, "is human being-there insofar as it is interrogated with respect to the character of its Being."[32] According to the early Heidegger, philosophy as hermeneutics is grounded in the free self-interpretation of human being-there or Dasein. When the early Heidegger contended that the philosophy of religion is illogical, he meant to suggest that the religious mode of human being-there does not allow for this kind of free or autonomous interrogation of its own Being. This is presumably because genuinely religious self-interpretation is in his view beholden to the message of revelation. As a result it has its own way of attesting to itself, one "which remains closed off in principle from any philosophical experience."[33] The implication is that philosophical discourse and religious discourse are ostensive in different ways. While the former expresses the self-showing of entities, including the self-showing of Dasein, the latter has in view primarily the relation between the divine and all other entities. To combine these two discourses would be to conflate two disparate ways of expressing the Being of entities. Moreover, by treating religion as an object of philosophical inquiry, one risks ignoring the ways in which the ostensive or expressive character of philosophical discourse differs from that of religious discourse. In effect the idea of a philosophy of religion is the idea of a hybrid discourse that is internally inconsistent, as it combines two antithetical ways of interrogating entities.

This view of the break between philosophy and religion, announced in 1922 and upheld repeatedly thereafter, accounts for why Heidegger initially thought he could fault Descartes for de-theologizing Thomistic concepts while enlisting the results he obtained in reading Paul and Augustine to develop new philosophical categories. If by secularizing Thomas, Descartes simply furthered the historical degradation of truth, Heidegger by contrast sought to counter this degradation by recasting the results of his own interpretation of Christian faith or "religious life" while sketching the existential categories found in *Being and Time*. He did so under the twin assumptions that the latter text would assuage rather than exacerbate the negative effects of secularization, and that whatever is truly religious in this or that theological work would remain uncorrupted by the philosophical "indications" generated by it. This is precisely why Heidegger would have rejected out of hand the suggestion that his own readings of Paul and Augustine resemble in any way Descartes's readings of Thomas or that they potentially intensify rather than mitigate the effects of secularization. Rather than contributing to the degradation of truth over time, Heidegger argued, his hermeneutic method followed clues left behind in earlier texts pointing the way toward the investigation of concrete life or existence on its own terms.

In this sense Heidegger's dismissal of the philosophy of religion as a pure illogicality is strategically important. It upholds the legitimacy as well as the originality of those concepts which, as I plan to show, emerged from his readings of theological sources. The particular derivations of these concepts are described below using the language of de-theologization, which I have intentionally borrowed from and turned against Heidegger in order to specify the ways in which his early writings repeat and transform various "sentences" in Augustine. In spelling out the procedures and effects of de-theologization, the first half of this study demonstrates that the repetition of these sentences had far-reaching effects upon Heidegger's thought, some of which appear to unsettle the central presuppositions underpinning Heidegger's analyses of human finitude. For this reason the first half of the study pays close attention to the rhetorical means which the early Heidgger used to protect his claims to exclusivity, uniqueness, and originality. In part this entails recognizing that Heidegger's claims to be doing "first philosophy" were initially more delicate than he was willing to admit, especially in his earliest courses, in which Christian theology is sometimes described as a separate and potentially competing fundamental science. And indeed, by troubling these claims, one of the ultimate aims of the present study is to slowly recuperate, over the course of the entire inquiry, the specific account of the philosophy of religion that Heidegger rejected as an oxymoron.

Chapter 1 below considers Heidegger's 1920–1921 reading of the Pauline epistles, explaining how it contributed to the formation of hermeneutic phenomenology while arguing that it is ultimately responsible for the fact that the discrepancy between religiosity and hermeneutics dogged Heidegger in subtle ways over time. Here I argue that the extreme form of guilt Heidegger uncovered in Paul, though designed to function as a model for elucidating temporality, calls into question the basic presuppositions Heidegger sought to establish in his phenomenological writings. It should be emphasized here that in making this observation I am not interested in faulting Heidegger's philosophy for supposedly failing to live up to his own highly stylized and idealistic portrait of Pauline Christianity. A criticism such as this one would be at best uninteresting. Much more important is the question of how the discrepancy between philosophy and religiosity cast its shadow on everything that followed in its wake and eventually influenced the terms in which guilt is handled in *Being and Time*.

The longest shadow was cast not by the reading of Paul but by the 1921 reading of Augustine's *Confessions*. For this reason, and for the reason that so many of Augustine's concepts reappear over time in Heidegger's works, even when Augustine is not explicitly discussed or cited, I have chosen as my primary reference point the material discussed in chapter 2 below, which examines the 1921 seminar course entitled "Augustine and Neoplatonism." This chapter spells out the role that Augustinian *confessio* initially played for Heidegger as he sought to undo the effects that Cartesian metaphysics had upon modern philosophers such as Husserl. Here I argue that Heidegger's investigation of the *Confessions* positioned Augustine as a predecessor—a philosopher of concrete life or what Heidegger called *facticity*, a figure who points the way toward reversing the ill effects of modern metaphysics.

This role is short-lived, however, for reasons that are clear. During the time that Heidegger was scrutinizing Augustine, he also began scrutinizing Aristotle. And in Heidegger's courses the rise of the one coincided with the fall of the other.[34] From 1921 until the publication of *Being and Time*, Heidegger paid far more attention to Aristotle than he did to any other philosopher. Chapter 3 thus situates the transposition of Augustinian terms into Heidegger's descriptions of human finitude from 1921 to 1926 against the backdrop of Heidegger's more extensive engagement with Aristotelian ethics and ontology. In so doing it shows how the discrepancy between Heidegger's vision of religiosity and the constructive use he ultimately made of it was mapped onto his reading of Greek sources. This investigation sets the stage for a reconsideration of the use of testimony in *Being and Time*.

Chapter 4 outlines the ways in which the conceptual genealogies articulated in the first three chapters interact with the 1927 treatise, explaining how its connection with the *Confessions* advances as well as disrupts the preparatory analysis of Dasein. In the introduction to *Being and Time*, Heidegger famously argues that the history of philosophy has hindered the philosophical investigation of concrete life, and that philosophers, especially modern ones, have unwittingly concealed its true configuration while borrowing from other, foreign domains of research the concepts they have applied to human existence. For this reason historical research in philosophy must be *destructive*—not in the sense that such research must annihilate the past, but rather in that it must stake out the positive contributions of traditional sources to contemporary inquiries. A destructive interpretation approaches philosophical concepts cautiously, with the intention of dissolving the concealments engendered by their history. It identifies the "primordial experiences"[35] in which philosophical concepts first take shape and in which concealments first arise. Moreover it shows that the history of philosophy is marked by a series of *transfers* or *transpositions* through which concepts tailored for specific forms of inquiry become disconnected from these domains and are then applied in separate domains.

In exploring the links between *Being and Time* and the *Confessions* it is impossible to avoid the sense that we are taking up Heidegger's method of hermeneutic destruction, adopting its conceits while turning them back against *Being and Time*. This adaptation of hermeneutic destruction, however, differs from the original by virtue of the fact that it does not lay claim to the "primordial experiences" in which Heidegger first began questioning Being. Instead it studies how certain concepts in *Being and Time* took shape in order to show that Heidegger's first way of building up the question of Being was designed to keep at bay competing notions of human finitude that could just as easily be derived from its genealogical sources. If anything, then, this investigation identifies alternative experiences of finitude that Heidegger rejected or that he constituted as non-primordial as he put forth the finitude of Dasein as the ontic foundation for all ontological inquiry.

In this sense, chapter 4 takes its cue in a highly specific manner from Hannah Arendt's *Love and Saint Augustine*. At the moment Arendt pivots in this work from outlining a tension in Augustine to seeking its resolution, she cites Heidegger. She contends that in his 1929 essay "On the Essence of Ground," Heidegger draws a distinction between two senses of world (*mundus*) in Augustine—the world as created, and the world as object of illicit desire. Concerned with the latter, he supposedly neglected the former, leaving "uninterpreted"[36] the world as created. In its context the remark invites us to read Arendt's account of created being as a tacit criticism of Heidegger. For our purposes it can be used to render explicit the full effects of de-theologization by showing that Heidegger inevitably left some aspects of religiosity behind while transposing others into his hermeneutic phenomenology. That is to be expected, of course, but the effects of this selection on *Being and Time* are far from obvious. The goal of chapter 4 is to show that these effects account for why this treatise repeatedly disqualifies, yet never fully vanquishes, the suspicion that human existence is fundamentally disjointed and—to adopt Heidegger's phrase—potentially "irretrievable" in and for itself.

In the narrative recounted here, this suspicion matters not only because it seems to have haunted Heidegger's early readings of Paul and especially Augustine, but also because Heidegger indulged it after *Being and Time*, forcing him to revisit his early de-theologization of Augustine. Karsten Harries once remarked that "from beginning to end we meet in Heidegger the admittedly shifting and evolving tension between what I want to call a theological and philosophical strand."[37] A key part of this evolving tension is the subtle and hitherto unnoticed role played by Augustine and Augustinian locutions in Heidegger's later works. The second half of this study is devoted primarily to the contested notion of the "Turn" in Heidegger's thought. More specifically, it handles the ways in which the later Heidegger in his efforts to revamp the question of Being sought to manipulate Augustinian formulae that appear in his early writings. Here I contend that whereas the early Heidegger repeated Augustinian "sentences" with the intention of expunging theology from contemporary philosophical inquiry, the later Heidegger rewrote these same repetitions in an effort to distance himself from modern metaphysics in its onto-theological constitution. In his later writings, Heidegger subtly exploited the tension created by his own indebtedness to a Christian theological archive. More specifically, the instability inherent in those of his concepts with identifiably "Augustinian" origins allowed Heidegger to subtly imbue these concepts with critical force in his later works.

Chapter 5 advances this argument on two fronts. First, it documents the often surprising connections between Heidegger's brief return to Augustine in 1930 and his posthumously published prewar writings, particularly as it informs his 1936–1938 treatise entitled *Contributions to Philosophy*. Over the past decade the latter text has been the object of growing interest among scholars of the modern European philosophical tradition, many of whom have underscored its centrality to the later Heidegger.[38] By focusing on this often obscure and dense work, chapter 5 demonstrates that key parts of the altered versions of Dasein and temporality that emerged in the works of the 1930s are prefigured in Heidegger's reading of *Confessions* 11, including the new determination of Dasein in terms of displacement and "restraint" (*Verhaltenheit*). It shows that these prefigurations are taken up in novel ways in Heidegger's attempt to reconceptualize the ecstatic dimensions of time. Second, it explains how this "other" de-theologizing repetition of Augustinian anthropology which took place in the 1930s targets the presuppositions guiding its 1921 antecedent, suggesting that Heidegger could not go forward after *Being and Time* without restaging his initial attempt to separate the thinking of Being from its religious and theological past.

The question is thus to determine what role is played by various conceptual reiterations of Augustinian terms in Heidegger's later writings. The fact that Heidegger utilized Augustine in his 1946 essay entitled "Anaximander's Saying"[39] to shed light on the earliest trace of Being in Western philosophy is just one sign among others that these reiterations carry a significance that becomes apparent only when they are interpreted as part of the history of concepts developed here. And this speaks to a larger dynamic internal to the Heideggerian corpus, which I discuss in two interconnected ways in chapter 6 under the heading of retraction. Chapter 6 discusses the later Heidegger's tendency to redefine the meaning of Being in terms of retraction as part of his attempt to carry out an "immanent criticism"[40] of his own philosophical trajectory. It argues as well that this self-criticism heralds the strangely muted resurgence of re-signified Augustinian terms in the later Heidegger's debate with Nietzsche, the so-called last metaphysician and the philosopher who allegedly completed the project of modernity launched by Descartes. The goal of chapter 6 is not simply to pinpoint the ways in which Heidegger's response to Nietzschean metaphysics echoes the original juxtaposition in his corpus between Descartes and Augustine; it is also to ask what this inquiry tells us about Heidegger's analysis of nihilism, his rejection of Nietzschean voluntarism, and his desire to distance himself from modern metaphysics in its onto-theological constitution. Thus chapter 6 poses the question of de-theologization on the grandest scale in Heidegger's corpus.

If this tightly focused yet interdisciplinary study of Heidegger has any larger significance, it is surely tied to the sense that Heidegger's complex and shifting relation to theological sources has exerted a heavy influence on recent debates in and around philosophy, religious studies, and theology in their Anglo-European contexts. Not only is this influence clear in recent instantiations, predominantly in the French context,[41] of what Jean-Luc Marion has called the "Augustinian quarrel;"[42] it surely reaches far beyond this. In many instances scholarly efforts to parse the distinction between philosophy and theology, or the religious and the nonreligious, have been in part determined by the need to respond productively to Heidegger's thought and his assessments of previous thinkers. This "obligatory passage,"[43] as Levinas put it, yields in this case a modest proposal regarding the status of the philosophy of religion in its contemporary continental setting.

In this setting, the philosophy of religion—or religions, depending on the context—is no longer fully governed by the set of concerns often associated with its formation as a discipline in classical or modern sources.[44] Though its development runs parallel to the constitution of religion as quintessentially modern object of inquiry, many eighteenth- and nineteenth-century European thinkers viewed the philosophy of religion mainly as a subgenre of philosophical inquiry strictly analogous to other such subgenres, including the philosophy of art, of literature, of science, and of history. Yet the dual tendency among modern European scholars to define the philosophy of religion either as the application of a pre-established autonomous mode of critical or rational reflection upon the representative texts of a given religious tradition—i.e., the *philosophy* of religion—or as a specific set of discursive practices embedded within a tradition—i.e., the philosophy *of religion*—has been offset of late by scholarship that emphasizes the more pressing concern to interrogate the shifting sets of historical, cultural, and ideological forces that have shaped modern conceptions of rationality and largely dictated the terms in which modern thinkers repudiate religious discourse and practice even as they exhibit a continued fascination for religion.[45] This more expansive approach targets the relatively close and often tortured relationship between reason and revelation in their Kantian and post-Kantian delimitations. The study of this history makes room for a range of competing agendas among scholars of various stripes presently engaged in a wide array of interrelated forms of inquiry targeting the increasingly nuanced role of religion in contemporary political and intellectual debates. In part these forms of inquiry have contributed to the general rise of interest in the relationship between religion and historical materialism, in political theology, and in inquiries concerning the afterlives of twentieth-century European humanisms and deconstruction.[46]

The present study of de-theologization, though focused almost exclusively on Heidegger's thought, exemplifies a specific approach to the philosophy of religion and its position in contemporary continental philosophy and critical theory. In this context, the philosophy of religion is not simply the philosophical elucidation of a religious worldview nor is it the examination of the logic undergirding the set of truth claims specific to religious texts. In short it is not merely a particular mode of analysis that takes religion as its pre-established object of inquiry. Alongside this notion of the philosophy of religion, which is admittedly a prevalent and legitimate one, it is possible to define this field of inquiry as the critical examination of the historically conditioned and highly regulated sets of statements and rhetorical strategies that allow modern thinkers to separate themselves from imaginatively constructed religious traditions while nevertheless continuing to draw upon the resources of these same traditions in novel ways. The philosophy of religion is the discourse that examines how these processes of separation and dependence play out over time. Thus its primary objects of inquiry are the strategies that thinkers employ to differentiate putatively secular forms of inquiry from their nonsecular counterparts. In this instance, our concern to focus on these strategies has led us to defer consideration of Heidegger's attempts to overcome metaphysics, or to occupy its age differently, until the very end of the study, for the sake of showing that the terms in which he delineated the end of metaphysics are implicated in the dynamic of de-theologization spelled out at length over six chapters. This concern ultimately explains as well why the present study neither defends nor disparages the process of separation and dependence it strives to describe, but rather confines itself to the much more difficult though admittedly more modest task of understanding how it works.

CHAPTER ONE

Heidegger's Paul

INTRODUCTION

"At least I tried. The guiding notions which, under the names 'expression,' 'experience,' and 'consciousness,' determine modern thinking, were to be put in question with respect to the decisive role they played."[1] With these words Heidegger reflected upon his early Freiburg lecture courses (1918–1923) more than thirty years after they were delivered. By the time he published these remarks in 1958 as part of a "quasi-fictional"[2] confession entitled "Dialogue on Language," the hermeneutic phenomenology spelled out in *Being and Time* had receded from his view. The treatise that made him famous had also propelled him into a series of endless revisions, sending him in search of a way to directly interrogate the meaning of Being in general. In the "Dialogue" we learn that the project articulated in *Being and Time* had originated with a series of rash attempts to jettison "the sphere of subjectivity and of the expression that belongs to it."[3] In hindsight these attempts seemed ill-advised, primarily because their goal was unattainable: "Nobody can in just one single leap take distance from the predominant circle of ideas, especially not if he is dealing with the well-worn tracks of traditional thinking—tracks that fade into realms where they can hardly be seen."[4] But if in this manner the later Heidegger sought to disparage his very first lectures and seminars at Freiburg, he nevertheless revealed their guiding thread, suggesting that his inquiry into the relation between expression and existence was the crucible in which *Being and Time* first took shape as well as the guiding line for his meticulous early readings of ancient, medieval, and modern texts.

The present chapter considers Heidegger's 1920–1921 winter lecture course entitled "Introduction to the Phenomenology of Religion" in this light, underscoring the irreducibly ambivalent status of religion in Heidegger's earliest critiques of the relation between expression and experience. Just prior to his disavowal of the philosophy of religion in 1922, Heidegger wagered that the phenomenological investigation of what he called "primordial Christian religiosity" could reinvigorate contemporary philosophical analyses of lived experience. This wager is particularly evident in the manuscript for Heidegger's winter 1920–1921 lecture course, the bulk of which is devoted to commenting upon Paul's first and second letters to the Thessalonians. It is clear that Heidegger believed for a time that these two texts, 1 and 2 Thessalonians, could actually help to clarify contemporary philosophical accounts of temporality by providing sound guidance for the conceptualization of historical becoming. At issue here is the fact that in its attempt to establish Paul as model for conceiving time philosophically, the commentary on 1 and 2 Thessalonians generates a hidden dilemma in Heidegger's work that never got resolved, but that nonetheless set the stage for Heidegger's painstaking de-theologization of Augustinian anthropology in 1921.

The dilemma as I describe it below is a function of the role that Pauline eschatology briefly played for the early Heidegger, whose interest in religiosity was directly related to his sense of the potential, and potential shortcomings, of Husserlian phenomenology. It is well known that by the time Heidegger began lecturing on religiosity in 1920 he was already convinced that Husserl had reopened the possibility of articulating a science of lived experience, even as he worried that Husserl's methodological breakthroughs were jeopardized by his uncritical reliance upon Cartesian metaphysics. In pitting Pauline eschatology against contemporary philosophical and historicist conceptions of time, Heidegger aimed to capitalize on these breakthroughs while revamping the concept of life underpinning them. And yet the attempt to utilize primordial Christian religiosity as a model to be emulated necessarily wound up casting this religiosity in the role of an enemy to be vanquished. The present chapter thus identifies the subtle ways in which primordial Christian religiosity functions as a mimetic rival for Heidegger in his handling of New Testament sources, one that is displaced through the development of Heidegger's hermeneutic phenomenology.

The real significance of Pauline eschatology in the context of Heidegger's early Freiburg lectures comes into view only if we see that in the "Introduction to the Phenomenology of Religion" Paul is made to embody the redemptive suffering of the crucified Christ. This typologizing of Paul, however, is far from self-evident in the course manuscript. I argue below that it emerges only if we retrace Heidegger's rather submerged and highly suggestive treatment of the Pauline *katechon*, the obscure figure identified in 2 Thessalonians 2:6–7 as holding off the end time, delaying the coming of the man of lawlessness or Antichrist. It is the constitutive role of the *katechon* in the structure of Pauline eschatology that accounts for the fundamentally ambivalent status of religiosity for Heidegger, as this structure threatens to overturn the very philosophical presuppositions Heidegger wanted it to confirm. To advance this argument, the present chapter maintains a tight focus on the years 1919–1921. Rather than turning directly to Heidegger's exegeses of Pauline texts, it begins with a brief but detailed look at the conception of human life these exegeses were meant to ratify. It then spells out the argument of Heidegger's 1920–1921 "Introduction to the Phenomenology of Religion." In a last step it highlights the tightly regulated circulation of concepts through which Heidegger sought to establish the primacy of his own notion of contemporary historical becoming by appealing to the alleged source of primordial Christian religiosity.

THE HERMENEUTICAL INTUITION

In his authoritative study of the early Heidegger, Theodore Kisiel underscores the crucial significance of the 1919 War Emergency Semester (*Kriegsnotsemester*) course (KNS 1919), entitled "The Idea of Philosophy and the Problem of Worldview,"[5] as paving the way for the analysis of existence elaborated in *Being and Time*.[6] Added to the German academic calendar to accommodate an influx of students returning to university studies from military service, the course provided Heidegger with the chance to articulate his own account of phenomenology as a descriptive science. Before an audience largely unfamiliar with the finer points of Husserlian methodology, Heidegger crafted an intricate defense of the unity of lived experience. Set forth in vitalist terms indebted to the late nineteenth-century German life-philosophy and the work of Wilhelm Dilthey, the defense places in sharp relief the view of self-consciousness that the 1920–1921 commentary on Paul was meant to corroborate. The core of the defense consists in demonstrating that concepts do not necessarily interrupt the flow of experience, nor do they portion it out into discrete yet ultimately falsifying snapshots of an unbroken but otherwise inaccessible whole. On the contrary, concepts can in fact allow the intentional subject to resonate with its experiential contents and thereby to achieve a sort of genuine self-possession.

The controlling metaphor of resonance provided the foundation upon which Heidegger would eventually construct the figure of human *Dasein* or "being-there" in subsequent essays and lecture courses. If we take a close look at the KNS 1919 lecture course, we can discern the sense in which Heidegger's attempt to circumscribe the psychic realm as the primary object of philosophical inquiry was part of an effort to overhaul the basic procedures of Husserl's account of phenomenological reduction.[7] This will also afford us the chance to specify the sense in which phenomenology could be a science of *the historical*—a capacity which the early Heidegger was also willing to extend to certain discursive treatment of religion: "History in its most authentic sense is the highest object of religion, religion begins and ends in it."[8] Thus before turning to religiosity in the early Heidegger we must first explain the sense in which phenomenology, as a science of the historical, is hermeneutics.

The KNS 1919 lecture course begins with Heidegger pointing out the many problems that proliferate around contemporary philosophical uses of the term *worldview*. Heidegger rejects the assumption that philosophy is or should be the science of values.[9] Seeking to rebuff depictions of philosophy as inductive metaphysics he sets out to redefine the relation between truth and validity. The notion, he argues, that philosophy's goal is to achieve a specific "worldview," a metaphysical viewpoint from which the world is interpreted in a universally binding sense, is a common though mistaken notion of philosophy's true potential. According to Wilhelm Windelband, scientific discourse posits normative axioms in the service of establishing their a priori validity.[10] In reply, Heidegger asks "whether truth as such constitutes itself in an original worth-taking."[11] If the phenomena of truth and value derive their sense from the most concrete level of experience, then they must be traced back to a level at which first-person experience is not already deformed by the intrusion of theory or the objectification of experiential contents. When life is lived to the fullest extent possible, the "I" simply lives "in" the world as it is encountered, without overlaying values upon things. Does this "I" encounter what is intrinsically of value by positing values to itself? Does the valuable here take the form of an object or prescription that stands over "me" for whom it is binding? "Clearly not," Heidegger replies. "I experience value-relations without the slightest element of an 'ought' being given. In the morning I enter the study; the sun lies over the books, etc., and I delight in this. Such delight is in no way an ought; delightfulness as such is not given to me in an ought-experience. I ought to work, I ought to take a walk: two motivations, two possible kinds of 'because' which do not reside in the delightful itself but presuppose it."[12] The two modes of taking delight stand opposed here, in an opposition that furnishes the basic schema elaborated by the rest of the course.

In one mode, the phenomenon of delight is constituted by the act of positing the valuable by abstracting values from the vital flow of experiential contents. When lifted from the immediate richness and intensity of the experiential flow, valuing becomes synonymous with the act of positing norms that reflect back upon life from above it. The value as so posited has been disconnected from the concrete experience of what is truly valuable for me. Superimposed upon concrete life, it is given as if from elsewhere. But the valuable need not be encountered in this manner as standing above me, abstracted from the vital flow of life. In a more basic mode of experience, I can encounter what is delightful, and thus what is of value for me, from within the vital flow of experience and thus as marked by its radical particularity. At this level I do not necessarily posit something as delightful so much as I simply delight in it. This seemingly trivial observation matters greatly in the KNS 1919 course precisely because it implies that not all forms of reflexivity entail abstracting or standing apart from the simple intention of life in its devotion to experiential contents. The "I" who simply delights in the delightful has not yet morphed into the theory-laden "subject" who relates to the world through a veil of normativity. This dichotomy between two modes of value is the linchpin in Heidegger's argument that philosophy is primordial science, by which he means that it is a descriptive science of the fundamentally vital unity of cognition and sensation, the science of the primordial intention of life in its intrinsically meaning-conferring identity. This identity takes shape as what Heidegger calls the "pre-theoretical" level of existence—"theory" being for Heidegger a modification or a "de-vivification" of an originally vital impulse that refers back to its source in a more basic form of being toward entities in general.[13]

When Heidegger adopts the language of life-philosophy in referring to lived experience as concrete, he has in mind not only the concrescence of experiential contents woven together as a coherent and meaningful totality, but also the fact that this totality is ineluctably marked as *mine*. When I adopt a theoretical posture toward what is valuable or true, I place it at a distance from me. Standing opposite the content of my experience, I have already departed from the simple intention of living "in" something. This minimal alienation puts me at a distance from my Being as a historically particular entity, which is why the theoretical realm points back toward something more original and alive, something not yet objectified or *"removed [ent-fernt]*, lifted out of the actual experience."[14] The theoretical gaze, which turns experiential contents to stone, entails a relation with things that is literally evacuated of vitality. Its objective correlate is the thing-experience or *Dingerfahrung* which constitutes the natural scientific relation to entities.[15] And just as concrete life does not conform to the category of thinghood, so too the subjective correlate of thinghood is characterized as an altered, de-vivified form of experience devoid of all reference to the particularity of the historical individual: "The historical-I is de-historicized into the residue of a specific 'I-ness' as the correlate of thinghood."[16] By opposing theory and the pre-theoretical, Heidegger assumes the burden of showing how a descriptive science of experience could possibly be pre-theoretical. He also must account for why it seems that life cannot maintain itself for long at a pre-theoretical level, why it so easily degrades into theory.[17]

Rejecting the primacy of theory, Heidegger seeks to redefine what he calls the "psychic." He argues that unless it can be proven that the psychic is given as an autonomous and identifiable sphere of experience, the science of self-consciousness will remain no more than a fiction. This is the real dilemma confronting Heidegger in the KNS 1919 lecture course, which culminates in the question concerning the origin of all rational principles. Are rational principles intrinsic to pre-theoretical life? If so, does this mean that life is self-structuring? Or as Heidegger asks: "Can the axiomatic problems, the questions concerning the ultimate norms of knowing, willing, and feeling, be demonstrated in the psychic itself? Do I stand in the psychic as in a primordial sphere? Is the genuine origin or 'primal spring' [*Ur-sprung*] to be found here?"[18] His response to this question comes in the form of a vehement defense of the view that any descriptive science worthy of the name must express its object without distorting it, and that it must bolster one's original standing in psychic sphere. The examined life is not simply transparent to itself; it is in fact a richer, *more intense* version of the unexamined life.[19] Far from paralyzing life or breaking it up into a series of approximations, conceptual determination vivifies the very impulse it seeks to capture.

To access the life he presupposes to be self-vivifying, Heidegger must first show how life can overcome thing-experience, or what he calls "the sole supremacy of the sphere of things."[20] By 1919 Heidegger had already ascribed to life the tendency to reduce the manifold senses of Being to the notably de-vivified meaning of the object. And he had already determined that the psychic realm is not at all a "thing," since thinghood is constituted outside the pre-theoretical realm. At issue, then, was to determine the domain of experience in which "I" may encounter myself primordially as living in the world, starting with environmental experience. As with the analysis of value, the founding interconnections of worldly experience are not superimposed upon the events of which they are comprised. The world is first and foremost an event—an idea Heidegger seeks to capture in the phrase *"es weltet"* (it worlds). In everyday life I need not first assemble the component of my experience in order for them to take on meaning; I do not first have to add up the features of a desk—wooden surfaces arranged at right angles to each other, having mass, extension, color, etc.—before I encounter it as the coherent meaningful totality I call a "desk," but rather the world in its eventhood is such that in my vital spontaneity I live "in" and "toward" it as a meaningful totality. Thus I am there already along with the world: "in this living-towards there is something of *me: my* I goes out beyond itself and resonates *with* this seeing. . . . More precisely: only through the accord [*Mitanklingen*] of this particular *I* does it experience something environmental, where we can say that 'it worlds.' Wherever and whenever 'it worlds' for me, I am somehow there."[21] The ability of the "I" to resonate with its experiential contents represents the earliest definition of the event in Heidegger's corpus. It is likewise the foundation for his understanding of human "being-there" or Dasein.

The pre-theoretical domain of vital experience described in the 1919 lecture course is what Heidegger elsewhere calls *facticity* (*Faktizität*), or alternatively *factical* (*faktisch*) *Being* or *factical life*. These terms crop up in Heidegger's early lecture courses just after the 1919 course and play a key role in his investigation of religiosity, which is designed to confirm the sense of lived experience as resonating with its experiential contents. These terms designate the unique way in which life is "there" alongside itself, distinguishing its way of being a fact from all other species of being a fact. The being-there of life in and for itself is philosophy's main object of inquiry: "The object of philosophical research is human 'being-there' [*menschliche Dasein*] insofar as it is interrogated with respect to its character of Being. The basic direction of philosophical questioning is not externally added and attached to the interrogated object, *factical life*."[22] In a review of Karl Jaspers's *Psychology of Worldviews*,[23] Heidegger asserts that the way in which "I" have myself allows me to scrutinize my own way of Being: "What turns out to be important here is accordingly the fact that I *have myself*, i.e. the basic experience in which I encounter myself as a self. Living in this experience and gearing myself to its very sense, I am able to question after the sense of my 'I am.'"[24] This dynamic is what he calls elsewhere "the refined disposition for attentively listening in on the immediate life of subjectivity."[25] When Heidegger specifies how the "I" has itself, distinguishing its mode of self-possession from the possession of external objects,[26] he contends that human beings never possess themselves as stable or steady entities, but rather they can have or possess themselves only to the extent that they "worry" (*bekümmern*) deeply about themselves.[27]

Virtually all of Heidegger's early lecture courses from 1920 on highlight the constitutive role of worry in vivifying experience. In one way or another they all suggest that human beings can attain genuine self-standing in the world only by setting out to fulfill their own potentialities, putting themselves at risk of not living up to these projected possibilities. This is one key aspect of what Heidegger calls *being worried*: "Experience is . . . living participation, being worried, so that the self has a certain standing in this worry."[28] By actualizing its ownmost potentialities, the "I" can achieve a standing in the world that the early Heidegger would call a genuinely "historical"[29] one.

When Heidegger claims in KNS 1919 that something of the "I" lies within this dynamic of living-out-toward the world, the structure of experience he espies is clearly worked out in opposition to Husserlian transcendental reduction, which he sees as failing to do justice to the strong link between intuition and comprehension. In §57 of *Ideas, First Book*, entitled "The Question of the Exclusion of the Pure Ego," Husserl clarifies the status of the phenomenological ego in its transcendentally reduced state. Following Kant, who determines the "I-think" (*cogito*) as that which accompanies all of my representations, Husserl argues that after carrying out the transcendental reduction "we shall not encounter the pure ego anywhere in the flux of the manifold mental process which remains as the transcendental residuum."[30] Here the implication is clearly that the pure ego constituted by reduction is never objectively there for itself in its reflection upon experiential contents. For his part Heidegger doubts that this argument represents the final word on the prospect of determining the ego's mode of being through simple inspection of experiential contents. Though he does not deny Husserl's argument that the ego "cannot in any sense be a really inherent part or moment of the mental processes themselves,"[31] he rejects the terms of this description while suggesting instead that the ontological specificity of vital experience contains an intrinsic reference to the particularity of the ego which, though it is not a really inherent part of experience, nonetheless opens the way to a descriptive science of historical becoming. Thus the Being of the "I" *is* indeed somehow there for itself, and this Being can be brought within the purview of simple inspection, even if its presence cannot be registered in the mode of self-reflection.

The concept of "resonance" in the KNS 1919 lecture, an implicit rejoinder to Husserl, provides some indication of the fact that the historical specificity of first-person experience cannot simply be bracketed from the dynamic process that reveals the self-givenness of things in their essences. For Husserl, the self-apprehension of the *cogito* is a function of its capacity to reflect upon the stream of mental processes itself.[32] Heidegger's concept of resonance in KNS 1919, on the other hand, seeks to uncover the self as apperceived in the intentional relation that characterizes all environmental experience. To show how this is so, Heidegger adapts the technical Husserlian distinction between generalization and formalization in arguing that the "I" is directly affected by its own Being. In §13 of *Ideas, First Book*, Husserl contends that all conceptual classification takes one of two forms. When I generalize, the series of categories I place in sequential order is arranged as a hierarchy of abstractions. The abstractions are so ordered that they express an ever-increasing distance from the concrete particulars to which they refer. I advance through this sequence and so arrive at the highest levels of abstraction. But when I *formalize* particulars, I must proceed in a different manner. Rather than passing through levels of abstraction I jump directly from the experience of *this* particular entity to the simple act of affirming its presence before me as a formal "something whatsoever." For Heidegger this latter affirmation of the entity as a formal-logical something is nothing vague or empty, but instead it marks a sort of affirmation that altogether avoids the hierarchy of abstract categories through which the mind must pass when it generalizes. When I simply affirm something as *being-here* before me I do not pass through a set of materially bound generic concepts. In formalizing I do not leap away from lived experience and into abstraction, but rather I simply affirm that, *yes, there is something here before me, here I stand before something that is a fact for me.*

In this simple affirmation of a *this-here*, the *for-me* is experientially highlighted. It is emphatically present as an intrinsic feature of concrete experience. Formalization can thus be interpreted as an index for the highest potentiality of lived experience. And the ability to formalize indicates that discursive forms inhabit lived experience from the bottom up. Far from being "an absolute interruption of the living-relation,"[33] conceptualization actually facilitates the dynamic conceptual process of appropriating experiential contents as well as the process of self-interpretation which Heidegger in short order began calling hermeneutics. In this sense, formalization is the vehicle through which life can encounter and study genuine norms in the domains of knowing, willing, and feeling. The root of all lived experience, this gesture of the "out-toward" constitutes the world as a meaningful and coherent totality informed by conceptual discursiveness. All theoretical formations and all scientific constructs must be seen to arise from, and to revert back upon, this pre-theoretical gesture of the out-toward, which, as the origin of life's intrinsic meaningfulness, signifies the pre- of the pre-theoretical.

Toward the end of the KNS 1919 course Heidegger identifies this movement out toward the world with the vital impetus in an effort to purge Husserlian reduction of its allegedly objectifying tendencies while clarifying the concrete connection between experience and expression. The structure of resonance Heidegger outlines in the last pages of the course manuscript achieves this aim by displacing Husserl's description of the self-givenness of essences. In his 1907 Göttingen lectures, Husserl describes pure seeing or intuition as the counterpart of essences in their self-givenness. The goal of the transcendental reduction in these lectures is to constitute pure seeing as the act that captures the pure givenness of essences. The intentional seeing that captures this givenness is according to Husserl entirely devoid of the sort of conceptual productivity that he associates with discursive understanding. The pure seeing of essences, in other words, must involve "as little *understanding* as possible, as much pure intuition as possible (*intuitio sine comprehensione*). Indeed we are here reminded of the speech of the *mystics* when they describe the intellectual act of seeing that contains no discursive knowledge."[34] The analogy between the receptivity of pure seeing and the Christian theological motif of learned ignorance[35] is meant to highlight the extent to which the intentional act carried out in the reduced state is for Husserl free from all possible contamination by discursive judgment.

For his part Heidegger doubts that the passivity attributed to the intentional act of pure seeing is a legitimate ideal, as he suspects that it grows out of a desire to bring vitality to a standstill. In the KNS 1919 lecture course the self-understanding of life is already described as a kind of projection; the "I" which resonates with its own seeing goes beyond itself in order to meet experiential contents. The self-reflexivity of the vital flow is constituted by the unbreakable bond between these two components. Underscoring the self-reflexive unity of life is precisely what is at stake in identifying intuition as *hermeneutical*: "The empowering experience of experience [*Erlebens des Erlebens*] that takes itself along with itself is the understanding intuition, is the *hermeneutical intuition*, the originary phenomenological back-and-forth formation of the recepts and precepts from which all theoretical objectification, indeed every transcendental positing, falls out."[36] In being-toward what is experienced, the "I" does not leave itself in the lurch. The relevance of this is that far from preventing access to the essences of things, the reflexive character of life is precisely what opens access to them. On its basis I can express the Being of things in discursive formulations that actually intensify, rather than interrupt, the flow of life as *mine*.[37] Thus the formulae Heidegger uses to describe the reflexivity of the vital impulse, including the "hermeneutical intuition,"[38] run directly counter to the opposition Husserl establishes in 1907 between intuition and comprehension.[39] Heidegger suggests that even in its receptivity the ego remains vitally active, constituting the meaningfulness of concrete experiences by cross-referencing them, knitting them together as a coherent totality. Husserl's 1907 description of truth slants toward objectivity, Heidegger suggests, whereas life in its pre-theoretical breakout into an always already meaningful world is nothing objective. The KNS 1919 lecture course ends by arguing that the concept of self-consciousness must be jettisoned in favor of a more apt expression of "the primordial intention of genuine life, the primordial bearing of life-experience and life as such, the *absolute sympathy with life* that is identical with life-experience."[40] The primordial intention of life is identical with its primordial bearing. This implies for Heidegger in 1919 that the "I" possesses itself through absolute sympathy with itself in such a way that it can interrogate its own Being without theoretically deforming it.

Whether or not philosophy has at its disposal the terms it needs to describe this mode of self-possession is a much thornier issue: "we will see," he writes in the "Introduction to the Phenomenology of Religion," "that through the explication of factical Dasein, the entire traditional system of categories will be blown up—so radically new will the *categories of factical Dasein* be."[41] Indeed the search for a whole new set of categories capable of describing the intention of life non-theoretically is exactly what motivated Heidegger's investigation in 1920 of primordial Christian religiosity insofar as this latter object of inquiry was meant to provide a foresketch of how factical life experience is a conceptually self-determining totality.

THE ESCHATOLOGICAL PROBLEM

Heidegger's 1920–1921 "Introduction to the Phenomenology of Religion" is a hybrid affair, consisting of a detailed discussion of his own phenomenological method followed by a set of exegetical reflections on Paul's letter to the Galatians and his first and second letters to the Thessalonians. The shift from one to the other, spurred by student complaints that the first half of the course had failed to examine religious texts, led Heidegger to argue that Paul's earliest extant letters exhibit the essential unity of Christian belief and practice. Though the turn to Paul was initially improvised, it was directly linked to the major methodological dilemma highlighted in the first half of the course, which spells out Heidegger's phenomenological method of formal indication.[42] In neither contemporary philosophy nor religious studies, we learn in this first half, do scholars adequately theorize the essence of historical becoming. As a result it is up to phenomenology to clarify these discourses by asking the following question: "How does the historical stand with regard to factical life existence itself? Which sense does the historical have in factical life existence?"[43] But when Heidegger speaks of *the historical* in this context he is mainly interested in showing how the past as such stands in relation to the concretization of factical life experience in the present. That is, he is primarily orientated toward attaining the specific concept of temporality that can serve as the meaning of human being-there. The question of history in the "Introduction to the Phenomenology of Religion" is meant to ratify and to supplement the KNS 1919 lecture course by conceiving the vitality of experience in temporal terms. It is by reading Paul, Heidegger contends, that we first uncover the true meaning of historical becoming as temporality.

This claim assigns to Paul a curious, if short-lived, role in Heidegger's burgeoning method of hermeneutic destruction. The method of destruction was just taking shape at the moment when he offered the "Introduction to the Phenomenology of Religion." A portion of the summer 1920 lecture course, entitled "Phenomenological Destruction"[44] advances the claim that, because Dasein is inherently prone to self-deception, philosophical research must adopt a skeptical view of all previous expressions of Dasein's Being. It must set out to "destroy" philosophical texts not by simply rejecting out of hand their conclusions, but by identifying the experiential conditions of possibility for the philosophical concepts they apply to human Dasein, pinpointing the ways in which these concepts conceal, rather than disclose, the Being they seek to express. This work of dismantling conceptual schemas is primarily positive in the sense that it is meant to facilitate the ontological examination of Dasein in the present by preventing contemporary philosophers from uncritically adopting the views of their ancient, medieval, and/or modern predecessors. The first Marburg seminar, given in winter 1923–1924, provides a schematic overview of hermeneutic destruction. According to it the task of destruction is to examine "how existence's self-obstructing is enacted in history."[45] More specifically it argues that the major motifs of destruction are geared specifically toward counteracting the forms in which self-obstruction has been manifested in ancient Greek, and in medieval and modern European, philosophy from Aristotle to the present. In a short document written in late 1922, Heidegger argues that by making historical inquiry into human being-there or Dasein less sure of itself, hermeneutic destruction renders contemporary Dasein's existence fundamentally questionable. It thereby aims to actualize existence in the form of genuine worry or insecurity.[46] This is not to say that hermeneutic destruction ends in pure skepticism. On the contrary, it is meant to show that factical Dasein, when rendered questionable, "must carry a sense within itself and thereby require for itself a particular lawfulness."[47] This lawfulness provides a grounding for the conceptual determinations comprising the structure of existence at a given historical moment. Because Dasein is fundamentally historical, these determinations cannot be conjured out of thin air, but instead they must be derived from the same historical tradition which hermeneutics approaches destructively in an effort to highlight Dasein's tendency toward self-obstruction.

Here we come upon what initially motivated Heidegger to read Paul. To uncover the lawfulness particular to existence, Heidegger's own method of hermeneutic destruction required him to identify a site of self-interpretation somewhat detached or distant from the metaphysical tradition he seeks to destroy, yet relevant enough to this tradition and its practitioners that it could arguably furnish a critical vantage point for dismantling and reconfiguring contemporary expressions of experience. Though the early Heidegger was often quite explicit about how this or that ancient, medieval, or modern thinker should be hermeneutically destroyed, the "Introduction to the Phenomenology of Religion" is tellingly silent when it comes to destroying Paul's writings. It argues instead that the structures of eschatological temporality at the heart of Galatians and 1 and 2 Thessalonians have been consistently misunderstood by biblical commentators and Bible scholars alike. As Otto Pöggeler remarks, this means that Paul's letters display for the early Heidegger "life's dominant structure in the significance of its performance rather than in the significance of its contents."[48] As such they exemplify the authentic sense of history from which the present has fallen away,[49] setting up Paul as the voice of conscience for contemporary philosophy, pointing the way toward clarifying how factical life experience "takes itself along with itself,"[50] to quote the KNS 1919 lecture course.

Now, if these are indeed the guiding intentions behind Heidegger's 1920–1921 reading of Paul, then two questions must inform our analysis.

The first is to determine whether or not the reading actually confirms these intentions. The second is to determine if the reading of a fundamentally religious text generates unforeseen conclusions that complicate the model of the hermeneutical intuition in philosophically significant ways. Since the bulk of the course manuscript is devoted to 1 and 2 Thessalonians, our efforts to answer these questions will have to focus on these two works.

Heidegger puts no stock in the arguments of scholars such as William Wrede, whose 1903 monograph *Die Echtheit des zweiten Thessalonicherbriefes untersucht*[51] disputed the Pauline authorship of 2 Thessalonians. Though he engaged contemporary biblical scholarship on Paul, leaning heavily on the work of Paul Deissmann, he argued largely on thematic grounds that 1 and 2 Thessalonians are authentically from the hand of Paul, that they are the earliest extant Christian writings, and that they moreover display a progression toward true Christian religiosity. Second Thessalonians, by these lights, bolsters the model of religiosity initially sketched in 1 Thessalonians. The "Introduction to the Phenomenology of Religion" thus aims to show, first, that 1 Thessalonians tells us what becoming Christian means, as it indexes the transformation in the structure of one's Being that necessarily occurs with taking on board the Christian calling; and second, that 2 Thessalonians explains how the act of awaiting the parousia or Second Coming of Christ counts as the full expression of what it means to become Christian. To this extent Heidegger's general approach to Paul remains indebted to the work of Franz Overbeck,[52] among others, as it is geared toward delineating the essence of Christianness or primordial Christian religiosity in the earliest extant Christian writings, by establishing Paul as an intermediary between the reader and the figure of Christ, a move that sets up Paul as the exemplar of faith, the one who renders intelligible what it means to follow Christ.[53]

The "Introduction to the Phenomenology of Religion" focuses on 1 and 2 Thessalonians not only because Heidegger assumes that they are the earliest Christian texts. It is crucially important as well that Heidegger reads these texts as drawing attention to the very "center of Christian life: the eschatological problem."[54] One of the main presuppositions guiding this reading of Paul is a version of an argument made by some of the late nineteenth- and early twentieth-century scholars cited in the course stipulating that the eschatological tendencies prevalent among the earliest practitioners of Christianity set these practitioners apart from "late-Judaism."[55] This dubious and essentializing opposition between early Christianity and late Judaism puts in historical terms the provocative yet conceptually crucial claim that Pauline religiosity cannot be understood unless we see that, unlike his late Jewish counterparts, Paul remains completely unconcerned with the question concerning *when* the parousia or Second Coming will actually occur. In Heidegger's terminology, Paul disregards the "object-historical level" of experience which is associated with the terms *Geschichte* and *Geschehen*. Instead his relation to the parousia takes shape primarily at the "absolute-historical level" of the pure event (*Ereignis*), the only level at which the calling to become Christian can be effective. For Paul, then, the Second Coming is primarily meaningful not as if it were a potentially datable historical happenstance that may or may not occur at some point in the future. To relate to the parousia in this manner would be to completely miss its religious significance, or as Heidegger writes: "We never get to the relational sense of the *parousia* by merely analyzing the consciousness of a future event."[56] By these lights the act of awaiting the parousia does not consist in expecting something to happen in the future: "The structure of Christian hope . . . is radically different from all expectation [*Erwartung*]."[57] The break between expectation and the enactment of eschatological awaiting runs throughout the course, dominating Heidegger's portrayal of every aspect of Christian religiosity. If to be Christian means being unconcerned with object-historical question of *when* the Second Coming will occur, this is primarily because the genuine stance of awaiting it at the absolute-historical level does not motivate raising this question. Religiosity at this level is bound up with different concerns, which Heidegger spells out as he slowly works through 1 and 2 Thessalonians.

Thus when Heidegger identifies the "eschatological problem" as the heart of Christian life, he suggests that early Christian communities quickly abandoned the fundamentally eschatological element of religiosity as they took stock of the historical success of Christianity as a movement: "by the end of the first century, the eschatological in Christianity was covered up."[58] And yet the demise of eschatological vigilance is not the sole, or even the primary, sense of the eschatological "problem" discussed in the "Introduction to the Phenomenology of Religion." The rapid decline in eschatological sentiment among early Christians is seen as symptomatic of, rather than strictly identical to, the so-called eschatological problem highlighted in the 1920–1921 lecture course.

Essentially the eschatological problem does not refer to the fact that the parousia fails to occur, thereby causing the early Christians to revise their expectations regarding the end times. This would be to view it as a purely object-historical affair. Instead, the somewhat submerged argument that takes shape in "Introduction to the Phenomenology of Religion" is that the experience of awaiting the eschaton at the absolute-historical level is internally divided, and thus prone to being abandoned by the Christian believer.

To get at the structure of awaiting, Heidegger walks a fine line between portraying religiosity in purely rational terms and granting the privilege of revelation as constituting the self-interpretation of religious faithfulness. In the remarks on method appended to the course, it is apparent that phenomenology stands in a complex and potentially antagonistic relation with the "religious life" it sets out to delineate. The argument of the course takes for granted that phenomenology and theology are disparate discursive domains, and it makes clear up front that the philosophical exegesis of biblical sources is limited to the extent that phenomenology must "renounce the last understanding that can only be given in genuine religious experience."[59] The assertion places Heidegger at a distance from his chosen subject matter, yet this distance is immediately overcome through a compressed chain of assertions about the nature of phenomenological description. Though phenomenology must renounce the last understanding given in religious experience, this is paradoxically what allows it to transcribe religiosity faithfully in non-revelatory terms. "It is uniquely proper to phenomenological understanding," Heidegger writes, "that it can understand the *not-understandable*, in that it radically *lets it be*."[60] This formulation is remarkable not only because it defines phenomenology as a *contradictio in adjecto*, but also because it presents the contradiction as guaranteeing the primordial status of phenomenological description over and against scientific objectivity.

It is not difficult to identify in positive terms the "last understanding" of religiosity which phenomenology must renounce, but which it recuperates precisely through this act of renunciation: this is the "mind of Christ" mentioned by Paul in 1 Corinthians 2:16 and identified in the last hours of the lecture as the true understanding of primordial Christian religiosity. The fact that this understanding is renounced yet *salvaged* by the phenomenological gaze is what allows Heidegger to claim, first, that he can access the absolute-historical level of Paul's stance of awaiting, and second, that this stance can be shown to produce a concept of temporality with contemporary relevance.

This recuperative function of the phenomenological gaze is taken for granted at every step in "Introduction to the Phenomenology of Religion." In §23 Heidegger transitions from a brief discussion of Galatians to the detailed exegesis of 1 and 2 Thessalonians that occupies him for the remainder of the course. To understand Paul phenomenologically, he suggests, it does not suffice to locate Paul in his historical context. What matters above all is that we must "enact the letter writing, or its dictation, with him."[61] Only then will phenomenological commentary be able to capture Paul's genuine religious experience "in its absolute unrepeatability."[62] From Heidegger's perspective the effect of this transposition is not that phenomenologists loyally rehash Paul's words, but instead that they shift themselves to the absolute-historical level from which these words are issued. The goal of this strategy is to use Paul in order "to gain a real and original relationship to history,"[63] which permits us to read the inquiry into Christian religiosity as confirming, and even deepening, the description of the hermeneutical intuition in KNS 1919.

In the "Introduction to the Phenomenology of Religion," Heidegger maintains that the pre-theoretical and philosophical concept of history as becoming-in-time must be gleaned from Paul's stance of awaiting the parousia, or as the central propositions of the course put it: "1. Primordial Christian religiosity is in factical life experience. Postscript: It is authentically [factical life experience] itself. 2. Factical life experience is historical. Postscript: Christian experience lives time itself. ('to live' understood as a *verbum transitivum*)."[64] Christian religiosity, factical life experience, history, and time are gathered up and strung together like beads on the same string, linked by the controlling hypothesis that Paul's eschatological vision allows us to grasp the problem of time in a concrete manner "entirely irrespective of all pure consciousness and all pure time."[65] Here we can guess at how the distinction between object-historical expectation and absolute-historical awaiting will bear upon the question of factical life. The lines quoted above suggest that a careful description of Christian religiosity promises to dislodge the question of time from the purely theoretical context in which Husserl examines it. The claim is a crucial one if only because the temporal dimensions of awaiting are not dealt with in Heidegger's courses prior to "Introduction to the Phenomenology of Religion."

The point is not that the lived experience of Christian religiosity is identical with time itself, but rather that temporality is *produced* by this religiosity. Heidegger is after the sense in which Christian religiosity gives rise to temporality, letting it be what it is in itself. On what basis, then, does Pauline Christianity *live* time transitively, as though it produces time in its pre-theoretical meaning? Heidegger looks to the eschatological problem at the heart of Christianity in an effort to show how this problem gives rise to temporality as such. Only in this sense can we understand why the eschatological problem is at the heart of Christianity for Heidegger. What matters to him is not solving the problem per se, but rather showing that one can wrench from the ever-intensifying experience of the problem *as a problem* the very essence of temporality in its purely phenomenal dimensions.

AWAITING AS TORMENT

The substantive reflections Heidegger offers on 1 Thessalonians focus on the nature of "proclamation" or the preaching of the good news as providing the overarching framework in which Pauline belief and practice take shape. A brief letter consisting of five chapters, 1 Thessalonians attracts Heidegger's attention mainly due to the compact meditation on the end times which opens its final section: "Now, brothers and sisters," writes Paul, "about times and dates we do not need to write to you, for you know very well that the day of the Lord will come like a thief in the night. While people are saying, 'Peace and safety,' destruction will come on them suddenly, as labor pains on a pregnant woman, and they will not escape."[66] The breathless and panicked tone of the prose, Heidegger surmises, not only controverts the arguments of Schrader and Baur that the letter is not authentically Pauline, but it also underscores something crucial about what it means for Paul to be the slave of Christ: "Paul lives in a peculiar torment (*Bedrängnis*), one that is, as apostle, his own, in expectation of the second coming of the Lord. This torment articulates the authentic situation of Paul. Every moment of his life is determined from out of it."[67] It is clear for Heidegger that Paul's torment is bound up with his relation to the Thessalonians themselves. We get a glimpse of this torment in the very first lines of the epistle. In the words of thanksgiving Paul offers toward the outset of 1 Thessalonians, Heidegger espies the twofold structure of Christian experience: "You became imitators of us and of the Lord, for you welcomed the message in the midst of severe suffering with the joy given by the Holy Spirit. And so you became a model to all the believers in Macedonia and Achaia."[68] The Christian vocation inaugurates a specific form of experiential becoming that entails its own form of knowledge as conviction.

The call reconstitutes the Being of the Christian, in the sense that his or her existence is reoriented toward the event of the call as "having-become"[69] Christian. Borrowing the metaphor of resonance employed in the KNS 1919 lecture discussed above, Heidegger argues that the flow of Christian life is not entirely congruent with the structure of vital experience apart from the call. Religious life is constantly relayed back to the experience of having-become, which now accompanies it at every step, generating an existential structure that can be interpreted as a precursor to Heideggerian thrownness. The Christian is enjoined to confront the future by referring it to the wellspring of the past: "Having-become is not, in life, just any incident you like. Rather, it is incessantly co-experienced [*ständig miterfahren*], and indeed such that *Being* [*Sein*] is now *Having-become* [*Gewordensein*]."[70] Here the act of extending oneself into the future is formally described as a reversion upon a deep past—deep not because of its peculiar distance from the present, but because of its power to determine the entire course of life ensuing from it as well as its having befallen the individual from an indeterminate elsewhere.

The self-knowledge enjoined by this recursion upon the past is more or less obscure in the commentary on 1 Thessalonians. At first Heidegger refuses to give it any content; we must look ahead to the 2 Thessalonians commentary in order to see it revealed more fully as tied to the notion of the *katechōn*, the one who "restrains" the end times and puts off the parousia.

For the time being, however, we can note that for Heidegger it is equally important to connect the novel schematization described in 1 Thessalonians to the assertion in verse 6 that the Thessalonians must receive Paul's message "in great grief or affliction [*Trübsal*] with the joy given by the Holy Spirit [*en thlipsei pollē meta charas*]."[71] The sense of the joy conferred by the Holy Spirit is eventually explicated in the lecture course as part of the commentary on 2 Thessalonians. At the outset Heidegger focuses on why Paul refers to the Thessalonians' having accepted his message in great grief or affliction. Following the major conceit of the course, this grief has nothing to do with the object-historical level of experience, and so cannot refer to what is presumably an obvious contender for its occasion, namely, the persecution of Christian communities. Heidegger insists rather that at the absolute-historical level great grief or affliction is indeed the *mode* in which the Christian calling is heard and appropriated. The Thessalonians are not grieved because they are confronted with practical obstacles. Instead they are grieved because the hearing of the Christian message entails an inner struggle that is launched by hearing the message of hope which they have received and which they are now enjoined to preach to others.

Advancing line by line through 1 Thessalonians, Heidegger underscores that the "having-become" of the Christian entails *dechesthai ton logon*, "accepting the word" proclaimed by Paul. Though such acceptance consists outwardly in learning or receiving the standards of Christian living, in its essence the Christian calling is rooted in a hidden drama that transforms the Christian's basic disposition into a great grief borne by the sense that the present life consists essentially in lack: "The acceptance or 'taking-on' consists of entering into the distressful *lack* which is life."[72] It is impossible to overestimate the significance of this grief in the present context. Its centrality for Heidegger is never in doubt as he makes increasingly clear that grief is linked to the hidden source from which the concept of temporality will eventually emerge in the commentary on 2 Thessalonians.

This emphasis on grief as divinely bestowed opens a whole series of oppositions running throughout Heidegger's reading of both 1 and 2 Thessalonians that are meant to establish despair as coequal with, if not as the form of, Christian hope. This effort to equate hope and despair takes two identifiable forms. The first pertains to Paul's relation to the Thessalonians. As the one who proclaims a message of hope, and who seeks to encourage the community at Thessalonica, Paul intervenes within the lives of those to whom he preaches: "for Paul," Heidegger suggests, "the Thessalonians have an absolute significance."[73] Citing 1 Thessalonians 3:7 Heidegger paraphrases Paul, suggesting that his fate as an apostle rises and falls based on whether or not the Thessalonians accept his message. Paul's very Being is said to depend entirely upon the authentic enactment of Christian religiosity on the part of those to whom he writes. The second person is thus the locus of hope: "*You* [the Thessalonians] are my hope in the Parousia. *You*, in what you have now become and are becoming, are so through my apostolic proclamation, my concernful enactment in regard to you, that is to say, *you are* my real being."[74] At the same time, Paul's torment is a function of his struggle to empower others to remain vigilant in awaiting the parousia. If the Thessalonians hold out in their Christian vocation to await the parousia properly, then Paul can rest assured that he is carrying out his mission. But if they fail to remain vigilant, then Paul will have failed in his mission to announce the good news.

To borrow Heidegger's terminology, the content-sense or the "what" of Paul's Being is entirely exhausted by the enactment-sense or "how" of the Thessalonians' Being. Because it is never certain *if* the Thessalonians will stand fast, Paul remains in constant jeopardy. This is *the* crucial aspect of the eschatological problem, as the grief Heidegger registers in Paul based on 1 Thessalonians is grounded in this experience of radical uncertainty, which spreads itself out, enveloping Paul's entire mission as an apostle. Paraphrasing the message of his letter, Heidegger writes that Paul effectively conveys the following to the Thessalonians regarding their mission as Christians: "If it fails, it is *my fault;* and therefore I can*not bear* it [*kann ich es nicht aushalten*]. I am restless concerning you, for I do know where you and I 'lie' . . . and the *tempter* is at work!"[75] We see here how the eschatological problem takes shape for Heidegger as a worry or concern that has little to do with awaiting the actual return of Christ as a future event, and everything to do with the responsibility the Christian must assume with respect to it.

In a second facet of the problem, not only does Paul hold himself responsible for the lives of others, he also believes that the present delay of the parousia depends upon his own enactment. Here we return to the point laid out above, namely that the absolute-historical stance of awaiting does not motivate the question concerning *when* the parousia will occur. This is because, according to Heidegger, at the absolute-historical level the question concerning *when* immediately reverts back upon the one who poses it, provoking the question concerning *how* the individual Christian awaits the parousia. In asking *when* Christ will come, the Christian is primarily concerned with asking him- or herself *how* he or she awaits this coming. Heidegger draws upon 1 Thessalonians to resolve genuine Christian vigilance into two component parts, "awaiting" and "serving." Here the futural element of primordial Christian religiosity consists not in looking toward an approaching event, but in redoubling the interrogation of the present with a glance back at the event of having-become Christian. In awaiting the parousia the Christian's desire that something happen on an object-historical level must take shape as a self-accusation at the absolute-historical level. The transfer of energy from desire to self-accusation, or from the question of when Christ will return to the question of how I am awaiting this return, is what Heidegger calls "fate."[76] The fact that this sense of insufficiency grows in direct proportion to the authenticity of awaiting implies that the Christian who awaits the parousia is fated to find him- or herself increasingly guilty for its delay.

This explains why Heidegger views eschatology as a *problem* in Christianity, one that goes to the heart of what it means to lead a religious life. Paul exemplifies primordial Christian religiosity to the degree that he feels himself to be somehow responsible for the delay of the parousia. The more he lives out his calling, the greater and more poignant is the grief he experiences in awaiting the parousia. The fact that Paul has not done enough to prepare the way for the parousia is actually what forms the basis for his sense of personal guilt. Heidegger's Paul sees the "I" as incurring others' guilt, taking upon himself the sins of the world. His grief is said to be unbearable not because it is quantitatively excessive, but because it increases in direct proportion to the enactment of religious life. The more apostolic Paul is, the more guilty he becomes.

This view of religious life as torment determines how Heidegger approaches Paul's experience as a letter writer. For Heidegger the immense guilt that is tied to the character of Paul's mission is detectable not only in the content of his message but also in the panicked and urgent tone of his prose. When Heidegger sets out to write the letter along with Paul he does not want to lose sight of this panicked tone. He is chiefly concerned with transposing the phenomenological gaze itself to the level at which Paul's confession of infinite guilt is put to work, which is also the place from which Paul seeks to encourage the Thessalonians to cultivate the kind of personal responsibility and guilt he attributes to himself.

In the first paragraphs devoted to 2 Thessalonians Heidegger argues that Christian conversion is virtually meaningless at the object-historical level and that it only takes on significance with respect to absolute history or the *Ereignis*. The break between these two levels is mapped in various ways, filling out the portrait of Christian hope as a species of grief. Initially Heidegger correlates the covering up of genuine Christian eschatology with the reduction of all understanding to representational ideation. That is to say, when the Christian falls away from genuine Pauline vigilance, then he or she posits the eschaton in an imagistic or representational manner, as though the image in the mind succeeded in bringing close something that remains, in the terms of the event, quite distant: "In talk without qualification of 'representation,' one misrecognizes the fact that the eschatological is never primarily idea."[77] The suspension of representation implies that the vigilance of awaiting is irreducible to expectation, as we have seen above. But if the Christian does not represent the end, then how is the parousia "there" as a term of relation within the experience of true awaiting? The course manuscript does not allow one to answer this question beyond stipulating that the parousia functions nonrepresentationally as the ground of absolute responsibility.

As he protects the distinction between the object-historical and the absolute-historical in part by excluding from the latter mode of enactment forms of testimony pertaining to the former mode, Heidegger gives the impression that one cannot detect in an objective sense the "enactment character" of genuinely religious awaiting. Phenomenologically speaking it is only from within the awaiting itself that its presence and directionality can be detected, or as he puts it: "that which has the character of enactment is only co-possessed, and cannot for itself be objectified [*verge-*

genständlich werden]."⁷⁸ The unmistakable adaptation of Husserlian terminology is crucial here. For Husserl the realm of consciousness is unified by the ego. In reflecting upon consciousness as a whole the ego renders present the sum total of elements comprising this whole, and these elements are then said to be present in the mode of presentification (*Vergegenständlichung*). At the same time the ego carrying out this reflection nevertheless remains absent from the totality of representations rendered present by it. The ego remains on the near side of all presentification, and is thus inaccessible within the realm of reflection it generates.⁷⁹

In making use of technical Husserlian terms Heidegger in fact argues here that the truly religious awaiting is marked by a kind of self-occultation. Though he affirms that enactment of Christian awaiting is "co-possessed" or somehow present to itself, he falls back upon notions of self-dispossession⁸⁰ to specify his mode of presence-to-self, suggesting that in the experience of awaiting Christian religiosity is present to itself paradoxically in the form of absence. To illustrate this he alludes in passing to mystical theology,⁸¹ assigning a fundamentally apophatic dimension to experience of awaiting, not only to language concerning it: "The complex of enactment can be explicated neither positively as a mere course of happenings, nor negatively through some negation or other. The thoughts of negative theology grew from similar motifs of the 'beyond yes and no.'"⁸² The apophatic dimensions⁸³ Heidegger assigns to absolute history provide the grounds for his argument that Christian hope is typified by the kind of grief discussed above. In line with this, Heidegger maintains that the only proof of a Christian calling is the experience of affliction. The Thessalonians, he maintains while speaking in the person of Paul, "must be despairing, because the affliction increases, and each stands alone before God. It is these to whom Paul now answers that affliction is an *endeigma* [proof] of the calling; the others he sharply rejects."⁸⁴ On this basis it is clear that the eschatological problem in Christianity has to do with a self-occultation caused by the confluence of expectation and grief, hope and despair. The stakes of Heidegger's wager that Christian religiosity ratifies the fundamentally reflexive character of the hermeneutical intuition spelled out in KNS 1919 now come into view: the radically uncertain and potentially self-occluding character of religious awaiting places it at a distance from the kind of objectivity that Heidegger associates with theoretical sciences. Yet in holding up this experiential uncertainty as the model for the enactment of lived experience, Heidegger means to emphasize its structural overlap with the hermeneutical intuition. He thereby risks inadvertently setting up religious awaiting in its negative dimensions as a potential foil for his argument in favor of the fundamental self-reflexivity of lived experience.

THE PAULINE "I" AND THE *KATECHŌN*

If the problem of an immense Christian guilt slowly emerges in the commentary on 1 Thessalonians, then in the commentary on 2 Thessalonians the problem reaches its climax as it is tied to the drama of a vicarious suffering. It is unclear, however, how Heidegger proposes to extract from this permanent crisis the sense of historical becoming as temporality. In turning to his commentary on 2 Thessalonians, the link between guilt and temporality comes into view, as does the kind of joy that is available to the Christian who properly awaits the parousia.

Heidegger begins by asserting that 2 Thessalonians expresses a more extreme form of panic or worry than the one evinced by 1 Thessalonians. He then reasons that Paul's tension has grown, and that his torment now revolves around the obscure figures mentioned in 2 Thessalonians 2:1–10, the man of lawlessness or the Antichrist on the one hand, and on the other the enigmatic *katechōn*, the one who restrains the Antichrist and thereby puts off the day of the Lord. "Now we request you, brethren," Paul writes,

> with regard to the coming of our Lord Jesus Christ and our gathering together to Him, that you not be quickly shaken from your composure or be disturbed either by a spirit or a message or a letter as if from us, to the effect that the day of the Lord has come. Let no one in any way deceive you, for it will not come unless the apostasy comes first, and the man of lawlessness is revealed, the son of destruction, who opposes and exalts himself above every so-called god or object of worship, so that he takes his seat in the temple of God, displaying himself as being God. Do you not remember that while I was still with you, I was telling you these things? And you know what restrains him now [*kai nun to katechon oidate*], so that in his time he will be revealed. For the mystery of lawlessness is already at work; only he who now restrains [*ho katechōn*] will do so until taken out of the way. Then the lawless one will be revealed whom the Lord will slay with the breath of His mouth and bring to an end by the appearance of His coming; that is, the one whose coming is in accord with the activity of Satan, with all power and signs and false wonders, and with all the deception of wickedness for those who perish, because they did not receive the love of the truth so as to be saved.[85]

Paul never reveals the identity of *what* or *who* does the restraining in this passage, nor does he disclose the identity of the man of lawlessness mentioned here. This in part explains the allure of this passage for ancient, medieval, and modern commentators. The recent resurgence of interest among theoreticians working outside biblical studies in the figures of the *katechon* or *katechōn* is linked mainly to its significance in twentieth-century political theology. The German theorist Carl Schmitt, for example, follows the precedent set by Tertullian when he interprets the *katechōn* as the positive historical function of political empires. On this reading the *katechōn* consists in a worldly or decidedly secular power invested in staving off the chaos of the end time. Paul Metzger and Ernest Best have shown that this modern version of the tendency to associate the *katechōn* with Rome or with political sovereignty more generally represents just a small spectrum of opinions on 2 Thessalonians in the history of Christian biblical exegesis.[86]

The the mystery of the *katechon* lies at the very heart of Heidegger's commentary even though its centrality is not readily apparent. The commentary revolves around this mystery even though Heidegger following Paul never explicitly unmasks its identity. Nevertheless Heidegger's specific way of deriving temporality from Christian religiosity only makes sense if we see that the anonymity of the *katechon* on his reading is not entirely indeterminate, but rather its identity can be inferred by pinpointing its function as the inner principle of religious life, the ground or source from which the temporality of awaiting arises and to which it returns.

The route Heidegger takes to isolate the function of the *katechōn* is a circuitous one. For starters, he approaches 2 Thessalonians 2:1–10 by mapping the Pauline man of lawlessness onto the bifurcation between objective history (*Geschehen*) and absolute history (*Ereignis*) running throughout the course. The man of lawlessness mentioned in the passage is for him the Antichrist: "The appearance of the Antichrist is no mere momentary happening [*vorübergehendes Geschehen*], but rather something upon which one's fate is decided—even for those who are already believers."[87] The ability of the Christian to recognize the Antichrist is conferred by the Holy Spirit. Only those who await the parousia in absolute lack or distress will be able to discern the identity of the man of lawlessness. The concept of faith underpinning Heidegger's understanding of 2 Thessalonians is mentioned earlier in the course: "Faith not empty as a state and as yielding a final bliss, rather enactmental relation of the concerned entry to the future; being-dead since the beginning of the end of time. . . . Faith is: *dying with Christ.*"[88] Now, the Pauline theme of faith as dying with

Christ provides the lens through which Heidegger reads 2 Thessalonians. And it will eventually allow us to understand how it is that, according to Heidegger, Christian religiosity *produces* time or lives it transitively.

The commentary slowly works toward this goal by linking 2 Thessalonians 2:15, in which Paul admonishes believers to "stand firm and hold to the traditions" they were taught, with 1 Corinthians 7:24, which expresses a similar dynamic: "each one is to remain with God in that condition in which he was called," as Paul writes. The reading of 2 Thessalonians thereby provides Heidegger with an occasion for fully spelling out the condition in which the Christian awaits the parousia. In 1 Corinthians 7:29-31, Paul explains more fully how the Christian should stand firm: "But this I say, brethren, the time has been shortened, so that from now on those who have wives should be as though they had none; and those who weep, as though they did not weep; and those who rejoice, as though they did not rejoice; and those who buy, as though they did not possess; and those who use the world, as though they did not make full use of it; for the form of the world is passing away." Heidegger cites the passage in order to explain how eschatological time illuminates the essence of history, taking his cue from the notion that the critical time or *kairos*[89] has grown short for Paul. He then links the structure of the kairos to the theme of dying with Christ. It is here in conjunction with the schema of the world as passing away that we get a fuller picture of how Christian experience brings forth temporality, as the sense of history as becoming in time that Heidegger associates with the Pauline kairos promises to shed light on the function, if not the identity, of the *katechōn*. Thus far in the commentary Heidegger has been intent to show that Christian eschatology involves suppressing the sense of the future as consisting solely in datable events that have yet to occur. By contrast in the final sections on 2 Thessalonians he redoubles his effort to prove that Christian religiosity consists of a joyous grief that constitutes the schema of the world as passing away.

For Heidegger the structure of the kairos or critical time has little to do with time considered as a flux or time in its protensive and retentive capacities as described by thinkers such as Husserl. Earlier we noted that in his discussion of conversion Heidegger portrays the act of awaiting the parousia, the futural dimension of Christian life, as equivalent to the dynamic of being continuously thrown back upon the event of "having-become" Christian. The Being of the Christian is distended toward the future in such a manner that this Being reverts immediately upon its past, rendering its present highly unstable and insecure. Here in connection with the Pauline kairos, the roots of the threefold ecstatic temporality spelled out in *Being and Time* first become discernible in an outline of eschatological time that will be retained in Heidegger's subsequent writings on hermeneutic phenomenology. The sense of the future as a radical recursion upon the past; the repeatability of the past in its thrown character; the form of the present in its uncertainty as the birth of the historical—all of these themes are present here in nascent form within the discussion of 1 Corinthians as it is used to elucidate 2 Thessalonians, with a crucially important caveat. Here the Pauline kairos reveals that the alteration of the temporal schema caused by Christian conversion is one that increases the *brokenness* of life instead of revealing the *unity* of time's threefold ecstatic structure: "Christian life is not straightforward but is rather broken [*gebrochen*]: all surrounding-world relations must pass through the complex of enactment of 'having-become' so that this complex is then co-present, but the relations themselves, and that to which they refer, are in no way touched."[90] The kairos is time lived in terms of its brokenness. But what does brokenness mean in this case? For starters, it is clear that the christianization of temporality for Heidegger hollows out the content of life, robbing one's worldly standing of significance to such a degree that Paul counsels no change in one's station. And yet the compression of time seems to be effected by a sense of brokenness that has nothing to do with the relation between the objective and absolute levels of history, but that instead pertains exclusively to the event-like character of religiosity. What connects Heidegger's brief remarks on 1 Corinthians to his overarching commentary on 2 Thessalonians is the theme of mortification, the definition of faith as dying with Christ that is mentioned in connection with Galatians. If we keep this definition of faith as dying with Christ in view, we can solve the riddle of the *katechōn* in the commentary and use it to discern the sense in which awaiting gives rise to temporality.

For Heidegger, as we have said, the Christian does not stand back from the schema of the world as it passes away, but rather the Christian in his or her ipseity belongs to this schema, and so this ipseity persists as part of the form of the world that is now passing away. Though Heidegger does not cite the Pauline or deutero-Pauline letter to the Ephesians, whose author admonishes his readers "to put off your old self, which is being corrupted by its deceitful desires," and "to put on the new self, created to be like God in true righteousness and holiness,"[91] he plays upon the crucial motif of faith as mortification in order to think eschatological awaiting in the form of expiation or atonement, the dying away of the old self. The sense of brokenness at play in Christian life is further specified in the commentary by modifying the Eckhartian theme of detachment,[92] which Heidegger maps onto the Pauline critical time in glossing 1 Corinthians. Heidegger subtly modifies the theme in order to speak of detachment or isolation as clarifying the experience of time opened by the Pauline kairos: "The isolation [*Abgesondertsein*] of Christian life sounds negative. Properly understood the complex of experience can be grasped only out of the origin of Christian life-context. . . . With brokenness, the anguish and gloominess of the Christians is still intensified; it has entered into the innermost realm."[93] These lines suggest that the Christian stance of awaiting is affected internally by a certain experience of brokenness. They also suggest that this sense of brokenness must be situated against a level at which Christian religiosity remains unbroken albeit in a manner that does not reconstitute its unity or harmony: "In Christian life there is, however, also an unbroken life-context, on the level of spirituality which has nothing to do with the harmony of life."[94] From this we see that Heidegger views the brokenness of Christian life in terms of the process of mortification whereby the old sinful self is passing away as the new redeemed one is born. We also infer here that the division between sin and redemption is rooted in a more fundamental vitality that does not vitiate, but rather intensifies, the experience of brokenness in question.

The true import of these lines comes from what they reveal about the rather submerged set of claims Heidegger advances in his commentary on 2 Thessalonians. Everything in this commentary hinges upon Heidegger's effort to explicate the proper meaning of the *spirit* or *spirituality* for Paul. This effort is highly relevant for understanding the relation between the phenomenology of religious life and the model of vital experience described in the KNS 1919 lecture course. The main issue is this: if according to the KNS 1919 lecture course intuition and understanding are structurally unified in all experiential contents, then the universal validity of this structural unity should extend to religiosity as well. If, as Heidegger indicates, the explication of religious life should assist the phenomenologist in grasping the nature of lived experience, then we should fully expect the description of Christian spirituality connected with 2 Thessalonians to display the kind of unbroken vital unity that characterizes the reflexivity of the hermeneutical intuition in KNS 1919 as I outlined it above. In fact Heidegger's discussion of the fractured character of Christian life is merely a first sign that the view of spirituality advanced in the final sections of "Introduction to the Phenomenology of Religion" confirms the model of the hermeneutical intuition in KNS 1919 only in the sense that it puts this model on an endless trial. And this alerts us to the fact that if Heidegger's portrait of Christian religiosity winds up justifying in his own eyes the basic presuppositions of his hermeneutics it will not do so by conforming to any preset pattern, but by constantly tearing away at the foundations of this hermeneutics, submitting them to the most jarring and violent form of solicitation.

In §32 of the manuscript Heidegger notes that the conversion experience, the touchstone of all genuine religiosity, "exceeds human strength. It is unthinkable out of one's own strength. Factical life, from out of its own resources, cannot provide the motives to attain even becoming Christian."[95] The event of becoming Christian is not ascribable to Christian life itself. It is rather the product of an alien work that Heidegger attributes to the Pauline spirit or *pneuma*. More importantly this calling must be seen as signifying the *indwelling* Spirit as the ground of all Christian enactment. When Heidegger speaks of the unbroken life-context of Christian enactment, he has in mind this spirit or *pneuma* as the ground of religiosity and thus as a feature internal to it: "The *pneuma* in Paul is the basis of enactment."[96] The assertion greatly complicates any attempt to align Christian religiosity with the self-reflexive character of the hermeneutical intuition, as it effectively thinks the divine as the animating principle of human volition. The language Heidegger uses to explicate this basis of enactment is influenced by his reading of medieval scholasticism. The view of the Spirit he adopts in this course is arguably indebted to the series of notes and sketches compiled years earlier for an undelivered lecture course on medieval mysticism.[97] In this earlier context the analysis of Cistercian spirituality in particular is geared toward showing that in Bernard of Clairvaux among other writers the soul must constitute itself as "the place for God and the godly,"[98] the vessel through which divine power is active in history.

The vision of the apostolic life that emerges in the 2 Thessalonians commentary is in line with this, as the basis for the experience of awaiting the parousia in Paul depends on the illuminative grace and its noetic effects in a manner similar to the early Heideggerian reading of Cistercian and late medieval Spanish mystical texts. In a tight sequence toward the end of the commentary on 2 Thessalonians, Heidegger first reasserts his portrayal of the spirit as the ground of Christian enactment. He then immediately identifies the Christian with the *anthrōpos pneumatikos*, the one who is taught by the Spirit or, as he puts it, "the one who has appropriated a certain peculiar property of life."[99] This reading depends on a strong notion of the Holy Spirit as conferring prevenient and operative grace upon the created soul. In connection with this, Heidegger ties the reading of 2 Thessalonians to 1 Thessalonians, filling in the reading of 1 Thessalonians 1:6 we noted above, in which Paul describes becoming Christian as an acceptance of the word "in great despair with the joy of the Holy Spirit." Whereas the commentary on 1 Thessalonians focuses on the meaning of despair, the commentary on 2 Thessalonians in its discussion of the spirit focuses on the theme of joy.

What then is the meaning of religious joy in this context? Its significance can be discerned here only if we focus on the figure of the "spiritual man" in Heidegger's remarks, which gives rise to a highly idiosyncratic reading of the *katechōn* in 2 Thessalonians. The basic premise of the 2 Thessalonians commentary is that the spirit confers knowledge upon the one who accepts the Christian message. The one who is spiritual, as Paul writes in 1 Corinthians 2:15, "appraises all things, yet he himself is appraised by no one." In Heidegger's paraphrase of this line, the centrality of the knowledge conferred by the Spirit is brought to the fore: "The complexes of enactment themselves, according to their own sense, are a knowledge. . . . According to its essence, 'knowledge' requires 'having the spirit' [*pneuma echein*]."[100] Heidegger's brief discussion in §§32–33 of spiritual knowledge is meant to elucidate Paul's proclamation of the Antichrist in 2 Thessalonians 2. Only by taking on the burden of eschatological distress, by repositioning oneself within life as affliction and grief, can the Christian discern sin and recognize the man of lawlessness.[101] But this repositioning merely makes it possible to recognize the Antichrist. It does not guarantee that the Christian will indeed recognize him. This is why for Heidegger Paul admonishes the faithful in 1 Thessalonians 5:21 to "examine everything carefully, and hold fast to that which is good." And with this need for vigilance we come to the crucial moment in Heidegger's commentary.

Heidegger notes that in 2 Thessalonians 2:6–7, Paul reminds the Thessalonians that they know exactly who or what is restraining the Antichrist. In other words, following Heidegger's gloss, Paul does not identify the *katechōn* because it is not necessary to do so for his audience. The Thessalonians know perfectly *who* or *what* puts off the end times. From Heidegger's perspective the knowledge concerning this delay is conferred upon them by the spirit. It is the spirit as the ground of Christian enactment that alerts those awaiting the second coming to the fact of its delay. Moreover it is actually *having the spirit* that constitutes the *factuality* of this delay. From this, one can infer that the *katechon* is actually at the root of Christian enactment, and that when Paul appeals to the Thessalonians' knowledge of its identity he is actually referring them back to the enactmental ground of their own awaiting. Concerning the *katechon* as the enactmental ground of Christian awaiting, Heidegger writes: "From this complex of enactment with God arises something like temporality to begin with. II Thess. 2:6–7: 'and you know what is now restraining him [*kai nun to katechon oidate*]'—for the mystery of lawlessness is already at work."[102] In short, the *katechon* or *katechōn* designates the locus from which temporality is produced by primordial Christian religiosity in the form of awaiting.

Does this mean that for Heidegger the indwelling Spirit is the *katechōn*? All signs seem to point in this direction, even if Heidegger does not explicitly acknowledge it. In his monograph Metzger notes very few precedents in the early Church for interpreting the Holy Spirit as the *katechōn*.[103] Slightly more common is the tendency to equate the *katechōn* with the divine will or with God himself. Yet Heidegger comes closest to the former construal by arguing that we must pay close attention to the fact that Paul links the *katechōn* to the drama of religious enactment at the level of absolute history, and that he sees this drama as closely linked to the experience of the present as radical subjective uncertainty.[104] While glossing 2 Thessalonians 2:3, Heidegger suggests that in its essence Christian facticity is clarified through "an increase of the highest anguish."[105] To this he adds that this anguish is bound up with the emphatic sense of the present in which the mystery of lawlessness or sin is already at work. On this reading, the "now" of eschatological time is thus the "now" in which sin has taken root: "To the Christian only the '*now*' (*to nun*) of the complex of enactment in which he really stands is to be decisive."[106] The notion that the Christian equates his or her own complex of enactment with the mystery of sin fits well with Heidegger's earlier suggestion that Christian life is one of an ever-intensifying inner affliction.

This is indeed the linchpin in Heidegger's argument concerning the authenticity of 2 Thessalonians. If the Thessalonians know all too well who is restraining the man of lawlessness, it is because they are painfully aware that the present consists primarily in anguish. To this extent their experience mirrors that of Heidegger's Paul, who sees himself as needing, and failing for the time being, to live in such a way as to bring about the parousia: "There are those in the congregation [at Thessalonica]," Heidegger writes, "who have understood Paul, and who know what is crucial. If the *parousia* depends upon how I live, then I am unable to maintain the faith and love that is demanded of me; then I approach despair. Those who think this way worry themselves in a real sense, under the sign of real concern, as to whether or not they will hold out until the decisive day. But Paul does not help them; rather he makes their anguish still greater."[107] The fact that those who possess the indwelling Spirit approach despair is a sign of just how radically uncertain they are regarding their enactment of awaiting.

Such an approach to 2 Thessalonians is at odds with a more recent philosophical treatment of the Pauline corpus. In *The Time That Remains*, Giorgio Agamben follows Paul as well as Heidegger by refusing to grant "any positive valuation of the *katechōn*."[108] And though he criticizes Schmitt's tendency to associate the *katechōn* with the historical agency of political entities, he exhibits this tendency in its most extreme form while at the same time reversing its valence. The *katechon* is not, according to Agamben, political power in its stabilizing force, insofar as it staves off the chaos of the end times. It is rather the political as the "force that clashes with and hides"[109] the messianic suspension of the law. In this sense the *katechon* refers indefinitely to every constituted form of authority that rejects the promise of the parousia. If we follow Agamben's reading of 2 Thessalonians, then the *katechōn* or *katechon* would stand outside of, and ultimately in opposition to, the situation of eschatological awaiting. The unveiling of its mystery would coincide with the appropriation of a new form of power or force, one that "assumes the figure"[110] of the messianic as lawlessness, i.e. weakness as a form of virulence. By contrast Heidegger does not extract the *katechōn* from the stance of eschatological awaiting. Whereas Agamben views messianic lawlessness or inoperativity as an apolitical force standing in opposition to the political figure of the *katechōn*, Heidegger interprets the *katechon* as that which opens the experience which Agamben equates with the messianic.

The real import of the fact that Heidegger equates this figure with the indwelling Spirit as the ground of Christian enactment—implying that the Spirit itself puts off the parousia, renders Christian awaiting radically uncertain of itself, and opens the present as affliction—is that this interpretation clarifies the sense in which Christian spirituality for Heidegger can be thought of as unbroken, though without harmony. If according to Heidegger having the Spirit means knowing that the parousia depends upon how "I" live and thus experiencing oneself as guilty for the sins of the world, then presumably this knowledge alerts one to the fact that the affliction one endures in the present is divinely ordained. In short, the Pauline pneumatic self understands that the critical time or kairos consists in a kind of mortification, a putting to death of the old self. The reason why those who genuinely worry themselves approach despair is that they enter most deeply into the experience of the present as mortification. And yet to follow the contours of Heidegger's reading is to acknowledge that this despair is compatible with the kind of joy given by the spirit. The unity of Christian spirituality in this reading is a *unio spiritus*, the spiritual union between the soul of the Christian and the indwelling divine Spirit. It is only by acknowledging the specific form in which this spiritual unity is experientially enacted that we can understand the Heideggerian contention that Christian religiosity gives rise to time.

The commentary on 1 and 2 Thessalonians describes the union of Christian spiritual life as taking shape in a pattern with unmistakably temporal dimensions, according to which the act of anticipating a future event throws the Christian back upon a deep past, raising the question of whether or not one has truly accepted the Christian calling. This dynamic interplay between past and future opens the present in a form of affliction in which the pneumatic self, as responsible for the delay of the parousia, takes upon itself the sins of "the world." One is tempted to claim here that the strong bond between temporality and being-guilty characterizing primordial Christian religiosity anticipates the prominent role that this bond eventually plays in *Being and Time*, as I shall discuss in chapter 4. To make this claim, however, would be to risk overlooking the more immediately meaningful point, which is that in his effort to show how Christian religiosity generates time, Heidegger has effectively figured the experience of the present for Paul along the lines of a joyous vicarious sacrifice or inner crucifixion. Heidegger's Paul is actually a type for the crucified Christ, the *verus imitator* of the one who takes away the sins of the world. And the spiritual unity which his Paul urges the Thessalonians to cultivate likewise figures mortification as an inner crucifixion.

In other words, the structure of temporality that emerges in the "Introduction to the Phenomenology of Religion" is unmistakably cruciform. Thus when one arrives at the end of the commentary on 1 and 2 Thessalonians one has the distinct impression that in his effort to glean the meaning of temporal becoming from New Testament sources Heidegger has just pulled off an interpretive feat of impressive proportions: his commentary manages to install the cross as the very center of historical becoming, while barely mentioning the gospel narratives and without alerting its readers to just how profoundly it revolves around the central unnamed event of crucifixion, taking it up speculatively just as the young Hegel did in his *Faith and Knowledge*.[111]

RELIGIOSITY: EXEMPLAR AND RIVAL

"Real philosophy of religion arises not from preconceived concepts of philosophy and religion. Rather, the possibility of its philosophical understanding arises out of a certain religiosity—for us, the Christian religiosity.... Why exactly the Christian religiosity lies in the focus of our study, that is a difficult question."[112] So begins the concluding paragraph of the "Introduction to the Phenomenology of Religion." Having claimed that Paul allows us to sketch historical becoming as temporality, Heidegger then struggled to justify this choice. The task of a "real philosophy of religion," he asserts, "is to gain a real and original relationship to history, which is to be explicated from out of our own historical situation and facticity."[113] At the same time, however, a real and original relationship to history is the condition for a real philosophy of religion: "At issue is what the sense of history can signify for us.... History exists only from out of a present. Only thus can the possibility of a philosophy of religion be begun."[114] The reasoning here is circular: a real philosophy of religion is possible only on the basis of an original relation to history, which in turn is the precondition for a real philosophy of religion. We could perhaps dismiss the contradiction were it not for the fact that it adequately reflects the situation that emerges once we read Heidegger's commentary on Paul alongside his initial descriptions of hermeneutics. From this contradiction we can offer the following observations by way of conclusion.

First, that the reasoning behind Heidegger's inquiry into religiosity is at base circular suggests that by placing the phenomenology of religious life in its context, a circularity comes into view that anticipates the hermeneutic circle which Heidegger identifies in *Being and Time* as the precondition of ontological inquiry. At the outset of the 1927 treatise Heidegger concedes that there is a manifest circularity to his existential analysis, which formulates the question of Being by first defining an entity in its Being.[115] But here in early 1921 he indicates by contrast that the phenomenology of religious life has not yet actualized "the possibility of a real philosophy of religion,"[116] if only because it still aims to cultivate a real relationship with history.

Second, the observation that Heidegger's "Introduction to the Phenomenology of Religion" ends by laying bare its circular logic cannot count as a formal objection to its findings any more than the manifest circularity behind *Being and Time* disqualifies ahead of time the results obtained by analyzing Dasein. The point here is not to suggest that this inquiry lacks coherence, but rather to observe that its circularity precedes the rise of the one mentioned in *Being and Time*, which is rendered productive in that it seeks to make explicit the implicit understanding of Being which forms Dasein's experience at every step. Whether the transition to the latter circularity involves displacing and overwriting the former one remains to be seen. Here it is important to note, however, that less than two years after his highly subtle exegesis of Paul, Heidegger altogether disowns the philosophy of religion on account of its incoherence, arguing that this philosophy would impossibly have to straddle the border between two antithetical domains or regions of experience entirely shut off from one another. According to the 1922 formulae, the "pure illogicality"[117] of the philosophy of religion provides the basis for its disqualification. When measured against the sophisticated strategy of the Paul commentary, however, we can see that what Heidegger calls the illogicality of the philosophy of religion had been its real strength in 1920–1921, the mark of its privileged capacity to bring forth an original relation to history.

Third, the eventual repudiation of the philosophy of religion functions here to indirectly confirm the discrepancy between the aim of the Paul commentary and the results obtained by it. On the one hand, by confirming the link between guilt and temporality this commentary makes a real contribution to the philosophy that takes shape in the early lecture courses. Neither the KNS 1919 course nor the review essay of Karl Jaspers's *Psychology of Worldviews* ever manages to pinpoint time as the constitution of the "I am." Neither text, moreover, identifies the role played by guilt in constituting time as the meaning of factical life. By contrast the Paul commentary is almost singularly focused on achieving these goals, as Heidegger seeks a new vocabulary for defining factical life as temporal becoming. On the other hand, these goals are achieved only by borrowing an account of Christian life marked by a disparate kind of unity whose motive force is conferred by an indwelling figure of the divine. On this point it is not difficult to see that the concept of temporal being Heidegger gleans from primordial Christian religiosity is tied to an absolutely non-representable source beyond the confines of a strictly secular account of rationality, the presence of which threatens to overturn the notion of self-possession Heidegger elsewhere defends and to overload the religious believer with an exorbitant responsibility which this believer could never appropriate. To this extent Heidegger's Paul commentary works at cross purposes: it seeks to illustrate temporality along the lines of the unified self-reflexivity characterizing vital experience, even as it views Christian religiosity as a disharmonious yet unbroken spiritual unity rooted in the inner presence of a divine principle. The combination of these two trajectories imparts to religiosity a vacillating and unsteady presence in Heidegger's early lecture courses.

This unsteadiness extends as well to textual sources deemed to be religious, allowing them at times to confirm and at other times to contest the primordial structures of existence as they take shape philosophically in Heidegger's corpus. Though the early Heidegger devotes little attention to it after 1921, this dilemma is greatly exacerbated by his 1921 commentary on Augustine's *Confessions* to which we now turn, which re-inscribes the circular logic broached here in the final lines of the commentary on Paul.

CHAPTER TWO

The *Cogito* Out-of-Reach

INTRODUCTION

On September 13, 1920, Heidegger wrote a letter to a twenty-three-year-old Karl Löwith, advising him on how to prepare for the upcoming term. At the time Heidegger planned to conduct a practicum on Descartes's *Meditations on First Philosophy* alongside his lectures on Christian religiosity. In his response to Löwith, Heidegger indicates that from his perspective the two courses were thematically linked, as they were both devoted to the curious task of "reversing" Cartesian self-consciousness: "For the '*cogito*,'" Heidegger writes, "*all of Christian philosophy* comes into question for me, since I want to see it *backwards*, look at it *in verso*, so to speak. It is only important that you know something of the other metaphysical treatises and the *Regulae*, so that the perversity of [Descartes's] epistemological resolution can be studied."[1] These lines mark the emergence of a crucial theme in the early lecture courses. Starting in 1920, Heidegger would labor for years to reevaluate Descartes's argument in the *Meditations* "that the proposition, *I am, I exist*, is necessarily true whenever it is put forward by me or conceived in my mind."[2] And this reevaluation is precisely what motivated his critical confrontation with Augustine in 1921.

A subsection of *Being and Time* §43 entitled "Reality as an Ontological Problem" does a slightly better job of explaining the stakes of "reversing" the *cogito*, as it indicates that Heidegger grants the validity of Descartes's argument while assigning it a novel meaning: "If the 'I think, I am' [*cogito sum*] is to serve as the basic point of departure for the existential analytic of *Dasein* then it needs to be turned around. . . . The 'I am' is then asserted first, and indeed in the sense that 'I am in the world.'

53

As such an entity 'I am' in the possibility of Being towards various ways of comporting myself—namely, thoughts [*cogitationes*]—as ways of Being alongside entities-within-the-world. Descartes, on the contrary, says that thoughts [*cogitationes*] are present-at-hand, and that in these an *ego* is present-at-hand too as a worldless *thinking thing* [*res cogitans*]."[3] By early 1922, Heidegger had already outlined his argument that Descartes perverted the nature of self-consciousness by inferring its ontological meaning from the undetermined objective standing of thought-contents.[4] Having overlooked what the KNS 1919 lecture calls the pre-theoretical level of lived experience, Descartes assumed that thinking consists in relating myself to thought-contents set before the mind's eye, and that the ego as the possessor of thought-contents has the same kind of Being as do these representations. The *cogito*, properly speaking, is a thinking thing, a *res cogitans*. To view it in reverse would mean, for Heidegger, not only to reject the notion that the *cogito* can be construed as a thing, or something present-at-hand in Heidegger's language; it would mean reopening the inquiry into the enigma of its ontological status for the first time in the modern European philosophical context.

The 1920–1921 reading of Paul in "Introduction to the Phenomenology of Religion" fails to mention Descartes, yet the connection Heidegger draws in his letter to Löwith between reversing Cartesian self-consciousness and reinterpreting Christianity is a crucial one. The close tie between them is borne out by the fact that on multiple occasions from 1920 to 1931 Heidegger suggested that a critical retrieval of Augustine of Hippo's anthropology could provide the resources for undoing Descartes's alleged perversion of the *cogito*.[5] This arguably explains why in the early Freiburg lecture courses Heidegger speaks of the "independent value" of Augustine's well-known *Confessions*,[6] and why his summer 1921 seminar entitled "Augustine and Neoplatonism" consists of a line-by-line gloss on Book 10 of the *Confessions*. In the seminar manuscript's final pages Heidegger reveals that the entire course is animated by the hidden aim of fighting back against Cartesian subjectivity: "Descartes watered down Augustine's thoughts. Self-certainty and the Having-of-Oneself [*das Sich-selbst-Haben*] in Augustine's sense are wholly other than the Cartesian evidence of the *cogito*."[7] Here the opposition between Descartes and Augustine mirrors the disjunction between modern forms of philosophical subjectivity and Heidegger's own hermeneutics. The two thinkers are said to be diametrically opposed on what is meant by having-a-self (*das Sich-selbst-Haben*).[8] But in what sense is Augustine's account of self-certainty wholly other than that of Descartes?

The present chapter argues that a careful reading of "Augustine and Neoplatonism" demonstrates that Heidegger does indeed uncover a "reversed" *cogito* in the pages of the *Confessions*, and moreover that his singular concern to show that Augustinian confession engenders a specific mode of self-possession left a profound mark in his nascent hermeneutic method. Modern scholarship has demonstrated the pitfalls of applying contemporary concepts to ancient and medieval sources. As Brian Stock contends, "Augustine has no term for the elusive notion of the self,"[9] but rather he frequently designates it with various pronouns or terms such as intellect (*mens*), mind (*animus*), soul (*anima*), and spirit (*spiritus*). This is precisely why, I contend, Heidegger enlists Augustine to counteract the prevalence of Cartesian metaphysics among his contemporaries. As I explain, Heidegger tries to show in "Augustine and Neoplatonism" that Augustine's search for God led him to characterize human existence as a species of nothingness, one that Heidegger sees as ontologically opposed to the Cartesian self. Thus in 1921 it is Augustine who is said to anticipate the novel "self-experience"[10] which Heidegger seeks to recover by destroying the modern philosophical foundations of subjectivity. But as with the exegesis of Paul, we must ask whether or not Heidegger's attempt to extract from a theological text a critique of contemporary accounts of subjectivity works at cross-purposes with itself. What fascinates the early Heidegger about Augustine is the connection he espies in the *Confessions* between self-interpretation and self-renunciation. As I show, however, the version of self-renunciation he attributes to Augustine in 1921 is tied to a prohibition against self-representation that unsettles Heidegger's attempt to make use of it philosophically as an antidote to Descartes.

THE *COGITO* "*IN VERSO*"

To set the stage for "Augustine and Neoplatonism," it is first necessary to gain a fuller picture of Heidegger's concern to "reverse" the Cartesian *cogito*. Let us recall that in the Second Meditation Descartes employs a method of hyperbolic doubt to arrive at his famous conclusion: "So after considering everything very thoroughly, I must finally conclude that this proposition, *I am, I exist*, is necessarily true whenever it is put forward by me or conceived in my mind."[11] As I mentioned above, Heidegger does not dispute the validity of the assertion. Instead he adopts it as a "point of departure"[12] in *Being and Time*. In doing so he takes issue with the fact that, in the Second Meditation, Descartes immediately interprets the Being of the ego as a thinking thing: "I am, then, in the strict sense only a thing that thinks; that is, I am mind, or intelligence, or intellect, or reason—words whose meaning I have been ignorant of until now. But for all that I am a thing which is real and which truly exists [*res vera et vere existens*]."[13] What Heidegger calls the "perversity" of Descartes's epistemological resolution is perhaps best captured by this last phrase, which identifies the ego as a "*res . . . existens*," or an existing thing. The formula conflates two ways of Being that Heidegger takes to be fundamentally divergent—thinghood, which characterizes objects present-at-hand, and existence, which describes the ontological meaning of human being-there. Heidegger's wager is that starting with Aristotle metaphysical concepts have been geared toward thinghood, leaving existence more or less uninterrogated.

Along these lines, to reverse the *cogito* means to interpret the "I am" as a unique way of Being in its own right, first, by refusing to interpret it as a thing and, second, by developing a whole new set of categories to describe existence as an enigmatic way of being thrown into the world and being able to project possibilities before itself. To accomplish this task Heidegger argues that he must first destroy the modern philosophical subject by uncovering its ontological inadequacies.[14] Through historical inquiries designed to unsettle the Cartesian view of self-consciousness, he contends, contemporary philosophers can avoid the mistake of interpreting existence "in an indifferent, formally objective, uncritical and unclarified sense, one that has no genuine relation to the *ego*."[15] Although idea of reversing the *cogito* is discussed in the early Freiburg lecture courses directly following "Augustine and Neoplatonism," it is not until Heidegger arrives at Marburg that he systematically engages Descartes's *Meditations* in a seminar setting.

In the first Marburg lecture course, entitled *Einführung in die phänomenologische Forschung* (*Introduction to Phenomenological Research*), in the winter semester of 1923–1924 (WS 1923–1924), Heidegger devotes most of his attention to Descartes "and the Scholastic ontology that determines him."[16] Here we encounter the earliest version of the standard charge Heidegger would level against Descartes: under the sway of the mathematical sciences, Cartesian metaphysics enacts "a fundamental repositioning in the basic determination of a human's being,"[17] while simultaneously leaving intact the "old ontology . . . as a self-evident foundation."[18] This repositioning involves taking over Thomas Aquinas's concepts of truth and understanding while assigning to human volition capacities that Thomas reserves for the divine, resulting in what Heidegger calls "an extreme Pelagianism of theoretical knowing"[19] that establishes the *cogito* as the firm and certain foundation of a universal science. Henceforth, Heidegger asserts, modern metaphysics prioritizes a single mode of being as the meaning of Being in general—namely, being as *being-certain* or mere ascertainability, which the early Heidegger associates with presence-at-hand or *Vorhandensein*.[20]

While this approach requires Heidegger to situate Descartes carefully in relation to Thomas, it also leads him to align himself with Augustine: "We will make the sense of [Descartes's] idea of truth more accessible for ourselves by orienting 'truth' to existence itself, and asking *in what sense truth pertains to 'existence' at all*. It is the Augustinian question of the *relation of veritas and vita*."[21] Here we cannot fail to notice that the destruction of Cartesian metaphysics Heidegger attempts in WS 1923–1924 is placed under the banner of a question deemed to be Augustinian. Given that Heidegger argues that Cartesian metaphysics is a form of Pelagianism, it is hardly surprising that he aligns himself with Augustine. At first glance, however, this alliance seems at best peripheral to Heidegger's main concerns in criticizing Descartes, if only because the WS 1923–1924 course contains no substantive analysis of Augustine. In point of fact Heidegger's reading of Descartes solidifies his alliance with Augustine in a surprising fashion, as his reading of the *Meditations* is designed to show that the Augustinian question itself—namely, "in what sense does truth [*veritas*] pertain to existence [*vita*]?"—is the only legitimate form of the *cogito*. That is to say, the "I" has itself only to the extent that it directs this question at its own Being, radically undermining its sense of security.

To anticipate our reading of "Augustine and Neoplatonism," this dynamic of having-oneself by radical self-interrogation is the form of selfhood that Heidegger claims to uncover in Augustine, for whom the "having-of-oneself is, as factical, such that it enacts an endangering [*Gefährdung*] of itself and thereby builds itself up."[22] In fact a similar conclusion is reached in the *Introduction to Phenomenological Research* as Heidegger seeks to avoid resolving Cartesian doubt into objective self-certainty and to reassert the legitimacy of the Augustinian *quaestio* as the authentic Being of self-consciousness.

This strange assertion requires elucidation. In §§39–45 of WS 1923–1924, Heidegger dwells on Descartes's Second Meditation, rehearsing the method of hyperbolic doubt. Here he studies the figure of the *cogito* at the point of its emergence. By the beginning of the Second Meditation, let us recall, Descartes has placed all external reality, including the evidence of the senses and of memory, along with body, figure, extension, and motion, under the supposition of falsehood. Now the prospect of an all-powerful deceiver threatens to undercut Descartes's efforts to establish the existence of any entity with absolute certainty. Heidegger dwells upon this moment of extreme skepticism in which Descartes's search for certainty enters an "end situation" and is incapable of advancing any farther.[23] As the search reaches an impasse, Descartes confronts a kind of nothingness: "At the end of the path, the search [for certainty] is so positioned that it is placed before 'nothing' and before 'the nothing' of its own possibilities."[24] Ironically this search attains its goal here in being forced back upon itself, as the one searching becomes present to himself as "out-for-something" (*auf-zu*), lingering in the state of hyperbolic doubt: "[Descartes] is not only placed *before the nothing*, but also placed *in the nothing of any possibility* of still encountering something. The search is before the nothing and it itself is placed into the nothing, and yet is still characterized as out-for-something certain."[25] Heidegger argues that this phenomenon of being "out-for-something" is nothing other than the intentional structure of subjectivity.

It is only when hyperbolic doubt reaches its highest pitch that Descartes is finally "pressed to make a leap to see"[26] this structure for what it is: "All the search can encounter now is the *being of the one searching itself*. . . . The search can now find only the *Searching-Being itself* [*Suchendsein selbst*], which contains in itself its *Being*. . . . The *esse* of the very *res* that I come across is the sort of being that must be expressed by the *sum*, 'I am.' Not something like the discoverability [*Vorfindlichkeit*] of doubting as a *res* is what is found, but rather the fact [*Tatbestand*] that an *esse* is given along with the doubting."[27] The Cartesian *ego* emerges here in its essence as the fact of reflexive self-discovery in the search for true knowledge. But as the reading of Descartes Heidegger advances three years later, in his winter 1926–1927 lecture on "The History of Philosophy from Thomas Aquinas to Kant," makes clear, the cognitive self-confrontation that occurs here for Descartes is "not an intuition of a given, but the discovery of a state-of-affairs."[28] All that can be deduced ontologically speaking about this essence according to the 1923–1924 course is that the ego is somehow "there along with itself," that its essence affects it in the mode of self-doubt. Thus in the 1923–1924 text Heidegger faults Descartes for too quickly concluding that the being of the one searching can be determined as a thing, or more specifically a "thought-thing" (*Denkding*),[29] when in hyperbolic doubt the essence of the ego affects it as a "fact" (*Tatbestand*) that is fundamentally enigmatic and undetermined.

By these lights the *ego cogito* is formally nothing other than this mysterious being-given-to-oneself or pure self-affection. What Heidegger calls the "out-for-something" (*auf-zu*) is a structure that stands in for the ego's intentional directedness toward the world. Though this directedness is not objectively experienced by the ego it is nevertheless "there" for it in the mode of self-affection. For Heidegger the great breakthrough of the *Meditations* is the discovery that the ego has an immediate, nonobjective access to its own intentional directedness, and yet Descartes grasps neither this essence nor the ego's relation to it in an ontologically appropriate manner. This explains why the destruction of the *res cogitans* in 1923–1924 is chiefly concerned with its reflexive form. Heidegger argues not only that the ego consists in intentional directedness toward experiential contents but also that this directedness is underpinned at all times by an unthematic, implicit, and essential reflexivity that must be designated as such. The *cogito* is thus always a *cogito me cogitare*, "I think myself thinking," or a "having-oneself-along-with-oneself" (*das Sich-mit-habens*): "*Cogito* does not simply mean: 'I ascertain something that thinks'; instead, it is a *cogitare*, indeed, such that I myself have this entity along with thinking."[30] Or as he puts in 1926–1927: "the essence of the *cogitatio* [is] *conscientia*, consciousness, thinking-with-oneself [*sichmitdenken*]."[31] Thus, when Descartes invokes a foreconcept of being to determine the Being of the *cogito sum*—that is, when he simply assumes that the chief mark of its Being is the fact that it is discoverable and thus certain—he allegedly covers over this basic existential stance of "having-oneself-with-oneself."[32]

Years later in the *Nietzsche* volumes, Heidegger identifies this unique way in which I am always "directed back"[33] at myself, or facticity,[34] as the ontologically legitimate core principle of the ego as the form of representation in general: "Descartes says that every *ego cogito* is a *cogito me cogitare*; every 'I represent something' simultaneously represents a 'myself,' a me, the one representing (for myself, in my representing). Every human representing is—in a manner of speaking, and one that is easily misunderstood—a 'self'-representing."[35] By winter 1923–1924 Heidegger already attributes the misunderstanding of self-representing to Descartes without appealing to the Kantian definition of the "I" as the form of all representation but by arguing that in the *Meditations* Descartes glimpsed yet immediately elided the phenomenon of "respectiveness" or *Jeweiligkeit*. For the early Heidegger this concept signifies the radically finite and historically particular nature of first-person experience. In each and every case, the "I" has its own Being, in the sense that it has been delivered over or thrown upon this Being, which it must then appropriate or project before itself in terms of possibilities to be achieved. Respectiveness is irreducible to self-consciousness, even in the entirely indeterminate sense in which Kant saw the transcendental ego as accompanying the empirical ego: "no talk of accompanying [*Begleiten*] gets at the authentic factuality [*Tatbestand*]."[36] Instead a radical reversal of perspective is needed in order to resist determining respectiveness ontologically as a *res* or a thing.

It is crucial that in 1923–1924 this reversal yields the insight that self-having is achievable for the respective, factical individual only in the mode of self-interrogation. The destruction of the *res cogitans* accomplished in the *Introduction to Phenomenological Research* concludes with the assertion that the ego has itself precisely to the extent that it calls itself into question, that it *factically enacts* the Augustinian question concerning the relation between life and truth. Along these lines hyperbolic doubt is overcome not when the ego finally concludes that it *truly* exists, but only when it maintains itself *as* the question, "Am I, do I truly exist?" This argument first appears in the early Freiburg lecture courses directly following "Augustine and Neoplatonism," in late 1921 or early 1922 for example: "The formal indication of the 'I am,' which is the indication that plays the leading role in the problematic of the sense of the Being of life, becomes methodologically effective by . . . becoming actualized in the demonstrable character of the *questionability* ('restlessness') of factical life as the concretely historiological question, 'Am I?'"[37] In this earlier context it is clear that the act of maintaining oneself in this state of restless self-interrogation offers the only way to avoid falling back upon the ontological category of presence-at-hand in defining the self: "The peculiarity of the actualization of this question [Am I?] is precisely the fact that, as a matter of principle, it does not answer the question with a pure, simple, and perfect 'yes,' which would then obviate any further discussion of life, or with that kind of 'no.'"[38]

A similar conclusion would be reached directly following the *Introduction to Phenomenological Research* in Heidegger's famous 1924 lecture, "The Concept of Time." Although the lecture defines *Dasein* as the "fullness of time" (*die volle Zeit*)[39] or as "temporality itself" (*Dasein ist . . . die Zeitlichkeit*),[40] it crucially argues that these definitions are taken seriously only to the extent that they are expressed in the form of the question. In this context the phenomena of death and finitude are first broached in order to test the hypothesis that Dasein is "there" factically for itself such that it can interpret its Being as a whole. If finitude means that part of Dasein is always yet to come and additionally that when Dasein, as a finite entity, comes to its end in death it is no longer "there" for itself,[41] then in what sense does its Being constitute a totality that is available through self-interpretation? The unity of Dasein's existence will be the focus of my critical rereading of *Being and Time* in chapter 4 below. Here I only want to note the following in passing. The 1924 argument that the finitude of Dasein challenges but does not overturn the presupposition that existence is a totality available to Dasein depends upon the assertion at the very end of the lecture, which is that Dasein's Being is meaningful as temporality only from within the stance of self-interrogation: "Who is time? More closely: are we ourselves time? Or closer still: Am I my time? In this way I come closest to [my Being as time], and if I understand the question correctly, it is then taken completely seriously. Such a question is thus the most appropriate manner of access to and of dealing with time as in each case mine. Then *Dasein* would be: being-questionable (*Fraglichsein*)."[42] The conclusion echoes the one reached in the commentary on 1 and 2 Thessalonians, which shows that religiosity constitutes temporality in a cruciform experience of guilt, though in that earlier context Heidegger does not attribute to Paul or to Christian religiosity the formal determination of Being as being-questionable.

The latter determination resembles exactly the destruction of the *res cogitans* in the *Introduction to Phenomenological Research*. In contrast to Descartes, Heidegger asserts that the *ego cogito* must be taken "in the sense of a *formal indication*, in such a way that it is not taken directly (where it says nothing), but is related to the respective concrete instance of what it means."[43] The fact that the *ego cogito* must remain open and labile suggests that Heidegger's destruction of Descartes is designed to come full circle. Having started out by submitting Descartes to the Augustinian question concerning the relation between life and truth, Heidegger implies that this very question is a form that can adequately express the ontological "fact" of having-a-self. This question is not simply the banner under which Heidegger places the 1923–1924 destruction of the Cartesian *res cogitans*; it is also the positive yield of the destruction itself, the expression of a primordial act of existing in which I am confronted with my own existence in the world. Thus, between the 1920–1921 project designed to extract the concept of temporality from Paul and the 1923–1924 reinterpretation of self-consciousness in terms of facticity we can locate the formation of being-questionable, *Fraglichsein*, as the leading indication of selfhood by underscoring its thematic connection with Augustine. But as with the reading of 1 and 2 Thessalonians, the question we must put to the 1921 seminar "Augustine and Neoplatonism" is whether the results generated by a commentary on a religious source adequately reflect the philosophical aims for which this commentary is initially undertaken.

TWO MODES OF *CONFESSIO*

In course manuscripts from late 1921 or early 1922, Heidegger calls this ever-intensifying experience of self-interrogation the "restlessness"[44] of factical life. Broached in detail in "Augustine and Neoplatonism," the existential category of restlessness in Heidegger's subsequent writings bears all the marks of its Augustinian heritage. At first glance, however, it is not entirely obvious that this seminar crucially contributes to the development of Heideggerian hermeneutics.[45] In their published form, the manuscript materials for "Augustine and Neoplatonism" are rather limited in scope: a short preface discussing Dilthey, Harnack, and Troeltsch is followed by a main part consisting of a line-by-line commentary on *Confessions* 10.1–39 that is supplemented by two indices containing digressions on Augustine's letters, sermons, and other writings. But a closer look at the manuscript tells a different more complex story.

I argue here, first, that Heidegger's commentary on Augustine is designed to achieve a philosophically crucial goal, as it provides a first sketch or a "fore-understanding" of the phenomenon of having-a-self, which Descartes allegedly perverts in his *Meditations*. The procedure employed to achieve this goal is similar to the one Heidegger adopts in reading Paul. That is, he interprets the *Confessions* hoping to isolate its religious core. He then derives from the enactment of its religiosity the structure of genuine self-possession, which in this case he gleans paradoxically from Augustine's act of renouncing his "self" in the search for God. Second, I argue that the form of self-renunciation Heidegger uncovers in this search attributes to Augustine a radical prohibition against self-representation. This allows Heidegger to enlist Augustine philosophically as a bulwark against Cartesian metaphysics, but it raises the possibility that the philosophical aims guiding the Heideggerian reconstruction of Augustinian anthropology may be incongruent with the critical forces it sets in motion. To take stock of this dilemma we must briefly follow the crooked trail Heidegger blazes in his effort to isolate the ontological standing of the Augustinian soul as a species of nothingness (*nihil, Nichts*) before God.[46]

The portion of "Augustine and Neoplatonism" that concerns us is thus the commentary on *Confessions* 10. Composed during the last decade of the fourth century C.E., Augustine's *Confessions* consists of thirteen books, the first nine of which recount Augustine's life story leading up to his conversion to Christianity in 386 and the death of his mother Monica in 388. The tenth book marks a shift away from the narrative component of the *Confessions* toward the examination of crucial theological themes, including the search for God recounted in Book 10, the discussion of time and eternity in Book 11, and of heaven and earth in Book 12 and creation in Book 13. In "Augustine and Neoplatonism," Heidegger justifies his decision to focus on the search for God in Book 10 by noting that this book is set apart from the other twelve as it records Augustine's attempt to confess, not what he was in the past or what he will be once he is established in the form in which God created him, but rather what he is now in the "in the very time of [his] confessing."[47] The analogy between this act of confessing oneself in the present, which Augustine calls the "fruit of confession,"[48] and the Heideggerian notion of hermeneutics as the self-interpretation of factical Dasein should be clear. Not unlike the self-interpretation of Dasein, this confession is contemporaneous with its theme and takes aim at itself, attempting to disclose "what I am and what I continue to be."[49] But for Augustine this stance of confession is crucially subordinated to the more fundamental goal of answering the question: "What do I love when I love my God?"[50] Thus the mode of self-interrogation Heidegger isolates in Augustine is not an autonomous form of self-exploration. It is subordinated to the search for God, just as the analytic of Dasein in *Being and Time* is subordinated to the aim of building up the question of the meaning of Being in general.

Buried in Heidegger's initial review of facts concerning *Confessions* 10, we find the central conceit around which his commentary is structured: the so-called fruit of confession is actually a compound substance. There are two diametrically opposed ways of searching for God, and thus interrogating the self, in the book.[51] The 1921 commentary attempts to account for the gap between the two by dividing Augustine's search for God into an "earlier" and a "later" set of considerations on the nature of the self. This novel approach to the search for God breaks up the text into a first portion running from Chapter 1 to the excursus on memory that ends in Chapter 19. In these chapters, Heidegger suggests, Augustine slowly realizes that he is searching for God as though God were an object or as though his intuition of divine presence might be fulfilled experientially in such a way that he could say of God: "this is what he is."[52] The excursus on memory, however, alerts Augustine to the essentially idolatrous dimensions of this way of searching. Augustine then switches gears and adopts a different way of going after God, and along with this, a different manner of confessing what he is in the present.

This latter way of searching for God is the real focal point of the commentary and the portion in which Heidegger first sketches the genuine mode of self-having and discerns as well a series of categories that will eventually find their way into his analytic of Dasein. Spelled out in Chapters 20 to 39, this second or later mode of *confessio* is not simply "more thorough, more detailed, more complete, more secure, and better" than its earlier counterpart, but rather it is carried out according to an entirely different "direction of grasping, means of grasping, and enactment of grasping."[53] Thus in tracing Augustine's passage from one mode of *confessio* to another, it is not a question of delineating the so-called tripartite structure of the *confessio*—understood as the confession of faith, the confession of sin, and the confession of praise—but rather of demonstrating that this triple form of confession may be enacted according to one or the other way of searching for God. Moreover it is a question of showing that in the second way, which is almost entirely taken up with exploring the various forms of temptation the soul undergoes in its worldly sojourn, Augustine succeeds not in rendering God present as an object but instead in rendering himself present to God by "making of himself a question."[54] This is the general framework for Heidegger's commentary, which reaches its climax in the analysis of this second mode of confession.[55]

To reach this climax Heidegger first has to explain why Augustine initially goes astray as well as how he extricates himself from the earlier, idolatrous way of searching for God. Part of this explanation involves the claim that Augustine's *Confessions* cannot be approached in a neutral fashion but must be submitted to hermeneutic destruction. From Heidegger's perspective, the earlier mode of confession, which is oriented toward intuiting the divine, is symptomatic of the fact that Augustine finds himself enmeshed in philosophical and religious worldviews prevalent during late antiquity, and that he uncritically adopts certain objectivizing tendencies from the milieu of Christian Platonism informed by Stoicism and Plotinian metaphysics. Heidegger draws evidence for this charge from Augustine's treatise *On Christian Doctrine* among other texts, in which Augustine describes creation as consisting of a hierarchy of entities, some of which have more Being, and thus are more real, than others. From this hierarchy Augustine derives a table of values meant to dictate proper relations among beings.[56]

Regardless of whether this is an accurate reading of Augustine its real import lies in the fact that it motivates Heidegger to level the charge of "*axiologization*" (*Axiologisierung*)[57] against the Augustinian corpus. Axiologization refers primarily to the ontological ordering of entities in terms of their rank, their arrangement in a hierarchy that assigns value to entities based upon how much Being they possess or how real they are. At the top of hierarchy stands the being par excellence, the most real entity, which is the only entity that can be said properly to be. Heidegger does not argue that Augustine's views of reality and of God are entirely determined by the tendency to reify Being in these terms. His real concern is to show that the truly religious dimension of Augustine's search for God can be brought out only if one first "destroys" this metaphysical scaffolding that supports it. This critique proves to be quite damaging to the edifice of Augustinian thought, as a great majority of Augustinian concepts are targeted for destruction and are thus stripped bare of their allegedly axiologizing tendencies. Such basic features of Augustinian thought as the doctrine of God as *summum bonum*, the hierarchy of creation, the universal pursuit of happiness, and the human desire to rest in God—all of these are bracketed or even dismissed in "Augustine and Neoplatonism" as though they belonged to some external pagan framework overlaid upon the lived experience of Christianity.[58]

Like all acts of hermeneutic destruction, the reading of Augustine aims at something positive. In "Augustine and Neoplatonism" it is crucial to see that the real target of destruction is simultaneously the concept Heidegger seeks to retrieve above all others. And this is Augustine's account of what it means to enjoy God. The *fruitio Dei* or enjoyment of God is most profoundly marked by Augustine's objectivizing and axiologizing tendencies. And yet it is precisely by expunging these tendencies that we can bring into view the genuinely religious core of *fruitio* and of joy or rejoicing (*gaudium*) more generally, allowing us to see the sense in which the religious stance of Augustinian confession can serve as a fore-sketch of facticity.

The point cannot be emphasized enough, since it guides Heidegger's commentary on Chapters 20–39: the work of destruction in "Augustine and Neoplatonism" is carried out by distinguishing between two senses of the *fruitio Dei*—one to be destroyed, the other to be salvaged.[59] The former sense is that of resting in God, which Heidegger seeks to expunge entirely from Augustine's anthropological and soteriological frameworks, and which he associates with the tendency to treat divinity as though it could be constituted as somehow present to the soul.[60] From the moment when the search for God gets underway early on in Book 10 to the point at which it stalls halfway through the book, when Augustine begins to suspect that he is searching incorrectly, it is for Heidegger this inadequate sense of *fruitio Dei* that leads the way. That is, when Augustine first turns to creation hoping to find God, and then turns inward to find God within the soul, he is dominated by the sense that he will at some point happen upon God as though God were some*thing* that could be present to the soul. It is only when the cataloguing of memory's contents fails to turn up the divine, but equally fails to overturn the conviction that God somehow resides in the mind—in other words, by *Confessions* 10.19—that Augustine slowly begins to consider the possibility that perhaps he is far from God, whereas God is closer to him than he is to himself.

The latter sense of enjoyment, the one Heidegger wants to salvage, comes to the fore here in the middle chapters of Book 10, and it leads the way for the remainder of the book. This notion of enjoyment is formed by assigning a positive meaning to the privation of rest, finding in *restlessness* or *Unruhigkeit* the principle of mobility which the texts of 1920 and 1921 associate with Christian religiosity: "The *fruitio* in Augustine is not the specifically Plotinian one, which culminates in intuition, but is rooted in the peculiarly Christian view of factical life."[61] The claim is striking, since it grants legitimacy to the Christian view of life as entirely depriving intuition of its experiential primacy.

By these lights Augustine is a thinker of restlessness, of the radical insecurity that characterizes human finitude. To anticipate the direction in which "Augustine and Neoplatonism" will develop the positive sense of restlessness, deploying it against the privilege of intuition, we can say that "Augustine and Neoplatonism" salvages the factical sense of enjoyment or *fruitio* by explicating it in terms of love, the most sustained discussion of which appears in a gloss on *Confessions* 10.34, where Augustine juxtaposes the carnal "pleasure of the eyes" to the spiritually purified gaze of the "invisible eyes." In the first *Tractate on the Gospel of John*, Augustine discusses cleansing or purifying the heart in connection with the Beatitudes as the condition for seeing God.[62] Heidegger, in turn, explicates this theme by glossing Sermon 53, where Augustine, meditating on Matthew 5:8, "Blessed are the pure in heart, for they will see God," advises his flock to turn inward and scrutinize themselves in order to become pure:

> Think of the face of the heart [*facies cordis*]. Force your heart to think about divine matters, compel it, drive it on. Anything that occurs to it in its thinking which is like a body, fling it away. You cannot yet say, "This is what he is"; do at least say, "This is not what he is." When, after all, will you say, "This is what God is"? Not even when you see him, because what you will see is inexpressible.[63]

Because everything hinges for Heidegger upon isolating the Augustinian *visio Dei* from what he calls the Plotinian sense of enjoyment (which allegedly culminates in an objectifying intuition of the divine), he equates the very work of purification mentioned in Sermon 53 with the ineffable visionless vision of God: "The self gains the enactmental condition of the experience of God. In the concern for the selfly life, God is present. God as object in the sense of the *facies cordis* operates [*wirkt*] in the authentic life of human beings."[64] The point here is that the command to think of the face of the heart precludes the intuitive capture of the divine. The ineffable God not only eludes vision, but this God also enjoins the soul to look away and to turn back upon itself. For Heidegger this means that the work of purification never results in illumination, or rather that illumination consists in nothing other than continuous purification.

To explain how the soul could possibly maintain itself in this state of perpetual purification Heidegger invokes the connection in Augustine's work between fear (*timor*) and love (*dilectio, amor*), appealing to Augustine's *Eighth Homily on 1 John* in which the act of love consists in a certain well-wishing, or *benevolentia*: "all love, my dear brothers, implies necessarily an element of goodwill [*benevolentia*] towards those who are loved."[65] Benevolence for Augustine is more complex than it first appears to be, not only because pride sometimes masquerades as benevolence but also because the soul can never be certain that charity reigns over pride.[66] This is why Augustine asserts that benevolence acts as a check on pride only when we will the neighbor to be our equal before God,[67] thereby ensuring that we help the neighbor to attain his or her true form as conceived by the divine mind: "You love in him, not what he is, but what you would have him be [*Non enim amas in illo quod est, sed quod vis ut sit*]."[68] According to Heidegger, Augustinian love is summed up in the very last phrase of this quote: "I will, that you be (you)," or *volo, ut sis*. This phrase appears just once in "Augustine and Neoplatonism,"[69] yet it shows up on multiple occasions in Heidegger's letters[70] and in his published philosophical works.[71] Augustine models this definition of neighborly love on God's love for creation. In *On the Trinity*, Augustine argues that to the extent that the word "Father" signifies the essential unity of the triune Godhead rather than a person of the Trinity, it refers to God's love for creation as a whole. Invoking John 16:27 as his proof-text, he explains that the broad use of the term "Father" refers to God "such that He loves us, that we may be [*quales amat ut simus*]."[72] The reason why Heidegger divides Book 10 in half, associating the first half with the pejorative sense of enjoying and the second with its positive or truly religious sense, is that he emphasizes to an extreme degree, in Lutheran terms, the Augustinian argument that the soul cannot love God or cling to God on its own, without divinely given grace preceding its action.

The distinction Augustine draws between chaste fear (*timor castus*) and servile fear (*timor servilis*) is thus crucial for Heidegger. This distinction resolves the tension between two potentially contradictory biblical passages. On the one hand, in the Vetus Latina Psalm 18:10 reads: "The fear of the Lord is pure, enduring for ever and ever." On the other hand, 1 John 4:18 states: "There is no fear in love. But perfect love drives out fear, because fear has to do with punishment." Augustine notes that servile fear, which is essentially the fear of being punished by God, is driven out by perfect love.[73] By contrast, chaste fear consists in desiring the good and is thus not apprehensive of evil things: "When you begin to long for good things, chaste fear will arise in you. What is chaste fear? Not letting go of the good. Listen: it is one thing to fear God lest he send you to Gehenna with the devil. It is another thing to fear God lest he retreat from you."[74] For Heidegger chaste fear comes into play with regard to *Confessions* 10.36, where Augustine asserts that in desiring to be loved and feared by others, the soul neither loves nor fears God chastely ("*non amare te, nec caste timere te*").[75] Heidegger, in short, finds a very clear textual basis for salvaging the positive sense of *fruitio* by linking it to chaste fear: "But when you fear God, lest His presence desert you, you embrace him, thus you desire to enjoy him (*cum autem times Deum, ne deserat te praesentia eius, amplecteris eum, ipso frui desideras*)."[76] Having established this link, it remains for Heidegger to show how Augustine enacts this desire in his second way of searching for God, inaugurating a second way of confessing himself from the middle to the end of *Confessions* 10.

RENUNCIATION AND THE END OF CARE

It is here in *Confessions* 10.20–39 that, according to Heidegger, Augustine glimpses "the great unstoppable distress of life."[77] The last half of "Augustine and Neoplatonism" rehearses the transition from servile to chaste fear, as reflected in the break between Augustine's first and second way of seeking God, in a manner that resembles the central conceit of Heidegger's commentary on 1 and 2 Thessalonians. In that context, the Christian who awaits the parousia is said not to ask *when* it will occur, but to focus solely on *how* to await it properly. Likewise, the argument in the 1921 summer seminar is that Augustine spends the first half of *Confessions* 10 searching for "what" God is, only to discover in the second half of the book that the crucial question actually concerns "how" he is seeking God. This shift in focus from the "what" to the "how" heralds Augustine's dethroning of intuition as the primary means for accessing divine presence. Heidegger explains this latter dynamic by showing how Augustine's second way of seeking God affords the soul the opportunity to achieve genuine *fruitio Dei* or enjoyment of God by rejoicing in truth. Thus the seminar reaches its climax in spelling out the sense of *fruitio* peculiar to Augustine's characterization of temporal life as radical insecurity or uncertainty.

This insecurity slowly takes shape through a line-by-line commentary on the text. For Heidegger, passages in Augustine's analysis of *memoria* had already proved that not all representations exist in the mind in the same manner, but rather there is diversity among the ways in which representations are retained and recollected. In Chapter 21, Augustine considers the possibility that the mind's knowledge of God's presence might be somehow connected to the memory of the happy life or the *vita beata*. The manner of being-represented characterizing the *vita beata* as a mental content is distinguishable from that of other mental representations.[78] Augustine notes that this mode of representation is unique among mental contents: "but we do have knowledge of happiness, and so we love it, yet still wish to gain it in order to be happy."[79] Here the memory of happiness unavoidably affects the will. In representing the *vita beata* to ourselves we cannot remain neutral with respect to it. Unlike in representing other mental contents, this representation necessarily elicits our desire to attain what it represents in present reality. To the degree that the memory of happiness calls forth a desire to be happy in the present, Augustine argues that the representation of the *vita beata* approximates the memory of joy (*gaudium*), though it is distinguished from the latter chiefly by the fact that joy is presumably something all individuals have experienced at some point in their lives, whereas Augustine is uncertain as to whether or not he has ever experienced true happiness.

When Augustine first defines happiness in Chapter 23 as taking "joy in truth" (*gaudium de veritate*), Heidegger initially glosses the definition by noting that it marks an "invasion of Greek philosophy"[80] into Augustine's theology, leading Augustine to define theological truth in fundamentally aesthetic terms. On this point, one of the crucial arguments of "Augustine and Neoplatonism" takes shape as Heidegger distinguishes between two senses of joy in the *Confessions*. When joy is linked to the criticism of Augustine's axiologizing tendencies, then Heidegger highlights the fact that Augustine often defines truth representationally as that which gives the soul rest. This fundamentally aesthetic and representational notion of truth, which treats the divine as the object of pleasure par excellence, is from a religious point of view entirely inappropriate to Christianity according to Heidegger. But when Heidegger opens his inquiry into the meaning of joy apart from its connection to the soul's resting in God, he simultaneously raises the possibility that the aesthetic and representational concept of truth Augustine allegedly takes over from Neoplatonic sources is not the primarily religious sense of joy in the *Confessions*. A different sense of joy is brought to the fore in Augustine's turn from the question concerning "what" God is to the question concerning how God must be sought.

The ambiguity in Augustine's understanding of enjoyment—and tied to this, his understanding of truth and divine nature—is a major concern in "Augustine and Neoplatonism," which comes to the fore in a discussion of the central interpretive dilemma Augustine faces in equating the *vita beata* with rejoicing in truth. In arguing that all human beings cannot but desire the *vita beata*, and that desiring to realize the *vita beata* in the present is an essential aspect of its being-represented to the mind, Augustine incurs the burden of having to explain why it is that so few human beings actually attain true happiness in the present life, as well as why truth is so often despised by the multitudes. Asking why preachers of truth are so often despised, Augustine notes that it is simply "because truth is loved in such a way that those who love some other thing want it to be the truth, and precisely because they do not wish to be deceived, they are unwilling to be convinced that they are deceived."[81] Though the fear of being deceived implies a love of truth, this same fear is ultimately an obstacle for the great majority of those who seek truth since "they love the truth when it enlightens them [*amant eam lucentem*], they hate it when it rebukes them [*oderunt eam redarguentem*]."[82] The apparent distinction between truth as illuminating and truth as rebuking builds upon the Johannine theme broached at the outset of *Confessions* Book 10 of "doing the truth" (*facere veritatem*), truth as something that one *does* rather than as something that pertains primarily to propositions. For Heidegger the break between these two kinds of truth marks the crucial moment at which Augustine gives up his desire to intuit the ineffable God and reorients his search by taking on board the divine rebuke, which he now puts to work in the mode of self-interrogation.[83] The act of privileging rebuking truth over illuminating truth marks a step along the way toward the goal of dislodging intuition as the primary means for accessing divine presence.

By Chapter 26, in other words, Augustine's search for God has been entirely redirected. As the excursus on memory generates the anxiety-producing insight that mind cannot contain itself,[84] it simultaneously lays bare the futility of searching for the divine as though it were a thing. This raises the possibility that God is uniquely "interior" to the soul in a manner that does not immediately translate into being experientially accessible. At this point Augustine's search for God is poised to reflect back upon itself in a manner that invites comparison with Descartes's search for apodictic certainty in his *Meditations*, though in Augustine's case the goal is to determine whether or not his manner of searching has prevented him from uncovering divine presence.[85]

One of the most crucial sections of "Augustine and Neoplatonism" handles Chapters 30–39, a portion of *Confessions* Book 10 in which Augustine explores temptation and sin. Following 1 John 2:16, Augustine divides temptation into three categories: lust of the flesh (*concupiscentia carnis*), lust of the eyes (*concupiscientia oculorum*), and worldly ambition (*ambitio saeculi*). In reading this section of *Confessions* Book 10, Heidegger is guided by two basic presuppositions.

The first is that in these chapters Augustine spells out a progression toward the genuine form of self-possession. The analysis of religious temptation, in other words, yields an account of having-a-self that closely resembles Heidegger's own notion of factical existence, though in the strictest sense this resemblance pertains only to the very last stage of the analysis, the one which handles worldly ambition. At the outset Heidegger does not tell us why he chooses to read the text in this way. We must await the end of his commentary to learn why he suspects that Augustine's discussions of the first two forms of temptation, fleshly concupiscence and the concupiscence of the eyes, do not broach the phenomenon of genuine selfhood, but rather focus solely on the related but separate themes of the self's sinful ways of relating to its surrounding world and to its own experience of mental contents. The implication is that it is only in examining worldly ambition (*ambitio saeculi*), the third form of temptation, that Augustine confronts the possibility of truly winning or losing the standing of genuine selfhood. Thus all the weight of Heidegger's presentation falls upon worldly ambition, as it is here that we are meant to discover the sense in which Augustine can be used to counteract the fallen, Cartesian manner of relating to the self.

The second assumption is much subtler and more difficult to understand, though it is in fact the controlling assumption of Heidegger's entire commentary. In Chapter 28 Augustine announces that human life is constant temptation. And in Chapter 29 he then implores God's mercy: "All my hope is naught save in Thy great mercy. Grant what Thou dost command and command what Thou will." Explaining the significance of these lines, Heidegger relates them to a passage in Augustine's *Expositions of the Psalms*:

[God] examines our heart and explores carefully to see that it is where our treasure is, that is, in heaven. He examines also our inward parts and explores carefully to see that we do not capitulate to flesh and blood but rejoice in God. Then he guides the just person's conscience in his own presence, guides it there where no human being sees [*ubi nullus hominum videt*]; he alone sees who discerns what each person thinks and what causes each person pleasure. For pleasure is the end of care [*finis curae delectatio est*].[86]

Though Augustine's commentary suggests that the just person receives divine guidance internally, it remains unclear whether this guidance remains hidden away from the just themselves, as though the gift of divine counsel is inaccessible even for those who are fortunate enough to have received it, or if it is safeguarded within the soul so that grace remains "on hand" or accessible for the justified soul. The issue of how grace is divinely given bears crucially upon key aspects of Augustine's thought: the development of his soteriology, his conception of freedom, as well as his account of nature and grace. In the present context the appeal to the *Expositions of the Psalms* matters mainly for a different reason, namely because it serves as the chief index for the concept of care, or *cura*, which Heidegger claims in later texts to have first identified in reading Augustine.[87] It is significant that this reference to the *Expositions of the Psalms* indicates that the end of care remains hidden from view even for those who are justified by grace. Heidegger leans heavily upon this dynamic of self-occultation in making sense of *Confessions* 10.30–39. The end toward which care tends is a blind spot from within the situation of caring, and it is by "worrying" over this blind spot, Heidegger contends, that for Augustine true selfhood is built up. Thus it is by deepening the sense of life as constant temptation, and doing so moreover while letting God remain unfound,[88] that Augustine slowly advances toward the stance of having-a-self.

Together these two interpretive principles direct Heidegger's attention toward the phenomenon of worldly ambition as harboring the leading sense of selfhood in the *Confessions*. In Chapter 36 of Book 10, this temptation is explicated in a very precise manner, as we are told that worldly ambition largely consists in "wanting to be feared and loved by men." Since communal life is unavoidably hierarchical, with some having more power than others, it is impossible to be social without fearing and loving others. And yet precisely because God alone is properly the object of chaste fear and perfect love, Augustine explains that the effects of succumbing to worldly ambition by desiring to be elevated to the status of the divine in the eyes of others are quite dire: "while we receive praises too eagerly, we lose caution and are caught up in them, and so separate our joy [*gaudium*] from the truth and place it in the deceitfulness of men: we delight to be praised and feared, not for Your sake, but in Your place."[89] Worldly ambition represents a direct challenge to God. In its very form it consists in having contempt for the creator God. Given that the soul can never be free of social life—even its own self-relation makes it possible to succumb to the desire to be feared and loved—Augustine is left to ask how the mind or soul can avoid separating its joy from God and depositing it elsewhere, entering into rivalry with the divine. Heidegger suggests that Augustine handles this question by dividing worldly ambition into two types. The first type, the "love of praise" (*amor laudis*), concerns the relation between the soul and its "communal world," or those neighbors in relation to whom the soul measures its worldly standing. The second type Heidegger identifies as the "private excellence" (*excellentia privata*) which consists in being pleasing to oneself, which he translates as "*Selbstwichtignahme*" (self-importance). In the case of self-importance, the communal world is inwardized or intellectualized as the soul plays the part of its own audience and now desires to be feared and loved by itself.

It is while addressing this second form of worldly ambition that Heidegger finally explains what is meant by genuine Augustinian self-possession and gives some indication as to how it "reverses" the Cartesian *cogito*. Rehashing Chapter 39, Heidegger outlines four ways in which the soul puts on airs before itself. The entire weight of his commentary is now brought to bear upon these four species of private excellence along with the sense of true selfhood Augustine allegedly discerns while discussing them. Heidegger marks the four species as such in his gloss on the passage, which notes that those who exhibit private excellence:

> please themselves but they mightily displease [God]: (1) not because they are displeased with things not good as though they were good, but (2) because they are pleased with things good as though they were their own; (3) or even if they rejoice in them as Yours, they think they have merited them; (4) or even if as proceeding wholly from Your grace, then not as rejoicing with their fellow men, but as grudging Your grace to others [*non tamen socialiter gaudentes, sed aliis invidentes eam*].[90]

The fourth and final form of private excellence provides the occasion for Heidegger to sketch genuine self-possession. In commenting on it Heidegger launches a remarkably stark criticism of self-representation. The criticism builds upon his earlier rejections of Augustine's "aesthetic" concept of truth and of his tendency to characterize the divine nature as a resting place for the pilgrim soul, yet it recasts these rejections in terms of a fundamentally religious prohibition against self-representation. The soul pleasing to itself fails to recognize that it is ontologically speaking nothing before God. The creature who puts on airs before itself plays the role of its own audience. In finding itself pleasurable it elevates itself to the status of being something real, something that has its Being from itself, and not from the creator God. The dilemma here is thus that in succumbing to worldly ambition the mind overlooks its creaturely nature. It fails to acknowledge that it is nothing before God.

Glossing the passage, Heidegger remarks:

> It is peculiarity of these four modes of self-importance that the self always sees itself before itself [*das Selbst sich vor sich selbst sieht*], positing [*vorsetzt*] its own self-world to itself and taking it to be decisively important, even if only in such a way that it is the one *in which* [*in der*] and *before which* [*von der*] grace and the *donum* are realized [*verwirklicht*]. But this means that it is precisely in that mode in which the self no longer attributes any achievements to itself that everything is relinquished in rejoicing before God [*alles aus der Hand gegeben wird in das Sichfreuen vor Gott*].[91]

We can see here that one crucial effect of succumbing to self-importance is substantivizing what Heidegger calls the "Selbstwelt" (self-world). In putting on airs before oneself, one plays the part of one's own audience. Heidegger radicalizes the discussion of worldly ambition to the point where he attributes to Augustine the view that even by recognizing oneself as having received grace one cannot avoid elevating oneself, or wanting to be feared and loved in an interior manner. That is, he interprets Augustine as arguing that by virtue of its capacity for self-reflection the mind is a factory of idols. Here it is the very *form* of self-reflection, to the degree that such reflection entails positing oneself before oneself in a manner that invalidates or nullifies the status of one's Being as a kind of nothingness before God, that leads the soul to *fall away* from God as the highest good and to rejoice in lesser goods.

On the basis of this passage we can see why for Heidegger Augustine succeeds in richly describing the crisis affecting creaturely existence: "Augustine clearly sees," Heidegger writes, "the difficulty and the ultimately 'anxiety-producing character' of Dasein in such 'having-of-oneself' (in full facticity)."⁹² This character results from the tension between two sets of claims. On the one hand, Augustine shows that true religious standing before God cannot be attained by the created mind since it requires the complete absence of self-reflection. Taking the passage above in its strongest sense, we might conclude that for Heidegger's Augustine the created soul cannot "see itself before itself," posit or represent itself to itself, without immediately taking itself as a false god. Merely by representing itself to itself, the self takes pleasure in itself and thus fails to rejoice in God. On the other hand, although Heidegger's Augustine maintains that suppressing all self-reflection or self-representation must be understood as a basic condition for rejoicing in God, he simultaneously argues that self-affection is an essential aspect of creaturely life—an insight that effectively condemns the soul to self-idolatry. In short, Augustine provides a compelling account of the real crisis afflicting the creaturely life because he manages to show that true religiosity exceeds human abilities, which renders this life fundamentally uncertain and marks it as a constant "being-troubled," or what Augustine calls *molestia*.

To put it in schematic terms, there are for Heidegger two ways in which Augustine sees the creature as inclined to objectivize itself. Either it delights in itself by merely recognizing itself as the recipient of grace, or the soul nullifies its charitable acts to the degree that it attributes these acts to itself, thus refusing to "share" them with others. This forceful reading of Chapter 39 casts Augustine in the role of applying an extreme version of Matthew 6:3 ("do not let your left hand know what your right hand is doing") to the soul's inner realm. It also greatly complicates the role of self-reflexivity in Heidegger as we have discussed it thus far. The claims I advanced above regarding Heidegger's take on Cartesian self-consciousness are in line with the set of claims discussed in chapter 1 above, in connection with the figure of the hermeneutic intuition in the KNS 1919 lecture course. In both contexts Heidegger repeatedly draws attention to the fundamentally self-reflexive character of factical experience, going so far in his reading of Descartes as to grant the basic validity of the claim that thinking is always an "I think-myself-thinking," i.e. that *cogito* is always a *cogito me cogitare*. In seeking to reverse the sense of this proposition by reformulating it as an interrogative, Heidegger aims to bring out rather than to cancel the fundamentally self-reflexive character of human Dasein.

However, the stark prohibition against self-representation attributed here to Augustine seems to go beyond the interrogative refashioning of self-affection and to take aim at the very form of self-reflexivity itself, raising the question as to whether or not religiosity as a phenomenon can be described in terms of the self-reflexivity Heidegger understands as fundamental to Dasein. Against the backdrop of this stark prohibition against self-reflection and/or self-representation, Heidegger argues that for Augustine no positing of mental content remains unaffected by illicit desire, leaving open the possibility that every act of self-attribution, even the simple affirmation of one's Being in the form of a question, launches a dynamic whereby, before God, "everything falls into the void . . . and everything is invalidated in regard to the *summum bonum*."[93] Thus the question raised here concerns the status of the question itself as the form befitting the intentional character of factical existence. For if in confessing before God no mental act remains untouched by concupiscence, even the dynamic of rendering oneself radically uncertain in one's Being, becoming a question to oneself, will be tainted by the desire to raise up the self as an idol.

It is thus here in connection with the radical prohibition against self-representation that we can discern the hidden contours of a genuinely religious form of self-possession. These contours belong to an anthropological figure that emerges briefly in the passage quoted above, which Heidegger subtly juxtaposes to the so-called theoretical Pelagianism of Descartes. The stringency of the prohibition against self-representation in the passage has a positive significance for Augustine to the degree that it allows him to understand what genuine *fruitio Dei* might look like. For starters, it would be devoid of all self-reflection, as we have been saying. But this negative criterion—the cancellation of all self-reflection, the privation of all self-attribution, and thus the nullification of every "for itself"[94] on the part of the creature who is ontologically speaking nothing before God—is not simply negative. It is described positively in the passage quoted above as "the mode in which . . . everything is relinquished in rejoicing before God [*alles aus der Hand gegeben wird in das Sichfreuen vor Gott*]."[95] But is not this *mode* the genuinely religious sense of being before God on Heidegger's reading? Is it not the religious mode of enactment par excellence? If so then we see that it is only when the soul is riveted to its own dereliction as a nothingness before God[96] that it can praise the divine without immediately coming back to itself, without getting caught up in the narcissistic recapture of the movement out toward the divine. In such rejoicing, the soul genuinely "has itself" paradoxically as having been relinquished or placed *out-of-reach*. Thus, the experience of self-renunciation Heidegger sketches here in Augustine invites thematic comparison with the conclusions reached in analyzing Heidegger's 1920–1921 commentary on 1 and 2 Thessalonians, in which Paul is figured as the crucified Christ. Here in the *Confessions* the link to crucifixion is by no means explicit, and yet the genuine sense of *fruitio Dei* Heidegger isolates in connection with *Confessions* 10.39—the act of rejoicing which consists in renouncing everything before God—is typologically linked to the figure of Paul as the true imitator of the crucified Christ.

Heidegger calls this act of self-renunciation before God "the last and most decisive and purest concern [*Bekümmerung*] for one's self."[97] In it we find the reason why he characterizes the Augustinian mode of having-a-self as wholly other than its Cartesian inheritor: the reversal of the Cartesian *cogito* in "Augustine and Neoplatonism" is neither a vague idea nor an implicit gesture, but rather a motif executed in a strikingly literal fashion. If to rejoice in God means placing everything "out of reach," and if in doing so one paradoxically attains selfhood by renouncing oneself, then the upshot of Heidegger's presentation of *Confessions* 10 is that Augustine attains true selfhood when he no longer claims to be some*thing* before God. In this renunciation the *cogito* is in fact reversed. In contrast to the Cartesian *res cogitans*, which ontologically speaking is for Heidegger an entity present-at-hand (*Vorhandensein*),[98] the mode of selfhood attained in relinquishing everything before God is that of an entity placed radically *out of reach* (*aus der Hand gegeben*). Thus, the conclusion reached in "Augustine and Neoplatonism" is that the search for God in *Confessions* Book 10 brings into view the self as an entity that is properly possessed if and only if it is given away, offered up in rejoicing before God. And the major significance of this fact is not that the Being of the self as so indicated in the *Confessions* is actually attained by Augustine, but rather that this indication can be used to determine, for the first time, the Being of the self that Descartes left "ontologically undetermined."[99]

THE "OUT-OF-REACH" AND THE "NOT-AT-HOME"

That Augustine's search for God engenders this kind of self-denial is a conclusion echoed years later in Hannah Arendt's *Love and Saint Augustine*. In Part 1, Arendt asserts that insofar as Augustine handles love as a kind of craving, there is a strong impulse on his part toward a final self-abnegation. Citing a line from Sermon 142—"God must be loved in such a way that, if at all possible, we would forget ourselves"[100]—Arendt underscores the connection between this impulse and the concept of self-possession that one can glean from the *Confessions*: "Just as true self-love," she writes, "can be actualized paradoxically only in self-hatred, so [self-] 'possession' can here only be actualized by oblivion."[101] Arendt ultimately concludes that the impulse toward oblivion is Neoplatonic in origin. At the same time, she argues that Augustine's impulse toward self-abnegation is not exhausted by this allegedly non-Christian drive toward self-oblivion but rather that it can affirm the resemblance between creature and creator: "In self-denial man acts 'as God' toward himself. He loves himself as God loves him, hating everything he has made in himself, and loving himself only insofar as he is God's creation."[102] For his part Heidegger reaches a similar conclusion in "Augustine and Neoplatonism," differing from Arendt only in the extent to which he emphasizes the idea that before God the creature is a species of nothingness, and that in this way it bears the mark of having been created out of nothing.

If we step back now from tightly reconstructing the central argument in "Augustine and Neoplatonism," then two points about its broader significance come into view. First, the figure of the Augustinian *cogito* out-of-reach enlarges the eschatological problem spelled out in the 1920–1921 commentary on 1 and 2 Thessalonians. The immense guilt heaped upon the Christian whose spiritual life consists in struggling to await the parousia correctly has a clear counterpart in "Augustine and Neoplatonism," in which Heidegger is focused less upon temporality per se and more upon the nature of factical experience. In the last section of the seminar manuscript, Heidegger argues that Augustine's search not only leads him to realize that he is far from God, but it brings him closer to God only to the degree that he experiences his own state as an ever-intensifying form of trouble or *molestia*. The ordeal which Augustine must endure is strictly analogous to the one Heidegger ascribes to Paul in 1920–1921: the closer he comes to God, the more acutely he registers his distance from God. The more "religious" he becomes, the more he realizes that he has fallen prey to illicit self-love. The dilemma is irresolvable without divine intervention, which signals for Heidegger that Augustine genuinely grasps the kind of infirmity that necessarily characterizes human finitude, which he expresses by arguing that the soul must become a great question to itself. That is, for Augustine the soul is "questionable," Heidegger writes, "in experiencing and having myself. 'Life'—a How of having, and indeed an experiencing of temptations. It is a *temptation*, it forms the possibility of losing and of winning itself."[103] By these lights the self can only be experienced as a question built up to a greater or lesser degree, one that can never be answered. This is the reason why "Augustine and Neoplatonism" argues that the phenomenon of Augustinian selfhood is constituted by what Heidegger calls *endangerment* [*Gefährdung*].[104] Endangerment refers to the act of risking oneself by entering into the paradoxical dilemma described above, that of continually experiencing one's distance from God as a way of approaching God.

The dilemma indeed corresponds to the immense guilt heaped upon the Christian in "Introduction to the Phenomenology of Religion," yet it arguably extends the eschatological problem traced in that context, rendering it all the more severe, to the degree that Heidegger now makes explicit in connection with Augustine something that was merely implied by his reading of 1 and 2 Thessalonians—namely, that the interior guidance divinely bestowed upon the believer remains experientially inaccessible from within the enactmental stance of faith. "Augustine and Neoplatonism" does this by explicitly thematizing the danger of recognizing oneself as the recipient of grace, first, by arguing that the "end of care" can be accessed only by divine intellection; and second, by arguing that the prohibition against self-representation is the positive criterion of genuine *fruitio Dei*.

The second crucial point about "Augustine and Neoplatonism" is tied to this extension of the eschatological problem spelled out in the Paul commentary. If we grant that the dynamic of endangerment as constituting genuine selfhood does indeed provide Heidegger with some indication or sketch of what it might mean to reverse the Cartesian *cogito*—and indeed, as we have seen, the textual evidence points in this direction—then it becomes virtually impossible to view the 1920–1921 phenomenology of religious life courses as a "false start,"[105] or as failing to hit its mark. On the contrary, the literal reversal of the Cartesian *cogito* in "Augustine and Neoplatonism" provides a benchmark with respect to which we can bring out its thematic and etymological links with those courses and seminars in the early Heidegger that pave the way to *Being and Time*.

Thus, before taking stock of these links, as I shall do in the next chapter by closely examining Heidegger's philosophical transcriptions of theological terms, it is necessary here to briefly situate the reversed Augustinian *cogito*, or what I am calling the *cogito* out-of-reach, alongside Heidegger's descriptions of factical existence as a species of nothingness in the texts of the 1920s. In his 1929 debate with Ernst Cassirer at Davos, Heidegger maintains that the question concerning the essence of the human being "leads man back beyond himself and into the totality of beings in order to make manifest to him there, with all his freedom, the nothingness of his Dasein."[106] These lines build upon similar passages in *Being and Time*, which will factor heavily into our analysis in chapter 4 below. Here I note that the strong association between facticity and nothingness crops up in Heidegger's early lecture courses just after "Augustine and Neoplatonism." In the third and final part of the winter 1921–1922 seminar manuscript, for example, Heidegger elaborates the basic categories of existence so as to highlight the ontological sense of nothingness befitting it: "Privation (*privatio, carentia*)," he writes, "is both the relational and the intrinsic basic mode and sense of the Being of life."[107] Far from defining factical life as rational self-sufficiency, the winter 1921–1922 course characterizes it as inherent neediness or lack. At the same time, factical life always finds itself in a surrounding world filled with objects that give the appearance of permanence and solidity. Precisely because factical life never possesses "self-sure Objectivity,"[108] the outside world of things beckons to it, seducing life into believing that it is ontologically the same as the objects it deals with. This self-deception represents a desperate attempt on the part of life to flee from itself. Positing itself as an object, life refuses to assume the radical insecurity of its own way of Being, freeing itself of the burden of having to be.

It is from this perspective that Heidegger first defines factical life in terms of *care*: "caring: to care for and about something; to live from [on the basis of] something, caring for it."[109] The tendency that care exhibits to secure its Being by taking flight into self-sure Objectivity reveals that life is fundamentally and self-reflexively concerned about itself. Its self-apprehension "is not original, but, instead, has passed through the 'it,' through an encounter with the 'it.'"[110] There is nothing to keep life as care, Heidegger suggests, from collapsing in upon itself—no check upon the hidden ways in which it takes refuge in objectivity and derives pleasure in fleeing from its finitude. This collapse is what Heidegger calls "ruinance" (*Ruinanz*).

Ultimately since life brings about ruinance on its own, this collapse furnishes the basis for arguing that life is a species of nothingness: "the collapse is not something foreign to [life] but is itself of the character of factical life and indeed is 'the nothingness of factical life.'"[111] To be clear, the sense of nothingness at play here is that of self-nullification. When in 1921–1922 Heidegger refers to factical life as a species of nothingness—when he argues that life is defined as privation or lack—he does not argue that life lacks this-or-that, as though it were lacking something which, if supplied to it, could complete it. Instead he defines care as the very movement of self-nullification, which is accomplished in the attempt to supply oneself with the self-sure objectivity that is fundamentally at odds with factical life. In this manner factical life sets out to prevent itself from actually occurring: "the nothingness of factical life is life's own proper *non-occurrence of itself in ruinant existence,* a non-occurrence brought to maturation by and for factical life itself, within life and without the surrounding world."[112] Life, according to this formula, is dead-set on rendering itself null and void. The drive toward self-nullification on the part of life is so extreme, Heidegger concludes, that we cannot subsume it under the general category of emptiness, but must think it in terms of a disastrous fall: "it is an emptiness which is precisely *disastrous* for the collapse itself."[113] According to such a formulation life must be grasped paradoxically as the privation of itself.

The crucial point here is that in its emphasis upon self-nullification, the winter 1921–1922 seminar elaborates, in what is supposed to be a non-theological fashion, a concept of nothingness profoundly indebted to the one that emerges in "Augustine and Neoplatonism." In both instances, the act of positing oneself as an object intervenes within the self-experience of the "I," becoming the source of a perverse pleasure and leading to the self's endless collapse. In both instances, factical experience is thought paradoxically as the privation of itself. If there is any difference between the two concepts of nothingness at play here, it comes down to the distinction between the kinds of falling movement Heidegger attributes to Augustine and to Dasein, respectively. Whereas in "Augustine and Neoplatonism" one has the impression that Augustine can do nothing of his own accord to prevent the defluxion of existence from gathering speed, and that instead he must rely upon a hidden divine intervention to save him from the ever-intensifying experience of *ruin,* the winter 1921–1922 course describes the philosophical act of self-interrogation as taking on the *anti-ruinous* function that "Augustine and Neoplatonism" must reserve for divine grace. That is, in describing factical life in terms of a disastrous collapse, it also repositions the mechanism by which life stops its downward plunge so that it is now internal rather than external to enactment itself.

Though it may seem like a small departure from "Augustine and Neoplatonism," this reinterpretation of self-interrogation as counter-ruinant has enormous methodological consequences for Heideggerian hermeneutics and for the role that the *question* plays within it. Subsequent to "Augustine and Neoplatonism," when he describes Dasein or factical life as "being questionable" Heidegger means to suggest that the very activity of self-interrogation may bring a halt to life's intrinsic inclination toward self-collapse. But this is not, after all, how he reads the *Confessions* in 1921. The point of "Augustine and Neoplatonism" is not to show that the act of confession actually halts the soul's tendency to slip away from truly rejoicing in God. If one interprets confession in this manner, then from Heidegger's point of view in 1921 one would necessarily fail to recognize that genuine *fruitio Dei* is freely bestowed by the divine, not achieved by the soul on its own. By contrast, when it comes to measuring its effects in the winter 1921–1922 course directly following "Augustine and Neoplatonism," then self-interrogation takes on a compensatory function that allows life to avoid collapsing in on itself: "A counter-ruinant movement is the one of the actualization of a philosophical interpretation. . . . It is precisely in *questioning* that factical life attains its genuinely developed self-givenness."[114] The gap between this formula and the figure of the *cogito* out-of-reach sketched in "Augustine and Neoplatonism" may appear to be small, but the fact remains that "Augustine and Neoplatonism" never ascribes to the religious subject the ability to disentangle the givenness of the self from its self-idolizing tendencies.

In other words, the difference between the *cogito* out-of-reach and the non-religious form of nothingness Heidegger attributes to facticity is consequential, as it transfers to Dasein the powers Heidegger associates with the indwelling Spirit in his reading of Paul, and with divine grace in his reading of Augustine. The fact that from late 1921 on Heidegger attributes counter-ruinance to factical existence itself dictates the terms under which his interpretations of Paul and Augustine can exert influence on his hermeneutic method. Shortly after the winter 1921–1922 lecture course Heidegger began referring to the essentially self-reflexive character of Dasein's Being—the way in which it always has itself or is a priori face-to-face with itself—as "disposition, mood" (*Befindlichkeit*) or self-finding, self-affection (*das Sich-befinden*).[115] In an often-cited text from 1924, he equates his own notion of *Befindlichkeit* with the Augustinian *affectio*,[116] a term signifying the impression by which the soul measures time according to *Confessions* Book 11. Setting up a rough equivalence among these terms, Heidegger would have us believe that the existential conception of *Befindlichkeit* or disposition is present in Augustine's writings, albeit in nascent form. But our reading of "Augustine and Neoplatonism" would suggest that such an equivalence is not operative in the 1921 seminar manuscript, and that when Heidegger subsequently reads his own notion of disposition back into the Augustinian text, the overall effect is one of greatly simplifying if not entirely obfuscating the textual lineage of his own concepts.

What is really at stake, philosophically speaking, in pinpointing this oversimplification? Why does Heidegger insist, starting in late 1921, that self-interrogation is potentially counter-ruinant?

The methodological significance of the latter view has its source in an *a priori* presupposition informing Heidegger's hermeneutic phenomenology. The winter 1921–1922 seminar makes clear that even if the factical "I" is always bent on evading itself and/or nullifying itself, it never actually manages to escape itself entirely: "In caring, life sequesters itself off from itself and yet in doing so does precisely not get loose from itself. . . . life is always seeking itself and does encounter itself precisely where it least expects—i.e., for the most part in its disguises."[117] The philosophical stakes of the assertion that life never fully escapes from itself even when it flees from itself are not always made fully apparent in the early lecture courses. During the early Freiburg and Marburg periods, Heidegger repeatedly argues against Descartes and Kant that the ego is affected directly by its own Being and that consequently the "I" can express its essence in conceptual fashion without distorting it. In his *Principles of Philosophy*, Descartes leaves little doubt that the finite intellect gains direct access to the attributes of entities, but never to substance: "Yet substance cannot be first discovered merely from the fact that it is a thing that exists, for this alone does not by itself affect us."[118] In 1925 Heidegger argues that Kant and Husserl adopted this position from Descartes without fully considering its implications: "Descartes says that we have no primary and original access to the Being of the entity as such. What Descartes expresses here in this way, that the Being of an entity taken purely for itself does not affect us, is later formulated by Kant in the simple sentence, 'being is not a real predicate'; that is, being is not a datum which can be apprehended by way of any kind of receptivity and affection."[119] Against the implicit Cartesianism of Kant, Heidegger insists, "there is indeed an entity which can be grasped directly and *only* primarily from its *Being* and, if it is to be understood philosophically, must so be grasped."[120] This entity is Dasein or factical life, which has the capacity to be affected by its own Being.

Here we pick up the thread of the argument that factical life is a species of nothingness. And moreover we pick it up as the argument takes shape in Heidegger's lecture courses just after "Augustine and Neoplatonism." In their earliest instantiations, the Heideggerian conceptions of anxiety and uncanniness are meant to justify the argument that Dasein, as a species of nothingness, is directly affected by its own Being: "Earlier, in analyzing Descartes' concept of the subject, I referred to his statement that we actually have no affection of being as such. But there is such an affection. . . . Anxiety is nothing other than the pure and simple experience of Being in the sense of Being-in-the-world."[121] The role assigned to anxiety in 1925 is taken over wholesale in *Being and Time*, in which anxiety allows Dasein to confront its Being-in-the-world immediately, without the intervention of anything worldly. But already in 1921–1922 Heidegger was committed to the view that the insecurity generated by self-interrogation could potentially allow Dasein to overcome all forms of self-deception: "[the *sum*] is an objectivity to be encountered first and foremost in questioning, and only thus can it be encountered concretely in any given case."[122] Here Heidegger already suspects that insecurity allows life to grasp itself appropriately. It was not until 1923, however, that he finds the solution to the problem in the figure of the uncanny self revealed by anxiety.

Here we come full circle by returning to the destruction of Cartesian metaphysics discussed above, the one accomplished in the 1923–1924 *Introduction to Phenomenological Research*. Immediately following this destruction of Cartesian metaphysics in the seminar manuscript, Heidegger suggests that existence is fundamentally at odds with itself because it is somehow a threat to itself: "What it defends itself against, the *threat*, lies in existence itself. The threat against which existence defends itself lies in the fact that it *is*. *That it is* is the threat of existence itself."[123] As in the 1921–1922 winter seminar, the totality of objects cared for by factical life is here described as providing a refuge against the unfamiliar threat that takes shape within life itself. This disturbance internal to life is nothing other than life itself, the burden of its having-to-be. Dasein comes face to face with this burden only when it can no longer hide behind what is familiar. In anxiety I am not confronted with this-or-that fear, but rather I come face to face with this unfamiliar threat, which is none other than the self in its "state of not being at home, uncanniness [*Unheimlichkeit*]. Uncanniness is the genuine threat that existence is subject to."[124] Linked to its conceptual precursor in the winter 1921–1922 seminar, this notion of uncanniness signifies a variation on the theme of life as nothingness: "Uncanniness is, if one asks what it is, *nothing*; if one asks where it is, *nowhere*."[125] Crucially what the winter 1921–1922 seminar identifies as the counter-ruinant movement of philosophical self-interrogation is here taken up into Heidegger's phenomenological description of anxiety as the state in which life confronts itself as a species of nothingness.

From a methodological point of view, uncanniness is supposed to confirm that the ego can access its Being directly. And in 1923–1924, Heidegger takes for granted that uncanniness is "the same phenomenon that Descartes took as the *cogito me cogitare* [the 'I think myself thinking'] . . . , and that Husserl developed as reflection."[126] Thus, when seen as part of Heidegger's argument in favor of a direct affection of substance, uncanniness provides in 1923–1924 something like a foundation for the Augustinian question concerning the relation between life and truth. Anxiety discloses the truth of existence to the extent that it displays existence as nothing and as nowhere, the uncanny threat inside myself from which I flee into the reassuring familiarity of everyday life. But in offering life the chance to confront this threat, the 1923–1924 reading of anxiety departs from the extreme form self-occultation that we detected above in the 1921 commentary on *Confessions* Book 10, retroactively transforming the latter into a potentially rival interpretation of human finitude.

CONCLUSION

With this observation we arrive at the heart of the issue. Although the debate with Descartes and his interpreters is what secretly drives Heidegger in "Augustine and Neoplatonism," it is also what accounts for the discrepancy between its results and the rendition of life as a form of nothingness that takes shape in Heidegger's courses from late 1921 to early 1924. Seeking to correct what he sees as an erroneous account of the self in modernity, Heidegger identifies the Augustinian *cogito* out-of-reach as the critical correlate of Cartesian self-consciousness. In so doing he remains unconcerned by any incongruence between the model of self-renunciation he attributes to Augustine and his own philosophical presuppositions concerning the structure and function of factical self-interrogation. The disparity between these two domains of research—the reading of religious texts and the formation of existential categories—is nonetheless discernible from late 1921 on, in the texts cited above. Here we can add, by way of conclusion, that this disparity is strikingly apparent in the appendix to the main portion of the winter 1923–1924 *Introduction to Phenomenological Research*.

That course ends on a fundamentally ambiguous note as Heidegger grants that his interpretation of uncanniness is provisional at best. In fact he suggests that any interpretation of uncanniness would have to be provisional. This is because uncanniness is "the condition of the possibility that something like *uncoveredness* lies in existence."[127] The phenomenon of uncanniness tests the powers of phenomenological description as it lies at the very limit of factical existence. For this reason Heidegger warns his students against putting too much stock in any one description of uncanniness. He concedes that his approach to it "is only a specific interpretation of the *here, is a merely specific way of dealing with uncanniness.*"[128] This frank admission changes the tenor of his analysis, first, because it leaves open alternative approaches to uncanniness; and second, because it suggests that Heidegger's decision to draw upon uncanniness in order to depict self-interrogation as potentially counter-ruinant may not be entirely justified on phenomenologically descriptive grounds, but may stem from his prior methodological commitments.

If we read this strange concession in light of the disjunction between the aims informing Heidegger's commentaries on religious texts and his attempts to formulate existential categories, then we can propose the following: the fact that existence is threatened by its own uncanniness may *but need not* prove phenomenologically, as Heidegger suspects, that self-interrogation is potentially counter-ruinant. In other words, nothing about Heidegger's early accounts of facticity as a form of nothingness, from 1921–1924, suffices to dispel on phenomenological grounds the suspicion that the care-structure he discerns is unavoidably self-occluding. This latter suspicion is in fact engendered by the readings of Paul and Augustine, yet its elision within the courses designed to formulate the existential categories of Dasein cannot be attributed solely to the difference between the religious dimensions of these readings and nonreligious context in which their findings are deployed. Thus, if the notion of existence as uncanniness sets the terms under which Augustinian terms are transposed into, and re-signified by, the hermeneutic of Dasein, it is also what retroactively bestows upon the figure of Augustine a twofold status in Heidegger's corpus, as one who anticipates and thus who authorizes the formation of a fundamental ontology, but also as one who threatens to turn it against itself.

CHAPTER THREE

The Remains of Christian Theology

INTRODUCTION

"My comportment in philosophizing is not religious, even if as a philosopher I can also be a religious person. 'The art resides precisely in that': to philosophize and, in so doing, to be genuinely religious."[1] So declared Heidegger in the first hour of his winter 1921–1922 lecture course, turning the page on the previous year's work. From now on he would no longer explicate theological or devotional works in an effort to gain a real relationship to history, nor would he explicitly draw upon Christian theological sources to offset modern philosophical trends. A case in point: the 1923–1928 Marburg courses contain extensive discussions of medieval Christian texts, and yet with the one exception of the oblique redeployment of the Augustinian question in the *Introduction to Phenomenological Research*, they seem not to ascribe to these texts strategies to be emulated. A decade would pass before Heidegger again revisited a Christian theological work in the hope of "opening a specific area of existence for philosophical consideration and inquiry."[2] And that encounter—a brief but significant reconsideration of Augustine in the early 1930s—would be the last of its kind in his corpus, notwithstanding allusions to Pascal, Eckhart, and the New Testament in his later works.[3]

And so, just weeks after completing "Augustine and Neoplatonism," Heidegger unceremoniously abandoned the project to which it belonged, and embarked on a more promising line of research. The beginner's level course on Aristotle's *De Anima*, offered in 1921 alongside "Augustine and Neoplatonism," had been a success. It would launch a whole series of investigations *toward* (*zu*) Aristotle. From 1921 to 1927 hardly a semester went by without Heidegger giving a course or a lecture on the Stagirite. The first Marburg course in winter 1923–1924, for example, elucidates the very concept of phenomenology by going back to Aristotle, while roughly half of the 1924 *Sophist* course deals with the *Nicomachaean Ethics* as a prolegomenon to reading Plato. But if the regress to Aristotle was undoubtedly the new focal point of Heidegger's historical research, the results obtained by it were necessarily marked by his early commentaries on biblical and Augustinian sources. In the present chapter, I examine the formation of Heidegger's existential categories—the concepts which in *Being and Time* comprise the structure of human existence—identifying the ways in which they come out of the "Introduction to the Phenomenology of Religion" and "Augustine and Neoplatonism." In his recent study of Heidegger's debate with Ernst Cassirer at Davos, Peter Gordon remarks that in his early lecture courses Heidegger "made use of religious experience as a clue for describing *Dasein's* existential structure."[4] A careful examination of the early lecture courses at Freiburg and Marburg confirms this remark, revealing the extent to which the configuration of Dasein's Being during the 1920s results from his de-theologizing, transposing, and transforming the categories first uncovered in his readings of Christian theological sources.

This examination also raises a twofold question concerning the strategy of de-theologization described below, which we will carry forward in our reading of *Being and Time* in chapter 4. First, if *Being and Time* ultimately seeks to clarify the structure of Dasein's Being by expunging from philosophy the "remains [*Resten*] of Christian theology,"[5] then exactly how, in detail, does the transposition and thus reintroduction of terms fraught with theological significance work toward this goal? Second, the crucial part of this supplementary work concerns the role played by the transposition of theological terms within Heidegger's destructive hermeneutic return to Aristotle. In *Being and Time*, Heidegger suggests that his own definition of existence as care grew upon him "in connection with his attempts to interpret Augustinian (i.e., Helleno-Christian) anthropology with regard to the foundational principles reached in the ontology of Aristotle."[6] At issue here is to flesh out this passing remark through a detailed analysis of concept-formation in Heidegger's corpus, one designed to determine precisely how the de-theologizing repetition of Augustinian terms interacts with the ontological principles Heidegger attributes to Aristotle, as well as those he lays down in his own texts. The result of this study will consist in a deeper appreciation of the tensions generated by the novelty of Heidegger's existential categories.

THE CRITICAL RETRIEVAL OF ARISTOTLE: A FIRST TRANSPOSITION

"It is my conviction that philosophy is at an end. We stand before completely new tasks that have nothing to do with philosophy."[7] We owe to the first Marburg seminar Heidegger's earliest declaration of philosophy's demise.[8] The theme most readily associated with the later Heidegger is actually the guiding line of the early courses, appearing here at the outset of the 1923-1924 *Introduction to Phenomenological Research*. Coming on the heels of two years spent investigating Aristotelian metaphysics, this course in 1923 uncoupled the search for new categories to express factical life or "existence" from the careful exegesis of Christian sources, reorienting it toward the origins of Western metaphysics. Now one of Heidegger's crucial arguments would come to the fore: philosophy's demise was encoded in its birth—a destiny discernible already in Aristotle, as it was he who set the tradition on the path it would follow until the present.

In its first version Heidegger did not explicitly link the end of philosophy to Nietzsche or Hegel. His point of reference was instead Husserlian phenomenology, as he sought to derive its potential as well as its limit from its Aristotelian inheritance. The summer 1923 course *Ontology: The Hermeneutics of Facticity* calls for significantly broadening Husserl's method so as to include among themes for investigation existence as well as Being itself. The broadening would spell the end of philosophy, since philosophy as it had been practiced since Aristotle was predicated on the forgetting of both themes. The contrast formulated in the first pages of the course manuscript set the tone for Heidegger's destructive regress toward Aristotelian ontology. On the one hand, "it was in phenomenology that a fitting concept of research first emerged."[9] Why? Because Husserl alone made it possible to study how various scientific disciplines constitute their objects of research as such. The breakthroughs achieved in the *Logical Investigations* permitted Husserl to study the objects of science via the acts that constitute them as such. This meant that phenomenology alone brought into view the objectivity of objects. On the other hand, the singular focus on constitution greatly hindered further development of phenomenological method. Limiting its scope to the objectivity of the object, phenomenology had deprived itself of the ability to interrogate anything that falls outside of its domain, failing to rise to the level of theoretical abstraction at play in objective representation.

The concept of presence Husserlian phenomenology took for granted turns out to be for Heidegger a truncated one. Applied indiscriminately to all beings, above all to the ego, it pertains exclusively to the theoretical realm. This is a sign for Heidegger that, while the study of acts of constitution opens access to objective representation, it fails to raise the question of "Being as such, i.e. *Be-ing which is free of objects*."[10] Thus the broadening of phenomenology proceeds from its narrow sense geared toward constitution to its wider sense "as something which includes ontology."[11] On the strength of subsequent testimony, we know that this broadening was tied to Heidegger's reading of Husserl's Sixth Logical Investigation. There, Heidegger believed, Husserl had preserved the memory of the Greek approach to Being: "Being," Husserl writes, "is nothing *in* the object, no part of it, no moment tenanting it, no quality or intensity of it, no figure of it, no internal form whatsoever, no constitutive feature of it however conceived."[12] That Being is *no* thing, that it *is* not—this would be a leitmotif for Heidegger from 1921–1922 on. Though Husserl paved the way to it, he nevertheless failed in Heidegger's view to follow it up by asking after the source of the leading sense of Being, the one that "is to guide the treatment of all problems in ontology."[13] In 1923 this source was indeed the being-there of the human being, or Dasein. Thus the inadequacies of phenomenology with respect to Being negatively affected its most concrete analyses by blocking access "to that entity which is decisive within philosophical problems: namely Dasein, from out of which and for the sake of which philosophy 'is.'"[14] It is from this perspective that Heidegger embarked on the "regress" toward Aristotle, having espied the need in phenomenological research for an extensive inquiry into "the history of Western human existence and the history of its self-interpretation"[15] guided by a critical reappraisal of Aristotelian ethics and ontology. Perhaps the clearest and most programmatic version of this regress appears in the 1922 Natorp Report, the first section of which offers an initial sketch of Dasein in its historical particularity: "the genuine object of research is *in each case always authentic facticity*, i.e., the facticity of one's own times and generation."[16] The focus of these historical investigations is obviously Aristotle, or more specifically Aristotle's explication of the human being to the degree that it suffered from certain fateful flaws that stem from human Dasein's capacity for self-distortion.

Let us recall that hermeneutic destruction is meant to identify the "objective sources'"[17] of ontological concepts in the concrete material circumstances of their historical origins. The Natorp Report highlights two aspects of Aristotelian thought as particularly pertinent to the initial obfuscation of facticity in the Greek metaphysical tradition. First, Heidegger contends that it is within the physical sciences or the study of natural phenomena that Aristotle hits upon the basic ontological concepts he applies indiscriminately to all philosophical objects of inquiry, ethics included. More specifically it was his success in studying movement or *kinesis* that furnished Aristotle with his general approach to beings: "those researches in which objects were experienced and thought in their basic character of being-moved and something like motion . . . provide the possibility of gaining access to the authentic motivational source of Aristotle's ontology."[18] Second, as Heidegger repeatedly remarks, Aristotle's method of philosophizing is one that relies upon "descriptive comparison and elimination,"[19] in that it seeks to elucidate the basic character of phenomena by comparing disparate interpretations of them.

The destruction of Aristotelian ontology targets both aspects of his thought, as it proceeds along the following lines of argumentation. On the first register, to the question, "as what kind of object was the human for Aristotle?," Heidegger retorts that human being for Aristotle is characterized as a particular form of movement, or what he calls "movedness." The concepts used to explicate this movedness are for the most part found in the *Nicomachaean Ethics*, particularly in the discussion of the dianoetic virtues in Book 6. Recent scholarship has left little doubt that Heidegger's hermeneutics of facticity owes a significant debt to his commentaries on the *Nicomachaean Ethics*.[20] If anything, the line of attack adopted here will reaffirm this argument while altering its sense. On a second register, because Aristotle views all phenomena through the prism of movement, reflecting their Being in concepts drawn from the natural or physical world, he can scarcely resist determining the preeminent sense of Being on this basis, namely by deriving it from the human being's native interaction with physical objects. In this interaction, the human being meets the world as consisting of objects of "dealings" or *pragmata* geared toward production. What truly *is* for Aristotle is the way of Being peculiar to the artifact in its solidity as a finished object.

Convinced that for Aristotle the concepts used to describe the creation of artifacts or products, *poioumena*, fundamentally determined his entire approach to Being, Heidegger maintains that "in Aristotle and after him *ousia* [substance] still retains its original meaning of the household, property, what is at one's disposal for use in one's environing world. *Ousia* means *possessions, what one has*."[21] It is here in the critique of Being as determined by the Aristotelian *poioumena* or *pragmata* that we find the origins of the classical Heideggerian criticism of metaphysics, which determines Being as constant presence. And the link Heidegger makes here between having and being-finished determines his assessment of every other concept in Aristotle. For Aristotle, "the primordial sense of Being is *being-produced*."[22] Such is the major insight of the Heideggerian critique of Aristotle. If Being is relative to production, then the human way of Being will be disclosed as something lacking solidity and/or completeness. When correlated ontologically with *ousia*, the human way of Being is destined to come up short and to compare unfavorably with the bewitching character of the artifact.

In its initial formulation the argument equating *ousia* with property highlights the fact that at the outset of Western metaphysics Aristotle, who first asks after the question of Being in general, covertly installs one sense of Being—Being as being-produced—as the standard against which all others must be judged. In the Natorp Report this conclusion allows Heidegger to isolate two further features of Aristotelian ontology. First, the allure of the finished object greatly affects Aristotle's account of intellection. Aristotle's ideal of pure perception, or what Heidegger calls "simple-looking-at" as a kind of rest, is achieved only by "freeing oneself from the concerns and apprehensions of going about those dealings directed to routine tasks."[23] The pure understanding tarries alongside entities in a detached and unbothered way. Its ideal form is *theoria* or contemplation, the pure intellection which Aristotle ascribes properly to the divine or *to theion*, the entity engaged solely in thinking itself: "This divine being *must* be pure perceiving, i.e. it must be free of *any emotional relation to its toward-which*."[24] From this perspective the simplicity as well as the self-equivalency of purely divine intellection derives from the interpretation of Being as being-produced no less than does the objectivity of the object.

Indeed this account of divinity as self-contained intellection is utterly crucial to Heidegger's critique of Aristotle. It is linked to a second feature of Aristotelian ethics, one that proves to be particularly influential throughout the history of Western metaphysics. For Heidegger the contrast between divine and human intellection in Aristotle is particularly pointed when it comes to *phronēsis* or prudence as a dianoetic virtue. As the mode of unveiling entities with regard to action, *phronēsis* for Heidegger must be seen as key to Aristotle's interpretation of the human as a form of movement: "What *phronēsis* brings into true safekeeping is the *toward-which* of going about those dealings that human life has with itself and the *how* of these dealings in their own being."[25] Prudence or practical wisdom discloses the relevance of entities to action; as a concrete form of reasoning it determines the goal of an action, or that for the sake of which an action is undertaken, and it sets out to determine how best to achieve this goal: "*Phronēsis* makes the circumstances of the actor accessible by keeping a firm hold on the *for-the-sake-of-which* of an action."[26] To put it succinctly, *phronēsis* is the real crux of the matter for Heidegger because its conceptualization is marked by two overlapping tendencies.

On one level, the analysis of pragmatic or practical reason in the *Nicomachaean Ethics* suggests that Aristotle hits upon a crucial feature of facticity, namely that in its dealing with the world "life is there [*da*] for itself in the concrete how"[27] of its dealings. It is impossible to overstate the significance of this simple insight that Heidegger ascribes to Aristotle, as it readily reflects the point of intersection between Aristotelianism and phenomenological hermeneutics. The Natorp Report concludes that Aristotle does indeed "bring this *being-found-along-with-itself* into relief"[28] as the essential characteristic of rational life. Thus it explains why Aristotle is the ultimate reference point for hermeneutic destruction, as well as why the elucidation of phenomenology takes its cue from him. Because Aristotle bestows upon the tradition, for better and for worse, the concepts it takes up in order to interpret the phenomenon of "having-oneself-with-oneself," his ontology must provide the grounds for clarifying this tradition, identifying its potential, even marking its limits.

On another level, even though Aristotle uncovers rational life as "there" (*da*) with itself in its dealings, the Natorp Report claims that he fails to determine this being-there in a positive manner. Instead, in the *Nicomachaean Ethics* and in other texts, its "ontological definition gets actualized through a *negative* comparison with another kind of being that is considered to be being in the *authentic sense*."[29] This being is of course pure intellection, the proper mark of divinity in its state of constant presence-to-self. Compared with the divine thinker, the human being seems fickle and lacking. Ontologically speaking, the human is "capable of being otherwise than it is and thus not necessarily and always what it is."[30] Aristotle, Heidegger suggests, leaves the human being fully undetermined in this capacity because he interprets it merely as privation of divine intellection. In the most pointed version of the argument, Heidegger suggests not only that Aristotle gives up on facticity, but also that in so doing he gives in to the factical tendency to flee from oneself, to cover over finitude while mistakenly trusting in its permanence. The belief has a tranquilizing effect. Though facticity "is anxiously concerned about developing its dealings" as it strives to secure its standing in the social and natural order, it nevertheless desires to relinquish "the care of directing itself to routine tasks" so as to be free from the dealings that occupy its time. In Aristotle's approach to practical knowing, Heidegger suggests, "the tendency of caring has *transposed itself* [*hat sich . . . verlegt*] into a 'looking at' for its own sake."[31] This transposition is the hidden genesis of the pure understanding, which implies that for Heidegger Aristotle's entire characterization of theological knowing moves in a falling direction, whereas his characterization of practical knowing remains undeveloped, and thus in need of further critical elaboration.

In a crucial final step, the Natorp Report informs us that this self-transposition on the part of life, its own intentionally "misplacing" care by adopting the stance of a pure, irenic "looking at" that seals life off from the world, is precisely what allows Aristotle to apply to factical life concepts originally meant to describe movement or *kinesis* as exhibited in productive kinds of dealings. The application of these concepts to factical life is symptomatic of the falling tendency whereby the "I" confuses itself with objects as finished or produced, tranquilizing or reassuring itself. In this sense, the indiscriminate use of concepts deriving from the movement of production proves that these concepts have lost the sense of their origins, and that they have done so through the pressure exerted upon them by the history of Western ontology. It is as if the concepts themselves have wandered off from their native lands and taken up residence is locations in which they are not welcome. It is in connection with Christianity that Heidegger highlights the detrimental effects of utilizing deracinated concepts: "Christian theology, the philosophical speculation standing under its influence, and the anthropology always also growing out of these contexts all speak *in borrowed categories that are foreign to their own domains of being.*"[32] In spite of this, we see in the Natorp Report that the first alleged "borrowing" or transposition of categories takes place in Aristotle, who is said to transpose his own categories from the *Physics* into the realm of ethics and politics so as to interpret the human being in its *nature*, sparking the need for new categories that can uproot and destroy categories that are foreign to the proper hermeneutic of Dasein.

DE-THEOLOGIZING AUGUSTINE: A SECOND TRANSPOSITION

If we examine the earliest sketches of factical life, those dating from the fall of 1921, the first thing that becomes clear is just how much experimentation was needed to generate categories comprising the structure of Dasein's Being. What concerns us here is primarily to show how often these experiments were informed by concepts taken over from "Augustine and Neoplatonism," as these concepts were often used to counteract the transposition Heidegger located in classical Greek sources.

In delineating these connections in a piecemeal fashion, we must work from the ground up. In so doing we can identify those structural components of Heideggerian care which recast Augustinian theologemes. The primary goal of such analysis is to demonstrate, first, that the re-signification and adaptation of terms Heidegger himself identifies as originally religious or theological is a key part of his strategy for undoing the effects of the transfer or dislocation of categories he espies in Aristotelian metaphysics; and second, it is to show how these re-signified terms interact with the basic presuppositions of Heideggerian hermeneutics. Thus, in studying these reappropriations I shall try to pinpoint what makes it possible for Heidegger simultaneously to renounce and redeploy, to efface and re-inscribe, the religious vocabulary he develops for himself in 1920 and 1921, making it reappear in his lecture courses from 1922 to 1927 as though preserved in suspended animation. In 1921–1922 Heidegger explicitly admits that some of his categories express in a nonreligious manner phenomena that first become visible within a religious framework. Arguing that temptation, for example, should be considered a mode of concrete life in general, he suggests that its concept emerges out of Christian experience in particular: "The temptative—not in a religious sense; for the experience of it to be alive, there is not required a basis in religious experience. To be sure, the temptative, as a character of movedness, first becomes visible through Christianity; visible: experienceable in factual life, able for *me* to experience it."[33] The claim that temptation first becomes visible through Christianity yet does not require "a basis in religious experience," marks a significant departure from the order of essence delineated in "Augustine and Neoplatonism," in which temptation is closely linked to the properly *religious* dimensions of Augustine's *Confessions* according to Heidegger himself. The departure belies the novel use to which Heidegger intends to put the categories in question. In its strict sense the term *de-theologization*,[34] used infrequently in the early lecture courses, describes the means by which these categories are formulated—namely, the movement by which a term or a relation is stripped of its theological reference and transferred out of a theological domain of experience in order to designate a universally valid, nonreligious structure of human being-there.

To constitute de-theologization in its strict sense as an object of inquiry, let us start by considering Heidegger's earliest accounts of factical life as they focus on fallenness or what will become the inauthenticity of everydayness in *Being and Time*. The conceptual roots of the inauthentic lay in the early Freiburg courses. While the concept of fallenness predates the 1921 *Confessions* commentary, the various outlines of its structure sketched between 1921 and 1927 unmistakably take up and transform certain aspects of Augustine's search for God. Consider the 1922 Natorp Report as an example. At its outset Heidegger begins spelling out factical life by describing what he calls circumspection, or the act of looking-about that uncovers the world, allowing life to get its bearings. "The movement of caring is characterized by the fact that factical life *goes about its dealings* with the world."[35] The analysis of circumspection is meant to show how factical life is "there" with itself in these dealings, and that it has always already uncovered the world for itself, as Aristotle saw. But what Heidegger wants to show is that factical life is inclined to "fall" in at least two senses. First, as I have mentioned, it tends to disengage from its dealings, giving up the direction of care, modifying itself into a disinterested and impassive gazing. The Natorp Report calls this "curiosity." Heidegger cites its Latinate root: "In the care of this looking, i.e. in curiosity (*cura* [care], *curiositas* [curiosity]), the world is there for one not as the withwhich of dealings directed to routine tasks but solely from the point of view of its *look*, its *appearance*."[36] Second, factical life falls into what it cares for. Delivering itself over to the world, it finds that it gets entangled in things, or absorbed by them: "What lives within the movement of caring is its inclination [*Geneigtheit*] toward the world as the propensity toward becoming absorbed in the world and letting itself be taken along by the world."[37] Both of these falling tendencies seem to emerge from *Confessions* 10 or at least from "Augustine and Neoplatonism."

In the first case we can point to *curiositas* as the second of three forms of temptation Augustine takes up from the Johannine tradition, whereas in the second case we can point to the substantive discussion of inclination and "being transported" in §13 of "Augustine and Neoplatonism," which addresses the first stages in Augustine's exploration of temptation. In this paragraph Heidegger shows that Augustine's analysis of fleshly concupiscence advances through a sequence in which the Latin verb *transire* plays a central role, culminating in the discussion of the "inclination of the heart" in *Confessions* 10.35. For Augustine when souls succumb to the concupiscence of the flesh they proceed *"outward* following after the things they have themselves made, interiorly abandoning Him by whom they were made, and destroying what He made in them."[38] This seems to fit quite well with the notion that factical life falls *in* to the world, though of course Heidegger never depicts falling-into the world as fallingoutward, mainly because he sees the "world" as a structural component of factical life or Dasein, and he sees Dasein as always already "outside" of itself.

Whereas the two initial determinations of falling in the Natorp Report seem to derive from "Augustine and Neoplatonism," the text also reproduces the tripartite structure of temptation in *Confessions*, albeit in a slightly altered form. This suggests that in speaking of cognate terms we are not dealing with simple equivalencies, and that it would be a massive oversimplification, if not a complete falsification, to argue that in transposing concepts Heidegger simply takes over this-or-that concept wholesale from Augustine. That is not at all how the de-theologization we are describing here actually works. The threefold movement of falling in the Natorp Report is not reducible to Augustinian temptation, though it can easily be referred back to it in order to take stock of how its nonreligious sense emerges from the religious phenomena that in part make it visible. This movement appears under the headings: (1) temptation; (2) tranquilization; and (3) alienation.[39] The correspondence between these categories and Heidegger's gloss on Augustinian *concupiscientia carnis*, *concupiscientia oculorum*, and *ambitio saeculi*, is readily apparent. As the first characteristic of falling as movement, temptation involves falling prey to possibilities drawn from the world. As such it resembles the loss of self in worldly content at stake in *concupscientia carnis* and highlighted by Heidegger in §13 of the Augustine commentary. The second characteristic, tranquilization, involves reinterpreting the circumstances of falling "as though they were situations of unworried security,"[40] and as such it remains linked to the modification of *cura* into *curiositas* which places the Augustinian soul at a distance from all worldly content, leaving it in a state of false security. Finally, through the movement of alienation, Heidegger writes, "factical life becomes more and more alienated from itself, and the movement of caring that has been left to its own devices and comes before itself [*vor sich selbst*] as the occurrence of life increasingly takes away the possibility that life can . . . bring itself into view."[41] This dynamic of coming-before-oneself is precisely the situation Heidegger analyzes in §16 of "Augustine and Neoplatonism," which addresses self-importance in *Confessions* 10.39, and which plays such a crucial role in showing how Augustine unveils full facticity.

The Natorp Report is not the first moment in which Heidegger experimented with subsuming Augustinian categories into his own description of factical life. The report itself was rather the result of a year spent doing just that. In the crucial third part of the winter 1921–1922 seminar, Heidegger provides a first glimpse at the structure of care. Here care designates "the basic relational sense of life in itself."[42] Initially the description of care is saturated with religious discourse, even as it designates the nonreligious concretion of life in general: "to live is to care about one's 'daily bread.' This must be understood very generally, as a formal indication. 'Privation' (*privatio, carentia*) is both the relational and the intrinsic basic mode and sense of the Being of life."[43] At the outset the phenomenon of care is placed at a certain distance from the interpretation of Being as value. And when the latter is traced back to its historical roots in Greek philosophy, care is meant to stand forth as recovering the basic manner in which life experiences the world. In this first sketch the world designates the content of lived experience, and as such it is always already included within the care structure. In his first attempt at delineating its categorial structure, Heidegger indicates that the kind of movement or movedness[44] proper to care is that of "unrest," or "inquietude" (*Unruhe*). Now the term *unrest* has an obvious parallel in the *Confessions* 1.1, though in its first mention Heidegger alludes to Pascal, not to Augustine.[45] And indeed Augustine is barely mentioned in the course at all.

The categories of care outlined here differ slightly from the version that appears in the Natorp Report, although the tripartite schema of care appropriated from Augustine is unmistakable. Factical life, we are told, relates to the world in three basic ways, which are designated *categories of relationality*—namely, by means of (1) inclination (*Geneigtheit, Neigung*), (2) distancing (*Abstand*), and (3) sealing-off (*Abriegelung*). These categories draw heavily from Heidegger's gloss on *concupiscientia carnis, concupiscientia oculorum,* and *ambitio saeculi,* respectively. In the case of inclination its Augustinian heritage is virtually self-evident: "This categorial sense, inclination, is included in the relationality of life itself and imparts to life a peculiar weight, a direction of gravity, a pull towards something."[46] In its inclination life encounters its world "as dispersion, as dispersing, manifold, absorbing, engaging, etc."[47] Both aspects of inclination have identifiable precursors in Augustine. The first recalls the well-known statement of *Confessions* 13.9: "My love is my weight: wherever I go my love is what brings me there"; and the second resembles the theme of dispersion running throughout the *Confessions* and first mentioned in 2.1: "I collect myself out of that dispersed state in which my very being was torn asunder because I was turned away from You, the One, and wasted myself upon the many." In its first categorial moment, care reveals that the "I" is always delivered over to, and lost in, the world as the content of its experience. This means that life fixes its own meaning as if it were no different ontologically speaking than the things it encounters:

"life . . . offers itself to itself in a worldly way, i.e. in the form and in the ontological sense of its world."[48] But even in the minutest details, the 1921 version of inclination depends upon and recasts the Augustine commentary of the preceding semester.

For example, in 1921 Heidegger speaks of life's *proclivity* toward pulling itself down, losing itself in the world: "This proclivity impels life into its world, rigidifies it, and brings to maturation a hardening of the directionality of life."[49] The first mention of hardening as an existential category is found in the 1921 *Confessions* commentary, which contains a brief discussion of the exposition of Psalm 55:6 in which Augustine refers to those who have "hardened their hearts against the Lord's admonition."[50] In these early drafts of factical life Heidegger criticizes Augustine while salvaging yet de-theologizing his terms. For his part, Heidegger never speaks of the world as the external world. For him, factical life lacks an inside and an outside. And yet he takes up the very terms that Augustine uses to express the difference between the internal and the external realms, since in his view they render visible the loss of the "I" within the content of the world. Whereas Heidegger seeks to detach this transfer from the theological and metaphysical presuppositions that cast the world as external, he seeks at the same time to retain the means to express this transfer as a form of actualizing lived experience. For a philosopher bent on revealing how "life itself is experienced essentially as world,"[51] Augustinian terms are indeed well suited for adaptation by means of de-theologization.

The same point holds in the case of Augustinian curiosity, which displays life as lost in its own medium, paradoxically shut off from the world by opening itself to it. The second category of relation discussed in the winter 1921–1922 course is what Heidegger calls "distancing" or *"Abstand,"* or life's tendency to detach itself from the world, to live such that it remains unaffected by what it encounters. Factical life encounters things as "before" it; in distancing, this "before" is "suppressed"[52] and life carries on unmoved by what it encounters. This suppression is the focus of Heidegger's 1921 gloss on Augustinian curiosity,[53] the purpose of which is to show that sensuousness has a different function in curiosity than it does in concupiscence of the flesh: here what matters is that the object of desire is not positioned *in carne* (in the flesh), such that I fall into it as content, but rather desire is directed at sensuousness as such or as experiencing *per carnem* (through the flesh).[54] In curiosity what is pleasurable is not this-or-that thing, but experiencing itself. Here factical life is similarly cut off from its content through distancing. The content now passes before it in a cinematic fashion so that gazing itself becomes the hidden object of pleasure.

As for sealing-off (*Abriegelung*), Heidegger defines it as deferring the genuine appropriation what is held in care or concern. Simply put, factical life refuses to face up to the truth. In this refusal what is held "before" one in genuine care is not entirely suppressed, but the "I" nevertheless turns away from it, running away from its destiny. In the Augustinian theme of *aversio Dei* or turning away from God, we find in large part the raw materials for Heideggerian sealing-off. Let us recall that in *Confessions* 10.23 Augustine tries to explain why truth so often provokes hatred. Some minds, he suggests, love the truth when it shines upon them, but hate the truth when it rebukes them. Of these minds, Augustine writes, "do not wish to be deceived and do wish to deceive, they love the truth when it reveals itself, and hate it when it reveals them." The human mind, Augustine concludes, desires "to keep itself concealed,"[55] even as it wants nothing to be concealed from it. The 1921 gloss on this passage contains earliest mention of life as sequestering itself (*sich-selbst-abriegeln*), as Heidegger simply translates Augustine thus: "Thus, human beings do wish that the 'truth' reveals itself to them, that nothing is closed off to them, but they themselves close themselves off against it [*sie selbst aber riegeln sich ab dagegen*]."[56] Just as for Augustine the human being cannot hide from God, so for Heidegger factical life cannot shake free of itself by sealing itself off.

The parallel is by no means immaterial. It sets up what is perhaps the crucial move informing Heidegger's early approach to care. Toward the end of the 1921–1922 course, Heidegger explains that the three categories of relationality we have just explored—inclination, distancing, and sealing-off—cannot possibly exhaust the framework of care, since they do not depict care as reduplicated. To study the full concretion of care, one must see that these structures are themselves taken up into the care-structure; they are cared-for, which means that care takes itself into care: "Caring is by itself contained in care; it is *be-cared for* [*be-sorgt*], itself assumed by caring, ap-prehended by caring."[57] This means not only that care is at all times marked by inclination, distancing, and sealing-off, but also that in order to delineate its categorial structure one must repeat the analysis of the care-structure, allowing for the fact that care is always enacted in the self-reflexive form of apprehension or concern with itself.

TRANSLATING TEMPTATION

"Being-in-the-world is in itself *tempting*."[58] The section of *Being and Time* that most closely resembles these early sketches of factical life is chapter 5 of Division One, entitled "Being-in as Such." In a section entitled "The Everyday Being of the 'There' and the Falling of Dasein," all of the categories we encountered above—temptation, tranquilization, alienation, and self-entanglement (akin to sealing-off)—are reproduced in a compressed form as Heidegger outlines the basic phenomenal characteristics of falling.[59] The analysis of falling as basic characteristic of existence makes clear that Dasein is "constantly torn-away"[60] from its proper Being, and that this constancy alone offers access to Dasein's way of Being. Thus we see reproduced in this section not only the very categories outlined in the 1921–1922 winter course, but also the basic presupposition they are originally meant to justify, namely that Dasein "has" itself, that it safeguards a memory of itself, even as it evasively turns away from itself. Having identified these categories as de-theologized versions of Augustinian terms, my goal in studying how they are deployed in *Being and Time* will be to focus on this thesis which Heidegger takes for granted, but which I wish to begin calling into question.

The link between Being-in (*Insein*) and the Augustinian tradition is made explicit in the 1925 "draft" of *Being and Time*: "What we have set forth here as the Being-in [*Insein*] of Dasein and characterized in greater detail is the ontological fundament for what Augustine and above all Pascal already noted. They called that which actually knows not knowing but *love* and *hate*."[61] In the 1927 treatise, a truncated version of this statement makes its way into §29 where it is subordinated to the assertion that philosophical insight into the affective life has failed to surpass Aristotle's *Rhetoric*.[62] This assertion elides Augustine as a reference point for the treatment of Being-in placed at the outset of Division One, which serves as a prolegomenon to the analysis of everydayness. What exactly is Being-in? In §5 Heidegger offers an initial explanation as to why Dasein is ontologically farthest from itself: "The kind of Being which belongs to Dasein is rather such that, in understanding its own Being, it has a tendency to do so in terms of that entity towards which it comports itself proximally and in a way which is essentially constant—in terms of the 'world.'"[63] The 1921–1922 course underscores the fact that the world is always already included within the care structure, and the adoption of Augustinian theologemes we have uncovered there is meant to clarify the sense in which factical life or existence is always bound up with, and thus lost in, its worldly content. *Being and Time* §12 sets forth Being-in as an "existentiale" or a category of facticity. In specifying that Dasein is in-the-world, Heidegger tells us, he does not mean to suggest that Dasein finds itself spatially inside the world, as though the world were a container. Irreducible to the spatiality of objects present-at-hand, Being-in as an existential refers primarily to Dasein as dwelling in the world—worldhood being an intrinsic element of Dasein's Being. As dwelling, Dasein is *in* the world in two basic senses: it resides in the world, and it looks after the world.

Though Augustine is nowhere mentioned in conjunction with the twofold determination of Being-in as residing (*habitare*) and as loving (*diligere*), the 1925 draft of *Being and Time* grants this connection without spelling it out, identifying Augustine as a thinker whose anthropology could account for, albeit within certain parameters, the phenomena associated with Being-in.[64] Chief among these phenomena is that of absorption. As dwelling and loving, Dasein is in the world in the sense of being alongside (*Sein-bei*) the world. And yet it is alongside the world in the sense that it is *toward* the world. That is, being-alongside the world means essentially "being absorbed in it."[65] This absorption afflicts Dasein's relation with others, as expressed in its absorption in the anonymous subject of everydayness, the *they* or *das Man*. It applies as well to Dasein's relation with innerworldly beings, the ready-to-hand or the present-at-hand, each of which concerns Dasein in a manner that sparks a forgetting of the ontological difference between Being-in-the-world and innerworldly beings. In §12 we likewise discover that Dasein's factical self-understanding is entirely determined by concern: "Dasein's facticity is such that its Being-in-the-world has always dispersed itself or even split itself up into definite ways of *Insein*. . . . All these ways of Being-in have *concern* as their kind of Being."[66] Because Dasein is toward the world in the sense that it is concerned in various ways with whatever it meets in the world, concern comes back again to one of the key implications of facticity mentioned above: Dasein is such that it understands itself "as bound up in its destiny with the Being of those entities which it encounters within its own world."[67] Thus, as we have seen, Dasein or factical life is not *toward* the world in the sense that it merely goes out to meet the world, but rather its very Being is intertwined with objects of concern. For the most part we find diffused throughout Division One of *Being and Time* various remnants of the categories taken over from the Augustine commentary to express this dynamic. The 1921–1922 account of distancing or *Abstand*, for example, is taken up into Dasein's everyday sociality in the form of *distantiality*. The latter concept appears in §27 where it denotes a fundamentally disruptive aspect of being-with others, namely that in everyday life Dasein is constantly beset by its concern over how it differs from others, "whether one's own Dasein has lagged behind the Others and wants to catch up in relationship to them, or whether one's Dasein already has some priority over them and sets out to keep them suppressed."[68] Such observations tell us very little ultimately regarding how the de-theologized concepts that were developed during the early Freiburg period inform the problematic of existential analysis. To get a handle on this we must consider the paragraphs in *Being and Time* devoted to the phenomenon of falling.

Although we have seen that these paragraphs reproduce almost verbatim the categories taken over from the *Confessions* commentary in 1921–1922, the debt to Augustine in this section of the text is not limited to the categories already mentioned, but rather it is evident throughout the threefold schema which displays falling as the fundamental movement of existence. For Dasein, falling is an equiprimordial structure of Being-in-the-world along with state-of-mind, understanding, and discourse. By the time Heidegger turns his attention to falling in §35 he has already spelled out the other three elements of Being-in. We learn from §29 that Dasein always has a mood, and that in its mood Dasein is brought before itself. If the disclosive power of moods extends far beyond that of self-knowledge and volition, this is because it entails a way of finding oneself that does not arise from seeking itself, but which is taken for granted ahead of time: "As an entity which has been delivered over to its Being, it remains also delivered over to the fact that it must always have found itself—but found itself in a way of finding which arises not so much from a direct seeking as rather from a fleeing."[69] This priority given here to the past tense informs the structure of understanding as well: "Dasein is such that in every case it has understood . . . that it is to be thus and thus. As such understanding, it knows *what* it is capable of—that is, what its potentiality-for-Being is capable of."[70] Likewise for Heidegger discourse is essentially the articulation of intelligibility, and as such it grounded in the disclosure of the world informed by affection and understanding.

The treatment of falling that begins in §35 is meant to reveal the kind of affection, understanding, and discourse that characterize everyday Dasein as delivered over to the anonymous "theyself" (*das Man*). Falling, we are told, "does not express any negative evaluation, but is used to signify that Dasein is proximally and for the most part *alongside* the world of its concern. This *absorption in* has mostly the character of being-lost in the public character of *the theyself*. Dasein has, in the first instance, fallen away from itself as an authentic potentiality-for-being-its-self, and fallen into the world."[71] Now the threefold structure of falling found here is comprised of "Idle Talk," "Curiosity," and "Ambiguity." These characteristics of everydayness designate its affect, understanding, and discourse, respectively. And though this tripartite structure does not correspond in the strictest sense with the forms of Augustinian temptation we examined above, these structural characteristics do draw heavily upon these forms in order to explain the peculiar sociality of Dasein's everyday life. Indeed, Heidegger devotes the middle of §36 entirely to Augustine, rehearsing the analysis of curiosity in *Confessions* 10.35.[72] And though Augustine is not explicitly mentioned in connection with the other phenomena comprising falling, there is ample evidence to suggest that their analyses likewise make use of de-theologized Augustinian terms.[73]

My main goal in establishing these connections is to point out that they all converge around a central concept. As with the early lecture courses, so it is with *Being and Time*: this central concept is the nothingness of existence, which is undoubtedly the nodal point around which a great many de-theologized Augustinian terms are gathered in the 1927 treatise. I believe that we can read this concept as highly overdetermined, much like the center of a dream according to Freud. The nothingness of existence is discussed primarily in §38, entitled "Falling and Thrownness." Though often overlooked, this paragraph is methodologically crucial to the analytic of Dasein, as it is here, while analyzing falling as a kind of movement, that Heidegger first hits upon "the whole existential constitution of Dasein."[74] Indeed, it is no accident that the three major phenomena in which the nothingness of existence is manifest concretely—anxiety, Being-towards-death, and conscience—appear in sequence only after the movement of falling is fully worked out, since these phenomena matter for Heidegger mainly as illustrations of Dasein's existential constitution. In what sense does falling reveal that existence is nothing? Which concept of nothingness is at play in falling?

In its average everydayness Dasein is fallen in the sense that it is fascinated by others and absorbed in their world, letting itself be guided by idle talk, curiosity, and ambiguity. The concept of negation at play in everydayness is thus one that afflicts the self primarily. In everydayness Dasein is not its self: "Not-Being-its-self functions as a positive possibility of that entity which, in its essential concern, is absorbed in a world."[75] And Heidegger does not fail to remind us that this species of not-being fulfills the directive, linked to Augustine, with which he opened the analytic of everydayness: "This kind of *not-Being* has to be conceived as that kind of Being which is closest to Dasein and in which Dasein maintains itself for the most part."[76] What follows in §38 is a brief discussion of those categories I have already mentioned—temptation, tranquilization, estrangement, and self-entanglement—which are repeated almost verbatim from the early lecture courses. Here they are accorded a peculiar significance. Up until this point, Heidegger argues, *Being and Time* has outlined the existential constitution of Dasein without going beyond it in order to "take note of its character as a phenomenon."[77] These de-theologized Augustinian categories allow him to do just that, however, as they point out the existential mode of Being-in-the-world as tied to the peculiar movement of Dasein: "This movement of Dasein in its own Being, we call its *downward plunge* [*Absturz*]. Dasein plunges out of itself into itself, into the groundlessness and nullity of inauthentic everydayness."[78] If we situate this description of Dasein's downward plunge alongside the 1921 *Confessions* commentary, we see that a similar dynamic is at work for Augustine, who is said to come face-to-face with "the most groundless plunge [*abgründigsten Sturz*]"[79] at the very end of his exploration of temptation. This is not to say that the two plunges are structurally identical. On the contrary, if we continue to read closely we can identify the ways in which *Being and Time* §38 overprints and effaces its Augustinian precursor.

It is clear, for example, that Dasein's existential plunge is neither a fall from a pristine state, nor is it a fall into a "bad and deplorable"[80] standing, as if it were akin to a state of sin. What it shares in common with the *status corruptionis* is that it is constant. And in §38 this constancy is converted into its phenomenality or visibility. Falling can be experienced because it constantly "tears the understanding away from the projecting of authentic possibilities."[81] Thrownness is the experience of self-negation as a phenomenon: "Thrownness, in which facticity lets itself be seen phenomenally, belongs to Dasein, for which, in its Being, that very Being is at issue. Dasein exists factically."[82] The last sentence has the character of a proof, as if up until this point it was not entirely certain in *Being and Time* that Dasein exists factically, i.e. that it is "there" with itself. And indeed this is the case: until the point in the treatise when the vortex generated by falling finally lets facticity be seen as such, the assertion that Dasein exists factically remains merely conjectural. But once falling exhibits Dasein as an entity that has lost itself and shows that this loss is given to be seen, then Heidegger can count the loss as a gain, recognizing it as the positive characteristic of everydayness.

This interpretation of falling is possible only because Heidegger limits ahead of time the concept of negation involved in everydayness. At the outset of §38 we are told that not-being-oneself is not the same as pure and simple non-being. The concept of negation at play in Dasein's everydayness is a relative, not an absolute one: "On no account, however, do the terms 'inauthentic' and 'nonauthentic' signify 'really not' [*eigentlich nicht*] as if in this mode of Being, Dasein were altogether to forfeit [*verlustig*] its Being."[83] On the face of it, the argument seems to be incontestable. Its first step consists in assuming that, since the absolute negation of Dasein's Being would imply its no-longer-being-there, it could never function as a positive existential characteristic. In a second step Heidegger suggests that since the nothingness at play in everydayness is a relative one, it "lets itself be seen phenomenally"[84] in thrownness.

Both steps, however, become less certain when read alongside the early lecture courses. On the one hand, *Being and Time* §38 presupposes that Dasein's falling never effects a "forfeiture" of its Being, yet this is precisely the possibility entertained in the 1921 commentary on *Confessions* 10.39, namely that factical life may indeed "fall" in a matter that somehow involves a disastrous loss of its Being. Augustine opens *Confessions* 10.39 by observing that men "are made vain" (*inanescunt*) when they are interiorly pleased with themselves before God. Heidegger interprets this line in the strongest possible terms. He argues that in being interiorly pleased with oneself, one is not simply made vain before God, but rather one is rendered null and void before God. The vain forfeit their very Being before God: "through this hidden 'movement' everything falls into the void [*alles ins Leere fällt*], *inanescit*."[85] As we have already seen, a similar account of a disastrous fall makes its way into the first lecture course after "Augustine and Neoplatonism": "the nothingness of factical life is . . . a void which is precisely *disastrous* for the collapse itself."[86] Regardless of whether or not Heidegger had these connections in view while composing *Being and Time* §38, his refusal there to leave open the possibility that the nothingness of everyday life might entail the forfeiture of Dasein's Being reads as a denial, a repudiation of an earlier, potentially more extreme version of falling. On the other hand, even if we could reconcile falling as an existentiale with its earlier versions, we must still consider the fact that, in 1921–1922 at least, falling was meant to show, as Heidegger puts it, that something like a "fulfilling intuition"[87] of factical life is a category mistake. Here in *Being and Time* §38, Heidegger now suggests that falling does indeed let itself be seen phenomenally as thrownness. This means that thrownness, though it cannot be construed as a fulfilling intuition of Dasein's existential constitution, is described in such a way as to defend the accessibility of Dasein's Being on phenomenological grounds.

Thus at the very least we can see that the chain of suppositions allowing Heidegger to unveil the existential constitution of fallenness results from a shifting set of conceptual choices all of which shore up the unity of falling. But here I would like to suggest that there is thus good reason to suspect that in its basic intention *Being and Time* §38 defends this unity by overwriting an earlier, more extreme version of falling that cannot be accounted for within the preparatory analytic of Dasein.

THE "LOGIC" OF DE-THEOLOGIZATION

This assertion takes aim at the conceptual sources of falling in *Being and Time*. Before developing it further, we must note that in the present context the logic of de-theologization presents us with a twofold enigma that must be explained in order to spell out the stakes of our suspicion.

On the one hand, it remains unclear how Heidegger hopes to keep his structures completely isolated from theological dogmatics when the fact remains that they are etymologically linked to experiential contexts that are inherently dogmatic, and when he in fact already admitted in 1922 that key phenomena themselves are first rendered "visible" within a decidedly theological context. On the other hand, by considering an admittedly limited range of concepts comprising everydayness, we have confirmed that Heidegger's existential interpretations of certain phenomena develop out of, and thus undeniably break with, their stated or implied religious antecedents. To that degree the repetitions we have tracked are designed to introduce novelty into the philosophical realm rather than sameness. The de-theologization of concepts is undoubtedly analogous to translation. And in the transfer of concepts and phenomena from one realm to another, the content in question is not simply repeated but fundamentally altered. The evidence as we have presented it does not allow us to ignore difference or to pretend that it does not exist, by asserting that Heidegger relies upon, or simply borrows from, Christian sources. This is why in studying de-theologization we are not repeating the false charge that Heidegger's philosophy is a "disguised theology" [*verkappte Theologie*].[88] Instead we are considering exactly how certain terms derived from an anthropological nexus which Heidegger himself identifies as *obstructing* the question of Dasein's Being can in fact be transformed and utilized to unblock it. And moreover we are trying to grasp hold of what motivated Heideggerian de-theologization to begin with.

In *Being and Time* §74, Heidegger asserts that previous possibilities of existence may be handed down from one generation to another as part of the basic constitution of Dasein's historical Being: "Repeating is handing down explicitly—that is to say, going back into the possibilities of the Dasein that has been-there."[89] Critical engagement with the historical past must be guided by the existential concerns of the present. This is an unavoidable consequence of the fact that Heidegger grounds understanding in the existential category of projection, arguing on this basis that true understanding never consists in reconstructing the past or reaching the intention of an author, but in providing for factical Dasein new potentialities-for-Being. We can get the past "right" only if we have first resolved in the present to take hold of our destiny. In so choosing itself, Dasein can genuinely repeat what is past. In repeating the past, however, Dasein does not simply mimic or bring back a prior form of existence. Rather, the genuine repetition of the past is the mode in which Dasein genuinely hands down or bequeaths itself to a future.

Heidegger thus distinguishes rigorously between *repetition* (*Wiederholung*) and *retrieval* (*Wiederbringung*): "But when one has, by repetition [*Wiederholung*], handed down to oneself a possibility that has been, the Dasein that has-been-there is not disclosed in order to be actualized over again. The repeating of that which is possible does not bring again or retrieve [*Wiederbringen*] something that is 'past,' nor does it bind the present back to that which has already been outstripped."[90] The past makes a claim upon the present, and the repetition of prior possible forms of existence heeds this claim. It thereby issues a rejoinder, a counterclaim, against the past. Three years prior to *Being and Time*, Heidegger had insisted upon the retrievable nature of the authentic past: "The past—experienced as authentic historicity—is anything but what is past. It is something to which I can return again and again."[91] Heidegger insists here that this capacity for return does not bear within it the possibility of an objective retrieval, a reanimation or return of the past. What *Being and Time* makes clear is that the past is something to which I can repeatedly return only to the extent that the past has already been taken up into the dynamic projection of existential possibilities.

In examining the logic of de-theologization we are paying close attention to the difference between repetition and retrieval. Heidegger's attempt to distinguish rigorously between the two informs his characterization of the way in which hermeneutics forms its basic categories of existence. But in asking how the transpositions of religious terms and structures into philosophy can facilitate the categorial determination of existence, we are also questioning the validity of a rigorous distinction between repetition and return. We do so in order to ask if Heideggerian repetition can avoid inadvertently conjuring or bringing back—i.e., retrieving in the sense of

Wiederbringen—prior or archaic forms of existential possibility that Heidegger intends to ground in their ontological significance.

This question takes aim at the assertion, on Heidegger's part, of the alleged discontinuity between the religious domain, as the point of origin for certain concepts and/or phenomena, and the existentiality of Dasein's Being as the target or point of arrival for transcribed concepts. We have already seen that in many instances the argument in favor of discontinuity elides differences which we want to imbue with philosophical significance, leading us to doubt the argument in favor of it. Moreover, the question takes aim at the assertions, on Heidegger's part, of the radical disjuncture between the religious domain opened by means of revelation and the philosophical realm in which the dogmatic histories of certain concepts are supposedly bracketed, reduced, or put out of play. We have already seen that in many instances Heidegger's acts of conceptual transcription seem to *retrieve*, and not just to repeat, the most dogmatic elements of the concepts he sets out to de-theologize. Thus we must account for de-theologization while pushing back against Heidegger's own self-descriptions throughout the early lecture courses, as these descriptions undoubtedly have a strategic function.

At the outset of the present chapter, I mentioned that in the introduction to the 1921–1922 winter course Heidegger suggests that his goal is "to philosophize, and, in so doing, to be genuinely religious."[92] Although this statement can be read as equating philosophy and religion, I proposed that we read it as evidence that the latter must come to displace the former. This reading is borne out by subsequent texts in which Heidegger expresses the relation between philosophy and religion in more antagonistic terms. In 1922, for example, Heidegger writes: "Philosophy, in its radical, self-posing questionability, must be *a-theistic* as a matter of principle. . . . The more radical philosophy is, the more determinately is it on a path away from God, yet precisely in the radical actualization of the 'away,' it has its own difficult proximity to God."[93] The atheism in question is a peculiar one, having nothing to do with materialism or with denying the existence of God. That this atheism depends upon having an intimation of God explains why it can take on a religious significance, as Heidegger points out: "in religious terms, [atheism] amounts to raising one's hand against God."[94] The break between theology and philosophical atheism does not concern the difference in content addressed by these two discourses, but rather it concerns chiefly the respective forms of self-interrogation characterizing them. Whereas theology involves throwing oneself upon God, philosophy involves the throwing life back upon itself.

Thus even if the facticity of the "I" who philosophizes is a religious one, when it is taken up into philosophical questioning the religious aspect of its experiential content is withdrawn from the form in which it is cast. As Heidegger puts it, the *asceticism*[95] of philosophy is such that it must step back from, or renounce, the living actualization of religion in order to identify its ontological foundations. While this does not preclude philosophy from taking religiosity as its object of inquiry, it ensures that if the religious were to appear within the philosophical domain then it could only appear by virtue of being constituted retroactively as that which is suspended within the rational realm. In its turn this suspension allows Heidegger to depict philosophy as genuinely religious or equivalent to the religious, precisely in virtue of renouncing this religious.

Although the early Heidegger was convinced that by exiting the anthropology of Christianity and the ancient world he could clarify both its and his own ontological foundation, he seems not to have considered the possibility that this very gesture of *exiting* may itself be an essential part of the secularizing process he meant to oppose. It is only later, starting in the mid-1930s, that he begins to express misgivings about the viability of *exiting* metaphysics. By contrast, during the period stretching from 1922 to 1927 Heidegger remains more or less uninterested in his own transposition of religious concepts and phenomena. And he scarcely reflects on how his own attempts to exit theology and to articulate the *end* of philosophy compare with related but distinct attempts carried out by his predecessors in the German tradition. Some brief attention to this question can help clarify for us the stakes of de-theologization.

In the preface to *Die Religion innerhalb der Grenzen der bloßen Vernunft* (Religion within the Boundaries of Mere Reason), Kant argues that philosophy can borrow from biblical theology without encroaching upon its domain provided that whatever philosophy borrows it uses for its own purposes and not for any expressly theological aim. No matter what Kant's political motives were in distinguishing rigorously between philosophy and revealed religion, he was confident that philosophy could scarcely overstep its bounds so long as it makes use of what is revealed by ascribing a meaning to it that is "suited to mere reason."[96] In this manner, philosophy can be sure that it imports nothing into biblical theology. Indeed it makes no claim at all upon the biblical theologian, but merely draws upon the history, languages, and books of all people "in order to confirm and explain its propositions, but only for itself."[97] For what purpose? Why would reason even bother to engage religious sources in this manner? The *Religion*, let us recall, is devoted to showing that the idea of God necessarily rises out of morality, and thus that there is a purely rational concept of religion. In its subjective aspect, religion for Kant is the sum of all duties as divine commands. What reason gains in borrowing from religious or theological sources, which for Kant means biblical sources, is of inestimable value for it, since Kant argues that Christianity in its historical and material aspects alerts reason to its supersensible vocation. Religion, then, provides moral perfection with a foothold in history. It launches rational freedom in history, even as it looks toward the emergence of reason from its religious beginnings.

The entire argument of the *Religion* presumes that concepts having merely practical use involve something intuitively unfathomable to us. In Kant's critical philosophy these concepts are grounded in the ideas of reason, which lack intuitive objects to which they correspond. Kant assumes that we must borrow from sensible history and from nature the images, symbols, and expression we need in order to render intelligible to ourselves the practical ideas of reason in its supersensible vocation. How is reason made aware of its freedom, such that the idea of moral perfection is launched in history? In the *Religion*, Kant suggests that the Bible is the means by which humans become aware of the idea of moral perfection generated by pure practical reason within them, and moreover that it is through the Christian religion that this idea slowly begins to be actualized in human history. It is not until the *Conflict of the Faculties* in 1798, however, that Kant fully spells out this position: "Christianity is the Idea of religion, which must as such be based on reason and to this extent be natural. But it contains a means for introducing this religion to human beings, the Bible."[98] This tells us that for Kant the Bible is the "vehicle"[99] of reason. It is the means by which practical reason comes to itself historically. In this sense philosophy is actually obliged to engage the Christian religion, first, in order to establish the cognitive means to think through the idea of moral perfection; second, to anchor the supersensible ideas to determinate concepts of reason; and third, in order to further the historical elaboration of practical reason by bringing the material aspects of religion in line with its rational concept. Thus, in the Kantian framework philosophical reflection upon pure practical reason arises historically from the Christian religion, in which the idea of moral perfection is first instantiated in history.

This conceptual move, which identifies Christianity as the chrysalis from which reason is born, was highly influential for the German Idealist tradition after Kant. We find similar arguments in Fichte, Schelling, and Hegel. In the *Phenomenology* as well as in the *Lectures on Religion*, Hegel argues that religion is the penultimate stage in the historical progression of Spirit toward absolute self-knowing. Religion falls short of philosophy in the single sense that it thinks in a representational mode by projecting into the beyond the absolute essence of Spirit as Self. Thus, religion differs from philosophy not in terms of its content, but merely in terms of the relation it maintains with that content. Spirit comes to know itself absolutely only by overcoming religion, negating it in order to restore it to its truth dialectically in the historical progression of Spirit toward itself.

Whereas Hegel depicts religious thought as mired in a representational mode of alienation from its true Being as absolute Spirit, we have shown that the early Heidegger seems to reverse this arrangement by locating in primordial Christianity an exemplary critique of representational modes of thinking, one that phenomenology must adopt as its own. To the extent that phenomenology takes on board this critique, it stands in line with the Kantian approach to religion, which portrays philosophy as appropriating a dynamic launched in history by the Christian tradition; as coming to know itself by maintaining a critical stance with Christian history; and finally as surpassing religion altogether—leaving Christianity behind while recognizing itself as true Christianity. As it does for Kant, Christianity for Heidegger renders visible phenomena which otherwise might escape the rational subject. One is tempted to argue that Heidegger tries to compress into a few short seminars the process of reason's self-discovery that Kant sees played out over millennia, as reason slowly disengages itself from the material conditions of its own emergence.

But this would be to disregard a key difference between the Kantian and Heideggerian approaches. Whereas for Kant the rational analysis of the Bible is geared toward securing the ideas and concepts generated by practical reason as objects of thought, rendering them thinkable by analogy, the Heideggerian destruction of religious texts has as its goal the recovery of factical life in its current configuration. As a result its critical re-appropriation of religious categories differs significantly in *formal* ways from the Kantian problematic. In the *Religion*, Kant argues that philosophy is free to borrow (*entlehnen*) from biblical theology. In the *Conflict* he goes further, arguing that philosophy is obligated to investigate teachings sanctioned by the theological faculty on historical or rational grounds. By contrast, in de-theologizing the religious expression of certain phenomena, Heidegger does not thereby purport to "borrow" from theological texts, but instead to destroy the "borrowed" (*erborgen*) categories that the Western tradition since Aristotle has applied to factical life. The ever-changing set of categories used to express existence, from the initial version set forth in late 1921 just after "Augustine and Neoplatonism" to the matrix of existentials described in *Being and Time*, are depicted as *not borrowed*. They mark the first time in history, in fact, that factical life has sought to interpret itself using its own categories, without "borrowing" from the natural world in order to make sense of human being-there. Nevertheless, our analysis has shown that the etymological links between the categories Heidegger describes as native to factical life and those he locates in Christian sources are quite extensive and undeniable. Are we to conclude that they are in fact "borrowed" from these sources? Merely posing this question puts us at a distance from the early Heidegger, who pointed out his debt to theological sources infrequently, and always as if to exorcise it. By answering it affirmatively, however, we risk losing sight of what is at stake in de-theologization, namely the ability to gain access to factical life as it bestows sense or directionality upon itself precisely by loosening the grip of Christian theology and the ancient world upon its conceptualization.

Here we may invoke a register entirely foreign to Heideggerian hermeneutics in a final effort to clarify the role of de-theologization in creating its central categories. We have shown above that the logic dictating de-theologization is not entirely in line with the limited set of observations Heidegger offers concerning it. And we have questioned the ways in which Heidegger marks continuity and discontinuity between his work and the theological sources to which he is indebted. To better understand the discrepancy, we enlist a mode of inquiry that seeks to determine how the incoherencies affecting discourse and language are regulated by certain laws of desire.

There is a strict, albeit limited, analogy between what Freud calls "the day's residues" (*die Tagesreste*) and what Heidegger calls the *remains* or "residues of Christian theology within philosophical problematics."[100] We have already demonstrated that even as Heidegger calls for radically expunging them from the field of philosophy, he draws upon these remains while building up the positive content of everydayness. In chapter 6 of the *Interpretation of Dreams*, Freud suggests that a dream is a compromise reached by various psychical systems. As the psychical apparatus functions like a reflex arc for Freud, the dream is a product of a retrograde movement or regression along its path. Among the various forces that contribute to its formation, Freud draws attention to the prominent role played by recent memory impressions, or the day's residues, in the content of any given dream. Such impressions, we are told, are indifferent, in that they have not yet been fully integrated into the network of associations comprising the field of the unconscious. The day's residues are thus well positioned to be taken up by the unconscious mind, and the unconscious makes use of them as representations in order to circumvent the censorship of the preconscious mind, thereby allowing repressed content to pass unnoticed into the field of conscious attention. Significantly, Freud does not describe the day's residues as borrowed by the unconscious, which re-signifies them in order to get its demands recognized. Instead he suggests that, by providing the representational site at which a compromise between unconscious demands and preconscious censorship can be reached, the day's residues must be seen as borrowing something: "the day's residues . . . not only *borrow* [entlehnen] something from the unconscious, when they succeed in taking a share in the formation of the dream—namely, the instinctual force [*Triebskraft*] which is at the disposal of the repressed wish—but that they also *offer* the unconscious something indispensable—namely the necessary point of attachment for a transference."[101] The limited analogy with the remains of Christian theology in Heidegger arises here, as it helps us make sense of how certain of his hermeneutic categories are generated.

We can say that for Heidegger the correspondence between the categories of everydayness and their Augustinian predecessors leads us to think of the latter as playing a role analogous to the day's residues in Freud's dream theory. Granted, the categories Heidegger seeks to re-signify are neither recent nor indifferent, but rather ancient and overlaid with a tangled set of associations. And yet when approached afresh with a view to revising phenomenology as a descriptive science of consciousness, they seem to *borrow* something from the facticity they are supposed to render visible, namely the force of expression that allows them to convey a sense of Being thoroughly passed over by the metaphysical tradition. For Heidegger, then, Augustinian anthropology takes on the force generated by the critique of representational thinking. It is imbued with the power of the "No!" that Heidegger directs at substantialist accounts of the self from Aristotle forward, above all at Descartes. In return, this anthropology furnishes a quarry in which new existential categories may safely be extracted, as it represents a point of contact between the present and the tradition in which it stands—a point of contact fashioned by the work of a censorship that adjusts them ahead of time to certain demands of intelligibility and legibility, certain sets of associations imposed upon them from elsewhere. To stay with the comparison, theologemes win in this manner a share in the formation of Heidegger's existential categories, albeit in de-theologized forms, just as the day's residues win a share in dream formation. And indeed, when they are put to use in this manner, the categories they yield bear a resemblance to the texts from which they derive, just as the content of a dream bears a resemblance to the memory impressions condensed and displaced in its formation.

The upshot of this comparison is not that Heidegger "borrows" theological categories to express the universal structure of existence in his Freiburg and Marburg lectures, but rather that a more complicated and less straightforward kind of transfer is at issue here. In the texts we are examining, those terms which are derived from theological sources are imbued with, or *borrow*, a force that strips them of their religious significance and permits them to be transposed into the existential constitution of Dasein, simultaneously imparting to them the critical force needed to dismantle the history of ontology. Thus, even though we can speak of de-theologization as the repetition, transposition, or transfer of theologemes, we cannot speak of the latter as *borrowed*. And indeed by speaking of theologemes as borrowing a critical force from, rather than as borrowed by, phenomenology, we can extend the analogy with Freud one more step.

Freud notes in *The Interpretation of Dreams* that the day's residues are in fact the real *disturbers* (*Störer*) of sleep. Because they have not yet been fully integrated into the mind's existing network of associations, recent memory impressions are wildcards in the sense that they threaten to disrupt the psychical apparatus, rousing it to vigilance by demanding its full attention. Thus the very thing that allows the unconscious to take hold of daily residues—namely, the fact that as recent impressions, they are also "indifferent"[102] ones—enables them potentially to throw off psychic equilibrium. In short, dream formation does not entirely rob the daily residues of their disturbing character. As the residues are taken up into new symbolic representation, they retain their capacity to disturb the psychic apparatus. The same is true, we suspect, of those existential categories Heidegger formulates by means of de-theologization.

A DISTURBANCE IN HEIDEGGER'S REGRESS

Here we find grounds for revisiting Heidegger's hermeneutic regress toward Aristotle, while paying close attention to the analysis of falling in *Being and Time*. The positive aim of the regress was to recover from Aristotle a pragmatic concept of truth in terms of disclosure. At issue is thus to understand how the logic of de-theologization contributes to this aim as well as potentially disrupts it.

As I have mentioned, by late 1921 or early 1922 Heidegger began focusing his attention upon Aristotelian ethics and metaphysics. The crux of the matter quickly became understanding the dianoetic virtues in *Nicomachean Ethics* 6.3, which Aristotle defines as follows: "the states by virtue of which the soul possesses truth by way of affirmation or denial are five in number, i.e. art (*technē*), knowledge (*epistēmē*), practical wisdom (*phronēsis*), philosophic wisdom (*sophia*), comprehension (*nous*)."[103] By examining these virtues as so many modes of concretely taking beings into "safekeeping," Heidegger proposes to liberate *phronēsis* from its subordination to *nous theōretikos*, the contemplative ideal form of cognition that Aristotle attributes to the divine thinker.

In 1922 we get a glimpse of what the concept of practical truth that Heidegger espies in Aristotle would look like if it were fully disconnected from the privilege of the contemplative ideal and the definition of Being as being-produced, upon which this ideal is based. Pragmatic truth entails reasoning in a concrete manner to achieve one's aim, or in Heidegger's words: "*Phronēsis* is the illumination of dealings that co-temporalizes and unfolds life in its *Being*." To this Heidegger adds: "*Phronēsis* makes the circumstances of the actor accessible by keeping a firm hold on the *hou heneka*, the 'for the sake of which.'" And finally: "*Phronēsis* moves toward the *eschaton*, 'the ultimate particular fact,' in which the concrete situation seen in these definite terms culminates at the particular time in question."[104] These three clues allow us to see, first, that practical reasoning entails making judgments concretely about entities and situations that can be otherwise than they are. This is the first mark of its difference from the contemplative ideal, which relates to that which is eternal and unchanging. Second, practical reasoning consists in grasping hold of a concrete situation in its entirety, starting from the purpose of action, or that "for-the-sake-of-which" all action must be undertaken. The syllogisms of practical reasoning are valid only if the final goal of action is held firmly in view at every step. This is reflected in the third line quoted above, which suggests that concrete reasoning grasps the significance of the particular while keeping a firm hold on the ultimate end of action.

Here we see that the critique of Aristotelian ontology registered above, namely that it obscures factical life by applying borrowed categories to it, does not fully apply to the description of practical truth Aristotle offers in the *Nicomachaean Ethics*. Heidegger seeks to recover from Aristotle's treatment of the dianoetic virtue a concept of practical truth as "nothing other than the whole unveiled moment (at the particular time) of factical life in the how of its decisive readiness for dealings with itself, and this how is within life's factical relation of concern to the world it is presently encountering."[105] In other words, the concept of *phronēsis* represents Aristotle's best attempt to show how factical life unveils itself in its Being as an articulated structural totality. Indeed the critical stance which the early Heidegger adopted toward Aristotelian ontology was always tempered by his confident belief that *phronēsis* was the key to reformulating the Husserlian doctrine of intentionality in terms of a phenomenological hermeneutics of Dasein. Over time this confidence grew stronger even as Heidegger changed his focus. In the summer 1924 Marburg lecture course, entitled *Basic Concepts of Aristotelian Philosophy*, Heidegger no longer brings to the fore the tendencies at play in Aristotelian philosophy toward prioritizing *pragmata* in the meaning of essence or *ousia* in general. At Freiburg he had flirted with arguing that Aristotle failed to access existence as such. By contrast we find this assertion pushed to the background in the 1924 summer course, which focuses instead upon the positive aspect of Aristotelian pragmatics and their relevance for clarifying the existentiality of human Dasein.

Here Heidegger finds himself preoccupied by a single theme: the relation practical reason maintains with the end or *telos* of action, that for the sake of which action is done. In pragmatics the concept of the end is equivalent with the good. Heidegger's task is to determine the structure of practical truth placed in relation with its telos: "The being of human beings is determined as concern; every care as concern has a definite end, a *telos*. Insofar as the being of human beings is determined through *praxis* (taking-action), every *praxis* has its *telos*; insofar as the *telos* of every *praxis*, as a limit (*peras*), is agathon, agathon is the genuine being-character of human beings."[106] The ontological equivalency between human being-there and the good as *agathon* is utterly crucial for grasping the stakes of Heidegger's destruction of Aristotle. This equivalency takes center stage in 1924: "The *agathon* is a determination of the being of human beings in the world. Therefore, through this analysis of the *agathon*, we will acquire a new clarification of the Dasein of human beings, specifically by referring this back to its limit, its *peras*, which is to say to the genuine being-character itself. On this basis, we will investigate the *agathon* more closely as a being-determination of human beings, a being-character of concern, and so of Dasein itself."[107] In practical reasoning, the being of the one who reasons is at stake in the reasoning itself. The contrast between *phronēsis* and *nous theōretikos* now works in favor of the former. The one who contemplates is at leisure, Heidegger reminds us, in the sense that he or she remains unaffected by the object contemplated—a lack of affection that reaches an apotheosis in the portrait of the divine thinker.

By contrast practical reasoning involves no such appeal to objectivity. The one who reasons about how to achieve an aim puts his or her Being at stake. In practical reasoning, one cannot reason well without being fully implicated in the reasoning process, and without risking one's very Being.

Heidegger's way of underscoring this is to equate the Aristotelian concepts of the good and the "limit" or aim (*peras*) of action with the Being-character of the human being. This equivalency is the origin of an existential determination of Dasein that caused Heidegger some problems after the publication of *Being and Time* and required clarification on his part: "The Dasein exists in the manner of Being-in-the-world and as such *it is for the sake of its own self*. It is not the case that this being just simply is; instead, so far as it is, it is occupied with its own capacity to be."[108] The statement makes the most sense when we read it alongside Heidegger's persistent attempts to equate the Being of Dasein with the Aristotelian *hou heneka*, or that for the sake of which action is undertaken. What comes to the fore in the 1924 summer course is the relevance of this equivalency for rethinking human finitude: "Dasein is *being-limited*."[109] Dasein is thus fully itself only in relating to its Being as fully at stake in its action.

The decision to equate the Being of Dasein with the Aristotelian concept of the good or *agathon* harbors an enigma that is not easily solved. I highlight it here to suggest that this decision goes to the very heart of our question concerning the stakes of de-theologization in the early Heidegger. The ontological stakes of this decision may be summed up by insisting upon the difference between the arguments of the religious life courses, which portray the Christian as fundamentally distant from the divine figured as an immanent, transcendent, or *highest good*, and the driving impulse behind Heidegger's research on Aristotetlian ethics, which identifies the meaning of the good or *agathon* with the being-character of Dasein. In the present context the question of de-theologization comes down to *this* difference, which concerns the contrasting ontological functions Heidegger assigns to the Aristotelian *agathon* and the Augustinian *bonum* vis-à-vis facticity.

The determination of the Aristotelian *agathon* as limit is spelled out at great length starting in the 1924: "*Peras*, the limit, determines the being-there of what is concerned. *The completion of concern is only possible in that what is concerned is there, that the concern is not grasping at straws, that concern has the character of the limit (peras).* Only in this way is it possible for a concern in general to come into its being."[110] In these lines Heidegger arguably has in view the connection between finitude and death, worked out at length in 1924 and reflected within the determination of Dasein as being-at-the-limit: "*Being-gone* is the most extreme mode of Dasein. . . . *Telos, teleion* has the character of limit, specifically limit in the sense of being, such that this limit determines beings in their 'there.'"[111] What does *being-gone* mean here? And how is it the most extreme mode of Dasein? The argument concerns death as the outermost *possibility* of Dasein, the most possible possibility and thus the one that cannot be outstripped. According to the 1924 lecture *The Concept of Time*, death in its existential conception is not simply or even primarily the end of life. Death stands before Dasein in a manner that allows Dasein to appropriate it as a possibility. In anticipating death Dasein grasps hold of its outermost possibility. Death is thus included in the phenomenal structure of anticipating death, allowing Heidegger to interpret it as a way of Being and not as the end of life.

The 1924 summer course *Basic Concepts of Aristotelian Philosophy* locates the ontological foundations of this view in Aristotle, as Heidegger argues that the end of action is rendered present as the most extreme limit of possibility through anticipation.[112] The ontological equivalency of Dasein and its end is carried forward in the crucial 1924–1925 winter course entitled *Plato's Sophist*, the first part of which contains the most detailed and most radical version of Heidegger's Aristotle: "in the case of *phronēsis* the object of deliberation is life itself; the *telos* or end has the same ontological character as *phronēsis*."[113] And further: "the *telos* of practical reasoning is . . . the *anthropos* himself . . . the proper Being of man is the *telos*."[114] It is by putting oneself at stake in action that the human being unveils itself as such.[115] The Aristotelian *phronimos* is "the one who deliberates in the right way . . . regarding 'what is conducive to the right mode of Being of Dasein as such and as a whole.'"[116] These deliberations concern "the right and proper mode of Being of Dasein,"[117] which is how Heidegger renders the Aristotelian *eudaimonia*. But what really matters here in Heidegger's reading of the *phronimos* is that the *end* toward which the *phronimos* relates is of the same ontological character as the Being of Dasein itself. In genuinely prudent action, the *telos* of the action is in fact disclosed and preserved as such, which is why, according to Heidegger, Aristotle concludes that *phronēsis* is "a disposition of human Dasein such that in it I have at my disposal my own transparency."[118] The 1924 summer course is already moving in the direction of equating practical reasoning with the phenomenon of conscience: "the *ergon* is there for the one who in concern is *present in himself* (*an sich selbst gegenwärtig*). . . . The human being may be defined with respect to genuine living and rising up into concern."[119] But we must await the *Sophist* course, however, before we discover its real significance: "*Phronēsis* is nothing other than conscience set into motion, making an action transparent. Conscience cannot be forgotten.... Conscience always announces itself."[120] The fact that practical reasoning is not susceptible to forgetting or *lēthē* proves for Aristotle that it cannot be considered theoretical knowledge or *epistēmē*. For his part, Heidegger takes this insusceptibility as signifying the constancy of human being-there-with-itself. And for him the homology between the unity of action in practical reasoning and the unity of finitude in anticipating death is instructive: in both cases the most extreme element of the relation in question—the end of action in the case of practical reasoning; death in the case of Dasein—is immanentized, included within an intentional impulse that constitutes this impulse as a whole. In noting this homology we gain a foothold in approaching the enigma mentioned above. The association Heidegger emphasizes in Aristotle between the Being of the actor and the end of action as *agathon* or the good is manifestly is in tension with our own depiction of the Augustinian *cogito* out-of-reach.

This opposition is emblematic of the deeper disturbance introduced into Heideggerian hermeneutics by the transposition of theologemes as I have outlined them here, as all of the latter are genealogically linked to a description of human finitude that seems to contest the one Heidegger seeks to isolate as a reader of Aristotle. For Aristotle, the *telos* as the good reveals itself only to the one who resembles it, and yet for Heidegger as a reader of Paul and Augustine resemblance is not propitious in the same manner, as the finite human being is never homologous with the good. It is difficult to fathom that Heidegger was unaware of this potential ontological discrepancy between these competing notions of the good—especially given the fact that he faults Descartes, as we have seen, for his theoretical Pelagianism—or that he did not register at least the potential disturbance it would seem to introduce into his view of human finitude. But can we surmise that in aligning himself with Aristotelian pragmatics Heidegger followed the "path away from God"—not in the sense that he chose atheism, but in the sense that he chose one account of human finitude over another? And that the extreme form of existential *brokenness* attributed to the Christian in 1920–1921 would be eclipsed by the portrait of existence as unified action that emerges from his reading of Aristotle? Regardless, the homology provides the overarching framework into which Heidegger introduces de-theologized terms, as it is directly linked to the modern figure whose anthropology reveals the need for a thoroughgoing categorial determination of human Being-there.

Let us recall that at the outset of *Being and Time* it is Kant who is faulted for having "failed to provide an ontology with Dasein as its theme."[121] The 1924 summer course informs us that the homology Heidegger locates in Aristotelian practical reason "is echoed in the *Kantian* definition of the human being: the rational essence exists as an *end in itself*."[122] And in 1928 when Heidegger repeats the assertion by arguing that Dasein exists for the sake of itself, in the sense that its Being provides the ultimate reference point for all use-value, he writes, "there comes to view the structural moment that motivated Kant to define the person ontologically as an end, without inquiring into the specific structure of purposiveness and the question of its ontological possibility."[123] The charge is echoed elsewhere in the same volume, when Heidegger suggests that if Kant had pressed on in exploring the meaning of being-an-end-in-itself, he would have seen that the human way of being has its own set of categories, fully distinct from those of nature.[124] The clear implication is that Heidegger's own analysis of purposiveness, drawn from Aristotle and opening onto the phenomenon of Being-towards-death, is designed to supplement Kant by elaborating the categories he should have discovered for himself.

In the context of the Aristotle courses, the figure of Dasein comes into view as fundamentally tied to the question of the limit or end as the site in which a being properly comes to rest: "Every being is determined in its being by the fact that it is a *limit*, the having-been-complete that has its limits. 'Limit' is not somehow determined by the relation of one being to another, but rather the limit is itself a *being-aspect in beings*; *peras*, limit, is its *site, its place, its being-produced, being-in-its-place*."[125] The fact that he repeatedly ties Aristotelian *entelechy* to the Kantian moral determination of man as end-in-itself should lead us to see that Heidegger's guiding question concerns once more, as it did in the Augustine commentary, the phenomenon of having-oneself-with-oneself. We find confirmation of this in the 1928 *Basic Problems*, "Formally it is unassailable to speak of the ego as consciousness of something that is at the same time conscious of *itself*, and the description of the *res cogitans* as *cogito me cogitare*, or self-consciousness, is correct."[126] But here we come to the crux of the matter, as we can now invoke to full effect the figure of the Augustinian *cogito* out-of-reach: the matrix into which Heidegger introduced de-theologized terms derived from Augustine is one in which the formal definition of Dasein as being-there-with-itself is defended at all costs. The defense is motivated, as we know, by the charge leveled against the metaphysical tradition, which remains forgetful of the distinction between the Being of consciousness and Being as presence-at-hand. But what is potentially lost in this arrangement is any view of finitude that would challenge the basic characteristics that allow Heidegger to distinguish ontologically between the former and the latter ways of Being.

The lodestar of hermeneutic phenomenology, Heidegger holds fast to the definition of human finitude as a having-itself with itself no matter how strenuously he attacks Descartes. The definition forms an unbreakable bond between the Cartesian *cogito* and Dasein, setting the stage for the analysis of falling in *Being and Time*.

CONCLUSION

We have arrived at two conclusions regarding de-theologization in the early Heidegger. First, the transposition of Augustinian terms has a positive and a negative function. First, it allows Heidegger to describe phenomena historically disclosed by, but not unique to, the domain of experience opened by Christian revelation. Second, this transposition functions negatively to immunize his formal descriptions of Dasein's Being from the critical force he originally attributed to their predecessors in Christian texts. In short, the transpositions themselves are tied to theological models that threaten to undermine the ontological principles Heidegger wants them to serve. Their elaboration within an ontological context determined by the regress to Aristotle functions to bracket the question of a finitude without limits posed in connection with the figures of self-renunciation explored in connection with Paul and Augustine. Thus, we must conclude that the categories of falling everydayness in *Being and Time* are deployed without regard for the full potential provided by their conceptual histories. Such a regard would include the possibility that these histories would unsettle rather than confirm the portrait of factical finitude they are meant to nourish. Indeed, we have demonstrated that these categories were transposed from a model of self-renunciation that does not fully align with the overlap between Heidegger's characterization of Aristotelian foundational principles and his own basic hermeneutic presuppositions.

We are thus faced with an either-or scenario: either the formal definition of self-possession uncovered in Aristotle and reflected in Heidegger's texts provides the proper ontological corrective against the excessive forms of guilt and self-renunciation Heidegger initially uncovered in Paul and Augustine; or the return to Aristotle elides the gap between the theologically informed categories constructed in the religious life commentaries and their de-theologized correlates in the hermeneutic categories of existence. Put otherwise, the critical force Heidegger initially attributes to Pauline and Augustinian religiosity is either neutralized or retroactively augmented by de-theologization. In either case, we have identified a subtle rift in Heidegger's early notion of finitude, which is shown to combine two anthropological registers that potentially ought to repel one another. The issue now is not only to determine how this affects Divisions One and Two of *Being and Time*, but also to gauge how the rift informs Heidegger's thought going forward.

CHAPTER FOUR

Testimony and the Irretrievable in *Being and Time*

INTRODUCTION

"So we are necessarily strangers to ourselves," Nietzsche wrote in 1887, "we do not understand ourselves, we *have* to mistake ourselves, for us the principle 'Each is farthest [*der Fernste*] from himself' applies to all eternity."[1] Forty years after Nietzsche pronounced this eternal principle, Heidegger took it to heart. The opening paragraphs of *Being and Time* leave little doubt that everyday life, though it is ontically closest to us, remains "ontologically the farthest [*das ontologische Fernste*]"[2] and is thus overlooked by philosophers from Aristotle to the present. Though he approves of Nietzsche's principle as an apt characterization of everyday life, Heidegger nevertheless disagrees with its central premise. Even if we are ontologically farthest from ourselves, he reasons, we are by no means condemned to mistake ourselves. As long as the entity that is ontologically the farthest from me is in each case *mine*, there is no need to conclude, *pace* Nietzsche, that I am bound to mistake myself or that I cannot confess the truth of my Being.

Quoting Augustine ("but what could be closer to me than myself?") Heidegger argues early on in *Being and Time* that, though we know that we are hidden from ourselves, we must nevertheless presuppose that a thoroughgoing hermeneutic of Dasein as the entity ontologically farthest from me is within reach: "not only must this entity," he writes in *Being and Time* §9, "not be missed in that kind of Being in which it is phenomenally closest, but it must be made accessible by a positive characterization."[3] Such is the goal Heidegger sets for himself at the outset of the existential analytic. To reach it he must explain how Dasein attests or gives testimony to its own Being as a unified structural totality—how, that is, it shows itself to itself, essentially dictating to itself how it ought to be interpreted. The passing reference to Augustine in *Being and Time* §9 is meant to justify his wager that Dasein bears witness to its Being as a unified whole. However, the fact that Heidegger uses Augustine to justify this wager even in passing sharpens the central question that emerges from the foregoing three chapters, while simultaneously shifting our focus to the theme of testimony in *Being and Time*. The preparatory existential analytic of Dasein revolves around the following question: can Dasein delineate its own Being as a unified totality? Is this Being *shown* to it such that Dasein can confess the truth of its existence? The project of *Being and Time* depends entirely upon identifying specific phenomenal evidence that warrants answering these questions in the affirmative. But our investigation thus far suggests that, at best, it remains to be seen whether or not the concepts derived from theological sources in the early lecture courses are suited to the task of shoring up the unity of existence.

In short, the philosophical question that emerges from this investigation is thus whether or not unity is a predicate of existence, or if every being is *one*. In *Love and Saint Augustine*, Hannah Arendt argues that according to Augustine's *Confessions*, "man can never have himself as a whole (*totum*). If he had himself as a whole he would have his Being. . . . However, since he was created so that his Being exists for him only as a source, man's concrete existence is governed by temporality in which he can never fully grasp himself."[4] Written in 1929, the remark could easily be interpreted as leveling an implicit criticism against Heidegger's *Being and Time*, published two years earlier. Our examination of the fundamental contexts in which the existential analytic takes shape during the 1920s now bears directly upon the question of its perceived success or failure in *Being and Time*. Whether or not the implications of Arendt's observation, above, were lost on Heidegger, the textual evidence suggest that Heidegger encountered difficulty integrating his vision of Christian religiosity into his own hermeneutic model of existence.

The present chapter argues that the tension between two registers of the existential analytic of Dasein—the one which affirms that Dasein can confess itself as a whole; the other which works toward this affirmation counterintuitively by shaking our confidence in it—reaches its highest pitch in the discussion of testimony in *Being and Time*, a discussion that centers on the twin themes of Being-towards-death and existential guilt. In order to secure the unity of existence, first, in the form of care and, second, in the complementary forms of time and historicity, the 1927 treatise must actively dispel the postulate of a fundamentally dispersed, forfeited or fractured self, one that does not lend itself to the kind of unification Heidegger calls *authenticity* or the *truth of existence*. Thus far our investigation into the sources of *Being and Time* has drawn attention to the role of the indwelling Spirit in the Paul lectures as well as the strong prohibition against self-representation (the *cogito* out-of-reach) in the Augustine lectures. Both figures, I have shown, raise the possibility that the human being as an entity is irreducibly disharmonious, and that unity is not predicable of it. I now intend to invoke this genealogical insight as corroborating evidence by associating the postulate of a fractured or disjointed self, to the degree that it is broached in *Being and Time*, with Heidegger's reading of these particular sources. In order to demonstrate that, despite an extensive effort to do so, it is impossible for Heidegger to fully dispel this postulate, this chapter retraces the steps *Being and Time* takes to show how Dasein testifies to the unity of its existence. I shall demonstrate, first, that the figure of the self as an irretrievable otherness reemerges at crucial moments in the course of Heidegger's exposition of factical Dasein and, second, that, in its ineffaceable character, this otherness can be read as the disturbing reemergence of the very theological possibilities of existence Heidegger aims to expunge from his philosophy.

THE OUTLINE: EXISTENCE AS A WHOLE

"The success of the preparatory interpretation of Dasein," Heidegger wrote in the summer of 1925, "in drawing out the structure of the Being of Dasein in itself is based upon this, that in the thematic development of the analysis this very entity—Dasein in its totality [*Ganzheit*]—is secured."[5] But what does it mean to secure the "whole" of Dasein, and why is it so crucial for Heidegger? It means, first, that any interpretation of this entity should be guided by the assumption that its structure "is something 'a priori'; it is not pieced together but is primordially and constantly a whole."[6] Second, it means showing that this structure can be phenomenally exhibited in full. At Marburg, Heidegger's insistence that human Dasein can access its Being as a whole grew in direct proportion to the strength of the arguments he crafted to refute it. The earliest discussions of Being-towards-death, as we saw in chapter 3 above, were designed to shake confidence in the presupposition that Dasein can get itself wholly into view, only so that the validity of the presupposition could ultimately be reasserted. Division One of *Being and Time* is largely preoccupied with "securing" Dasein's Being as a whole by sketching the outline of its structure as care. Division Two then re-interprets this whole by showing how it is enacted or concretized as a unity. The latter thus superimposes the unity of existence as time upon the structural totality of existence as care.

In *Being and Time* Division One the potential problems generated by constantly reaffirming the a priori cohesiveness of existence are overshadowed by the imperative to disclose the elements comprising its structure. This faith in the structural cohesiveness of existence is Heidegger's starting point in the Preface—a point, that is, which is famously a circle. "Inquiry, as a kind of seeking," Heidegger writes, "must be guided beforehand by what is sought."[7] If we seek to question Being, in other words, then its meaning must already be available to us in some way. How do we uncover the answer we already possess? We must first delineate the meaning of one being in particular; only then can we interrogate the meaning of Being in general. This circularity is irreducible; Heidegger famously adds that all formal objections to it fail to prevent concrete ways of investigating from getting up and running. Indeed the investigation is already afoot by the time this circularity is even mentioned in §2, which leads Heidegger to argue that the Being of the inquirer itself has ontico-ontological priority in building up the question of Being. Thus the bond between the act of questioning and Being itself forms the first ring in *Being and Time*.

Out of it Heidegger will unfurl a second one. After a long preparation he advances from existence to its intrinsic meaning as care. The direction in which he elaborates existence is determined at the outset, in §12: "The compound expression 'Being-in-the-world' indicates in the very way we have coined it, that it stands for a *unitary* [*einheitliches*] phenomenon. This primary datum [*Befund*] must be seen as a whole [*im Ganzen*]."[8] It is not until §41, almost halfway through the treatise, that Heidegger displays this whole as care [*Sorge*], or the "primordial context"[9] in which are woven together the various elements comprising Dasein's Being. Care is for Heidegger a threefold unity. As care, Dasein's Being is defined as: (1) already-in-the-world; (2) alongside-other-entities; and (3) ahead-of-itself. The resemblance this tripartite structure bears to the time as past, present, future, is unmistakable. In Division Two, Heidegger will take the former three features back into the phenomenon of primordial time, arguing that they correspond exactly with the ecstatic dimension of Dasein's Being as temporal stretch. But already from the outset Division One emphasizes the structural integrity of this "stretch." Expounding its structure, Heidegger emphasizes two of its aspects. First, the Being of Dasein is in each case *mine*. The phenomenon of "mineness" (*Jemeinigkeit*) stipulates that each Dasein is delivered over to itself, and must take over its Being as its own: "That Being which is an issue for this entity in its very Being is in each case *mine*. . . . Because Dasein has in each case *mineness*, one must always use a *personal* pronoun when one addresses it: 'I am,' 'you are.'"[10] It is precisely in this context where mineness determines ahead of time the existentiality of existence, defined primarily with respect to the future, that Heidegger first raises the question concerning the "who?" of everyday Dasein.

Section 12 establishes the rigorous difference between Dasein as Being-in-the-world and innerworldly entities. It is here that we encounter the first characterization of Dasein in terms of care—or at least, in terms of concern and solicitude, the two forms care takes in *Being and Time*. The analysis of worldhood that emerges out of this preliminary sketch redefines the nature of spatiality. In repositioning world as a phenomenon included in Dasein's Being, Heidegger dissolves the division between the inner and the outer worlds, and portrays Dasein as primordially outside of itself. Each element in Heidegger's discussion of worldhood emphasizes Dasein's structural cohesiveness, from the analysis of its environment to the spatiality characterizing existence.

It is not until the discussion of sociality, starting in §25, that Heidegger begins to challenge this cohesiveness. The fact that Dasein must always be addressed as "I am" or "you are," etc., instead of "it is," does little to answer the who-question, since this question never looks for the simple and empty formal "I" or "you," which, for Heidegger, serve merely to indicate the priority of unity over multiplicity in displaying Dasein as a self. In being with others, we succumb to fascination. The study of sociality, being-with-others, is primarily for Heidegger a chance to grapple with fascination: "Proximally and for the most part Dasein is fascinated with its world. Dasein is thus absorbed in the world."[11] To ward off this fascination while exposing it, existential analysis works over various levels of self-concealment at play in relation with others. Heidegger is famously suspicious of the "who" that lies at the bottom of average everydayness: "The 'who' is what maintains itself as something identical throughout changes in its experiences and ways of behavior, and which relates itself to this changing multiplicity in so doing."[12] We often mistake the "who" by conflating it with the ontological characteristics of more permanent things. In that sense we take the "who" as *subjectum*. But even when we resist doing so, the identity of the "I" is never straightforward: "It could be that the 'who' of everyday Dasein just is *not* the 'I myself.'"[13] An extensive and cautious analysis is necessary to avoid mistaking the "I" for the subject or as immediately identical with the "I myself." This is precisely why Heidegger starts with the assumption that authentic selfhood is attained only as a modification of the everyday identity of Dasein as "no one" in particular.

Behind this assumption lies Heidegger's conviction that Dasein has always already fallen prey to fascination with other Daseins and with the world, and that because of this the faith which philosophers place in the powers of self-examination and introspection is entirely misguided. What if the "I" exerting itself in reflective awareness is already distorted, such that its apparent correspondence with its image is of no help in determining the Being of the one reflected? In that case the givenness of Dasein to itself would depend entirely upon weaning it from various forms of seductive fascination. "But in that case," Heidegger concludes, "there is ontologically a gap [*eine Kluft*] separating the selfsameness of the authentically existing Self from the identity of that 'I' which maintains itself throughout its manifold Experiences."[14] The gap separates authentic selfhood from the featureless yet fascinating realm of the "who," suggesting that the self remains irreducible to whomever we nominate as an answer to the who-question. In the flow of Division One this gap is treated as a threat. Its emergence in §27 calls forth a concerted effort to defend the unitary primordial structure of Dasein's Being. The three equiprimordial characteristics of Dasein—state-of-mind, understanding, discourse—Heidegger explicates directly following his discussion of sociality are meant to underscore the point that the non-uniformity of Dasein does not imply that its Being is fundamentally fractured, but rather that it is always implicitly brought before itself as a whole.

Marked by state-of-mind (*Befindlichkeit*) Dasein has always already disclosed itself in a certain disposition or mood. Even when Dasein does not understand why a certain mood has befallen it, its mood necessarily results from a primitive self-discovery that outstrips all rational investigation. In the discussion of mood, Heidegger shores up the totality of Dasein by arguing that the affective means of disclosure surpass those of conscious self-reflection. In §29 he enlists the testimony of Augustine and Pascal in support of his view that self-affection reaches further than self-knowledge. This line of argument is oriented toward justifying the presupposition that, in a mysterious fashion, Dasein has always gained access before all else to the whole of facticity: "The mood has already disclosed, in every case, *Being-in-the-world as a whole, and it makes it possible first of all to direct oneself toward something.*"[15] The same holds for understanding, the second equiprimordial characteristic, discussed in §31: "As a disclosure, understanding always pertains to the whole basic state of Being-in-the-world."[16] Understanding pertains above all to projection.

It draws from the particular factical situation of Dasein those possibilities which it projects before itself. These possibilities stand toward Dasein as that "for the sake of which" it strives. Spanning the distance between thrownness and possibility, understanding discloses existence as a whole, setting the mark for all striving after possibility and allowing Dasein to seize upon "the full disclosedness of Being-in-the-world *throughout all* the constitutive items which are essential to it."[17] Thus whereas self-affection extends backward to encompass Dasein's Being as thrown, understanding extends forward as the futural stretch of possibility. The two are linked by discourse, the a priori structure of which is elaborated starting in §34. As a feature of discourse, interpretation is the act of articulating the "totality" (*Ganze*) of significations comprising the intelligibility of an entity. Here Heidegger's real concern is to show how language determines Dasein from the ground up. He defines assertion as "a pointing-out which gives something a definite character and which communicates."[18] This definition is motivated by the role that discourse plays in the architectonic of Division One. From it Heidegger infers that fallenness embraces Dasein's Being as a whole. Thus, along with self-affection and understanding, Heidegger uses his discussion of discourse to reassert the ontological priority of homogeneity over non-homogeneity, structural unity over modal non-uniformity, as he ever so slowly lays the phenomenal groundwork for care.

Each aspect of Dasein's Being fits together in order to set the stage for the analysis of anxiety. Why does Heidegger appeal to anxiety at the moment he confidently asserts, in the last line of §38, that by describing the structures of fallen everydayness he has finally obtained the phenomenal ground for a comprehensive view of existence as care? In anxiety the multiplicity characterizing Dasein's everyday identity is resolved in its formal simplicity as the gap between the self and the "who" disappears. In anxiety I am riveted to myself, deprived of all escape, yet simultaneously given to myself in the form of nothingness. Recalling a tradition that runs from Augustine to Kierkegaard and Freud, Heidegger suggests that anxiety lacks a proper object. It does not consist in fearing this or that, but rather in shrinking away from nothing in particular. Heidegger posits that this "nothing in particular" is in fact Dasein itself: "That in the face of which [Dasein] shrinks back must, in any case, be an entity with the character of threatening; yet this entity has the same kind of Being as the one that shrinks back: it is Dasein itself."[19] Is this threat equivalent to a self-reproach? Not at all. "That in the face of which one is anxious is completely indefinite."[20] This implies that Dasein is a threat to itself simply because it cannot shirk the form of nothingness in which it appears to itself in anxiety. In fleeing this nothingness, Dasein cannot avoid dragging it along with itself, which is why "in anxiety one feels *uncanny* [*unheimlich*]."[21] Uncanniness is thus the existential mode in which Dasein is individualized, becoming free to choose either for or against itself.[22] Having outlined the structure of anxiety, Heidegger tallies its elements, concluding that the total yields "the whole of Dasein."[23] The fact that the existential components of anxiety correspond exactly with the equiprimordial characteristics of Dasein sketched just prior to its analysis only confirms for Heidegger that Dasein's Being is indeed a tripartite whole.

In *Being and Time* Heidegger never advances beyond confirming that Dasein's Being must be conceptualized as a structural totality. The integrity of Dasein's Being is established at the outset of Division One. And in first displaying care, in §41, Heidegger describes this totality as a priori with respect to all of Dasein's factical situations: "Care, as a primordial structural totality, lies *before* every factical attitude and situation of Dasein, and it does so existentially *a priori*; this means that it always lies *in* them."[24] Although anxiety provides an initial confirmation of this structural totality, the rest of *Being and Time* is devoted to showing how this whole is concretely instantiated. To this end Heidegger retraces the "whole" of Dasein three times—first, as Being-towards-death; next, as the call of conscience; finally, as temporality and historicity. In each instance, he does not simply reassert the integrity of Dasein's Being. Instead he sets out to shake our confidence in the presupposition that Dasein is a whole, to show that this presupposition can withstand an onslaught of objections to it. This interplay between challenging and reasserting the integrity of Dasein's Being lends its rhythm to the existential analytic, yet it also instills in Heidegger a growing suspicion that this analytic fails to display on sufficiently phenomenal grounds the structural totality of Dasein.

Reflecting this growing suspicion, the penultimate chapter of *Being and Time* echoes in the form of a question the assertions put forth in §41: "Have we indeed brought the whole of Dasein, as regards its authentically *Being*-a-whole, into the forehaving of our existential analysis?"[25] This question remains unanswered in the very last chapter of *Being and Time*, which announces the "incompleteness"[26] (*Unvollständigkeit*) of the foregoing existential analytic. It is this sense of incompleteness that we want to study here, slowly lining it up alongside the results of our inquiry into de-theologization. This inquiry left us with the nagging suspicion that some of the concepts Heidegger uses to defend the unity of existence are not entirely well-suited to this purpose, if only because they are derived from experiential contexts that fundamentally deny this unity.

What is lacking at the end of Division One, after the analysis of anxiety, such that Heidegger balks at announcing the unity of existence, once and for all? "With the expression 'care' we have in mind a basic existential-ontological phenomenon, which all the same is *not simple* [*nicht einfach*] in its structure."[27] Anxiety yields an articulated whole. It thus provides a glimpse at the possible unity of existence. But because it reveals care as a manifold it is merely a sign or indication (*Anzeichen*) that the ontological question of Dasein ought to be pursued further, so as to "exhibit a *still more primordial* phenomenon which provides the ontological support for the unity [*Einheit*] and totality [*Ganzheit*] of the structural manifoldness of care."[28] This exhibition must meet two criteria. First, it must clarify the totality of presuppositions guiding the hermeneutic of Dasein. Second, it must "expressly assure [*versichern*] that the *whole* of the entity which it has taken as its theme" has been brought into view.[29] In short it matters little if existence appears as a potential unity, or as an abstract whole, when everything rests upon catching a glimpse of this whole as it is concretized.

The question of finitude arises in *Being and Time*, as it does in Heidegger's early lectures, precisely because death seems to ruin the prospects for getting the whole of Dasein into view. For Heidegger the phenomenon of death is initially a counterargument against the totality of existence. The argument is a familiar one: as long as Dasein exists, part of its life remains outstanding. When Dasein runs the entire course of life, then it comes to its end. When it comes to an end, nothing remains outstanding or still to come. But because Dasein ceases to be precisely at the moment of death, it is no longer "there" to capture the totality of experiences. Only by altering the meaning of death does Heidegger sidestep these arguments.

Among the various senses of ending, death has the least in common with "those which first thrust themselves to the fore."[30] These must be repudiated before the positive existential meaning of death can be assigned. Death is neither the fulfillment nor the simple disappearance of life. As an ending, the meaning of death derives from the futural aspect of care: "just as Dasein *is* already its 'not-yet,' and is its 'not-yet' constantly as long as it is, it *is* already its end too. The ending which we have in view when we speak of death does not signify Dasein's *Being-at-an-end*, but a *Being-towards-the-end* of this entity."[31] According to this formula, death is positively determined as a "way to be."[32] Even in the present, when a portion of life remains outstanding for it, Dasein is already its death. This paradoxical determination of death is unmistakable in its full existential conception, which equates death with Dasein's Being as possibility: "death, as the end of Dasein, is Dasein's ownmost possibility—non-relational, certain and as such indefinite, not to be outstripped. Death is, as Dasein's end, in the Being of this entity *towards* its end."[33] What matters most for Heidegger is showing that death is an integral component of anticipation. Death as possibility is an intrinsic part of Dasein's existential structure. Because death is already integrated into the dynamic movement of existence, the act of anticipating it concretizes care as an unbroken totality, without remainder: "In anticipation Dasein can first make certain of its ownmost Being in its totality [*Ganzheit*]—a totality which is not to be outstripped."[34] In one of its initial appearances in Heidegger's course manuscripts, the totality of care glimpsed in Being-towards-death furnishes the basic self-certainty of the "I": "This certainty, that 'I myself am in that I will die,' is *the basic certainty of Dasein itself*.... If such pointed formulations mean anything at all, then the appropriate statement pertaining to Dasein in its being would have to be *sum moribundus* (I am in dying)."[35] But the full sense of this certainty emerges only later in *Being and Time*, when Heidegger brings together death and conscience to reveal temporality as the meaning of care. The analysis of death thus ends on an ambiguous note: "Does Dasein ever factically throw itself into such a Being-towards-death? Does Dasein *demand* [*fordert*], even by reason of its ownmost Being, an authentic potentiality-for-Being determined by anticipation?"[36] The question leaves open a twofold possibility. Either Dasein fails in every case to project itself upon its death, or it anticipates death in a manner that remains disconnected from its particular set of factical possibilities determined by its thrownness. Confident that he has dispelled the latter possibility, Heidegger remains troubled by the former one. In the final paragraph devoted to Being-towards-death Heidegger dismisses this former possibility while briefly discussing the relation between anticipation and possibility. And yet without acknowledging it, he comes back to the figure of Augustine and to what Augustine represents in Division One.

We saw above that in §9 Heidegger associates the "ontological task which lies ahead"[37] with Augustine. This task consists of positively characterizing the dialectic of proximity and distance that marks the ontological specificity of Dasein's authentic selfhood. In the analysis of Being-towards-death Heidegger comes back to this dialectic in order to explain how Dasein anticipates death. To anticipate death consists in putting up with death as possibility. Does this mean expecting it? To expect something, Heidegger suggests, involves "looking-away from the possible to its possible actualization, but is essentially a waiting for its actualization."[38] Anticipating death, by contrast, does not entail awaiting its actualization, but instead it means coming close to death in a different manner: "as one comes closer understandingly [to death], the possibility of the possible just becomes 'greater.' *The closest closeness which one may have in Being towards death as possibility, is as far as possible from anything actual.*"[39] Since death signifies the impossibility of every existential stance, every way of relating to something, it "offers no support for becoming intent on something, 'picturing' to oneself the actuality which is possible and so forgetting its possibility."[40] Here death is said to be measureless in the sense that it offers nothing to the imagination, no firm ground upon which anticipation can slyly convert death's possibility into the imagistic objectivity of representation. The argument rests on the absolute break between non-imagistic anticipation and the imagism of expectation. Even if we doubt that this break is an absolute one, we can still see that death as possibility is measureless by virtue of its distance from the fixity of everything that is present-at-hand. The more one anticipates death, the more it grows as a possibility. And the closer one comes to it, the more it is revealed as ontologically farther from everything that is there before us in an objective sense.

Thus the allegedly Augustinian dialectic of self-opacity and self-revelation, first mentioned in §9, returns again in §53. It now justifies the decision to treat the anticipatory disclosure of death as the root of all existential possibility. But how is this decision justified, ultimately, if Being-towards-death does not on its own yield the concrete unity of existence? And what light is shed on this decision by our study of de-theologization?

TESTIMONY: THE UNITY OF CARE

The decision is justified by the testimony Dasein gives of its own potentiality-for-being-a-whole. As this alone displays the concrete enactment of care in its unity, we must approach this testimony by measuring it against the twin theological contexts that, we have shown, contribute to the structure of Dasein's Being—namely, the exorbitant guilt associated with Pauline eschatology, and the extreme self-renunciation associated with the Augustinian *cogito* out-of-reach. In *Being and Time*, however, this testimony is offered against the backdrop of the essential incompleteness of the existential analytic. Thus in retracing its formal features, we must determine how this testimony advances toward a specific kind of incompleteness, while warding off others whose connections with the theological roots of *Being and Time* we must make clear.

Among the major terms employed in the 1927 treatise, Heidegger is perhaps least cautious with his use of "testimony" (*Zeugnis*) and "attestation" (*Bezeugung*). This is puzzling, given that they play a major role in Division Two of the treatise. But unlike other existentials, they are never defined in their essence. The second chapter of Division Two grounds the unity of existence in Dasein's "Attestation of an Authentic Potentiality-for-Being,"[41] without spelling out the meaning of attestation ahead of time. We are thus on our own when it comes to discerning the meaning of testimony.

Early in Division One, testimony (*Zeugnis*) is included among a set of terms Heidegger distinguishes from signs. The sign, according to §17, is "an item of equipment whose specific character consists in *showing* or *indicating*."[42] Though the sign is something ready-to-hand, its use value must be distinguished from that of other tools. Its purpose is to manifest the general context of concernful dealings in which Dasein finds itself. The sign calls to our attention a referential totality constitutive of Dasein's worldhood, enabling Dasein to orient itself in time and space: "Signs always indicate primarily 'wherein' one lives, where one's concern dwells, what sort of involvement there is with something."[43] In this context indication is treated as a species of reference. The hammer and the act of hammering refer to something beyond themselves. They are always carried out *"in order to . . ."* The sign by contrast, though ready-to-hand, is not found alongside pieces of equipment such as the hammer, nor is its referentiality analogous to that of hammering. In Heidegger's terminology the sign "raises a totality of equipment into our circumspection."[44] Its purpose is to render this totality conspicuous. Even though the sign is embedded in a certain equipmental context, it rises up out of this context while uncovering the total network of references comprising its context. In this sense the sign provides the impetus for a panoramic view: the turn-signal of a car functions by illuminating an entire situation in its meaning. To give a sign is to reveal a totality in which various pieces of equipment have been assigned certain roles; to take something as a sign is to be led to this totality and to access it as a whole.

But if indication uncovers the set of assignments comprising the meaningfulness of the ready-to-hand, then how does the giving of testimony differ from the giving of signs? In short, what is testimony? The sign, in allowing Dasein to see that in a given context everything has its role, shows nothing less than "the ontological structure of readiness-to-hand, of referential totalities, and of worldhood."[45] If this is the essence of the sign, then testimony is excluded from its concept, as testimony cannot conform to the signitive indication in this mode of referring to the ready-to-hand. But can testimony function analogously to signitive indication within another "material" or existential context, one that is not primarily related to readiness-to-hand?

In Division One Heidegger contends that Dasein "attests" or "testifies" that its Being is defined pre-ontologically as care. In this instance testimony and attestation are used interchangeably. The testimony in question consists of a "historical" document that carries considerable rhetorical force in *Being and Time*, as it is meant to confirm for us that in defining existence as care Heidegger does not foist something alien upon Dasein, but rather he elucidates its pre-scientific self-understanding. Here to testify means little more than to express self-understanding, or as Heidegger puts it, to express oneself "primordially, unaffected by any theoretical interpretation and without aiming to propose any."[46] Testimony in this sense has a disclosive capacity analogous to that of signs. But rather than illuminating a totality of equipment, testimony consists in the self-expression that lights up the totality of Dasein's Being.

It is only in Division Two, however, that testimony is defined more precisely in two contexts. First, in opening the division, when Heidegger confidently asserts that the whole of Dasein can and will be brought into view, he suggests that Being-towards-death will eventually speak in favor of this whole. But whereas Being-towards-death proves that it is *de jure* possible for Dasein to be a whole, it does not display it *de facto* as a whole. Instead the analysis of death suggests that conscience will accomplish this, indirectly revealing the nature of testimony and attestation: "Manifestly Dasein itself must, in its Being, present [*vorgeben*] us with the possibility and the manner of its authentic existence, unless such existence is something that can be imposed upon it ontically, or ontologically fabricated. The attestation [*Bezeugung*] of an authentic potentiality-for-Being is given by conscience."[47] Thus attestation consists in unveiling, making present, not only what existence is, but *how* it is as well. If some aspect or mode of Dasein's Being is brought forth, in the sense that it is presented or professed (*vorgeben*), in a manner that allows us to pinpoint authentic existence, then this aspect or mode will be said to *attest* to Dasein's Being. Whereas the sign is referential in the sense that it points out something given as ready-to-hand, thereby illuminating a nexus of meaning, attestation is referential in an entirely different manner. It professes or purports to bring something forth without actually producing it as objectively given. At the outset of Division Two, then, Heidegger makes good on his earlier distinction between attestation and the giving of signs, as the analogy between them turns out to be a limited one. Testimony does not allow for the kind of intentional fulfillment characterizing the referentiality of signs; what it makes present is not presently given. Moreover, unlike the sign, attestation is identical with what it discloses. Its enactment does not differ from the Being of what it presents, whereas the sign is never identical with the context it illuminates.

This is where things stand with attestation and testimony when Heidegger turns to analyze conscience, arguing that it testifies to the unity of Dasein's Being as a whole. The call of conscience, according to §54, reaches Dasein in everyday life, making it possible for Dasein to return to its ownmost potentiality. Conscience reveals that Dasein has fallen away from its authentic existence. Conscience simultaneously interrupts the voice of the anonymous "who" of everyday life, allowing Dasein to cease "listening away" from its own voice. In heeding its call, Dasein makes up for its failure to choose itself, reclaiming the possibility of authentic selfhood. But in what sense does conscience, in giving something to be understood,[48] give testimony? Its ostensive function is specified in §56: "because Dasein is *lost* in the 'they,' it must first *find* itself. In order to find *itself* at all, it must be 'shown' [*gezeigt*] to itself in its possible authenticity. In terms of its *possibility*, Dasein *is* already a potentiality-for-Being-its-Self, but it needs the attestation of this potentiality."[49] The ostensive function of conscience is here modeled on the giving of signs. Thus, at the very moment Heidegger must rigorously uphold his own distinction between testimony and the giving of signs—at the moment, that is, when the distinction becomes methodologically significant for him—he treats Dasein's Being as if it were something that can be shown or indicated rather than simply professed.

The conflation of indication and presentment, *zeigen* and *vorgeben*, is subtle but fateful. Having carefully differentiated between them earlier in the treatise, Heidegger now claims that conscience gives testimony insofar as its voice indicates or shows something. But precisely because this voice indicates nothing other than Dasein's ownmost potentiality, the analytic of conscience cannot escape subtly reducing attestation to the giving of signs. This is not to say that the voice of conscience is ontologically the same as an item of equipment (i.e., a sign). Indeed it has its own way of indicating: "Conscience gives us 'something' to understand; it discloses."[50] In calling Dasein back to itself, conscience is "a giving-to-understand. In the tendency to disclosure which belongs to the call, lies the momentum of a push—of an abrupt arousal. The call is from afar unto afar. It reaches him who wants to be brought back."[51] Nevertheless even if conscience does not disclose by showing or indicating something present-at-hand, Heidegger cannot resist likening its mode of attestation to the giving of signs. And though the call of conscience goes from afar unto afar, this relation is still treated ontologically as a species of indication that resembles the giving of signs.

The reduction of attestation to indication is evident throughout the paragraphs on conscience.[52] It underscores the form of truth Heidegger wants to ascribe to existence: "To the call of conscience there corresponds a possible hearing. Our understanding of the appeal unveils itself as our *wanting to have a conscience*. But in this phenomenon lies that existentiell choosing which we seek—the choosing to choose a kind of *being-one's-Self* which, in accordance with its existential structure, we call *resoluteness* [*Entschlossenheit*]."[53] Resoluteness, as the truth of existence,[54] grounds the otherwise abstract portrait of authenticity uncovered in Being-towards-death. This figure of truth emerges only after Heidegger has cautiously analyzed the threefold structure of conscience—as caller, the one who issues the call; as called, the one who hears the call; and as the call itself, indicating a potentiality-for-Being—and has concluded that conscience is indeed the concretization of the care structure. The first ascription, conscience as caller, preoccupies Heidegger, as he is intent on proving that the anonymous caller of conscience is none other than Dasein itself. This proof is admittedly problematic. The caller of conscience, Heidegger argues, always remains utterly reticent. Its anonymity is never mitigated by the content of what it calls forth. But here anonymity is treated as a positive characteristic, the basis upon which the self is distinguished from all that is present-at-hand and ready-to-hand: "The peculiar indefiniteness of the caller and the impossibility of making more definite what this caller is, are not just nothing; they are distinctive for it in a *positive* way. They make known to us that the caller is solely absorbed in summoning us to something, that it is *heard only as such*, and furthermore, that it will not let itself by coaxed."[55] The anonymity of the caller is a function of the fact that the call itself is silent: "*Conscience discourses solely and constantly in the mode of keeping silent.*"[56] Though silent, the call cannot be misunderstood: "the direction it takes is a sure one."[57] In §57 this reticence provides the backdrop for arguing that the caller of conscience, "who is *no one* [*Niemand*],"[58] is in fact none other than the uncanny self that Dasein confronts in anxiety.

This inference is precisely what enables Dasein to attest to its ownmost Being as an *existentiell* unity. Earlier in §44 Heidegger had declared that truth is primarily not a property of things, but rather a mode of Dasein's existence. Truth consists in disclosure, *alētheia*. And Dasein is the being who discloses; thus primordial truth is "something essentially constitutive for Being-in-the-world as such. Truth must be conceived as a fundamental *existentiale*."[59] Now, by identifying the caller as self, Heidegger effectively concretizes the depiction of Dasein as disclosive, and of primordial truth as an *existentiale*. The caller of conscience is the concrete form of the uncanny self: "The call points forward to Dasein's potentiality-for-Being and it does this as a call which comes *from* uncanniness."[60] All that remains is to bring these components together and represent them as a unified whole, in which case the unity of existence will be simultaneously *indicated* and *professed*. This unified whole emerges only at the very end of the section on conscience, in the last lines of §60, where we learn that resoluteness, Dasein's most essential form of taking-action, is in fact the unity of care itself: "*Resoluteness however is only that authenticity of care, which is cared for by care [in die Sorge gesorgte] and possible as care.*"[61] Resoluteness, as authentic care, is the care of care. Having previously rejected the phrase "self-care"[62] as a tautology, Heidegger nevertheless employs this reflexive formula to express Dasein's Being as unified through conscience. In fact, he had hit upon this formula by 1922 if not earlier.[63] We find versions of it in the Marburg manuscripts leading up to *Being and Time*, where it is used to argue that facticity and existentiality, throwness and projection, are always linked to each other, as in 1926 for example: "In each of its concerns, Dasein is itself, as regarding its potentiality-for-Being, not the object of concern (*Besorgte*), but that which is taken into care (*Gesorgte*)."[64] In *Being and Time* the formula marks the culminating point of Heidegger's protracted effort to justify presupposing that existence is a priori a whole. It orients the remainder of the 1927 treatise. All that follows after it merely follows it up, as the analyses of temporality and history are specifically designed to confirm it.

FORSAKENNESS, MOURNING, AND THE CALL

The unity of care identified in section §60 is, on this reading, the hidden nerve center of *Being and Time*. It is the first instance in which care is exhibited as a concrete unified whole. The following sections double back upon its emergence, retracing the phenomenological evidence that occasions it. It is here most of all that our inquiry into de-theologization bears upon the composition of *Being and Time*, as it renders much less secure the evidence used both to justify this unity as well as to disqualify competing views of existence. Having reached the unity of care in §60, Heidegger believes that he has succeeded in showing that Dasein attests to its own Being as ontologically farthest from itself. And at this moment, the figure of Augustine once again haunts the existential analytic.

In §63 Heidegger confirms the thesis which he had attributed to Augustine in §9: "The way which we have so far pursued in the analytic of Dasein has led us to a concrete demonstration of the thesis, which was put forward just casually at the beginning—that *the entity which in every case we ourselves are, is ontologically that which is farthest.*"[65] But this so-called Augustinian thesis clashes with the evidence documenting the actual indebtedness of *Being and Time* to the *Confessions*, specifically as this indebtedness concerns the Augustinian *cogito* out-of-reach. In the 1921 commentary on the *Confessions* this anthropological figure is fundamentally ambiguous in a manner that arguably clashes with *Being and Time*. Let us recall that the form of self-renunciation Heidegger attributes in 1921 to Augustine is accomplished in relation to an extreme, theological, prohibition against self-representation. In that context it remains unclear whether or not the kind of "truth" Augustine attains in confessing himself effects the "gathering" up his existence into a unity. By contrast, in *Being and Time* Heidegger argues that the descriptive analysis of conscience is compelling enough that he can resolve the ambiguity in favor of existential unity. The self-forsakenness endured by Dasein does indeed show that the truth of attestation constitutes the unity of existence.

The divergence is a slight but utterly crucial one. Its legitimacy can be established on firm grounds, however, if we interpret the presupposition that Dasein's Being is a priori a whole, not only in light of the phenomenal evidence Heidegger selects to confirm it, but also with respect to the history of its conceptual formation, which contests this evidence. This history renders it much less certain that one is forced to adopt Heidegger's presupposition, let alone his phenomenological confirmation of it. A closer look at conscience shows that this conceptual history is reworked in its analysis precisely in order to dispel aspects of it that contest rather than confirm the unity of existence.

To begin with, the stretch exhibited by Dasein's Being in the analytic of conscience presents us with a problem that is structurally analogous to the one that afflicts the Augustinian *cogito* out-of-reach. In §54–60 this stretch has not yet taken on the form of temporality. It consists rather of the threefold identity of Dasein as caller, called, and content of the call itself. The coherence of this unity is grounded in the uncanny self-assurance of the caller, which shows itself as impervious to error. In the act of heeding the call, this assurance is immediately transferred to the one called. And it functions as the phenomenal ground upon which Dasein, as called, finds itself individualized. Now, Heidegger identifies this ground as the experience of forsakenness: "When the caller reaches him to whom the appeal is made, it does so with a cold assurance which is uncanny but by no means obvious. Wherein lies the basis for this assurance if not in the fact that when Dasein has been individualized down to itself in its uncanniness, it is for itself something that simply cannot be mistaken for anything else? What is it that so radically deprives Dasein of the possibility of misunderstanding itself by any sort of alibi and failing to recognize itself, if not the forsakenness [*Verlassenheit*] with which it has been abandoned to itself?"[66] Here the caller is fully immersed in calling. Its anonymity is put to work in, and exhausted by, the call itself. Likewise the one who hears the call must omit "the question of who the caller is."[67] This is so not because Dasein as called finds itself so obviously before the caller as the uncanny self that there is no need to ask the question. The question itself is inappropriate precisely because the relation between caller and the one called has the form of abandonment. But this means that abandonment is what cements the uncanny caller and the one called, and that to be individuated by the call of conscience is precisely to find oneself forsaken by none other than oneself—that is, by the caller who, in calling, remains the indeterminate "no one" (*Niemand*).[68] Now, there is nothing in Heidegger's early lecture courses that even remotely resembles this form of abandonment, apart from the function of reverberation in the 1921 gloss on *Confessions* 10. There we saw that Augustine's search for God culminates in a not-finding that throws the soul back upon itself, leading it to renounce itself in praising the hidden God. Here in *Being and Time* we find that the experience of forsakenness is woven into the fabric of care's unity. But in what sense could this inner forsakenness speak in favor of the concrete *unification* of existence? Of what sort is the forsakenness manifested here, such that it reduces the articulated structural multiplicity of care to its simplest form?

To work out the meaning of forsakenness, we must return briefly to the analysis of death, which yields the first and only other use of the term *forsakenness* (*Verlassenheit*) in *Being and Time*, and which presumes that the meaning of death is unveiled solely in the relation to my own death. The death of others cannot give me access to death in its proper sense. These deaths are rather so many trials from which I cannot glean the meaning of my own finitude: "The dying of Others is not something which we experience in a genuine sense; at most we are always just 'there alongside.'"[69] Though we cannot access the "loss-of-Being" which the dying person suffers, we do however experience the other's death as a changeover from life to death. In this changeover we may encounter the bodily remains of the deceased. These remains do not simply lie there before us, present-at-hand. The corpse can be honored or dishonored only because it is ontologically unique. The corpse, Heidegger argues, is not merely a body devoid of life, but it is fully imbued with the absence of life. The body of the deceased "is 'more' than a *lifeless* material thing. In it we encounter something *un-alive* [*ein . . . Unlebendiges*], which has lost its life."[70] Reversing Nietzsche's argument, Heidegger asserts that the dead are a species of the living. The deceased is the one who has "been torn away from those who have remained behind."[71] Though the body of the deceased is for us as "an object of concern in the ways of funereal rites, interment, and the cult of graves,"[72] this concern does not exhaust our relation with the deceased. Instead these acts of concern provide the occasion for our being-with the dead person in the mode of solicitude, the proper category of Dasein's sociality in general: "In tarrying alongside him in their mourning and commemoration, those who have remained behind *are with him*, in a mode of respectful solicitude."[73] But what does it mean to be with the dead? The description of mourning tells us something crucial about the nature of forsakenness in *Being and Time*. We can be with the deceased, Heidegger notes, even though "the deceased himself is no longer factically 'there.' However, when we speak of 'being with' we always have in view Being with another in the same world. The deceased has forsaken [*verlassen*] our 'world' and left it behind. But *in terms of that world*, those who remain can still *be with him*."[74] As in the analysis of conscience, forsakenness in this context provides the grounds for a certain kind of relation. The one forsaken remains behind; he or she is the survivor who belongs to the world forsaken by the dead. As forsaken, Heidegger insists, the survivor can nevertheless "be with" the deceased by means of mourning and commemoration.

From the experience of mourning, we can thus extrapolate the sense of forsakenness at play in conscience. The call of conscience places Dasein as called in a position analogous to the survivor who is abandoned or forsaken by the deceased. In conscience as in mourning, Dasein is forced to maintain its relation with the one by whom it has been forsaken. And it is forced to do so in a way that leads it to confront its own Being as being-in-the-world: "the call undoubtedly does not come from someone else who is with me in the world [*nicht von einem Anderen, der mit mir in der Welt ist*]."[75] As in mourning, I relate to the caller as one who is not "with me" in the world. Yet in §57 this privation is assigned the precisely opposite meaning from the one it receives in the case of mourning. Heidegger, that is, concludes from the negation of *Mitsein* involved in conscience that Dasein is marked by an inner forsakenness that shores up, rather than fractures its unity. But there is nothing about its peculiar phenomenality that dispels the idea that conscience is *strictly* analogous to the experience of mourning.

Could we not construe the anonymity of the caller as phenomenologically parallel to the *un-alive*, the non-finite or non-factical? Are there compelling reasons in *Being and Time*, apart from the presupposition that existence is a priori a whole, to interpret it not as analogous to the absence of the deceased Dasein but rather as strictly equivalent to the Being of the one called, the *life* of its life? In short, the analogy between the caller and the deceased Dasein presents us with an aporia Heidegger fails to acknowledge. The phenomenal evidence brought forth to identify the caller as self can be used to challenge no less than to confirm the unity of existence, as it leads one to analogize between the caller and the Dasein who is *un-alive*. Despite this, Heidegger is only concerned with the extent to which the caller's identity can be used to confirm the unity of existence. From this we can conclude that the inner dereliction that Heidegger uncovers in conscience—the experience of being forsaken by none other than one's self—has a phenomenological significance that is not fully exhausted by the end it serves in *Being and Time*.

Should we not, then, pursue the analogy between the status of the anonymous caller, its no-response, and the no-response of the deceased? The caller would then straddle the border between the factical and the non-factical. Like the Augustinian *cogito* out-of-reach, its ambiguity would remain irreducible to the binary opposition between factical existence and its privation. In this case, the caller would be akin to the experience of a mortality that cannot be converted into possibility, a no-response or an absence that motivates Dasein to take up its being-in-the-world in its entirety, while marking this entirety with an irreducible absence—an absence that renders its unity structurally impossible. As with the notion of the *un-alive* the non-factical character of the caller as oneself could never be converted into a way of being for the living, but rather the caller would be the no-response at the heart of the living, torn between temptation and vocation. This unresponsiveness would be "life-in-death—or should I call it death-in-life? I do not know (*nescio*)."[76] In short, the analytic of conscience fails to bring forth compelling evidence in favor of the presupposition that existence is a priori a whole. And this failure is signaled by the analogy between Heidegger's two uses of the term "forsakenness" (*Verlassenheit*). If we bracket the search for the unity of existence, then we can see that the analysis of conscience seems to produce the very gap or absence in facticity that Heidegger must elide in order to portray Dasein as ontologically *farthest* from itself.

The farthest? But have we not just shown that in *Being and Time* the deceased as un-alive is even farther away from Dasein than the caller, and that his or her absence is farther still than the farthest? In this sense, Heidegger would have inadvertently pointed out that the bonds of mourning outstrip the unity of existence as *mine*.[77]

GUILT AND THE IRRETRIEVABLE

"To hear the call authentically signifies bringing oneself into a factical taking-action."[78] The voice of conscience sets possibilities before me, Heidegger argues, and it is only when I resolve to enact these possibilities that I gain insight into my current state. Such insight cannot be achieved by reflective awareness of the present prior to the appropriation of my ownmost potentiality. It is only by heeding the voice of conscience that Dasein first *"gives* itself the current factical situation."[79] Though it is a concept of action, resoluteness is not the equivalent of practical reasoning, nor is it "a special way of behavior belonging to the practical faculty as contrasted with one that is theoretical."[80] Instead it is the root of both theory as well as practice. This root is simultaneously the true source of attestation in *Being and Time*: "As resolute, Dasein is revealed to itself in its current factical potentiality-for-Being, and in such a way that Dasein itself *is* this revealing and Being-revealed."[81] We have just measured the analysis of conscience against the study of de-theologization, questioning the function of forsakenness in rendering the unity of care. We did so, however, without mentioning the existential significance of guilt.

Here we can no longer ignore its role in constituting the unity of Dasein's self-understanding. Nor can we overlook the fact that the religious life courses render philosophically significant the discrepancy between theological and philosophical guilt that Heidegger mentions, but dismisses in *Being and Time*: "The Being-guilty which belongs primordially to Dasein's state of Being," he writes in a footnote, "must be distinguished from the *status corruptionis* as understood in theology." The latter, he continues, "has its own attestation [*Bezeugung*], which remains closed off in principle from any philosophical experience."[82] The very fact that this attestation of guilt remains closed off is eminently relevant if we wish to understand the existential significance of guilt in *Being and Time*. Once again, the issue here is not to reclaim a theological mode of attestation that is supposedly suppressed or denied within the existential analytic; it is rather to retrace the steps of the analytic, revealing the extent to which the conceptual choices dictating the composition of finitude in *Being and Time* are highly contingent, and motivated by a specifiable conceptual history.

The reflexive unity of care, first displayed in §60, is cast in terms of Dasein's ability to unveil its own Being. On this basis we can ask: when Dasein appropriates its own potentiality through conscience, when it thereby exists in a unified fashion, *as* what does it understand itself? The call of conscience, Heidegger observes, "either addresses Dasein as 'Guilty!', or, as in the case when the conscience gives warning, refers to a possible 'Guilty!', or affirms, as a 'good' conscience, that one is 'conscious of no guilt.'"[83] If we seek to identify its existential condition of possibility, we are straightaway confronted with the notion that conscience convicts. Whatever the content of the call, the call itself refers to my guilt, either by proclaiming that I am already guilty, or by referring me to the possibility of this charge. The importance of existential guilt in *Being and Time* cannot be overstated. It is the aspect of conscience that allows Heidegger finally to reach Dasein as a unified whole. It is thus the fragile bond conjoining the preparatory analytic of existence to the depiction of Dasein as primordial temporality. "Being guilty," Heidegger writes in §58, "constitutes the Being to which we give the name 'care.'"[84] It thus reveals the tensile strength of Dasein's Being as a stretched whole. Heidegger's account of existential guilt brings him closest to the theological origins of care. Because of this, it allows us to measure the distance between existential guilt and its religious precursors in Heidegger's early lecture courses. We can do this by leading the concept of guilt back to the material context from which it emerges, once again mimicking the Heideggerian method of destruction. The result of this effort will be to uncover within the analytic of conscience the unsteady repudiation of a fundamentally fractured existence which Heidegger's de-theologizations were meant to keep at bay.

The observation that conscience addresses Dasein as guilty does not imply that the sense of guilt at stake in this address is readily comprehensible. To attain the genuinely existential meaning of guilt, Heidegger must work toward the existential conception of guilt starting from its everyday senses, reading off the former from the latter by means of formalization. His aim is to show that guilt "lies in Dasein's Being as such"[85] and that being guilty is distinct way of Being. Indeed, this is Heidegger starting point: "Where then shall we get our criterion for the primordial existential meaning of 'Guilty!'? From the fact that this 'Guilty!' turns up as a predicate for the 'I am.'"[86] It is also the point to which Heidegger ultimately returns. Precisely because "guilty" turns up as a predicate for conscientious Dasein, Heidegger takes it for granted that guilt offers Dasein a way to be, i.e. that Dasein can *be* guilty. But is this so? Within which parameters does guilt show itself primarily as lying within Dasein's Being?

To answer this question we must track the method of formalization Heidegger uses as he extracts existential guilt from its everyday sense. To explain how guilt attaches itself primordially to the first-person, Heidegger first breaks up the ordinary meaning of guilt as "making oneself responsible for" (*sich schuldig machen*) into two basic forms that correspond to the fundamental division of care into concern and solicitude. To begin with, ordinarily guilt consists in indebtedness. To be guilty is to incur a debt by "depriving, borrowing, withholding, taking, stealing—failing to satisfy, in some way or other, the claims which others have made as to their possessions."[87] This notion of guilt derives from Dasein's dealings with innerworldly objects, and it thus bears upon Dasein's sociality as it pertains to concern (*Besorgen*). In addition, there is a notion of guilt that appears within the field of solicitude (*Fürsorge*). To be guilty can also mean being responsible for something, in the sense of "being the cause or author of something, or even 'being the occasion' for something."[88] Ordinarily, this aspect of guilt is tied to transgression or breaking the law, but it may signify as well Dasein's "responsibility for the Other's becoming endangered in his existence, led astray, or even ruined."[89] Here it is crucial to recognize that in formalizing guilt, Heidegger detaches it from indebtedness and transgression. In effect he argues that guilt is not necessarily related to these states, even if in its ordinary conception guilt is almost always bound up with them.

Allowing the twin notions of indebtedness and transgression to drop out of conceptualizing guilt, Heidegger retains two key insights informing its everyday meanings. On the one hand, he argues that guilt always involves "being the basis" for something (*Grundsein*). On the other hand, Heidegger argues that no matter how we parse guilt we encounter an element of negation or nothingness: "in the idea of 'Guilty!' there lies the character of the '*not*.'"[90] When I break the law, I have *not* done my duty. When I am indebted to the other, what I owe is something *missing* to him or her; and when I mislead the other, then I am the reason why the other is *not* living up to his or her potential. In each case, a "not" appears. According to its formal definition, existential guilt consists in "being-the-basis of a nullity."[91] Here it is crucial that we grasp the interconnection between these two sides of guilt—being-a-basis on the one hand, *nullity* on the other hand—since it secures for Heidegger the unity of care.⁹²

Of what sort is the "not-character" involved in being-guilty? Is it akin to negation as lack or privation—that is, the kind of negation we have just cited in connection with indebtedness and transgression? When Heidegger formalizes guilt, he raises "the ontological problem of clarifying existentially the *character* of this 'not' as a not."⁹³ At the same time, he commits himself to clarifying this "not" without relying upon ways of negation that are tied to presence-at-hand or to any other kind of Being apart from that of Dasein. Along with indebtedness and transgression, therefore, the notion of negation as privation or lack is left behind in the search for existential guilt. Heidegger appeals instead to the threefold structure of Dasein's Being. In each of its three aspects—facticity (thrownness), existence (projection), and falling (discourse)—this Being exhibits a form of nullity intrinsic to its very structure. First, there is the nullity involved in facticity or thrownness: "As being, Dasein is something that has been thrown; it has been brought into its 'there,' but *not* of its own accord."⁹⁴ Second, there is the nullity involved in projecting oneself, stemming from the fact that Dasein has always listened away from itself and failed to project itself authentically: "As being, [Dasein] has taken the definite form of a potentiality-for-Being which has heard itself and has devoted itself to itself, but *not* as itself."⁹⁵ Third, the twofold dynamic of thrown projection moves in a falling direction, and it prevents Dasein from fully taking itself over: "As existent, [Dasein] never comes back behind its thrownness in such a way that it might first release this 'that-it-is-and-has-to-be' from *its Being*-itself-Self and lead it into the 'there.'"⁹⁶ This last form of nullification calls for further reflection. Tied to the category of existence (and thereby to projection), it seems to be more severe than the other two.

It is one thing to say, regarding facticity, that Dasein is *not* determined in its "there" of its own accord, or that, regarding falling, it may not at times heed its own conscience. It is another thing altogether to say that Dasein, as existent, cannot span its own length, that it cannot lead its existence into its own factical "there." But this is the problem Heidegger confronts in the case of the third sense of nullification intrinsic to Dasein's Being. In this sense, Dasein is constituted by nullity precisely because, as a matter of structure, it seems unable to contain itself. Does this not imply a severe structural nullification, one that necessarily prevents Dasein from existing as a concrete unity? Confronted by this dilemma, it appears impossible to salvage the presupposition of existential unity.

And yet it is here that Heidegger insists most strenuously that we must hold fast to first principles. We must see that, having uncovered a sense in which Dasein's thrown basis eludes its projective capacities, we have found the touchstone for conceptualizing existential guilt:

> Thrownnness, however, does not lie behind [Dasein] as some event which has happened to Dasein, which has factually befallen and fallen loose from Dasein again [*ein tätsachlich vorgefallenes und vom Dasein wieder losgefallenes Ereignis*]; on the contrary, as long as Dasein is, *Dasein*, as care, is constantly its "that-it-is." To this entity it has been delivered over, and as such it can exist solely as the entity which it is; and *as this entity* to which it has been thus delivered over, it *is, in its existing*, the basis of its potentiality-for-Being. Although it has *not* laid that basis *itself*, it reposes in the weight of it, which is made manifest to it as a burden by Dasein's mood.
>
> And how *is* Dasein this thrown basis? Only in that it projects itself upon possibilities into which it has been thrown. The Self, which as such, has to lay the basis for itself, can *never* get that basis into its power; and yet, as existing it must take over Being-a-basis. To be its own thrown basis is that potentiality-for-Being which is the issue for care.⁹⁷

Just because Dasein cannot come back behind its own thrownness, he asserts, thrown facticity is not utterly inaccessible for it. Heidegger emphatically rules out the possibility that thrownness could be construed as an event that befalls Dasein yet falls away from it, fallen loose so that it becomes irretrievable. Yet he does so on methodological, as opposed to strictly phenomenological, grounds. Though the idea that thrownness occurs as a self-disappropriating event is rather striking, it is voiced here so that it can be prohibited. Why exactly? Undoubtedly Heidegger sets aside the metaphor of facticity falling loose because it seems to treat Dasein as present-at-hand, as though Dasein were a Tin Man whose parts can be tightened or loosened. But if we refuse to accept this analogy, then it becomes clear that the metaphor designates the very notion of finitude Heidegger cannot admit in *Being and Time* without giving up his search for the unity of existence. In other words, if thrownness were to befall, yet fall loose from, Dasein—if its event-like character were such that it remains radically inappropriable, absent in its essence from the life it launches—then existence would prove to be fundamentally discontinuous rather than continuous, broken rather than ecstatically stretched.

This is the not the first time Heidegger invalidates such a conception of thrownness. He does so as well in §57: "Existent Dasein does not encounter itself as something present-at-hand within-the-world. But neither does thrownness adhere to Dasein as an inaccessible and, with respect to its existence, an unimportant characteristic [als unzugänglicher und für seine Existenz belangloser Charakter]."98 As in §58 Heidegger insists defensively that even though thrownness may indeed become "closed off" or "covered up," it can never become so radically hidden that Dasein could fail to retrieve it. However, if we reflect on what is gained methodologically by disqualifying these twin notions of thrownness—on the one hand, as the inaccessible characteristic; on the other hand, the self-disappropriating event—then perhaps we can see what is motivating Heidegger's dismissals of finitude as fundamentally irretrievable in and for itself. These motives can be clarified by turning the tools of hermeneutic destruction against itself.

Though inadmissible in *Being and Time*, these overlapping notions of thrownness belong to "those primordial experiences" in which Heidegger achieved his "first ways of determining the nature of facticity."99 They are generated by "those primordial 'sources' from which the categories and concepts" of Heideggerian facticity "have been in part quite genuinely drawn."100 In other words, with good reason we are justified in tracing these two proscribed notions of thrownness back to the religious life courses, and in thereby destroying Heideggerian conscience by showing how it is both formed and deformed by its relation to rival conceptions of human finitude linked with Heidegger's earlier descriptions of being-guilty in its theological attestation. To see this, we must first consider how Dasein can take over its own basis.

Let us return to the quote above. If Dasein cannot come back behind its own basis, how can it take over this basis? How, in other words, does its basis offer to it something that Dasein can *be*? Projection provides the only means by which Dasein can take over its thrown basis. But how can Dasein take over its "past" by being futural—that is, by projecting itself toward its ownmost potentiality? It is tempting to believe that the more Dasein resolutely appropriates its potentiality-for-Being, the closer it moves to its thrown basis. In this sense Dasein would approach its basis as though it were an asymptote. It would approximate this basis while never actually coinciding with it. But this is not, on my reading, the vision Heidegger articulates.

When he emphasizes Dasein's incapacity to bring its basis under its own power, he underscores the gap separating projection from its thrown basis. At most Dasein can "be" its basis only in a negative fashion. It can be this basis by *not being it*: "Being-a-basis means *never* to have power over one's ownmost Being from the ground up. This 'not' belongs to the existential meaning of 'thrownness.' It itself, being a basis, *is* a nullity of itself."[101] If it is difficult to grasp the thought Heidegger conveys here, it is not because his way of putting it lacks precision. It is rather because the concept of self-nullification assigned to guilt in §58 resembles an apophatic discourse. Being-a-basis is thus a self-defeating act. If accomplished, it must be simultaneously affirmed and denied of Dasein. Because Dasein is fundamentally futural it can never actually come back to its thrown basis, nor can it approach this basis asymptotically by means of projection. Accordingly, Heidegger describes Dasein's thrownness as its null basis, yet he likewise describes the act of taking it over as "null projection." In this case, however, two negatives make a positive: Dasein can *not-be* its basis in such a way that it resolutely appropriates its ownmost potentiality, as projection offers the only way to take over one's thrown basis. The fact that disposition or mood unveils thrownness as a burden shows that we can neither coincide with, nor even approach, our own thrownness.

And yet Dasein may or may not project itself so as to achieve the right way of *not-being* its thrown basis. The logic of Heidegger's discourse—Dasein is its basis in *not* being it—yields a sense of negation that applies to existence alone. The negation at work in guilt is neither absolute negation (*nihil omnino*) nor negation in the sense of privation (*nihil privativum*). Rather it coincides with the ideal form of negation that emerges in Being-towards-death, wherein death offers Dasein a way to be.[102]

In being-guilty we glimpse the concrete instantiation of this ideal form of negation according to which *not-being-its-basis* constitutes Dasein's ontologically unique kind of self-constancy. We also see that, prior to all social relations, Dasein is guilty by virtue of its structural identity as thrown project. In its existential concept, guilt accrues to Dasein simply because self-nullification is the only mode in which it can be its basis. This means of course that nullification affects the very fiber of Dasein's Being: "*Care itself, in its very essence, is permeated with nullity [Nichtigkeit] through and through.*"[103] To put it otherwise, Dasein's guilt is inexpiable. It grows precisely to the extent that Dasein enacts its potentiality-for-Being, which is why guilt constitutes care.

The more resolutely Dasein projects itself onto its potentiality, the guiltier it becomes. But does the concept of negation involved in guilt fall under the jurisdiction of ontology? Heidegger poses this question at the very moment he concludes his discussion of self-nullification, and he remains unsure as to its answer: "Ontology and logic, to be sure, have exacted a great deal from the 'not,' and have thus made its possibilities visible in a piecemeal fashion; but it itself has not been unveiled ontologically."[104] The metaphysical tradition has never even made "a problem of the *ontological source* of notness."[105] And when it comes to guilt, Heidegger is cautious about the breakthrough he achieves in tying its species of negation directly to Dasein's existentiality. The phenomenon of being-guilty, he observes, "is more primordial than any *knowledge* about it."[106] Its roots run deeper than the reach of the understanding. When conscience brings us back to ourselves, we find not only that we are guilty but that we *had been guilty all along*: "does not the primordial Being-guilty make itself known rather in the very fact that guilt is 'asleep'?"[107] For good reason Heidegger suggests that the latency of guilt, which is made manifest only when guilt is awakened in conscience, accounts for the ontological obscurity of the "not" it entails. In the context of *Being and Time*, however, there may be other, extrinsic reasons why something obscure shows itself in Heidegger's analysis of guilt.

What goes unquestioned for Heidegger in *Being and Time* is that, in its primordial meaning, guilt is a *predicate* of the "I am." This is the starting point in §58, and it is the point to which Heidegger returns when he reinserts the existential conception of guilt back into the analysis of conscience. The entire edifice of existential guilt is constructed on this foundation that guilt is a predicate, and moreover that the true sense of guilt is reached by defining it precisely *as* a predicate. But does it not suffer from the conflation between attestation and the giving of signs, the Being of Dasein and the Being of an equipmental totality, that we identified earlier in the paragraphs on conscience? Conscience calls Dasein back to thrownness as its null basis; it likewise calls Dasein forth to its potentiality, so that, in existing Dasein takes over the entity which it already is. This interplay of calling-forth and calling-back summons Dasein to its ownmost being-guilty. In understanding the call, Dasein freely takes its guilt upon itself. This free act of volition is for Heidegger the basic condition for the possibility of all other guilt. As wanting-to-have-a-conscience, this free act is likewise the existential condition for the possibility of being good: "wanting-to-have-a-conscience becomes the taking-over of that essential consciencelessness within which alone the existentiell possibility of *being* 'good' subsists."[108] In connection with this free act of volition, Heidegger concludes that conscience manifests itself as an attestation of Dasein's Being, effectively concluding that in conscience Dasein exists as the sign of itself. But when Heidegger treats guilt as a predicate of the "I am" he treats it as an attribute, something that Dasein can *be*.

In the final analysis, however, if we treat the religious life courses as belonging to those primordial experiences out of which Heideggerian facticity has in part been genuinely drawn, then we relieve ourselves of the burden of having to present an alternative approach to Dasein's existential guilt. We can let Heidegger do this for us, allowing him to provide the means for destroying the unity of existence in *Being and Time*. Chapters 1 and 2 of the present study, above, endeavored to show that the pattern for inexpiable guilt in Heidegger's early lecture series was undoubtedly set by the religious life courses. First established through the Pauline figure of the "'I'" as *katechōn* in the winter of 1920–1921, it was reinforced through the Augustinian *cogito* out-of-reach in the summer of 1921. Conceptually speaking, *Being and Time* is closest to these courses when it takes inexpiable guilt as the ground for Dasein's attestation of its authentic potentiality-for-Being. Yet, in our destructive approach to existential guilt, its proximity to the figures of religiosity sketched in the religious life courses serves to sharpen three points of contrast between them.

First, the concept of nothingness or nullification (*Nichtigkeit*) Heidegger uses to describe existential guilt in *Being and Time* §58 pales before the one he uses to describe Pauline eschatological temporality. The latter, as read by Heidegger, is not so much as a predicate of the Christian "I am" as it is equivalent to the "I" itself—much in the way that Thomas Aquinas says that being is not a predicate of the subject "God," but identical with God as subject.[109] Second, the guilt Heidegger uncovers in Christian facticity is immense. It cannot be borne by the subject who labors under its weight. It thus offers nothing for the subject to "be." By contrast, the guilt described in *Being and Time*, like the concept of death to which it is attached, stands toward Dasein as something appropriable, something within its grasp. Third, this guilt is cut to fit the individual Dasein alone. It bears upon the guilt of an individual, and individualizes Dasein before the guilt that belongs to it alone. The immense guilt that emerges in 1921 as the very meaning of eschatological awaiting extends far beyond the facticity of the individual. And it has nothing to do with appropriating individual thrownness. Rather it attributes the "having-become" or *Gewordensein* that meets the Christian in his or her own individual thrownness to a source far beyond it. And it launches a process of expiation that grafts the failings of others onto the single individual. In the existential analytic, however, this radical extension of being guilty far beyond the parameters defined by thrownness remains utterly impermissible and/or irrelevant to the needs of fundamental ontology. When measured against the yardstick of Heidegger's own portrait of religious life, then, Dasein presents us with a watered-down conception of guilt. Though it may seem like an extreme position, the 1927 take on being-guilty is much less severe than its religious predecessor. In specifying that guilt must be treated as a predicate of the "I am" it issues a rejoinder against the former, shunning its excess.

Thus in two ways the Augustinian *cogito* out-of-reach likewise takes on a destructive function when compared with Dasein. First, let us recall from chapter 2 that in the 1921 course "Augustine and Neoplatonism" Heidegger portrays Augustine's search for God as yielding the insight that every act of self-predication necessarily amounts to self-idolatry. By contrast, in *Being and Time* guilt is above all a predicate of the "I am." When judged against its genealogical sources, this determination of guilt becomes suspect to the degree that it thinks guilt as a predicate. Does the determination of guilt as a predicate restrict its meaning? At the very least we can suggest that genealogically it neutralizes a competing conception of guilt present within Heidegger's own corpus, attenuating it so that it can function in *Being and Time* as a principle of individuation. From the perspective of the radical prohibition against self-representation Heidegger uncovers in Augustine, the guilt that shores up the existential unity of Dasein has been transformed ahead of time into something that can be grasped hold of and kept as one's own. But *Being and Time* gives no indication that the self-predication of guilt might be acutely problematic in this way. Granted, it is true for Heidegger that resolute Dasein is "something that keep silent . . . and does not keep on saying 'I.'"[110] Yet it is equally true that being-guilty is the basis upon which Dasein achieves its ownmost self-constancy. Which leads to the second sense in which the *cogito* out-of-reach acts—albeit at a distance—destructively upon Dasein: in §58 Heidegger argues that the act of choosing one's guilt confers upon Dasein the *existentiell* possibility of being good, which consists in wanting or willing to have a conscience. Such wanting signals for Heidegger "the taking-over of that essential consciencelessness within which alone the existentiell possibility of *being* 'good' subsists."[111] The destiny of the good is evidently tied to that of guilt. As the latter is reduced to the status of a predicate, so the former is made available to Dasein as a modal determination of its existence.

The recuperation of being good as an existentiell possibility is made possible by the fact that the meaning of guilt has been restricted, truncated, or watered down, ahead of time. Throughout the present study we have repeatedly noted that in the 1923–1924 *Introduction to Phenomenological Research*, Heidegger faulted Descartes for deriving the concept of truth from the search for subjective certitude. From that perspective the

Cartesian *regula generalis* provided evidence of the view that Descartes had fashioned his entire metaphysics in the form of an "extreme Pelagianism of theoretical knowing."[112] Here we would like to suggest that charge rebounds upon Heidegger in *Being and Time*, specifically in his willingness to treat the good as an existentiell possibility. Being-guilty, he writes in *Being and Time* §60, is Dasein's way of "letting one's ownmost Self take action in itself."[113] Seen from the perspective of the religious life courses, this existentiell possibility is a *contradictio in adjecto*. And its emergence in the existential analytic leaves Heidegger open to the charge of having articulated an extreme Pelagianism, not of theoretical knowing, but of *practical or existential* knowing, the knowing that comes by heeding the voice of conscience and that Heidegger highlighted in his effort to cast Dasein as the *alter ego* of the Cartesian subject.

CONCLUSION

One of the major presuppositions informing our reading of *Being and Time* is that neither of the two figures of irretrievability Heidegger seeks to bracket in the existential analytic—the inaccessible characteristic, the self-disappropriating event—goes unexplored in the early lecture courses. Rather, there is firm textual evidence to suggest that both figures, though unsettling in *Being and Time*, are at least examined in Heidegger's early commentaries on religious sources. Thus, from the genealogical perspective adopted here, their elimination by a treatise designed expressly to confirm the a priori unity of existence can hardly be treated as accidental. We surmise that from Heidegger's point of view the notion of an irretrievability that undercuts thrownness must be expunged from the inquiry into Dasein's Being on primarily methodological grounds. Nevertheless this expurgation of the irretrievable troubles the non-relational aspect of Dasein's guilt as well as the unity of care. It does so, to conclude, in the following four ways:

First, one implication of the claim that Heidegger's descriptive analysis of conscience is adjusted ahead of time to his search for the unity of existence is that he dismisses by force of methodological principle, rather than by dint of phenomenological description, the possibility that thrownness itself may be figured in terms of inaccessibility. Our inquiry, however, has linked this possibility to Heidegger's commentaries on religious sources, while suggesting that the dismissal of inaccessibility or radical self-occultation as the mark of thrownness is symptomatic of Heidegger's extensive critical engagement with the foundational principles of Aristotelian ontology.

Second, the concept of attestation in *Being and Time* ultimately remains entangled with the ontological meaning of reference and assignment. This entanglement suggests that within the context of existential analysis further work must be done to uncouple the categories of existence from the ready-to-hand and the present-at-hand. As we shall see below, however, it is only after *Being and Time* that Heidegger seeks to disentangle attestation from reference and assignment while rethinking the relation between Being and language—a move that confirms, retrospectively, the diagnosis of *Being and Time* offered here, as it provokes a thoroughgoing revision of the structure of Dasein's Being. That revision, to the extent that it involves the repetitive de-theologization of the categories we have studied thus far, will be our primary focus in the following two chapters of the present study.

Third, in suggesting that the principles Heidegger uses to defend the unity of existence are so many barriers he erects against its disunity, I mean to suggest as well that the existential analytic is disturbed by an alternative account of human finitude that cannot appear *as such* in its pages. By referring the phenomenon of being-guilty back to the hypothetical unity of existence and facticity, Heidegger effectively denies that any aspect of Dasein could be radically undisclosable yet relevant to the structure of existence. He thereby conceals the conceptual emergence of Dasein's Being from the radical prohibition against self-representation articulated in the religious life courses. Thus, a double suppression of this source is at work in *Being and Time*—one that targets an unspoken rival, the other that targets this unspoken rival as being of Heidegger's own making. But the suppression itself remains legible in the pages of *Being and Time*. And this is precisely because Heidegger advances toward the unity of existence by dispelling its possible refutations; in this sense, *Being and Time* is a text that seeks to head off its own hermeneutic destruction, specifically by integrating the principles of this destruction into the project it constructs, as so many adversaries to be defeated. Above all, these principles affect the unity of Dasein's selfhood, which is grounded in its "authentic potentiality for Being one's self,"[114] and is achieved when Dasein's conjoins its own being-guilty with an authentic anticipation of its death, the possibility of its own impossibility.

Finally, we have said that Heidegger rejects the notion of thrownness as an inaccessible characteristic without justifying this rejection phenomenologically. We can now connect this observation to the fact that in *Being and Time*, Heidegger never manages to shake the suspicion that something is awry or missing in his phenomenological description of nullity as permeating the care structure. *Actio in distans*: the suspension of irretrievability in one arena of the existential analytic affects one of its later stages. The suspicion is first expressed in general terms in §58, where Heidegger admits that the ontological meaning of "notness" (*Nichtheit*) remains entirely obscure. It then reemerges whenever Heidegger treats the unity of existence as if it has been confirmed once and for all. The attestation that conscience supplies suffices at the end of §60 to confirm the unity of care, yet it is only by bringing together death and conscience that Heidegger finally hits upon the self-constancy of Dasein in its ownmost potentiality-for-Being. But even here we would be wrong to suspect that further confirmation of Dasein as a unified whole is forthcoming in the treatise, despite the fact that it is a methodological requirement.

Let us recall, then, the note of incompletion upon which the treatise ends, for it will serve as our point of departure going forward. Heidegger closes the discussion of anticipatory resoluteness, the truth of Dasein's existence, by calling for its repetition. By *Being and Time* §66 we learn that the ultimate meaning of care is temporality, and that the entire structure of Dasein's Being must be reinterpreted in the form of time itself. Only by undertaking this reinterpretation, Heidegger argues, do we gain any insight into the "complications of a primordial ontology of Dasein."[115] At no point in *Being and Time*, however, do these complications seem to compromise the basic presuppositions guiding the existential analytic from its outset. But this is precisely the possibility Heidegger is forced to entertain after *Being and Time*, in an attempt to reconquer its territory. If we situate the Heideggerian inquiry into temporality in a context broad enough to encompass the primordial ontology of Dasein and its potential "complications," then we cannot fail to observe that the inquiry into temporality eventually gives way to questions whose significance eclipses the search for the unity of existence, and along with it, the hermeneutic orientation of phenomenology. This, in turn, provokes a forceful if veiled repetition after *Being and Time* of those concepts which owe their initial appearance in Heidegger to de-theologization. And in this manner, we have thereby furnished ourselves with a solid basis for broadening our inquiry by interrogating Heidegger's so-called Turn.

CHAPTER FIVE

Temporality and Transformation, or Augustine through the Turn

INTRODUCTION

On September 12, 1929, a few weeks after he delivered his inaugural lecture at Freiburg entitled "What Is Metaphysics?," Heidegger wrote a letter to Elisabeth Blochmann in which he discussed the singular importance of the Benedictine monastery at Beuron, in Baden-Württemberg, Germany, in his spiritual and intellectual development: "The past of human existence as a whole is not nothing, but that to which we always return when we have put down deep roots. But this return is not a passive acceptance of what has been, but its transformation (*Verwandlung*). So we can only abhor contemporary Catholicism and all that goes with it, and Protestantism no less so: and yet 'Beuron'—to use the name as a kind of shorthand—will unfold as the seed of something essential."[1] The question raised by the last line is an obvious one, as it invites speculation regarding exactly *what* is essential in this context, and whether or not it is essential *to* Heidegger's thought, specifically as we approach it through the lens of de-theologization.

The tone of the letter, coupled with what he took to be the portrait of Heidegger as a self-styled spiritual revolutionary, led the scholar Hugo Ott to speak of a "Beuron syndrome"[2] in the Heidegger-Blochmann correspondence, that is, a tendency to view its monastic setting somewhat romantically as facilitating spiritual renewal in a secular world. At the outset of the present study we mentioned Beuron briefly in connection with an unpublished lecture Heidegger gave in October 1930 on *Confessions* 11, Augustine's meditation on time and eternity. The present chapter examines this lecture in depth as part of Heidegger's exceedingly brief but significant reconsideration of Augustine in 1930–1931, a return that includes as well his winter 1930–1931 Freiburg seminar on the *Confessions*. The material included in these sources, though limited in scope, allows us to begin outlining a second de-theologization in Heidegger's corpus, one that is linked to a particular devotional schema Heidegger uncovers in Augustine's meditation on time. Evident in pre- and postwar writings in which Heidegger utilizes terms initially attributed to Augustine in his 1930–1931 commentaries on the *Confessions*, this second trajectory of de-theologization contributes in identifiable and unexpected ways to the so-called Turn in his philosophy. Though it is a contested category in Heidegger studies, I invoke the Turn while taking my cue from the 1946 essay "Letter on Humanism," in which Heidegger asserts that starting in 1930 he began overhauling both the question of Being and the figure of Dasein in an effort to reclaim the fundamental "standpoint"[3] of *Being and Time*. As he identifies this standpoint with the experience of the forgetting of Being, the Turn in its broadest sense designates the various ways, from 1930 on, in which Heidegger strives to rearticulate the basic concepts of his own philosophy in order to explain what it means that we forget Being, or that Being somehow *turns away* from Dasein.

Although it is true that after 1931 we do not find in Heidegger an extensive or even an explicit engagement with Augustine, the evidence presented here suggests that we can reconstruct in the writings of the 1930s and 1940s not only a critical engagement with the structures of *Being and Time* that derive from Heidegger's early commentary on the *Confessions*, but also a series of attempts to reconfigure temporality as well as the nature of the *question* in relation to what is revealed in his 1930–1931 reading of *Confessions* 11. For example the term "restraint" or *Verhaltenheit*, which in many contexts replaces "care" as the meaning of Dasein's way of Being in the later writings, emerges in 1930 as the translation of the Augustinian term *intentio animi*, the gathered intention of the mind toward eternity. The cumulative effect of de-theologizing terms such as these, a process rehashed here in detail, is that after *Being and Time* Heidegger simultaneously displaces and re-inscribes his debt to Christian theological sources in novel idiomatic contexts. Here I attempt to show that this debt plays two important roles for Heidegger during the 1930s and 1940s. First, to the extent that Heidegger, reflecting critically upon *Being and Time*, appears willing to grant that his commentaries on Augustine contributed to the formation of his fundamental ontology, his indebtedness to Christian sources furnishes an implied target for the immanent criticism to which he submits this ontology during the 1930s and 1940s. In 1963 Heidegger famously remarked that for thirty years he had focused entirely on submitting "*Being and Time* to an immanent criticism."[4] To show that the desire to carry out this immanent criticism is actually the driving impulse behind Heidegger's brief reconsideration to Augustine in 1930–1931, I begin here by examining the October 1930 Beuron lecture, spelling out its similarities to, and significant divergences from, the 1921 seminar "Augustine and Neoplatonism." Second, to the extent that this reconsideration of Augustine contributes to the formation of new concepts during the 1930s and 1940s, Heidegger cannot avoid re-inscribing his debt to the same theological sources that initially informed the fundamental ontology of *Being and Time*. This not only extends the dynamic of de-theologization into his later work. It also raises the question of what this repetitive re-signification means for Heidegger's thoroughgoing critique of metaphysics.

The present chapter pursues this question by uncovering salient connections between the 1930–1931 reading of Augustine and the 1936–1938 work entitled *Contributions to Philosophy*. Thus the highly unorthodox approach to the Turn adopted here consists in entering into Heidegger's later philosophy by starting out from its margins. This approach can be justified only in showing the hidden route that leads from the de-theologizing of Augustinian concepts to the central drama of the later work, which concerns the forgetting of Being itself. The steps involved in this demonstration mimic our analysis of de-theologization leading up to *Being and Time*, with the proviso that Heidegger now enlists the logic of de-theologization in undertaking an immanent criticism of his own philosophy. The final section below confirms the demonstration by showing that the brief reemergence of Augustine in Heidegger's 1946 essay "Anaximander's Saying" harbors a hidden significance that speaks to the trajectory outlined here. Thus, from start to finish we are concerned to show that Heidegger's fundamental commitment to pursue the question of Being forces him to stay closer to his theological roots than one might suspect.

AUGUSTINE REDUX

Among the texts documenting the slow transition away from the fundamental ontology of *Being and Time* and toward the thinking of the "Turn,"[5] the Beuron lecture and the 1930–1931 Augustine seminar would seem to be a minor affair. In highlighting this lecture, I suggest that its marginal status in the Heideggerian corpus belies its significance in two key senses. First, in fall 1930 Heidegger uncovers in *Confessions* 11 a transition or a "turn" from one mode of interrogating temporality to another that is subsequently taken up and altered in some of his most speculative prewar writings. The terms associated with this other or "deeper" mode of interrogation reappear in Heidegger during the second half of the 1930s, where they are used to redescribe temporality in connection with the so-called *transformation* (*Verwandlung*) of Dasein's way of Being—a theme that links these writings, strangely, to the transformative return to the past of human existence that Heidegger designates in 1930 using the shorthand, "Beuron." Second, Karl Löwith once remarked that "the transition from the analysis of time to the time of history which is characteristic for Heidegger's analyses of temporality, is not to be found in Aristotle or Augustine."[6] But the 1930–1931 documents on Augustine dispute this assertion, as they suggest that Heidegger did indeed find in *Confessions* 11 the means for articulating the being-historical mode of inquiry that characterizes his later works. However, it is crucially significant to note, as we shall explain, that when in 1930 Heidegger attributes something like a turn to Augustine in an effort to make sense of how temporality and eternity are related in *Confessions* 11, he does so in terms that reflect the argument of Hannah Arendt's 1929 monograph, translated as *Love and Saint Augustine*. Thus in focusing on the 1930 Beuron lecture we shall make sense of its argument by situating it in the context of a broader discussion.

Both the 1930–1931 seminar protocol on *Confessions* 11 and the 1930 Beuron lecture are identical in style and scope to "Augustine and Neoplatonism," the early Freiburg seminar that precedes them by a decade. Close commentaries on a single book of the *Confessions*, these documents advance a single argument that is strictly analogous to the 1921 reading of Augustine. In that earlier context Heidegger discerned a fundamental shift in Augustine's search for God, a transition from seeking God as an entity to constituting oneself as a question. In 1930–1931 this argument provides a template for reading *Confessions* 11. The 1930 Beuron lecture argues that Augustine moves between two ways of questioning time. On this basis it seeks to identify what is at stake in the second or deeper form of inquiry Heidegger locates in the second half of *Confessions* 11. By merely considering this text as worthy of inspection, Heidegger controverts the views he voices elsewhere; in the 1928 summer semester course we learn that Augustine is complicit in the forgetting of Being, that he relies upon Aristotle's conception of time, and that he offers no alternative to its vulgar meaning.[7] By contrast, the 1930 Beuron lecture—quoted liberally here to provide ample textual evidence drawn from an as-yet-unpublished source—takes Augustine as a foil for the metaphysical tradition, recasting him in the role he played for Heidegger in 1921: "What the *Confessions* are not," Heidegger asserts in the lecture, "*not* autobiography, not a self-analysis of mental experiences or a description of religious experiences, but rather [they pose the question], 'what is man?' as the question, 'what is God?' Contrast this with Hegel and otherwise with Nietzsche: 'God is dead—what is man?'"[8] This assertion once again cements Augustine's status as a forerunner to Heidegger. Behind it stands the opposition mentioned in the early lectures between Descartes and Augustine—an opposition explicitly reasserted in the 1930–1931 seminar protocol[9] and one that we shall explore further in chapter 6 below. In its immediate context the contrast between two ways of questioning man—one belonging to Augustine, the other belonging to Hegel and Nietzche—suggests that Heidegger's attempt to reposition himself vis-à-vis the project of *Being and Time* forces him to reimagine its conceptual or genealogical past, in part by modifying the "elsewhere" with respect to which this past identifes the *Da-* of Dasein.

Delivered before an audience comprised mainly of Catholic monks and clerics, the fall 1930 Beuron lecture explicates Augustine's approach to time and eternity based on two major presuppositions that are potentially unique to Heidegger. The first is that Book 11, Augustine's meditation on time, unifies the thirteen books of the *Confessions*. The book is not merely or even primarily a treatise on time, nor does it stand disconnected from the rest of the work, but instead it is what provides the essential "inner jointure [*Fügung*] of the *Confessions* as a whole."[10] Heidegger even contends that the meditation on time is the very ground of confession for Augustine: "The meditation on time as such, in its approach and in its results, is a *confessio*; it is not subordinated to any other [*confessio*], but rather through the meditation on time the *Confessions* reach their authentic depth, and in this deepest depth, their greatest width."[11] Indeed in Book 11 "the *Confessions* as a whole first reach their true aim, that is, their ownmost metaphysical ground."[12] To show how Augustine reaches this ground, the Beuron lecture focuses squarely on Augustine's famous saying in Chapter 14: "What, then, is time? If no one asks me, I know; if I want to explain it to a questioner, I do not know." The thematic centrality of Book 11 to the *Confessions* has gone unrecognized, Heidegger contends, because the tradition has utterly failed to grasp the significance of the ignorance Augustine expresses in these lines. Echoing Husserl's high assessment of Augustine on temporality, Heidegger contends that, "we are as yet quite far from exhausting the riches [of Augustine's meditation on time]. Hardly a single philosophical writer, if he speaks even in passing of time, fails to cite Augustine's words: 'if no one asks me, then I know; if I want to explain it to a questioner, I do not know.' Yet this dictum, around which revolves the entire difficulty of time-investigation, remains almost entirely misunderstood."[13] Heidegger crucially reinterprets this dictum as the key to understanding the relationship between time and eternity.

At the outset of *Confessions* 11, Augustine identifies his time-investigation as an exegesis of Genesis 1:1: "Grant me to hear and understand what is meant by *In the beginning You made heaven and earth.*" By the end of Chapter 5, Augustine has established that whereas the artist impresses form "upon a material already existent and having the capacity thus to be formed," the creator God does not simply translate form to matter, but creates everything from nothing in the eternal Word. Here the enigma of time is rooted in the mystery of divine utterance. If we wish to say what time is, Augustine surmises, then we must understand the manner whereby, through the eternal utterance of the Word, God brings forth all things. Understanding the relation between time and eternity thus hinges upon grasping the nature of this utterance, which poses two major problems for Augustine. The first revolves around understanding the eternal generation of the Word as it differs from the creation of temporal beings; the second is specifying how created beings stand with respect to the ideal forms in which they are made. These twin difficulties are referred to the plenitude of the Divine Word in the last lines of *Confessions* 11.7: "of Your Word nothing passes or comes into being, for it is truly immortal and eternal. Thus it is by a Word co-eternal with Yourself that in one eternal act You say all that You say, and all things are made that You say are to be made. . . . Yet all things You create by saying are not brought into being in one act and from eternity."[14] Heidegger acknowledges the centrality of this eternal "saying" as it determines the nature of time. Although he ranks it alongside Aristotle's *Physics* and Kant's *Critique of Pure Reason* as one of the three most important works on time in the history of philosophy, he maintains that *Confessions* 11 is, unlike the other two, not simply a treatise, but a document whose composition relates temporality to eternity. That is, he asserts that the meditation actually conveys Augustine back to the Eternal Word as the source of created being, allowing Augustine to attune his inner spiritual "ear" to the silence of the eternal Word. This attuning, in short, *is* time itself.

Not since the 1920–1921 lectures on Paul and Augustine had Heidegger publicly presented such a reading of a Christian theological text according to which its performative and referential aspects overlap so completely. In 1930–1931 seminar and in the Beuron lecture, Heidegger contends that *Confessions* 11, much like *Confessions* 10, is at first oriented ontically toward its object of inquiry. In first questioning time, in other words, Augustine treats it as a *thing* to be discovered. But when he fails to discover the meaning of time while searching for it as a quiddity, Augustine regroups and reorients his inquiry, eventually arriving at his destination by means of a detour.

The first half of *Confessions* 11, according to Heidegger, matters because it shows the futility of conceptualizing time as a "what" or an object that could be brought before us for inspection. All of the paradoxes of time stem from our tendency to deal with it as a measurable and divisible thing. In everyday life we reduce time to space. We speak of time as being long or short, yet when we set about conceptualizing time in this manner it quickly becomes apparent that the past is no longer, the future is not yet, and the present has "no extent of duration at all."[15] Augustine deduces that because we are aware of time passing and can take stock of this awareness, there must be "three times, a present of things past, a present of things present, a present of things future." Following the reduction of time to presence, however, Augustine is led in circles while trying to explain how time is measured, arriving at the empty tautology that "we measure time with time and in time,"[16] without providing any positive definition of time as time passing.

The impasse provokes an about-face, forcing Augustine to relaunch his inquiry on different grounds. In the second half of *Confessions* 11, Augustine stops treating time exclusively as something measurable or divisible into pointlike instants. The 1930 Beuron lecture directs attention to the outset of Chapter 17 as marking the first inkling of the transition: "Suffer me, Lord, to push my inquiry further (*amplius quaerere*); O my Hope, let not my purpose go astray." The transition is an amplification of the search for time. It marks a shift in questioning that revolves around the famous Augustinian definition of time as the distention or stretching of the soul, which appears in Chapter 26: "time is nothing other than *distentio*, but *distentio* of what, I do not know, and I would be very surprised if it is not tension of the mind itself."[17] The subsequent chapter of *Confessions* 11 confirms that time is indeed *distentio*. This is the same passage Heidegger quoted in 1924 before the Marburg Theological Society, associating his own notion of affection as *Befindlichkeit* with the Latinate term *affectio*: "In you, my mind, I measure time. . . . What I measure is the impression (*affectio*) which passing phenomena leave in you, which abides after they have passed by; that is what I measure as a present reality, not the things that passed by so that the impression could be formed. The impression itself is what I measure when I measure intervals of time."[18] The definition is put forth after Augustine rejects the view that time is the movement of the body.

For Heidegger the definition makes sense only if it is situated against the backdrop of a new way of interrogating time that, having been foreshadowed by Chapter 17, begins in earnest with *Confessions* 11.22, as it is here that Augustine first admits that no definition of time will hit the mark. The admission leads him to call upon divine assistance: "My mind burns to solve this complicated enigma. O Lord my God, O good Father, for Christ's sake I beseech Thee, do not shut off these obscure familiar problems from my longing, do not shut them off and leave them impenetrable but let them shine clear for me in the light of Thy mercy, O Lord." In the 1930 Beuron lecture, what is novel about these lines is that Augustine now subsumes the inquiry into temporality into the longing he directs toward eternity. The question of time is thereby taken up into the stance of prayer. And prayer is now seen as the mode of discourse associated with the ignorance concerning time Augustine voices in Chapter 14. It is by not knowing time, confessing this experience of the *nescio*, that Augustine finally redirects the meditation on time toward the Eternal Word.

In this experience of the *nescio*, the "I-know-not" what time is, the burning of the mind is not merely an intensified desire to articulate a definition of time. The *nescio* is instead for Heidegger the expressive act that transforms the desire to know time into something like an act of self-renunciation before God. Here we pick up the thread of the Augustinian *cogito* out-of-reach described in our previous chapters, as the act of beseeching God for mercy, for his help in seeking the meaning of time, is precisely what reveals to Augustine the nothingness of the present as the ontological poverty or emptiness of created being before God.[19]

Such is the central wager of the Beuron lecture, which transforms *Confessions* 11 into a mystical text in which Augustine casts himself onto God and comes to hear the silence of the eternal Word. By putting himself at the mercy of God, beseeching him to reveal time, Augustine slowly turns from *confessio* to its ground; Heidegger writes, "This profound not-knowing [*Nichtwissen*] [time] is that *deep questionability* in which I first question that which is worthy of being questioned, so that what is worthy of being questioned only *is* because I can and do question."[20] What matters here is not that Augustine's interrogation of time is redirected toward a different object or theme, as if some new realm of ontic experience is disclosed through prayer. Rather the experience of not knowing what time is actually constitutes time itself in the form of a novel question.

This inner connection between the question and prayer—or rather, *prayer* itself as the deeper form of questioning that Heidegger isolates in the latter chapters of *Confessions* 11—provides the framework in which Heidegger reinterprets the dual Augustinian themes of the dispersal of the soul and its being gathered in extending itself toward eternity. It also marks precisely the way in which Heidegger forces the Augustinian problematic to correspond with his pursuit of the meaning of Being in general. The approach to Augustine in the 1930 Beuron lecture and in the 1930–1931 seminar protocol takes for granted that the formal determination of prayer as a species of questioning allows for the analogy between religious and philosophical ways of searching for meaning. This wager imparts to the Beuron lecture its originality even as it circumscribes the Augustinian meditation, allowing it to serve as a critical commentary on *Being and Time* in two senses.

First, the transition described in the 1930 Beuron lecture from the question to the prayer marks the emergence of a self akin to, but ontologically distinct from, the Cartesian *cogito*. The Beuron lecture expresses the emergence of this Augustinian *cogito* in a manner that mimics its discovery in Descartes's *Meditations*. It is as if by ratifying the enigma of time Augustine becomes the very thing he is searching after: "What is it to seek or to question [*quaerere*]? Does it mean, 'asking' [*fragen*]? Seeking [is] searching for [*suchen nach*] or pleading [*nachsuchen*]—it is *imploring*, asking for something [*etwas erbitten*]—*Ask and it shall be given unto you*. . . . The Question [*Fragen*]—A cognizant seeking [*ein erkennendes Suchen*]—in Knowing the Truth—i.e. *to implore God* [for] the Unconcealment of beings."[21] This allows Heidegger to describe the emergence of an Augustinian self in and through prayer that mimics the irruption of the ego in Descartes's *Meditations*. In *Confessions* 11, Heidegger argues, temporality in the form of subjectivity is produced in the experience of the prayer such that the formal definition of the self can be given in a conclusion that states, "Therefore, 'I question,' or 'I am searching' [*quaero*]."[22] Here the *quaero* is meant to displace the *cogito*, just as the early Heidegger had sought to reverse the *cogito* by expressing its propositional form as a question. Prayer for Augustine is thus a more "primordial" form of seeking, one that outstrips its cognitive counterpart, revealing the ontological meaning of the soul as time: "To ask after time [is] to implore God for its unconcealment. To ask after time: that we are time itself. It is by imploring God that we authentically place ourselves in time, i.e. that we can be authentically temporal."[23]

Second, in the passage quoted above Heidegger asks if all questioning must play out as *cognizant seeking* or if there is a deeper way of asking questions. Answering in the affirmative, he then holds up *imploring God* (*erbitten, nachsuchen*) as the form of this deeper questioning. But the claim to undercut questioning as cognizant seeking necessarily takes aim at the definition of the question in *Being and Time*, contesting its presuppositions: "every inquiry is a seeking [*Suchen*]," Heidegger claims in the 1927 treatise. And he continues: "Every seeking gets guided beforehand by what is sought. Inquiry is cognizant seeking [*erkennendes Suchen*] for an entity both with regard to the fact that it is and with regard to its Being as it is. This cognizant seeking can take the form of investigating in which one lays bare that which the question is about and ascertains its character."[24] The structure of all rational inquiry described in 1927 consists of three major components: what is interrogated, or entities themselves (*Befragte*); that which entities are asked about, or their Being (*Gefragte*); and that which is to be found out by the inquiry, or the meaning of Being in general (*Erfragte*). Cognizant seeking thus takes aim at entities, interrogating their Being, with a view to the meaning of Being in general. At no point in *Being and Time* does Heidegger abandon this form of cognizant seeking, or claim that it is secondary with respect to a deeper form of questionability. Cognizant seeking is instead the mode of inquiry proper to Heidegger's fundamental ontology, which seeks to build up the question of the meaning of Being in general by interrogating the meaning of entities in particular.

By contrast, the 1930 Beuron lecture explicitly asserts that cognizant seeking is *not* the deepest form of questioning. It argues instead that for Augustine the mind *temporalizes* at a level of questioning more fundamental than that of cognizant seeking. By implication the 1930 Beuron lecture would convict the fundamental ontology of *Being and Time* in rather stark terms, while looking ahead to the "Turn" in Heidegger's own work. It would suggest, again by implication, that the entire problematic of existential analysis in 1927 remained at a level one step removed from the true temporalizing of questionability.

In the context of the 1930 Beuron lecture, the step beyond cognizant seeking is tied to the reading of Augustinian *distentio animi*, the temporal dispersion of the created mind. Though the 1930–1931 seminar protocol does not dwell on this issue, it is clear from the Beuron lecture that for

Heidegger the act of prayer, which is here figured as a redoubled interrogation of time before God, must be interpreted in a manner that sheds light upon the dialectical aspect of the mind for Augustine in its dispersion or *distentio*, and its attempt at self-gathering or *intentio*.[25]

The terms Heidegger uses in 1930 to document *distentio animi* play a central role in the experimental and posthumously published writings of the late 1930s. To see this we must look closely at how Heidegger defines past, present, and future in the Beuron lecture. In Book 11, Augustine famously resolves all three tenses to modes of the present—the present of the past, the present of the present, the present of the future. The Beuron lecture construes this scattered self-extending (*gestreute Sicherstrecken*) of the mind in three directions—memory (*memoria*), attention (*contuitus*), and expectation (*expectatio*)—as "the fundamental character of the active life, or the Being of human comportment."[26] In each direction this comportment is lived either genuinely or in a privative manner. Memory, according to the Beuron lecture, is either retention (*Behalten*) or forgetting (*Vergessen*); attention is making present (*Gegenwärtigen*) or letting-slip-away (*Vorbeigehen-lassen*); expectation is either awaiting (*Erwarten*) or renouncing (*Verzichten*).[27] One might expect that in the Beuron lecture or the 1930–1931 seminar protocol Heidegger would point out the similarities between his own account of time as threefold ecstatic stretching and the one associated here with *distentio animi*, yet Heidegger remains uninterested in this issue.[28] His attention is singularly trained upon the question of how, for Augustine, the mind recollects itself in stretching forth toward eternity. To interpret the twin figures of the mind as extended toward eternity and as gathered within itself, Heidegger once again appeals to prayer. Augustine begins Chapter 27 by addressing his own mind as follows: "Courage, my mind, and press on [*adtende*] strongly. God is our helper: he made us, and not we ourselves. Press on [*adtende*], where truth begins to dawn." In the dynamic of pressing on (*ad-tendere*) Heidegger espies the reversal of the mind's dispersion (*dis-tentio*) into multiplicity. That is, Heidegger interprets the intention of the soul, the ultimate expression of which is extension toward eternity, as a mode of this *at-tention*. The interpretation effectively equates the act of interrogating time with the enactment of true temporality: "Time [is] the distention of life [*distentio vitae*]. . . . And this means: gathering oneself together, stretching out toward eternity [*Gesammelt sich herausstrecken zur aeternitas*]."[29] The conclusions reached in the Beuron lecture are all tied to this insight. The assertion that prayer is the givenness of time echoes the conclusions of the 1924 lecture, in which Heidegger argues that the temporal Being of Dasein is exhibited in the form of question; it simultaneously displaces the latter argument by undercutting its mode of presence.

This displacement is evident in the lecture's conclusion, where Heidegger comes back to *Confessions* 11.14: "What is time? If no one asks me, I know. But if I want to explain it to a questioner, I do not know. This often-abused saying of Saint Augustine is not a witticism meant to reaffirm the difficulty of meditating upon time. Rather it is the presencing [*Anwesung*] toward an actual comprehension of time, arising from out of the deepest understanding [*Verständnis*] of its essence."[30] The implication here is that the true understanding of time consists in an ignorance raised to a fever pitch, the dereliction of a mind deprived of insight into its own condition and thrown back upon the divine in extreme supplication. In the 1930 Beuron lecture, this dark night of the soul is resolved by suggesting that not-knowing time eventually leads Augustine at the very end of *Confessions* 11 to a kind of quiescence or peacefulness which Heidegger calls "the gatheredness of *silent questioning*."[31] Prayer, in this sense, is nothing other than temporality in the form of a silent yet burning question, the force of a desire directed toward the Eternal Word.

Though one could read this concept of time as anticipating the Levinasian notion of time as the *à-dieu* or the *to-god* (even if the latter remains vehemently at odds in its intention with the notion of silent questioning developed here by Heidegger),[32] it is far more fitting to note the similarities between this definition of time as prayer and the arguments advanced in Arendt's *Love and Saint Augustine*, published the year before the Beuron lecture.

In Part I of that work, Arendt argues that in *Confessions* 11 the eternal essence "manifests itself 'inwardly'—it is the *internum aeternum*, the internal insofar as it is the eternal. And it can be eternal only because it is the 'location' of the human essence."[33] Heidegger ends the 1930 Beuron lecture with a similar claim. Though he refuses to explain exactly what he means by "silent questioning," his final remarks provide enough clues to solve the riddle. In a nod to his audience Heidegger traces the enactmental comprehension of time to the monastic experience of *lectio divina*: "This presencing should not be ignored by this lecture. But as a lecture [*Vorlesung*] it is only a rough guide to an actual reading [*Lesung*] in which the silent restraint [*Verhaltenheit*] of the heart is brought about wherein the reticence [*Verschwiegenheit*] of the Word speaks to us."[34] Though it might seem to be the case that Heidegger pulls up short here, refusing to divulge any useful information about the "locus" in which Augustine achieves the actual comprehension of time, his allusion to the heart is crucial as it is reminscent of Arendt's treatise, which underscores the importance of the heart in *Confessions* 11 while arguing that Augustine borrows Neoplatonic metaphors "divesting them of their specific mystical meaning,"[35] employing the temporal "Now" as a model for understanding eternity. Arendt cites *Confessions* 11.11 to suggest that the creature's heart links the finite soul to the eternal God, "Who will hold (the heart) and fix it [*tenebit illud et figet illud*], so that it may stand for a little while, and catch for a moment the splendor of eternity which stands still forever, and compare this with temporal moments that never stand still, and see that it is incomparable."[36] The last lines of the Beuron lecture seem to mimic Arendt's move, as Heidegger identifies the heart with the locus in which the mind or soul can listen to the eternal divine Word.

This listening refers to the enacted sense of temporality as the meaning of finite Being. The mind *temporalizes* or becomes time itself to the degree that it stands silent in corresponding with the "reticence" of the divine Word. The comportment in which the creature learns to hear this silence[37] is what Heidegger calls *restraint* or *Verhaltenheit*. From the side of the creature, it is what brings about the relation between time and eternity. Thus the clear upshot of Heidegger's rendering of *Confessions* 11 is that *restraint* or *Verhaltenheit* is Heidegger's term for the self-gathering of the soul or the *intentio animi*, its stretching-forth toward eternity, following Philippians 3:12–14, "not by dispersal, but by concentration [*non secundum distentionem, sed secundum intentionem*]."[38] If we follow his lead by equating this form of concentration with the silent questioning mentioned above, then we see that the last lines of the Beuron lecture tie up loose ends. What Heidegger calls *Verhaltenheit* or restraint is in fact the secret heart of Augustinian *intentio animi*. It is what Arendt calls the *internum aeternum*, the eternal insofar as it is internal. In short, in the 1930 Beuron lecture Heidegger takes up this theme in a manner that is not unlike Arendt. However, instead of determining the internal eternal as the pure fixity of an immobile instant, he presents it as a radical form of questionability understood as supplication before God, a more extreme version of religious "worry" or *Bekümmerung* out of which he developed the initial definiton of Dasein's existence as care.

THE MANIFOLD SENSES OF TRANSFORMATION

Virtually absent from the early lectures and seminars of the 1920s, the term *Verhaltenheit* or *restraint* plays a crucial role in Heidegger's later writings. From 1928 to 1935, we find only scattered references to restraint as designating the truth of intentionality.[39] Indeed the 1930–1931 seminar on Augustine and the 1930 Beuron lecture contain some of the earliest discussions of it in the Heideggerian corpus.[40] After the *Introduction to Metaphysics* (1935), however, the story changes dramatically. In the "being-historical treatises"[41] Heidegger wrote but did not publish during the mid- to late 1930s, including his *Contributions to Philosophy* (GA 65, 1936–1938) and *Mindfulness* (GA 66, 1938–1939), restraint supersedes care as the definition of Dasein's way of Being. In the *Contributions*, the terms in which Heidegger describes restraint closely track his characterization of it in the Beuron lecture: "Restraint is the ground of care,"[42] he writes at the outset of the 1936–1938 treatise, echoing his claim in 1930 that Augustine lays bare the ground of care in *Confessions* 11. In drawing attention to this similarity, our concern is not only to suggest that Heidegger's conceptualization of restraint forces him to reappropriate the genealogical sources of care in ways that are discernible in the being-historical treatises. It is also to examine from a critical perspective the parallels between two kinds of transformation Heidegger describes during this period—the one which in 1929 he names "Beuron," foreshadowing the theme of his 1930 lecture; the other which he puts to work seven years later in the *Contributions*. On this basis, we can discern what the logic of de-theologization contributes to Heidegger's efforts, during the 1930s, to find alternative ways of interrogating the meaning of Being itself.

As it is described in the *Contributions*, the shift from care to its ground entails detaching the question of Being from the cognizant mode of seeking adopted in *Being and Time*. It also entails reconceptualizing the structural totality of Dasein's Being. This reconceptualization is announced on the very first page of the *Contributions*, where it is characterized as an essential transformation of the human being: "The issue is no longer to be 'about' something, to present something objective, but to be appropriated over to the appropriating event. That is equivalent to an essential transformation [*Verwandlung*] of the human being: from 'rational animal' to *Dasein*."[43] A key part of this transformation involves reformulating the temporal stretch of Dasein's Being. It at this level that the conversion internal to *confessio*, described in the 1930 Beuron lecture as moving beyond cognizant seeking, informs the re-thinking of care in Heidegger's being-historical treatises. In what follows I propose to identify the ways in which the terms Heidegger utilizes to describe temporality in the Beuron lecture are transposed into his discussion of ecstatic temporality in the *Contributions*.

In chapter 4 we saw that *Being and Time* presupposes, first, that all ontological investigation is grounded primarily in the preparatory interrogation of the meaning of entities; and second, that in building up the question of Being this interrogation remains grounded in the direct confrontation with these entities. In the *Contributions* both principles are rendered questionable, under the guiding insight that what Heidegger calls Being in general—often designated by the archaic form *Seyn* or *Beyng*—has forsaken beings or turned away radically from them, and that as a result of this turning, Dasein can never actually recover or recollect its meaning such that the memory of Being would fully overcome its forgetting. The archaic term *Beyng* or *Seyn* thus has in view a relation with Being attentive to the priority of its concealment over its unconcealment, nondisclosure over disclosure, or what Heidegger calls the nonessence over the essence of Being. That Being is somehow radically extruded from ontic experience is a point broached in the later editions of the 1930 essay "On the Essence of Truth,"[44] which is perhaps why the "Letter on Humanism" dates the "Turn" in his work to 1930. The presumption that Being presences paradoxically in the form of absence fundamentally alters Heidegger's reading of the history of metaphysics, which he now interprets as consisting of a series of epochs in which Being as radically extruded from experience has been stamped by various conceptual determinations evincing the privilege of presence or *Anwesenheit* from the Pre-Socratics to Nietzsche.

As the ground of care, restraint in the *Contributions* signifies the deeper form of questionability required in order to further the inquiry into *Beyng* as ground of the history of metaphysics. And indeed the emergence of this deeper form of questionability, specifically as it pertains to the question of time, mirrors the role played by prayer in the 1930 Beuron lecture—an observation offered here in spite of the fact that the almost religious tone in which Heidegger often writes of restraint in the *Contributions* links up to his reading of Hölderlin as the poet who bears witness to the flight of the gods in modernity.[45] Restraint defines Dasein not only as enduring the withdrawal of Being, but also as it "is disposed toward the *stillness* of the passing of the last god."[46]

The formal similarity with Heidegger's description of Augustine places the difference between the two texts in stark relief: in the 1930 lecture restraint describes the soul as attuned to the silence of the Divine Word; here it refers to Dasein attuned to a disclosure devoid of all religious content—the passing of the "last god" being, for Heidegger, akin to the dazzling absence of divinities at the end of Western metaphysics. This double function of restraint not only suggests that its role in designating the theophanic aspect of Hölderlin's work remains, for Heidegger, predicated upon the evacuation of its originally theological attribution in Augustine's case. It also leads us to suspect that after *Being and Time*, Heidegger was forced in hidden ways to double back upon the conceptual roots of the treatise, repeating and modifying the logic of de-theologization I described in the first four chapters of the present study, in order to adapt it to the sense of Being as *Beyng* that slowly takes shape in his work during the 1930s. In turn, this repetitive re-signification of de-theologization itself provides a benchmark for understanding how it relates to the later Heideggerian critique of metaphysics as such.

The notion of Being as *Beyng*, the idea that Being itself turns away from and thereby abandons beings, first emerges as a major theme for Heidegger in the wake of *Being and Time*. In the writings of the late 1920s it is linked to the disclosive function of anxiety. In the 1929 lecture "What Is Metaphysics?," Heidegger suggests that anxiety brings us face to face with a nothingness irreducible to negation. Whereas in *Being and Time*, anxiety brings Dasein face to face with its own Being as a nothing and a nowhere, in 1929 it is said to bestow upon Dasein—to borrow a phrase from the 1943 "Postscript to 'What Is Metaphysics?'"—"the experience of Being as that which is other than all beings."[47] In order to show that anxiety lets us encounter a primordial nothingness prior to negation, Heidegger now grants in 1929 the possibility that beings are indeed afflicted with something like an absence of Being, and that Dasein experiences this loss more than all other beings. Although "the truth of Being entails that Being [*Seyn*] never prevails in its essence without beings, that a being never is without Being,"[48] this insight tells us nothing about how beings and Being go together. They are linked by a parting of ways. Being "gives every being the warrant to be,"[49] meaning that it grants beingness to beings as a whole; it lets them be. In so doing, Being takes leave of beings. It remains absent from the scene of beingness which it opens. This is precisely why scientific research, Heidegger argues, nowhere encounters Being. And yet in anxiety we confront the fact that Being lets beings be by abandoning them: "Without Being . . . all beings would remain in an absence of Being [*Seinslosigkeit*]. Yet such absence too, as the abandonment of Being is again not a null nothing."[50] Heidegger ceases to deny that beings are marked by an absence of Being, and he chooses instead to designate the essence of Being as a species of this absence. Anxiety makes manifest the slipping-away of beings as a whole; it also makes manifest the "nothing" or absence of Being that dispenses this slipping-away.

The argument is radicalized in the *Contributions* where restraint names existence as attuned to this absence of Being. As the ground of care, restraint consists in the disposition that arises through binding oneself to the abandonment of Being, preserving its loss by means of sheer force, a force that consists paradoxically in mirroring its bottomless depths by letting it go, bringing Dasein face-to-face with the fact "that beings *are*, and that *Beyng* has abandoned and withdrawn itself from all 'beings' and from whatever appeared as a being."[51] This withdrawal engenders an extreme scrupulosity on the part of Dasein, as Dasein must now contend with the fact that Being presences as privation or "self-denial" (*Sichversagen*) and that the truth of Being consists in "not granting itself" (*Verweigerung*).[52] The account of restraint Heidegger offers effectively equates the experience of Being with its forgetting, engendering talk of Being's oblivion.

If we prioritize the self-description of the "Turn" that appears in the 1946 "Letter on Humanism," which dates its first inklings to 1930, then we can get a sense of how crucial restraint is for Heidegger during the period stretching from the mid-1930s to the late 1940s. Thus far I have adopted the common and prevalent description of Heidegger's Turn as a turn from beings to Being, but this is by no means to emphasize a radical discontinuity between the early and the late Heidegger. On the contrary, the Turn in his thinking entails reframing the analyses of Dasein and Being by acknowledging the priority of the claim that Being makes upon Dasein, placing it in an ecstatic relation to the clearing of Being. At the same time, the "Turn" in its primary sense refers to something happening with Being itself: it is Being itself, as *Beyng*, that is said to "turn," in the sense that Being itself is what allows beings to be what they are while simultaneously turning away from them, in a manner disclosed by the slipping-away of beings experienced in anxiety. That there is a formal analogy between the questionability described in the 1930 reading of *Confessions* 11 and the one subsequently predicated of Dasein in its restraining relation to *Beyng* is signaled in the *Contributions*, which defines Dasein in terms that recall the analysis of Augustinian prayer as a form of seeking: "*Seeker, preserver, steward*—that is what is meant by *care* as the fundamental trait of Dasein. . . . The seeking is itself the goal."[53] But the evidence of structural parallels between the Beuron lecture and the *Contributions* is bolstered by a much stronger terminological overlap.

The extent to which Heidegger's retrieval of terms from the 1930–1931 rereading of Augustine facilitates his attempt to reclaim the locus of *Being and Time* can be illustrated by taking a closer look at his treatment of temporality in connection with the self-withholding of Beyng. The evidence linking Heidegger's 1936–1938 reconceptualization of time to Augustinian temporality is unmistakable. The Beuron lecture describes time as a threefold stretching whose ecstasies may be enacted in one of two modes: memory for Augustine is either retention (*Behalten*) or forgetting (*Vergessen*); attention is either making present (*Gegenwärtigen*) or letting-slip-away (*Vorbeigehen-lassen*); expectation is either awaiting (*Erwarten*) or renouncing (*Verzichten*).[54] In each pairing the latter term is the one Heidegger uses to designate distention, whereas the gathering of the soul consists in retention, making-present, and awaiting.

In the *Contributions*, Heidegger employs these same terms to describe the temporality of Dasein, except that he switches their roles: in a strict one-to-one correspondence, forgetting now takes the place of retention as the meaning of Dasein's primordial past; letting-slip-away takes the place of making-present as the meaning of Dasein's primordial present; and renouncing takes the place of awaiting as the meaning of Dasein's primordial future. The cumulative effect of this transposition marks the distance Heidegger travels in setting out from *Being and Time*, which affirms the existential conception of temporality as a tripartite ecstatic structure consisting of anticipation or being-ahead-of-oneself (the future), the repetitve taking up of one's thrownness or being-already-in-the-world (the past), and the resolute moment-of-vision or being-alongside other beings (the present). The *Contributions* does not give up on the idea of a resolute temporality, or a gathering-together of Dasein's Being. Nevertheless, it describes this gathering counterintuitively using the theological language of dispersion.

Let us consider this re-signification of dispersion more closely, following Heidegger in thinking time as a movement that proceeds by means of anticipation, recollection, and resolution—or, in other words, as the directional movement from the future through the past, and into the present. First, the redefinition of the authentic future in terms of renunciation matters most to Heidegger in the *Contributions*, according to which renunciation is the basic form of Dasein's relation with Being understood as restraint. This renunciation bears primarily upon the understanding as the capacity for projection. The futural character of Dasein's Being in the *Contributions* is recapitulated in terms that contrast starkly with *Being and Time*: "Dasein is appropriated as renunciation [*Verzichtung*]. Renunciation allows the refusal (i.e., the appropriation) to stand out in the open realm of its decisiveness. . . . Renunciation is originary standing: unsupported in the unsecured."[55] The passage from care to its ground has everything to do with the transformation of anticipation into renunciation—a movement that re-signifies the difference between *distentio* and *intentio* in the 1930 Beuron lecture. It is by letting go of Being, we are told, that Dasein paradoxically retains it: "renunciation is hardly a mere 'not-wanting-to-have' or 'leaving-aside' [*Auf-die-Seite-lassen*], but rather takes place as the highest form of possession."⁵⁶ Thus renunciation takes the place originally assigned by Heidegger to the anticipatory grasping of possibilities-for-Being on the part of Dasein.

Second, on the basis of this renunciation Dasein gains access to the history of metaphysics as the first beginning of philosophy from the Pre-Socratics to Nietzsche. Whereas in *Being and Time* Heidegger defines Dasein's relation to its past and its tradition in terms of repetition, here he reverses its valence to describe the genuine retention of the past paradoxically as a kind of *forgetting*. That is, the thinker who retains the past from the new comportment of restraint opened by the relation to *Beyng* is the one who *forgets* it in the right way. The authentic retaining of the past now consists in letting it go. This authentic retention does not consist in remembering or repeating previous "possibilities of *Dasein*."⁵⁷ Instead, in order to recollect the history of metaphysics as a whole, the thinker first "must have *forgotten*, in a creative sense, the *previous* way of asking about being, i.e. beingness. *This* forgetting is not the losing of something that is still to be possessed; it is the transformation into a more original stance of questioning."⁵⁸ Forgetting thus designates a relation with the past that surpasses and displaces the form of repetition described in *Being and Time*.

Third, in a final contrast with *Being and Time*, in which anticipatory resoluteness consists in grasping hold of potentiality-for-Being, the *Contributions* describes resolute action in the present not as a moment of vision but as a letting-slip-away. Whenever Dasein endures the self-withholding of Beyng as a form of *not-granting*, then Dasein becomes capable of enduring the defining event of late modernity as the "passing by" or flight (*Vorbeigang*) of the last god. *Contributions* §256, entitled "The Last God," is rife with references to this species of letting-be as letting-slip-away, in which Dasein lets the last god pass it by in the present. In the strange terminology of the *Contributions*, then, letting-slip-away (*Vorbeigehenlassen*) signifies the highest possible form of adhering to the last god in its passing: "essentially, the passing by of the god requires a constancy of beings and thus of the human being in the midst of beings. In this constancy beings in the simplicity of their respectively regained essence . . . first withstand the passing by and so do not still it, but let it run its course."⁵⁹ Thus, the strict correspondence between the terms used in 1930–1931 to describe *distentio animi* and the initial explication of restraint as the form of temporal finitude in the *Contributions* leads us to see that this latter temporal finitude inverts the temporal figure of anticipatory resoluteness described at length in Division Two of *Being and Time*. In this sense, Heidegger's indebtedness to Augustine allows him to "renounce" this figure while retaining it, re-grounding it against this new experience of the self-withholding of Beyng. In this context we can thus speak of a *dispersed* temporality taking shape in the *Contributions*, a concept of time according to which authentic temporality is nothing other than an intensification of its dispersal.

But does not this imply that, in part, the criticism which the *Contributions* levels against *Being and Time* stems from Heidegger's desire to think temporality otherwise than it is described in the 1927 treatise? The clandestine reappropriation of Augustinian *distentio animi* in the *Contributions* bears directly upon the crucial question concerning the relation between Dasein and temporality during the 1930s. This reappropriation suggests that, by abandoning the so-called cognizant search for the Being of beings, Heidegger cannot avoid reopening the question concerning the relation between temporality and primordial finitude. The centrality of this question in Heidegger's later works cannot be disputed. What we have shown is that one cannot understand this centrality without appealing to the persistent eccentricity of an eclipsed theological provenance.

FROM TIME TO ETERNITY

In short, to grasp the stakes of this second retrieval of Augustinian anthropology, we must now situate it in a larger framework, allowing us to see how the rethinking of temporality during Heidegger's middle period emerges out of the early works, leading to the 1946 essay "Anaximander's Saying," where the strange reappearance of Augustine reveals the real stakes of the implicit critique the middle Heidegger levels against the description of ecstatic temporality in *Being and Time*. In the present section I build up the first side of this framework by showing how the early Heidegger never really succeeds in detaching time and eternity in his early writings. And in the next section I show that Heidegger's account of *Beyng* eventually requires him to "destroy" the Augustinian origins of Dasein.

Let us resituate the dispersed temporality described above in the broadest context. When in 1924 Heidegger first committed himself "to understand time in terms of time"[60] he did so under the assumption that he needed to liberate the investigation of time from the metaphysical tradition by correcting two of its major mistakes. The first consists in viewing time as little more than the pale shadow of eternity, a privative mode of the "standing now" (*nunc stans*) classically ascribed to the divine. Couched in the language of theology, the charge placed Heidegger at a distance from philosophy as well, since, as he would claim thirty years later: "all metaphysics thinks of Being as eternity and independence of time."[61] The second consists in delimiting the question of time by tailoring it to the investigation of present-at-hand objects. The very first lines of *The Concept of Time*, the lecture delivered to the Marburg Theological Society in 1924, proscribe the act of determining the meaning of time by investigating "its comportment to eternity,"[62] subordinating its Being to the perpetual plenitude of a timeless ideal. The lecture interrogates time in connection with the movement not of natural entities, but of Dasein in its Being-towards-death, furnishing the basis in *Being and Time* for redefining primordial temporality as the threefold ecstatic stretching of Dasein's Being, a conclusion signaled in the very last lines of the winter 1926–1927 lecture course, *On the History of Philosophy from Thomas Aquinas to Kant*.[63]

This unity of this stretch refers to Dasein's Being as running-ahead-of-itself (future), being-already-in-the-world (past), and being-alongside-other-entities (present). Though it cannot be denied that this conception of temporality is animated by a desire to uncouple time and eternity, there is nevertheless a crucial ambiguity in its conception, one that develops across a range of texts written during the 1920s, which in part explains how Heidegger, having categorically dismissed eternity from all philosophical consideration in 1924, profited from revisiting *Confessions* 11 in 1930–1931. This ambiguity is signaled in the last paragraph of *Being and Time*. As Derrida has rightly noted,[64] this paragraph does not sum up or conclude the treatise so much as it interrupts it, breaking off its search for the meaning of Being. Having previously portrayed ecstatic temporality as time in its primordial sense, Heidegger comes to doubt the validity of this assertion. Having presupposed at the outset of the treatise that the question of Being must be built up by interrogating one entity in particular, i.e. Dasein, he wonders in §83 if every ontological investigation requires an ontic foundation. Here the prospect of a hyperbolically finite temporality, one that is even more fundamental than time understood as the ecstatic stretching of Dasein's Being, is entertained in conjunction with two possibilities: either, Heidegger suggests, the existential analysis of temporality as it appears in Division Two of the treatise needs to be repeated, clarified, and confirmed; or it must be abandoned in order to disconnect the question of primordial temporality from Being-towards-death and conscience, and to pose this question in conjunction with a more radical conception of finitude. In fact, both possibilities are linked to the question of eternity—which is never fully reduced within Heidegger's early writings—despite the fact that they clearly attest to his desire to extract the question of time from its classical philosophical and theological frameworks. Under the guise of a more primordial temporality, the question of eternity was destined to reemerge in the wake of *Being and Time*, paving a way forward by pointing back to the *Confessions*.

We can see this more clearly, and we can explain further how Augustinian *distentio animi* contributes to the formation of a novel understanding of time in the 1930s if we briefly examine the formation of ecstatic temporality leading up to *Being and Time*, highlighting the question of eternity as it appears in the margins of this treatise. The template for ecstatic temporality sketched in the 1924 lecture places it at a distance from natural time or world time, the everyday clock time "in" which events take place.[65] The point-like character of clock-time, the time we measure and reckon with in everyday life, is not time in the true sense of the term for Heidegger. As an indefinite manifold of duration, time is divided up more or less arbitrarily according to our needs. In everyday life we measure the passage of time as if it is comprised of discrete parts. When we reckon with time in this manner, we make use of homogeneous time, a time in which the now-point of the present is arbitrarily fixed, and no single point takes priority over any other. For Heidegger this conception of time obscures the fact that "human existence has already procured a clock prior to all pocket-watches and sundials."[66] Thus, prior to reckoning with time as a homogeneous flow, we have implicitly understood time in a different manner. The act of intending the now has a meaning above and beyond measurement. When I intend the present moment, Heidegger suggests, the "now" I express in each case references the "me" for whom it is there. I am there along with the now I intend, and this being-there is implicitly co-intended in my act of expressing the now as such. Because temporality is prior to the act of parceling it out in a piecemeal fashion, my most basic relation with the Being of temporality is bound up with the recursion back upon myself included in every intentional act. There is a profound connection, an identity even, between time and the "mineness" of existence: "Am I myself the now and my existence time?"[67] The question is posed at the outset of the treatise, yet Heidegger never answers it. Instead he sets out to show that the question itself is the form in which temporality is given as identical with Dasein. Already in 1924, we discover a version of this argument: "Time is Dasein. . . . Dasein is time, time is temporal. Dasein is not time, but temporality (*Zeitlichkeit*)."[68] The assertion that time is temporal is no mere tautology for Heidegger; instead it signifies that temporality as the meaning of Dasein's Being, the structures of which are broached in spelling out Being-towards-death, must be seen as separate from time in its everyday sense.

The portrait of Dasein's specificity composed in 1924 is largely retained in 1927. On the first page of *Being and Time* we are told that its provisional aim is to bring forth time as the horizon for the understanding of Being, by which Heidegger means that the temporalizing of Dasein's Being must be seen as the condition for the possibility that something like Being is given. And yet the theme of temporality is broached late in the treatise. It is only after the totality of Dasein's Being is displayed in the progression leading from falling and anxiety to Being-towards-death, and after it is matched by the unity of care displayed in conscience, that Heidegger finally raises the question of time, informing us plainly in §61 that the "totality, unity, and development of those fundamental structures of Dasein which we have hitherto exhibited . . . are all to be conceived as at bottom 'temporal' and as modes of the temporalizing of temporality."[69] It is here that we first come across the interpretation of care as a temporal phenomenon, the threefold stretching of Dasein as ahead-of-itself, already-in-the-world, and alongside-other-entities. The fact that Heidegger refers to these three ways in which Dasein's Being is stretched as the ecstasies of time does not impinge upon their interconnectedness. In its existential meaning, the term *ecstasy* designates "the original unity of being-outside-itself that comes-toward-self, comes-back-to-self, and makes present. In its ecstatic character, temporality is the condition of the constitution of Dasein's Being,"[70] which implies that the dispersal of Dasein's being as it is stretched in three directions is never enough to disrupt the unity of its full constitution as an existential totality.

This unity, however, is more enigmatic than one might suspect, and the decision to defend it pits Heidegger against the tradition in which he locates himself. When he conjoins presence-to-self and temporality in the 1924 lecture, for example, Heidegger effectively argues that time consists in self-affection, though not in the manner of what Kant calls transcendental apperception. In his 1925–1926 lecture course entitled *Logic: The Question of Truth*, Heidegger affirms with Kant that time is self-affection, but he suggests as well that hermeneutic phenomenology alone discerns its true structure. As the pure form of inner sense, time for Kant designates the way in which the mind is affected by its own activity. From Heidegger's perspective time as self-affection refers to the activity by which "I" first put myself in a position to intuit the given, constituting myself as able to encounter what is not me. The "I" is both subject and object of the affection in question. The source of the affection is what Heidegger calls the "now-sequence," the active previewing of the given as the root of schematization; its target is the "I" established in its intentional receptivity. The former, which remains implicit and un-thematic in all experience, corresponds to the nontemporal aspect of the Kantian "I" as transcendental, which Heidegger redefines here as temporal through and through.

This self-affection seems to be paradoxical for two reasons. First, its target is constituted by the spontaneity that supposedly takes aim at it, implying that this target is both earlier and later than its source. Second, the "now-sequence" as the source of temporality forbids the very presence of the "I" it constitutes, placing it under a representational ban: "the now-sequence," Heidegger remarks, "affects in such a way that it lets something be seen—but un-thematically, as if the now-sequence itself were constantly retreating and disappearing [*ständig zurücktretend und verschwindend*] in its constant referring-to. This affecting is thus something like a constant putting-oneself-aside [*Auf-die-Seite-treten*]."[71] The suggestion that time is self-affection in the form of an originary retreating, its referential function stemming from its capacity for disappearance, recalls the aporia discussed by Aristotle in *Physics* 4. There Aristotle suggests that when we define the "now" as a part of time, and time as comprised of "nows," we cannot avoid relegating time to the category of things that "are not" (*to mē on*). Along this line, the "now" in its utter simplicity lacks duration, and the present has no space. Heidegger avoids this pitfall by appealing to the existential constancy underpinning the now-sequence which is grounded in the reading of inner sense as analogous to a constant retreat. Like Aristotle he does not prove that time necessarily has a share in Being, but instead he presupposes that it "is," and on this basis he seeks to delineate both its essence as well as its manner of Being.

This appeal to constancy, however, is hardly unproblematic. For one thing, the 1925–1926 *Logic* lectures make use of the very phrase to describe time that the *Contributions* will prohibit. Above we saw that renunciation in the *Contributions* cannot be conceived of as a leaving-aside (*Auf-die-Seite-lassen*), whereas here time is configured as precisely the act of putting-oneself-aside so as to let the other emerge. The use of this term in the 1925–1926 analysis of time suggests that Heidegger construes its source as self-affection on the basis of an unacknowledged precomprehension of time. To define temporality's manner of Being in terms of constancy is necessarily to define time in terms of time. It is to borrow a specific determination of the temporal in order to make sense of temporality in its universal form. This original "borrowing" allows Heidegger to identify self-affection as the form of temporality, but it has the unintended effect of rendering provisional every possible explication of this form. For Heidegger, then, as a reader of Kant, to be an "I" is to be able to disappear constantly, to step aside without end, thereby allowing what is other than me to take center stage. This ability to clear the way is the source of all autonomy; it is also the root of temporality. Akin to the moment of vision in 1927, the now-sequence broached in 1926 is set apart from the common conception of the "now," and yet its chief characteristic, no less than the common conception it supplants, consists in its apparent permanence.

The same dynamic informs Heidegger's account of letting-beings-be subsequent to *Being and Time*: "To engage oneself with the disclosedness of beings is not to lose oneself in them; rather, such engagement unfolds as a retreating [*Zurücktreten*] before beings, such that beings might reveal themselves with respect to what and how they are."[72] In the *Logic* lectures Heidegger does not shy away from acknowledging the difficulty involved in giving voice to this retreating as a mode of Being as he ascribes a spectral quality to it: "the preview of the now is implicit [*unausdrücklich*]. It is a letting-something-encounter-us—i.e., a making-present—that passes through the now."[73] Certainly if time is conceived as flux, that which is "in" time is said to flow from the future, through the present, and into the past. But that is not how Heidegger thinks of it. Refusing to speak of the flux of time, he nevertheless has his eye on a "passing-through" prior to everything in time—namely the spectral character of the unthematic retreat which opens the present while canceling itself, reducing itself to the negligible presence of an absence constantly retained.

The upshot of this analysis is that it reveals Heidegger's dependence on—at the very least—the infinite in his very attempts to describe a radical finitude. Thus in Heidegger's description of the now-sequence, it would be more appropriate to substitute the terms *endless* or *infinite* for the adjective *constant*. In 1925–1926 Heidegger undoubtedly would have denied that time as self-affection involves recourse to in-finitude, and yet it seems that Heidegger cannot in fact describe the way in which Dasein opens itself up to other entities without reference to language and concepts that defy the terms of finitude. Recourse to the infinite under the guise of a standing absence is finally unavoidable in Heidegger's retrieval of Kantian time as pure self-affection.

This is confirmed by two further observations. First, the ground of Dasein's Being is quickly reinterpreted after *Being and Time* as an "abyssal ground" (*Abgrund*),[74] a ground deprived of all fixity or firmness. Second, in the late 1920s Heidegger revisits the question of the infinite and speculates on its appropriateness as a predicate of Dasein. The 1929 treatise *Kant and the Problem of Metaphysics* strongly asserts the finitude of Dasein: "there is nothing which even the idea of the infinite creature recoils from as radically as it does from ontology."[75] In the Davos debate, however, Ernst Cassirer calls Heidegger's bluff, accusing him of renouncing "the form of absoluteness which Kant advocated in the ethical and theoretical" realms, and of thereby misreading Kant by forcing his notion of subjectivity to conform to a preconceived notion of human finitude. When Cassirer asks Heidegger if the moral personality in Kantian ethics does not involve ascribing some notion of the infinite to the human being, Heidegger is forced to concede the point, admitting that, indeed, in Kant as in his own philosophy, "the human being has a certain infinitude in the ontological."[76] The admission is striking, yet it gives ground only so that Heidegger can immediately take it back by reasserting the prevalence of finitude: "the human being is never infinite and absolute in the creating of the entity itself; rather, it is infinite in the sense of the understanding of Being. But, as Kant says, provided that the ontological understanding of Being is only possible within the inner experience of beings, this infinitude of the ontological is bound essentially to ontic experience so that we must say the reverse: the infinitude which breaks out in the power of the imagination is precisely the strongest argument for finitude."[77] In a highly qualified manner, the text identifies the understanding of Being as a kind of infinitude, implying that Being is somehow more finite than finitude itself. Though Heidegger immediately retracts this concession, putting forth his version of the Kantian claim that the conditions of experience are equal to the conditions of objects of experience, he nevertheless raises the suspicion that Dasein's primordial temporality is somehow linked with an obscure conception of excessive finitude or in-finitude, and that its structure must be re-described as such.

Being and Time bears out this suspicion in a manner that leads straight to the question of eternity. Though easily overlooked, this question reemerges in its last pages as Heidegger is searching for phenomenological confirmation that the ecstatic temporality he has described is in fact time in its primordial form. I noted above that Heidegger's first step while discussing time in 1924 was to divorce it from eternity. Here we must admit that this move did not preclude Heidegger from exploring the prospect of redefining eternity along with time. At the outset of the 1924 lecture Heidegger assures his audience that his reflections are not theological, yet he leaves open the possibility that they can be understood theologically, in the sense that "a consideration of time can only mean making the question concerning eternity more difficult."[78] More difficult indeed, but not altogether impossible; a cryptic footnote appended to the penultimate paragraph of *Being and Time* revisits the issue: "The fact that the traditional conception of 'eternity' as signifying the 'standing now' (*nunc stans*) has been drawn from the common way of understanding time and has been defined with an orientation towards the idea of 'constant' presence-at-hand, does not need to be discussed in detail. If God's eternity can be 'construed' philosophically, then it may be understood only as a more primordial temporality which is 'infinite.' Whether the way afforded by the *via negationis et eminentiae* is a possible one, remains to be seen."[79] This note sows seeds of destruction in Division Two of *Being and Time*. The prospect of a more primordial temporality casts a shadow over the entire analysis of its existential conception. Though Heidegger relegates it to a footnote, the prospect cannot be bracketed or ignored by a treatise bent on identifying primordial temporality as such. The spectral presence of an infinite temporality is grafted onto the figure of God's eternity; together they are made to *pass through*, and so *disappear from* the problematic of finite temporality they threaten to disrupt.

The footnote thus foreshadows Heidegger's subsequent attempt in the *Contributions* to replace the temporal schema characterized in *Being and Time* with one that is more radical. This shift toward a more extreme version of finite temporality was achieved incrementally, during the late 1920s and early 1930s, in terms that echo the conclusions reached in *Being and Time*, as Heidegger nevertheless began to suspect that the question of Being would give way to the thinking of *Beyng*. The 1930 connections between the *Contributions* and the Beuron lecture provide a crucial glimpse at how Heidegger would pursue the question of a more primordial temporality after *Being and Time*, as this connection provides a basic orientation for assessing his trajectory. The full import of dispersed temporality as its primary yield is realized only after the *Contributions*, however, in an essay where Augustine makes a brief but telling appearance.

BEING AND *FRUITIO*: THE WAY OF EMINENCE

Heidegger's 1946 essay "Anaximander's Saying" is the product of more than a decade spent researching pre-Socratic philosophy. In *The Life of the Mind*, Hannah Arendt highlights its importance by noting that, along with the "Letter on Humanism," it is one of only two texts that provide a glimpse of Heidegger's thought in the immediate postwar context and that, of the two, it is the only one to break new ground.⁸⁰ The essay stands in line with the effort in the *Contributions* to rethink temporality as the horizon for understanding the meaning of Being. Moreover, in working out a concept of time as fundamentally disjointed, it further elaborates the more extreme stretch of dispersed temporality that first takes shape in the prewar writings in connection with the de-theologization of the 1930–1931 commentary on Augustine.

What interests me here is the way in which this essay portrays Augustine as a necessary point of reference for Heidegger in rethinking temporality. Whereas the *Contributions* surreptitiously repurposes a terminology first deployed in reading Augustine, the "Anaximander's Saying" renders explicit the criticism of *Being and Time* implied by this terminology at the moment it reintroduces Augustine into the conversation. It does so in order to elevate, as if by means of the same *via negationis et eminentiae* mentioned in *Being and Time*, the leading sense of existence as care reached in the 1921 commentary on Augustine to the level of Being itself, designating its "presencing" as a form of withdrawal, so that it comes to determine Being rather than Dasein. This is the final step in the argument I advance here, in an effort to build up the destructive force of the critical thrust Heidegger directs at *Being and Time* from the perspective of 1946.

The title of the essay, "Anaximander's Saying," refers to the fragment whose meaning it aims to decipher, as Heidegger discerns in Anaximander one of the earliest traces of Being in Western thought: "But that from which things have their arising also gives rise to their passing away according to necessity; they give justice and pay penalty to each other for the injustice according to the ordinance of time. [*ex hōn de hē genesis esti tois ousi kai tēn phthoran eis tauta ginesthai kata to chreōn · didonai gar auta dikēn kai tisin allēlois tēs adikias kata tēn tou chronou taxin*]."⁸¹ Citing John Burnet, Heidegger suggests that only a portion of the phrase's latter half is attributable to Anaximander, yielding a pared-down version of the saying as follows: "according to necessity; for they pay one another punishment and penalty for their injustice [*adikias*]."⁸² The fragment, we are told, deals with the theme of presencing—the arising and decaying of beings, as well as the manner in which Being stands with regard to beings as a whole. The first clause of the saying, Heidegger argues, names presencing itself. It contains the oldest word for Being in Western thought: "necessity" or *to chreōn*. The second clause deals with what presences, or beings in their manner of presencing. Thus, the truncated form of the fragment names the ontological difference between Being and beings.

Heidegger uses Anaximander to portray the dawn of a history that is now closed, its intrinsic possibilities having been exhausted by Hegel and Nietzsche. The fragment reveals the destinal character of Being in its epochal determinations; we are told that in its earliest trace Being "disappears into its still concealed truth,"[83] and that its presencing is overshadowed by beings. As a result, humanity is destined to go astray or to err in its interpretation of itself and of other beings. The exploitation of the natural world at the hands of modern technology counts as just one attempt among many to fill the void left by Being's absence—an absence Heidegger names the *epochē* of Being[84]—as it entails violently forcing upon beings a standard of our own making. Yet in its strongest sense the argument stipulates that because human beings cannot overcome error, they are necessarily deprived of insight into what is historically essential: "what happens historically is necessarily misinterpreted."[85] This implies not only that human beings are out of step with their own history, but also that time itself is disjointed.

Citing Theophrastus, Heidegger notes that Anaximander has been criticized in the past for using "moral and legal concepts"[86] to depict the natural processes of coming-into-being and passing-out-of-end, birth and death. The goal of the 1946 essay is thus to reinterpret the terms *dikē* and *adikia*, justice and injustice, by stripping them of all moral, legal, and juridical connotations.

In trying to render *dikē* or *justice* as a non-juridical and properly ontological term for the presencing of beings, Heidegger launches a thinly veiled attack on the philosophy of Nietzsche. The "Anaximander's Saying" essay begins by explicitly rejecting Nietzsche's translation of the fragment, while juxtaposing to Anaximander's early thinking of Being a "late aphorism"[87] from Nietzsche's 1885 notebooks. In chapter 6 below, I shall explore in more detail Heidegger's attempt to destroy Nietzsche's conception of time as the Eternal Return, which Heidegger construes as theological in a metaphysical sense. Here I want to pay close attention to Heidegger's attempt to translate Anaximander's early saying of Being, since it necessitates re-inscribing, in subtle fashion, the debt to Augustinian sources exhibited by *Being and Time*.

The first step in this re-inscription involves rendering the terms *dikē* and *adikia* not as *justice* and *injustice*, respectively, but rather as *jointure* (*Fug*) and *disjointure* (*Unfug*). Heidegger interprets the Greek *dikē* as the harmony or order of becoming, the articulated conjoining of beings as a whole, or what he calls the "jointure-giving order."[88] On this reading *dikē* designates temporal becoming as an ordered process, one that corresponds to the vision of the natural world as a nexus of conditioned causes. Arising and decaying, beings are enjoined in an orderly manner into the passing of the present, which offers them passage as they arrive in and ultimately depart from the world. *Adikia* is the opposite of this ordered conjoining or harmony; it designates a disorder or disjointure afflicting the temporal flow. It, too, rightly passes for an ontological determination of temporal becoming, which implies that time itself cannot be determined in an ontologically adequate manner without acknowledging that something has gone awry with beings, that becoming is fundamentally disjointed.

It is important to see here that the gloss on Anaximander follows the pattern set by the *Contributions*, as it radicalizes the depiction of time as an ecstatic stretching in order to depict the unity of temporal becoming negatively as always already de-structured or deranged. This derangement of temporal becoming seems at first in 1946 to be attributed to beings as a whole, which refuse to give ground to one another: "The dis-jointure consists in the fact that what stays awhile tries to have its while understood only as continuation. Thought from out of the jointure of the while, staying as persistence is insurrection on behalf of sheer endurance."[89] And yet this insurrection is possible only because jointure and disjointure are adjoined to one another by Being itself. In other words, Being itself is responsible for the fact that time is fundamentally unhinged.

The fact that beings can rebel against presencing implies that they are also capable of facilitating it, allowing beings to be enjoined as a whole. Beings give the gift of *dikē* when they concede to other beings the presencing allotted by Being itself. The issue at stake for Heidegger is to describe this species of giving, which has nothing to do with rendering "justice" to other beings and which is irreducible to giving them their due. The excessive form of giving as conceding or giving place consists in letting-them-be, withdrawing or renouncing my place so that the other can take his or her stand. This relation to disjointure does not take the form of "penalizing" beings for stepping out of line with temporal becoming, as Nietzsche's translation would have us believe. In the latter half of the essay Heidegger finds in the Greek *tisis*, which normally designates a payment by way of recompense, the leading indication of what it means for beings to give jointure or to let others be. Indeed, the meaning of *tisis* or "payment" becomes one of the two foci of his investigation, as it describes the proper presencing of beings. The other focus is the word *necessity* or *to chreōn*, which Heidegger assigns to the presencing of Being itself.

The question is now how to translate these two terms for a present-day reflection upon Being at the end of metaphysics. Heidegger first proposes to render *tisis* by his own concept of care or *Sorge*. Arguing that in its non-juridical sense the Greek *tisis* should be translated by the German *Schätzen* or "to esteem," Heidegger then identifies its leading sense with the German *Rücksicht* or consideration, providing a loose etymological basis for invoking the Middle-High German word *ruoche* equivalent to the English root *reck-* in the word *reckless*: "The Middle High German *ruoche* means 'solicitude,' or 'care.' Care concerns itself with another so that this other may remain in its essence. This concerning itself, when thought of as what stays awhile in relation to presencing, is *tisis, Ruch*. Our word *geruhen* belongs to *Ruch*, and has nothing to do with *Ruhe* [rest]. 'Geruhen' means: to esteem something, to let or allow it to be itself."[90] Care as *Ruch* signifies a "handing over of presencing" (*Aushändigen*),[91] an act of conceding time and place to the other that maintains itself in and through this concession. If giving jointure consists in acknowledging the other, then *tisis* or *reck* refers to this giving, insofar as it is retained in one entity's handing over of presencing to another entity.[92] Rather than interpreting Anaximander as stating that beings pay penalty to each other for injustice, Heidegger argues that for Anaximander beings take each other into care with a view toward healing the disjointure inherent in temporal becoming. In this sense genuine "reck" or care for beings consists in giving jointure for the sake of surmounting disorder.[93] The surmounting of disorder cannot be achieved simply by caring for beings, since Being itself adjoins disjointure. Anaximander's word for the presencing of Being is, according to Heidegger, *to chreōn* or *necessity*. The term names Being insofar as it hands out or dispenses both jointure as well as the "reck" which takes jointure into care.

We have no direct access, Heidegger suggests, to the meaning of the Greek *to chreōn*. And yet because this earliest saying of Being makes a claim upon us, it is incumbent upon us somehow to allay its obscurity. Heidegger does this by translating *to chreōn* with the German *"Brauch"* or *use*. His reasons for this choice are not clear initially, as they are not supported by the meanings normally attributed to this Greek word. Nevertheless we are told that for Anaximander, Being itself means "use" or "usage." Precisely because the latter term is no less obscure than the ancient saying of Being it translates, Heidegger proposes clarifying it by borrowing a term from Augustine:

> to use is to brook [*bruchen*], in Latin *frui*, in German *fruchten, Frucht*. We translate this freely as "to enjoy," which, in its original form, means

to take joy in something and so to have it in use. Only in its secondary meaning does "to enjoy" come to mean to consume and gobble up. We encounter what we have called the root meaning of "use" as *frui* when Augustine says, "*Quid enim est aliud quod dicimus frui, nisi praesto habere, quod diligis?*" ['For what else do we mean by *frui*, than to have on hand something beloved?'] *Frui* contains: *praesto habere*. *Praesto, praesitum* means in Greek, *hypokeimenon*, that which already lies before us in unconcealment, the *ousia*, which presences awhile. Accordingly, "to use" says: to let something that is present come to presence as such. *Frui, bruchen*: to use, usage means: to hand something over to its own essence, and, as so present, to keep it in the protecting hand.[94]

It is Augustinian *fruitio*, surprisingly, which enables us to decipher the root meaning of the earliest word for Being in Western metaphysics, opening a path for grasping an archaic meaning of Being. In its immediate context, this citation links the present discussion to the genealogical origins of *Being and Time* while at the same time tethering Augustine to the reading of Anaximander.[95] The highly specific role played by this citation can be fixed under the following three headings: presence, translation, and temporality.

Presence. Augustinian *fruitio* names how Being itself "presences" (*west*) or how it stands toward beings. Presencing in this context refers to the side of Being in its self-withholding that bespeaks of its relation toward beings. We cannot fail to note the privileged role that *fruitio* plays here: as the point of contact between the end of metaphysics and the earliest saying of Being, *fruitio* names how Being comes to presence as handing out jointure to beings. This use of the Latinate term is not capricious: its conceptual link to *to chreōn* in Anaximander is even more substantial in Heidegger's texts than one can gather from this passage. Appearing elsewhere in a 1942 seminar manuscript,[96] it hearkens back to the 1921 seminar "Augustine and Neoplatonism." In chapter 2 above, I uncovered the link there between *fruitio* as a mode of comportment and the Augustinian *cogito* out-of-reach. While this latter phrase designates the self-renunciation which the early Heidegger associated with genuine religiosity in 1921, *fruitio* in 1946 once again comes back to the hand, which in this case concerns the handing-out (*Aushändigung*) of jointure by which Being keeps beings safe by giving them away. Heidegger argues that the meaning of necessity or *to chreōn* for Anaximander derives from the Greek word for the hand (*hē cheir*).[97] He suggests in addition that Augustinian *fruitio* says the same thing, as it signifies the act of taking hold of something while releasing it, having it on hand (*praesto habere*) by renouncing it. But what is at stake in maintaining that Augustinian *fruitio* sheds light on the earliest saying of Being in Western metaphysics, that it renders this saying intelligible from the standpoint defined by the forgetting of Being?

Whether Heidegger acknowledges it or not, the act of equating *fruitio* with Anaximander's *to chreōn* unavoidably refutes the meaning he ascribed to *fruitio* in 1921. In chapter 2, I argued that Heidegger uncovered in *Confessions* 10 a notion of the *fruitio dei* or enjoyment of God that he took to be a forerunner of factical existence. In that context *fruitio* functioned as a predicate of the created soul or mind, not a predicate of the divine as highest good. By analogy we could say that *fruitio* was meant to be a predicate of factical existence, albeit one that always remained out of its reach. But by contrast *fruitio* in 1946 is no longer a predicate of facticity or existence. It is instead predicated of the presencing of Being itself: "*Frui* is now no longer predicated of enjoyment as human behavior [*Verhalten des Menschen*]; nor is it said in relation to any entity whatever, even the highest. Rather, 'usage' now designates the way in which *Being itself* presences [*wie das Sein selbst west*] as the relation to what is present."[98] Without referring to the conclusions of "Augustine and Neoplatonism" it would be utterly impossible to recognize the self-repudiation on the part of Heidegger that takes place in these lines. The seemingly trivial act of equating *fruitio* with the presencing of Being marks a reversal of the highest order in Heidegger's trajectory, as it transfers to Being a predicate which the early Heidegger had originally ascribed to existence. The "Anaximander's Saying" thus convicts retrospectively the early predication of *fruitio* of having foisted upon an entity, Dasein, a meaning properly ascribable to Being alone. But by convicting the initial de-theologization of the 1921 commentary on Augustine, it extends the charge as well to the portrait of Dasein it nourishes. The clues offered in 1946 suggest, then, that the "Anaximander's Saying" implicates Heidegger's early concept of care as *Sorge*, and *Being and Time* along with it, in the forgetting of Being. Which is not to say that in 1946 Heidegger simply disowns the early concept of care, but rather that he exploits it destructively, extrapolating from it the leading sense of Being as presencing. From the finitude of care he derives the more-than-finite or infinite presencing of Being: "the correlate of the epochal character of Being we can experience most immediately is the ecstatic character of Dasein."[99] Here the transfer of *fruitio* from Dasein to Being opens access to the earliest saying of Being as an infinite temporality, a finitude of Being more finite than the finitude of Dasein.

Translation. When it comes to the three terms under consideration—

to *chreōn* in Anaximander, *fruitio* in Augustine, and *Brauch* for Heidegger—we are obviously dealing with the question of translation. Announcing his desire to arrive at what is said in Anaximander so as to preserve his translation "from arbitrariness,"[100] Heidegger finds himself caught in a double bind: "We are bound to the language of [Anaximander's] saying and we are bound to our own native language. In both respects we are essentially bound to language and the experience of its essence."[101] In this rendering the bond of language is irreducible to "the standard provided by all philological and historical facts,"[102] and it must be experienced in the present before the past can be made intelligible. Only a poetical saying of Being can respond to the claim made upon us by Anaximander's ancient saying of Being. To render this trace legible, Being must first be poeticized in the present: "Thinking says the dictation [*Diktat*] of the truth of Being."[103] Here the bond with Being is itself a violence, or rather, as Heidegger puts, the bond "retains the appearance of violence." A twofold violence, no doubt: by refusing to let Being withdraw completely in its self-erasure, thinking "forces its unbroken essence into the open region,"[104] doing violence to Being by interrogating it. In addition, thinking as the interrogation of Being is necessarily invested with errancy, and so it is destined to do violence to Being in missing its mark.[105] Heidegger is clear about the fact that the historical dimensions of the errancy afflicting the earliest or Greek sayings of Being affects present-day interrogations of Being: "the Greek is buried away and appears, right up to our times, only in its Roman stamping [*Prägung*]."[106] Through this process the meaning of reality "becomes objectivity."[107] It is only by retracing the steps of this history, Heidegger surmises, that we can access the Greek way of thinking. Here the Latinization of the Greek experience of Being is an interment. The Latin stamping of the Greek experience of Being preserves the oblivion of its earliest traces, conveys them to the present precisely as obliterated. In this sense, Heidegger's allusion to the Latin *fruitio* is by no means accidental. It is necessitated by the Latin interment of Being in objectivity, which is furthered by Cartesian metaphysics. The invocation of *fruitio* aims at exhuming these traces from their Roman tomb. This task can be achieved not only by abjuring the interpretation of reality as objectivity, but also by retracing the process by which the earliest traces of Being are obliterated in the history of the West. The irony here is that Heidegger cannot diagnose the Roman stamping of Being without repeating it, by using a Latinate term to render intelligible the earliest Greek saying of Being.

In this regard, the brevity of Augustine's reappearance in "Anaximander's Saying" is essential to its meaning. Like the presencing of Being it names, the reinscription of *fruitio* in Heidegger's texts seems to coincide with its erasure. In line with this, the strong connection in 1946 between the German *Brauch* and the Augustinian *fruitio* is severed in subsequent discussions of usage as an ontological predicate. In *What Is Called Thinking?* for example, *Brauch* as a name for Being is derived from the German mystical tradition, and laid at the feet of Eckhart, who is identified as the forerunner of Hölderlin and Trakl.[108] In this manner, the original link to Augustinian *fruitio* is severed, ironically, by the invocation of a medieval Augustinianism, as Augustine goes unmentioned there in the analysis of the "high sense of *use* [*Brauchen*]"[109] as a term for Being.

Temporality. The role of *fruitio* in 1946 bears directly upon the prospect of a more primordial or infinite temporality hinted at in *Being and Time*, in two ways. First, when Heidegger recasts his notion of whiling or sojourning on the basis of Being as presencing, he thinks the temporal dimensions of what presences in an extreme form of distention. Though still committed to the view that finite time temporalizes as a unified whole, he now describes what presences as marked by an incline (*Gefälle*) that places it in relation to presencing as that from which it necessarily falls away. This is akin to saying that presencing simultaneously conditions the relation with Being and assures that this relation takes the form of forgetting, letting-slip-away, and renouncing. In short, the "Anaximander's Saying" ratifies the concept of temporality put forth in the *Contributions*. It suggests that the gatheredness of finite time in its threefold extension intensifies, rather than simply reverses, the distention or dispersal of finite time.

Second, the latter dispersal is now situated alongside the obscure figure of an even more primordial or in-finite temporality. In the final pages of the "Anaximander's Saying" Heidegger identifies Being with the infinite: "Usage, however, disposing order and so containing that which presences, hands out boundaries. As *to chreōn*, therefore, it is at the same time *to apeiron*, the infinite, that which is without boundaries since its essence consists in sending the boundary of the while to that which presences awhile."[110] In its relation with beings, Being lacks its own "while." It is never present there before us: "*The infinite/limitless is the beginning of beings* [*archē tōn ontōn to apeiron*]. What is without limits is not disposed by order and reck. It is not one of the things that are present, but rather *to chreōn*, the necessary."[111] In the 1941 *Basic Concepts* lecture course, Heidegger's meditation on the infinite as word for Being is much more extensive than in his published essays. There the self-withholding of Being is equated with infinitude. It is also identified with the sense of temporality as more finite than finitude itself. The positivity of an 'in-finite' temporality opposed to duration and irreducible to the instantaneity of the instant must not be expressed merely in terms of privation, but set against the self-withholding of Being as an active force of resistance against duration.[112] Being, in this sense, does not last or perdure, and yet it is still temporal. It comes to presence in a manner that has nothing to do with the instantaneity of the instant.

CONCLUSION

But here we must finally ask: is a temporality without duration even thinkable? If so, then as what? The *Contributions* addresses this issue while linking Dasein's temporality with the question of eternity: "The eternal is not what ceaselessly lasts, but rather that which can withdraw [*sich entzieht*] in a moment so as to recur later. What can recur: not as the *identical* but as the newly transforming, the one and unique, i.e. *Beyng*, such that it is not immediately recognized, in this manifestness, as the same."[113] The passage identifies eternity with *Beyng* which has no duration. This marks a shift in Heidegger's understanding of Being as a priori: in *Being and Time* the search for the meaning of Being was guided by the assumption that this meaning could be recovered by means of a process akin to anamnesis.[114] But in the *Contributions*, Heidegger no longer expects that *Beyng* will reveal itself apart from its withdrawal. Instead he surmises that Dasein retains this withdrawal to the extent that it is transfigured by it, allowing its manner of Being to correspond with it. In line with this, primordial temporality is recast against the act of retrieving Being in its immemorial oblivion, allowing us to grasp hold of Being as *Beyng*. Heidegger argues that this renunciation is the correspondence between Dasein and *Beyng*, the real transformation of Dasein into a new entity he designates as *Dasein*. The latter comportment consists in a "mirroring of the 'turning' in the essence of Being itself."[115] Crucial to the *Contributions*, this mirroring effect informs Heidegger's characterization of the ontological difference in the "Anaximander's Saying" as well. In both texts authentic temporalization consists not in the threefold stretch of past, present, and future, but in that which makes this stretch possible to begin with.[116]

Herein lies the debt to the 1930–1931 commentary on the *Confessions*, the legacy of *transformation* from Beuron to the *Contributions* which marks the switch to the language of restraint and renunciation in the later Heidegger. That the de-theologization of the Augustinian *intentio animi* is brought to an initial fulfillment in the *Contributions* is signaled by the attempt in the "Anaximander's Saying" to articulate a dispersed temporality while surreptitiously repudiating the early definition of existence as care in a manner that draws upon its genealogical sources as if upon some ancient code. Unlike the first retrieval of Augustinian concepts, this second de-theologization is scarcely registered as such in the texts that accomplish it. Its full significance can be clarified only if we insist upon its centrality in Heidegger's most crucial debate during the 1930s—that is, in his debate with Friedrich Nietzsche.

CHAPTER SIX

On Retraction

INTRODUCTION

In 1947, faculty members at Freiburg University, working in conjunction with the Allied occupying forces, considered dismissing Heidegger for his well-documented participation in Nazi politics during the 1930s. With his professional fate hanging in the balance, Heidegger enlisted the support of old friends, including the New Testament scholar Rudolph Bultmann. Though Bultmann and Heidegger were colleagues at Marburg during the 1920s, their correspondence slowed considerably during the 1930s, coming to a virtual standstill in 1941.[1]

On Bultmann's telling, their ensuing postwar reunion ran smoothly until the last possible moment, at which point he offered a parting remark that took Heidegger by surprise: "'Now you'll have to write a retraction, like Augustine, not the least for the sake of the truth of your thought,' I said. Heidegger's face became a stony mask. He left without another word. . . . I suppose one must look for a psychological explanation."[2] In *Martin Heidegger: A Political Life*, Hugo Ott argues that this anecdote exemplifies Heidegger's postwar reluctance to confront the possible political implications of his philosophy. As Ott understood it, this refusal can be indexed conceptually. Having rejected the correspondence theory of truth, Heidegger scarcely fathomed why it might be necessary to disavow his earlier views: "If the concept of truth is seen in terms of Heidegger's understanding of immanent being, then there is nothing to retract."[3] Ott thus suggests that Heidegger's face was set in stone long before the encounter with Bultmann, justifiably arguing that Heidegger was never capable of heeding Bultmann's advice.

As we saw in chapter 5, however, by 1936 Heidegger had already elevated retraction, self-withholding, and self-renunciation to the status of first principles, relying upon them to enact the Turn and to construe Dasein's relation to what he had begun calling *Seyn* instead of *Sein*, *Beyng* instead of *Being*. Indeed, the lexical range of terms applied to Being in the *Contributions* reflects an almost singular obsession on Heidegger's part to characterize Being as "that which retracts"[4] from beings, and to rethink Dasein in the form of a self-renunciation that mirrors this self-withholding. From the point of view adopted here, this observation sharpens rather than blunts Ott's criticism. It suggests that rather than censuring this or that aspect of his philosophy—that is, rather than writing *pace* Bultmann "a retraction, like Augustine"—Heidegger chose instead to ontologize retraction, elevating it as a leading ontological predicate and thus as one of the focal points of his later work. At issue, then, is to study the effects of this elevation as part of the "immanent criticism"[5] to which the later Heidegger submitted the philosophy of *Being and Time*.

In 427 C.E., toward the end of his life, Augustine wrote his *Retractationes* in order "to reconsider from an uncompromisingly critical perspective" everything he had written over the previous fifty years and "to single out for censure"[6] whatever he found lacking. Doubtless we have nothing of the sort from Heidegger, despite his tendency after the war to construct multilayered and complex scenes of confession, as in the quasi-fictional "Dialogue on Language," included in his volume *On the Way to Language*.[7] The irony of this text, among others, is that it arguably contributes to the "leaden silence"[8] Heidegger maintained about his political life before and during the Second World War, the weight of which has only increased with the release of his "Black Notebooks."[9] This silence leads us to interrogate the ways in which the concepts of self-withholding, retraction, renunciation, and revocation function in Heidegger's later works to extend, modify, and reclaim the conceptual scaffolding deployed in his early works. In turning now to consider the ontologization of retraction in later Heidegger, our claim is that, rather than utilizing the logic of de-theologization to explain the relation between Heidegger's philosophy and his own extensive participation in political life during the 1930s, we must employ this logic to demonstrate on conceptual grounds that in its most rigorous implementations this ontologization radicalizes the aspects of Heidegger's work it is meant to expunge. To this extent, the ontologization of retraction in the later Heidegger is the real destiny of hermeneutic destruction in the context of the Turn in his thought. And to the degree that this destiny involves re-inscribing his indebtedness to religious sources, it is also the destiny into which the figure of Augustine is swept up in his work.

"Thinkers," Heidegger wrote in 1929, "learn from their shortcomings to be more persevering."[10] If for Augustine retraction meant censuring the past and thereby marking discontinuity within a corpus, for Heidegger the thematization of retraction mobilizes an immanent criticism in a manner that allows him to defend the unity of his corpus from start to finish. On this basis, the present chapter argues that the themes of retraction, renunciation, and self-withholding are bolstered in Heidegger's later writings by a series of instances in which he reconceptualizes the nature of testimony while once more shifting his debt to Augustine. In chapter 5 we saw that in 1946 Heidegger transferred an Augustinian predicate from Dasein to Being to clarify the "earliest saying" of Being. Here it is crucial to note that this transfer belies the real target of the polemic launched in Heidegger's work during the late 1930s and early 1940s: Friedrich Nietzsche.

That the confrontation with Nietzsche would trigger the repetitive re-signification of those elements in Heidegger's thought initially forged in critical conversation with Augustine stands to reason. This re-signification is fated by Heidegger's parsing of the history of metaphysics. According to this history, Nietzsche, by interpreting Being as Will, exhausts the intrinsic possibilities of Western metaphysics and thereby proves that he is the modern philosopher most rigorously committed "to the subjectivity posited by Descartes."[11] Now, the path we have traced thus far offers a unique perspective on Heidegger's rejection of Nietzsche's voluntarism. And it alerts us to the fact that Heidegger, whether knowingly or not, may have been able to utilize his indebtedness to Augustinian textual sources in his efforts to resolve the crisis inaugurated by his insight into the abandoning of beings by Being. We have seen that as early as 1923, Heidegger faulted Descartes for his "theoretical Pelagianism,"[12] that is, for ascribing autosalvific capacities to human cognition, even as Heidegger strategically aligned himself with an Augustinianism of his own making. To this we must add that the opposition between Augustine and Descartes does not disappear in the 1930s; it resurfaces in connection with the brief 1930–1931 return to Augustine: "Descartes is only oriented toward knowledge and certainty, whereas Augustine is oriented toward the whole man."[13] In this instance the sustained opposition to Descartes anticipates the *Nietzsche* lectures of the late 1930s and early 1940s, in which the opposition finds its full expression. In the current context we can approach this opposition, and thus the polemic with Nietzsche, as providing a framework for the ontologization of retraction as well as the privilege of self-renunciation in refiguring Dasein.

The fact that this refiguring of Dasein is carried out in critical conversation with the categories used to articulate the care-structure in *Being and Time* binds it ineluctably to the destiny of the second de-theologization we began spelling out in the last chapter. One indirect consequence of the reading developed here is that it relativizes the changes in Heidegger's thinking brought about by the Turn insofar as these are shown to re-launch the conceptual mechanisms we have already uncovered at work in Heidegger's corpus.[14] The argument here proceeds in three steps, in an attempt to pick up the thread of the Augustinian *cogito* out-of-reach as it informs the debate with Nietzsche. First I argue that during the 1930s, in an effort to overhaul the question of Being, Heidegger retracts the "violent presentation"[15] of Dasein put forth in *Being and Time*, effectively *destroying* and re-signifying the care-structure outlined in the early works in order to rearticulate Dasein non-volitionally in a manner that privileges self-renunciation. Second, I contend that this re-signification of the care-structure, which reinterprets care as restraint or *Verhaltenheit*, involves enlisting the Augustinian sources of care in novel ways to contest Nietzsche's concept of truth. Finally, this re-inscription of Heidegger's indebtedness to these sources can best be understood as contributing to his attempt to outdo Nietzsche in rejecting Christian Platonism.

RETRACTION AND THE DESTRUCTION OF CARE

Every genuine questioning "transforms itself,"[16] Heidegger writes in 1935. The question of Being is no exception. In chapter 5 we saw that in the 1946 essay "Anaximander's Saying," Heidegger confers upon the essential occurring of Being a crucial predicate drawn from the theological sources of care, as he uses the Augustinian term *fruitio*, in an eminent sense, to clarify the earliest saying of Being in Western philosophy. To grasp the full significance of this transfer, we must examine the link Heidegger makes between Anaximander's earliest saying of Being and Nietzsche's determination of Being as Will to Power, the last saying of Being in Western metaphysics. This latter marks for Heidegger "the summit of the completion of Western philosophy."[17] The sense of volition at play in the determination of Being as Will, which Heidegger gleans from Nietzsche's 1885 notebooks, coalesces around the primacy of subjectivity after Descartes: "to stamp becoming with the character of Being—that is the highest will to power."[18] This power determines the meaning of beings as a whole only in conformity to a volitional intention that precedes them. Nietzsche allegedly thinks Being in terms of pure presence, and he likewise thinks volitional subjectivity as its exemplar. Being is thus "the mode of presence in which the Will to Power wills itself and secures its own presencing as the Being of becoming."[19] This determination absolutizes the forgetting of Being afflicting the entire metaphysical tradition. And this absolute forgetting of Being motivates Heidegger's discussion in 1946 of Being as the *eschaton*.

When it comes to the forgetting of Being, the fault does not lie with Nietzsche alone. Nietzsche is able to reduce the meaning of Being to Will precisely because Being, during the epoch of modern metaphysics, "disappears into its still concealed truth."[20] It thereby eludes Dasein's grasp to the extent that it "veils itself with itself," [21] condemning thought to err with regard to it. The ontological transfer of *fruitio* from care to Being is thus a way of responding to, or dealing with, the disappearance of Being in modernity. To spell out this "eschatology of Being,"[22] Heidegger must exhibit Dasein in its relation to the self-veiling of Being. This exhibition results from a whole series of transformations to which Heidegger submitted the question of Being during the early to mid-1930s. In this section I argue that this series provoked a reorganization of the care-structure that necessitated destroying its initial formulation in the early lecture courses. The transfer of *fruitio* from Dasein to Being is just one sign of this negative approach to care. But this approach does not entail rejecting the concept of care. Rather, the destruction of care paves the way for its reappropriation in the context of Heidegger's later account of the history of Being.

Indeed, this reappropriation sets the stage for Heidegger's surreptitious rearticulation of Augustinian terms in combating Nietzsche. The strict identity of Being and nothingness encapsulated in the 1946 formula the "eschatology of Being" arguably has its roots in the "meta-ontological"[23] approach to Being that Heidegger outlined in the late 1920s. *Kant and the Problem of Metaphysics* suggests that the main task for philosophy is no longer to render explicit the transcendental structures of existence, but rather to interrogate "the essential connection between Being as such and the finitude in human beings."[24] Whereas *Being and Time* had sought to describe finitude as a unified structure in preparation for interrogating Being in general, Heidegger now suggests that the very analysis of finitude will go astray unless it is conducted in tandem with the inquiry into Being. Henceforth the figure of Dasein is determined, to an ever greater extent, starting from the side of Being.

The 1929 lecture "What Is Metaphysics?" seeks to counteract the metaphysical exclusion of nothingness from fundamental ontology, and in so doing to determine Dasein starting from the meaning of Being as nothingness. In a compact sequence the 1929 lecture ascribes to anxiety the capacity to disclose this meaning. In anxiety, beings as a whole elude our grasp. Receding from us, however, they do not simply disappear. Anxiety makes Dasein hover in its inability to "get a grip" on things. In this uncanny state, beings slip into indifference, yet their slipping away hems in. As a fundamental disclosure of beings as a whole, the "no hold on things" in anxiety unveils Being as that nothingness which thrusts the slipping-away of beings upon Dasein. In anxiety I cannot take hold of Being any more than I can grasp beings as slipping away from me. Nevertheless, anxiety shows Being and beings as differentiated inasmuch as Being is "essentially repelling. But this repulsion is itself as such a parting gesture toward beings that are submerging as a whole."[25] The 1929 lecture argues not only that anxiety achieves the ontological difference, but also that it is only when Being and beings are unveiled as belonging together in difference that Dasein can care for beings properly: "Only in the nothing of Dasein do beings as a whole, in accord with their most proper possibility—that is, in a finite way—come to themselves."[26] It is thus only in anxiety that Dasein holds itself out toward Being as the nothing. Thematically speaking, it is a short step from Being understood as a parting gesture to the extensive thematization of Being as self-withholding and retraction in the *Contributions*. Nevertheless the path that Heidegger followed from 1929 to 1935 was anything but straight. The formulae outlined in the 1929 lecture, which equate "holding-oneself-out" toward Being with metaphysics,[27] temporarily recede from view in the early 1930s. Its subsequent resurgence in the mid-1930s is crucially important since, as I explain below, it is linked to the de-theologizing repetition of Augustinianism spelled out in chapter 5 above.

In the intervening years the question of Being was overtly politicized. In the summer of 1933, for example, Heidegger grafted the question of Being onto the spiritual-political concerns of the German *Volk*: "The German people is now passing through a moment of historical greatness; the youth of the academy knows this greatness. What is happening, then? The German people as a whole is coming to itself, that is, it is finding its leadership."[28] The 1933 summer course manuscript argues that the question of Being prepares the German people for uncovering its historical destiny. The points of contact established between ontology and the political destiny of Germany led Heidegger to emphasize the bond between German culture and its Greek heritage. This blatant anthropologism of the question carries unmistakably racial and militant overtones: "the question of man must be *revolutionized.*"²⁹ Though its political dimensions recede from view by the end of 1934, the call to revolutionize the "question of man" and of Being would leave its mark on Heidegger's work going forward. From 1933 on Heidegger insisted that questioning Being would be seen a path-breaking activity, and that the thinkers of Being must stand in the avant-garde of a world-historical destiny.

The first chapter of the 1935 *Introduction to Metaphysics* provides one of the most extensive analyses of questioning in Heidegger's entire corpus. Though its arguments do not fully reflect the political concerns of the 1933 course, they nevertheless work toward revolutionizing the "question of man" and of Being: "Why are there beings at all instead of nothing?" The opening line of the course manuscript identifies this as "the first of all questions,"³⁰ the highest question in terms of rank, and thus the one that is necessarily included in every other question. Borrowed from Leibniz, this "why-question" proceeds in two directions at once. On the one hand, the question recoils upon the one who poses it. Those who ask the why-question cannot be shielded from it: "What is asked in this question rebounds upon the questioning itself, for the questioning challenges beings as a whole but does not after all wrest itself free from them."³¹ The why-question is genuinely posed to the extent that "it poses itself to itself,"³² which, according to the 1929 lecture, is the mark of a genuinely "metaphysical"³³ question. On the other hand, the why-question is not limited by metaphysics, or rather it reveals the full reach of Dasein's transcendence toward Being. In a comment inserted into the 1953 edition of the 1935 text, Heidegger reminds us that the why-question takes aim not only at beings, but primarily at Being. The 1953 addendum signals the need to disentangle the question of Being from that of beings. It reminds us that the "fundamental question (*Grundfrage*) of the lecture course is of a different kind than the guiding question (*Leitfrage*) of metaphysics."³⁴ The question, "Why are there beings at all instead of nothing?" harbors within it a new mode of interrogating Being which Heidegger calls the "pre-question": "the leading into the asking of the fundamental question . . . must first awaken and create the questioning. Leading is a questioning going-ahead, it is a 'pre-question.' This is a leadership that essentially has no following."³⁵ Here the why-question is no longer linked to the spiritual-historical destiny of the German *Volk* as it was in 1933. The link is severed not by rejecting but by radicalizing the theme of leadership in interrogating Being. The leading question projects thinking beyond the term of beings, to the question of the truth of Being itself: "From the fundamental question of metaphysics, 'Why are there beings at all instead of nothing?' we have extracted the pre-question: 'How does it stand with Being?'"[36] Thus the 1953 codicils which Heidegger inserts into the 1935 *Introduction to Metaphysics* mark retrospectively a rupture, a break between the question of Being and the metaphysical question concerning beings as such. In the 1929 lecture these two questions are intertwined; by 1935 Heidegger had begun pulling them apart.

The division between them, signaled at a distance in the 1953 remark, is the main concern of the 1936–1938 *Contributions*. The text puts to work a "wholly other questioning"[37] of Being. As this latter question, not unlike the "pre-question" of Being mentioned in the *Introduction to Metaphysics*, deals primarily with the self-withholding of Being, it establishes the theme of retraction at the heart of Heidegger's thinking. Between the prewar turn to the self-withholding of Being and the 1953 codicils on this turn, Heidegger would experiment with abandoning the *form* of the question altogether, as in the 1941–1942 text entitled *The Event*: the relation with *Beyng* as such in this text is characterized as an "overcoming of questioning."[38] At the same time, this overcoming hyperbolizes the mode of interrogation Heidegger now associates with the epoch of metaphysics: "the overcoming of questioning is not a transition into questionlessness," he writes, adding that it is rather *"more of a questioning* than any question."[39] Already in the *Contributions* the difference between this hyperbolic questioning of Being and what precedes it is evident at the level of Dasein. Whereas the 1929 lecture pushes forward the analysis of anxiety evident in *Being and Time* while leaving the care-structure unaltered, the *Contributions* envisions a transformation of Dasein's Being guided by the following principle: "The more *un-being* [*je unseiender*] humans are," Heidegger writes, "the less they adhere obstinately to the beings they find themselves to be, the nearer they come to Being."[40] Here the logic of negation affects Dasein's Being no less than it affects Being itself. The two are now seen to correspond to each other by virtue of turning away from each other. The discontinuity with previous instantiations of Dasein should be clear: although *Being and Time* ascribes an ontico-ontological privilege to Dasein in the question of Being, it never claims that Dasein should be as *un-being-like* as possible. In suggesting that Dasein must mirror the self-withholding of Being the *Contributions* marks the passage from care to restraint, *Sorge* to *Verhaltenheit* in terms of a self-disavowal or self-renunciation of Dasein.

During the postwar period Heidegger ascribes to the figure of the poet, in the person of Stefan George, the experience of a self-renunciation that allows language itself to bestow presence on things.[41] But this is not the first time Heidegger broaches this theme. The obsession with self-renunciation is evident already in the first pages of the *Contributions*, in a section entitled "Preview," where we learn that restraint discloses Being as occurring essentially by denying itself: "in restraint . . . there reigns a turn toward the hesitant self-denial [*Sichversagen*] as the essential occurrence of Beyng."[42] Self-withholding is to Being what self-denial is to Dasein. As *Beyng*, Being comes to presence only in its withdrawal, retracting itself from experience and provoking a concomitant self-denial on Dasein's part. Self-denial thus marks the moment in which Dasein is transformed or *displaced* into the comportment Heidegger calls "Da-sein."

To explain how Da-sein is affected by the self-withholding of Being, Heidegger at first figures this affection as a species of negation, referring to it in starkly negative terms. It is ultimately in the stillness of a new kind of silence that Da-sein comports itself toward *Beyng* as the "pre-essential essence of Being."[43] To the extent that the latter signifies a species of absence designated by negative terms alone, Heidegger relies upon the two terms *self-withholding* (*Verweigerung*) and *refusal* (*Weigerung*)[44] to designate it. In so doing, one of his points is to argue that this abyssal self-withholding is paradoxically the ground in relation to which Da-sein's ecstatic understanding of Being must be reconfigured. Put otherwise, the *Contributions* points to self-withholding and refusal in order to answer the pre-question of Being posed in the *Introduction to Metaphysics*, i.e. the question that asks, "how does it stand with Being?"

On this basis it then asks if the sense of Dasein's Being must be revised. For it is clear that the portrait of Dasein as "Da-sein" in 1936–1938 is not entirely consonant with the 1929 analysis of Dasein's Being grounded in anxiety. They differ in two ways. First, in the case of Being, the *Contributions* radicalizes the 1929 description of Being as repelling beings, as Heidegger now maintains that Being withholds itself to the point of absence. Second, in the case of Da-sein, the *Contributions* radicalizes the 1929 dynamic of shrinking back before Being. It does so by reconfiguring care as restraint—a comportment whose dispositional mode is *displacement* or *Verrückung*, a radically ecstatic experience of being cast out of oneself. The tie between restraint and displacement suggests that in the *Contributions* the ecstatic dimensions of existence are pushed to their breaking point, as Heidegger struggles to rearticulate the structural distention that characterizes Dasein's Being as a stretch. And this is exactly what motivates him once again to critically reappropriate the theological origins of care and to contest its limits as these are portrayed in *Being and Time*.

The modification of the care-structure outlined in *Being and Time* is in fact the precondition for transposing Dasein into the entirely "new" questioning of Being. Put otherwise, this modification is not tantamount to rejecting care, but rather it heralds the reorganization of its structure within the problematic spelled out in the *Contributions*. The first step in transforming Dasein in the *Contributions* consists in what Heidegger calls the "original negation" of Dasein, the purpose of which is to reconstitute Dasein so that it becomes "the same in kind as that refusal which deprives itself of any accompanying,"[45] i.e. what Heidegger now calls "Beyng." This negation is the "meaning of destruction occurring in the transition to the other beginning."[46] It thereby signals Heidegger's desire to re-orientate the hermeneutic destruction by explicitly, if subtly, targeting his own texts. By refashioning itself to correspond with Being as refusal, Dasein does not assuage the forgetting of Being,[47] so much as it prepares the way for interrogating Being as forgotten. Only through this new correspondence between Dasein and Being, we are told, can one glimpse the "complete unfolding"[48] of metaphysics. The novelty of the *Contributions* is thus unmistakable when measured against the form of questioning Being that characterizes *Being and Time* as well as the 1935 *Introduction to Metaphysics*. In the latter context Heidegger still argued, as he did in 1927, that Dasein can never break free of beingness entirely. By contrast, in the *Contributions* he insists that in the act of interrogating Being, Da-sein must achieve "the *complete detachment [Ablösung]* from Being as beingness and as the most general determination."[49] The fact that this detachment pertains to the beingness of Dasein no less than it does to every other being provides the clearest indication that for Heidegger the destructive reappropriation of Dasein marks the transition from philosophy to a new kind of "thinking."

The conceptual significance of this detachment must not be overlooked. In what sense does restraint in the *Contributions* differ *structurally* from care in *Being and Time*? For starters, the intentional structure of restraint indicates that in the *Contributions* Heidegger aims to uncouple care from entities as such. *Being and Time* describes care as "a relation to entities within-the-world,"[50] which is precisely what Heidegger has in view when he elsewhere asserts that "care is always concern and solicitude, even if only privatively."[51] But by 1936 the privative mode of care would be brought forward. In *Mindfulness*, for example, Dasein is said to "attest to the deepest belonging" to Being by *"being-away"* from beings.[52] This break between care and beings reflects Heidegger's desire to exhibit a form of ontological inquiry that extends beyond the question of beingness and that is paradoxically called restraint. This desire motivates the depiction of care in the "Letter on Humanism" as "the care of Being."[53] What is not entirely clear, however, in the "Letter on Humanism" is that Heidegger could not portray care as the care of Being without first reorganizing care as form of, and in its relation to, beingness.

Heidegger's effort to think Dasein as detachment, broadening its intentional structure to show how it can interrogate Being apart from beingness, is perhaps most evident in the role assigned to displacement in the later works. Let us recall that in the 1946 essay "Anaximander's Saying," Heidegger links his own conception of care as *Sorge* to the Middle-High German *ruoche*, equivalent to the English *reck-*, as in *reckless*.[54] In its immediate context this leads Heidegger to argue that care is primarily grounded not in a relation with an entity as what is presently there before us, but in a relation to something prior, i.e. Being itself. Drawing on a passage from Homer, Heidegger compares the thinker of Being with Calchas, the Argive seer, mentioned in Book 1 of the *Iliad*, whom Heidegger takes to be emblematic of post-metaphysical thinking. Calchas, Heidegger argues, is not dominated by the proximity of beings. As the seer, he is simultaneously "the madman. But what is it that constitutes the essence of this madness? The madman is outside. He is away [*weg-sein*]. We ask: away to where? And from where? Away from the mere crush of what lies before us, of the merely presently present, and away to the absent."[55] Here Calchas exemplifies the thinker of Being who goes beyond the presently present (beings as a whole) and ecstatically relates to what is unpresently present (Being).

This ecstasy is akin to a form of madness. In going beyond what is present, the thinker of Being is cast beyond the confines of the care-structure in its ontic orientation. Such a thinker is mad, Heidegger admits, inasmuch as he or she is literally deprived of ontic forms of care, *ver-rückt*. Calchas transcends the present in a manner that allows him to speak the truth of the here and now. Calchas, Heidegger writes, "is able to find his way back from the away, back to what is present here and now, namely, the raging plague."[56] This valorization of ecstasy as akin to madness, a retreat from the crush of the present, sets the tone for all subsequent attempts on Heidegger's part to expand the care-structure. As Löwith notes,[57] Heidegger identifies displacement, the disposition of restraint in the middle writings, as a form of madness. Calchas appears to be mad from the perspective of those who are trapped within what lies before them, yet Heidegger sees him as the contemplative "who in an exceptional sense belongs to the totality of what presences."[58] The image of Calchas as a mad, truth-speaking visionary does not stand alone in Heidegger's texts. It is linked with other representations of madness in the middle and later writings that delimit the space from which reason as such can be interrogated and reworked. These representations are grouped around two poles. On the one hand, Heidegger cautions us against interpreting displacement as signaling a radical privation of the care-structure: "If we appraise the reflection on the displacement [*Verrückung*] of man from the standpoint of sound common sense and its predominance, we will reject it as deranged [*verrückt*], to play cleverly with a word."⁵⁹ On the other hand, when he indicates that displacement fulfills the function previously assigned to anxiety, that of disclosing Being in its difference from beings, he affirms that displacement designates "the plight of the abandonment of Being,"⁶⁰ something for which "we have no measure and no space—at least not yet—and we therefore force it into disfiguration or disguise if we speak about it by means of language as constituted hitherto."⁶¹ In its strongest sense this latter thesis is a tacit admission that within his current lexicon Heidegger can broach displacement either by disfiguring it or by way of negation.

In "Nietzsche's Word: 'God Is Dead,'" the way of negation is more salutary than it is pernicious, as it allows Heidegger to graft his own description of nihilism onto the Nietzschean death of God. In *The Gay Science* §125 Nietzsche famously narrates the brief tale of a "madman" who seeks God while proclaiming his demise. In his gloss on the passage, Heidegger considers Nietzsche's madman to be a forerunner of Dasein's displacement: "In what way is this man mad? He is *dis-placed* or *de-ranged* [*verrückt*]. He is moved out of the level of erstwhile man on which the ideals, now grown unreal, of the supersensory world are passed off as real while the opposite ideals are being realized. This *dis-placed* or *de-ranged* man is moved out [*hinausgerückt*] beyond erstwhile man. In moving out, nonetheless, he has only fully moved into [*eingerückt*] the predetermined essence of erstwhile man, to be the *animal rationale*."⁶² Having left behind "erstwhile man," or the human as theorized in the modern metaphysical tradition since Descartes, the Nietzschean madman, who shores up the ruins of the tradition he delimits, represents a failed displacement for Heidegger. This failure reflects Nietzsche's alleged inability to perceive the essence of the European nihilism whose onset he nevertheless manages to identify. Though Nietzsche describes this onset as the devaluation of all values, Heidegger contends that devaluation is symptomatic of a deeper truth: "the essence of nihilism," Heidegger contends, "consists in the fact that there is nothing going on with Being itself."⁶³ Thus, while moving beyond "erstwhile man," the Nietzschean madman nevertheless cannot envisage the true ground upon which he stands. The madman instead follows a predetermined path that reinforces the metaphysical conception of man as rational animal, remaining blind to the ontological foundations of European nihilism.

By contrast, Heidegger sets the Nietzschean critique of Christianity in its broadest terms, interpreting the death of God as the "decomposition" or de-essentialization (*Verwesung*)[64] of the supersensory. When ideal forms lose their binding force, the actual entities whose meanings they guarantee are likewise deprived of their sense. The vanished authority of the divine is replenished from the sensory realm as the latter is unfastened from the supersensory. The death of God allows the realm of the divine to be overwritten by a new, insurmountable form of sovereignty, namely, the "over-reaching"[65] of subjectity, the volitional will of the subject that secures its own self-certitude by means of a fiat. Heidegger insists that the Nietzschean figure of the Overman, the one who dispenses new values from out of the Will to Power, does not simply occupy the position of the vanished God. He maintains instead that the decomposition of the divine is the ground of idolatry. From now on, the *position* of God serves as the null-place where hyperbolic forms of sovereignty arise. This process of continuously re-inscribing hyperbolic forms of sovereignty at the site formerly occupied by God is for Heidegger "far more uncanny" than the Nietzschean devaluation of all values: "This place for God can remain empty. In its place, another one that corresponds to it metaphysically can open up, one that is identical neither to the essential realm of God nor to the essential realm of man, who, however, is again entering into a distinctive relationship with this other realm."[66] Two responses to this decomposition are possible. The first, spelled out by Nietzsche, consists in responding to the demise of the supersensory by valorizing strength, willing the demise of the weak, and desiring ever more power—in short, the transvaluation of all values, according to which the human subject is the measure of all things.

The other path is the one Heidegger believes that he is following in the *Contributions*, which consists in resituating the meaning of beings as a whole alongside the self-withholding of Being. This other path requires Heidegger to render Dasein in terms that are analogous to the Nietzschean madman, the thinker of the death of God, while simultaneously detaching this madness from the twin Nietzschean doctrines of the Overman and the Will to Power. The result is Heidegger's "negativistic"[67] approach to human subjectivity grouped around the dynamic of displacement, which I am approaching here under the rubric of the destruction of care. This destruction is not so much a rejection of madness in Nietzsche as it is an attempt to conquer its territory, which is situated beyond the limits of rationality.

This conquest is the positive goal of the original negation of Dasein mentioned above. Let us recall that Heidegger targets Nietzsche as giving voice to the unthought essence of modern scientific technology,[68] in the sense that the Will to Power and the Eternal Return describe the world as "an unending disaggregation and reaggregation of forces without any purpose or goal,"[69] as Iain Thomson writes, beyond the self-perpetuation of these forces. Though Nietzsche loses touch with nihilism by prioritizing the question of value, he nevertheless makes clear to Heidegger that a thoroughgoing critique of metaphysics must start by divorcing itself from existing conceptions of reason: "Thinking does not begin until we have come to know that the reason that has been extolled for centuries is the most stubborn adversary of thinking."[70] The shortcoming of Nietzsche's madman is thus not that he goes mad, but rather that he fails to hold out in his madness so as to return from it in the manner of Calchas.

Heidegger accepts that the displacement of Dasein, if it is judged from the vantage point of reason, will undoubtedly resemble a species of madness. This is the conclusion reached by Kant in his "Essay on the Maladies of the Head," which analyzes "that type of mental disturbance which is called madness and which, if it is more serious, is called derangement [*Verrückung*]."[71] The latter disturbance primarily afflicts our concepts of experience, according to Kant, or the forms of judgment we use to distinguish the internal from the external world, the rational from the irrational. From the mid-1930s on, Heidegger often implies that the thinker of Being possesses mantic powers akin to those he eventually ascribes to Calchas, empowering this thinker to step beyond the limits of rationality. In the 1937–1938 course *Basic Questions*, for example, he describes those who care for Being as offering themselves up as a "silent sacrifice,"[72] consecrating themselves wholly to Being.[73] Precisely because the contemplation of Being cannot be undertaken from the perspective of reason as it has thus far been conceived in Western philosophy, there is an intrinsic connection between this contemplation and the risk of madness: "the ones who suffered such contemplation," Heidegger writes, "were prematurely torn away from the sanity of their Dasein—and this in wholly different ways in their own respective domains: Schiller, Hölderlin, Kierkegaard, van Gogh, Nietzsche. . . . These names are like enigmatic signs, inscribed in the most hidden ground of our history."[74] We cannot fail to notice here that these enigmatic signs serve as cautionary tales for Heidegger if only because they do not return to sanity after having taken flight from their Dasein. The implication is that if one could withstand the contemplation of Being and afterwards return to sanity, one would solve the riddle posed by these names.

By rehabilitating the term *displacement* or *derangement*—a term Kant associated with enthusiasm—Heidegger cannot avoid including his own prior portrayals of the care-structure among the aspects of rational discourse that he must abandon if he wishes to reorientate ontological inquiry toward Being as self-withholding. In the *Contributions*, this reorientation generates a "sigetic" [75] approach to Dasein, a keeping silent about its structure. Elsewhere this sigetic or silent approach to Dasein leaves its mark on Heidegger's portrayals of the new beginning of philosophy after Nietzsche. In the *Basic Questions*, for example, Heidegger argues that in this new beginning Dasein "cannot even be mentioned, because it would immediately be interpreted as an object and the determination of the essence of truth would be denigrated."[76] But lest we think that Heidegger holds back or *retracts* Dasein in the new beginning for fear that others might misinterpret what is said about it, he is clear in the *Contributions* that this retraction is primarily grounded in a desire to refashion Dasein in the mode of *Da-sein*, i.e. the one that corresponds exactly to the the self-withholding of Being, or Beyng.

It is impossible not to notice that this refashioning simultaneously deprives Dasein of its meaning while leaving it perfectly intact. This strange repetition in which expropriation coincides with appropriation allows Dasein to be "kept in silence."[77] But even here silence takes on the meaning of a permanent self-contestation, since in order to interrogate Beyng, Dasein must continuously negate itself, or enact a "surrendering" or an "emptying-out [*Entäußerung*]"[78] that allows it to mirror Being by denying "itself to the point of the abandonment by Being."[79] The centrality of this dynamic to ontological inquiry allows Heidegger at moments to define care by its opposite—namely, as carelessness or unconcern. The reversal is part of the logic of destruction, applied to care, which we establish here as a first step in elucidating the return of Augustinian concepts in the debate with Nietzsche.

The *Discourse on Thinking* (the translation of Heidegger's booklet *Gelassenheit*) notes, for example, that the term *Gelassenheit* or *letting-be*, borrowed from Eckhart, carries "the sense of 'composure,' 'calmness,' and 'unconcern,'"[80] terms which directly oppose the early Heideggerian determination of care as concern or *Bekümmerung*. On at least two other occasions Heidegger develops the theme of "carelessness" at length. In the

1942 *Parmenides* seminar Heidegger rereads the Myth of Er in a manner that allows him to equate being "care-less" [*Sorg-los*] with the activity of the thinker who attends to Being as "withdrawing concealment."[81] And in the essay "Why Poets?" Heidegger goes further. Taking his cue from Rilke, he argues that beings as a whole are "without care," or "*sine cura*."[82] Here the term *carelessness* functions to reverse the valence bestowed upon care as *Sorge* in the 1920s. Put otherwise, care in "Why Poets?" designates what *Being and Time* calls inauthenticity, whereas carelessness denotes letting-beings-be: "Care has here the nature of deliberate self-assertion along the ways and by the means of absolute self-production. We are without this care only when we do not set up our essence exclusively in the precinct of production and command, of utilization and defense."[83] The dynamic of "being without care" now takes over the role previously assigned to care as concern and solicitude in Heideggerian hermeneutics. And rather than identifying this reversal, Heidegger simply transfers onto carelessness the Augustinian genealogy he first assigned to care in 1924–1927, invoking Pascal as an authority.

From our vantage point the transfer not only reveals the resilience of this genealogy, but it also reveals its centrality to the destruction of care sparked by Heidegger's desire to elaborate the fundamental correspondence of Dasein with the self-withholding of Being. Thus, having established that the negation of Dasein is the meaning assigned to hermeneutics in achieving this primal correspondence, it is now necessary to show how this "hermeneutics" can be accomplished in Heidegger's later works only by further extending the life of the concepts Heidegger seems to take back or retract.

NIETZSCHE AND AUGUSTINE

In *The Life of the Mind*, Hannah Arendt argues that Heidegger's condemnation of modern metaphysics as a nihilistic pursuit of power over entities has its origins in a personal crisis of conscience: "In Heidegger's understanding, the will to rule and dominate is a kind of original sin, of which he found himself guilty when he tried to come to terms with his brief past in the Nazi movement."[84] Arendt argues that the effects of this self-reckoning are legible in the second half of Heidegger's *Nietzsche* volumes, which include prewar materials drawn from Heidegger's 1936–1940 lectures as well as writings composed during and after the war. In these volumes, Arendt suggests, Heideggerian care "changes its function radically."[85] Whereas in *Being and Time* Heidegger had interpreted care within the framework of anticipatory resoluteness, he now adopts the Eckhartian language of letting-be, or *Gelassenheit*, to designate care in a thoroughly non-voluntaristic manner. Arendt portrays the switch as a tacit confession on Heidegger's part. Yet the evidence presented above suggests that it is the product of a fundamental methodological commitment to rethink the question of Being that has its roots in the years following *Being and Time*. The novel function of care Arendt observes in the *Nietzsche* volumes is in fact the *terminus ad quem* of the destructive reappropriation of care outlined above. While confirming Arendt's observation, we must also show that Heidegger's attempt to recast care in opposition to "the will to rule and dominate" requires him to silently oppose Augustine to Nietzsche. Mindful that scholars have identified significant problems with the 1961 *Nietzsche* volumes,[86] I draw on them here to show that in criticizing Nietzsche's conception of truth, Heidegger's descriptions of ontological inquiry remain linked to an Augustinian definition of faith. The destruction of care thus involves switching the valence of its genealogical roots, disconnecting them from the care-structure spelled out in *Being and Time* while linking them to care as letting-be. This entails subtly invoking Augustine's formulae as so many bulwarks against Nietzsche's doctrine of the Will to Power.

Augustine's uncanny relevance to the question of nihilism in Heidegger's middle writings is evinced by the very last line of the 1930–1931 seminar protocol on *Confessions* 11. In a cryptic remark Heidegger notes that in his meditation on temporality Augustine reaches the crucial insight that forgetting "lies already in the essence of retention as a mode of retention itself."[87] It is difficult to overstate the importance of this realization for Heidegger in the wake of his 1929 lecture "What Is Metaphysics?" The upshot of the 1931 seminar on *Confessions* 11 is that according to Augustine the mind retains divine presence paradoxically by forgetting it. In turn, this forgetting is taken positively as a deeper way of intending divine presence. This model of intentionality gave Heidegger some way of thinking by analogy how Dasein retains Being as nothingness. In the context of *Being and Time*, Heidegger never fully relinquishes the Platonic motif of anamnesis: "if Being, which has always already been understood 'earlier,' is to become an express *object*, then the objectification of this *prius*, which was forgotten, must have the character of a coming back to what was already once and already earlier understood."[88] The same cannot be said of texts written after the 1930–1931 Augustine seminar. Granted, Heidegger's postwar works defend the efficacy of devotional recollection or *Andenken* as providing access to the truth of Being. Nevertheless, during the 1930s he often characterized forgetting itself as a positive way of relating to Being—as in *Mindfulness*, where Dasein falls prey to a forgetting that "cannot be demarcated vis-à-vis the rememberable."[89] The point here is that by admitting the absolute primacy of concealment over unconcealment, Heidegger simultaneously changed the function of forgetting in his work, effectively arguing that Dasein retains the self-withholding of Being by means of a "a distinctive *not-retaining* retention."[90] The argument echoes the one reached in the *Contributions*: "Knowing Being does not rest on an *anamnesis* as determined since Plato, but rather on a forgetting."[91] And it is subsequently reaffirmed in the *Parmenides* seminar of 1942, in which Heidegger at first blames Plato for falsifying the nature of memory and forgetting,[92] and then argues that forgetting must be reexamined as a positive mode of retention.[93]

The fact that Heidegger associated Augustine with the positive meaning of forgetting as a mode of retention provides an initial indication for understanding why Augustinian formulae return in his debate with Nietzsche. The association remains more or less submerged in the *Nietzsche* lectures, and yet when Heidegger mobilizes the positive sense of forgetting *against* Nietzsche, in order to show that Nietzsche failed to grasp the ontological foundations of European nihilism, he falls back upon what he learned in reading Augustine.

To see this we must briefly outline the allegedly Cartesian dimensions of the Nietzschean project, as the re-signification of Heidegger's debt to Augustine occurs in the service of linking Nietzsche to Descartes: "What begins metaphysically with Descartes initiates the history of its completion through Nietzsche's metaphysics."[94] This completion is accomplished through Nietzsche's reduction of the ego to force. That Nietzsche adopts a univocal concept of force, under the heading of the Will to Power, in order to put truth into question experimentally actually proves for Heidegger that he belongs on the same metaphysical ground as Descartes. For both thinkers, Being means representedness,[95] or being established in thinking. Both thinkers supposedly determine the meaning of Being starting from subjectivity. They each describe as true what is most firmly fixed in the realm of the *cogitationes*. For Descartes the *cogito* functions as a bulwark against radical skepticism, whereas for Nietzsche the healthy, strong spirit who dispenses new values adopts the stance of a subject who demands that all beings conform to its will. When Heidegger argues that for Descartes, Being means representedness, he suggests that the major concern of the Cartesian metaphysics is to secure the self-certainty of the human being as the ground of every intention, activity, and thought. For

Descartes "everything that is certain of itself must in addition guarantee as certainly given that being *for* which every representation and intention, and *through* which every action, is supposed to be assured."[96] The driving force behind Descartes's determination of Being as representation is the need to secure the *cogito* in its mastery over all other givens. In the *Nietzsche* volumes Heidegger attributes this drive to Nietzsche himself, while arguing that the revaluation of values, as a function of the Will to Power, expresses in its purest form the metaphysical truth of modern scientific technology as the "enframing" (*Gestell*) of all beings, their determination in terms of use value.

The enframing of beings rests upon the power of the image. Accordingly Heidegger strongly emphasizes that the act of representing an entity by situating it as an image or object before the mind's eye cannot be viewed as an innocent act. It is rather a minimal exertion of power over the entity so depicted. To represent an entity means to set it "before one and to make what has been set in place [*das Gestellte*] secure as thus set in place."[97] The represented entity provides the subject with a point of reference for its own self-willing, a locus for its own realization as an active presence in the world. Thus no matter how often Nietzsche seems to repudiate the ego, in Heidegger's eyes he nevertheless succeeds only in reinterpreting the Cartesian *cogito* in psychological terms as the Will to Power.[98] This prevents Nietzsche from accessing the sense in which European nihilism is grounded in Being itself. And it also prevents him from grasping the true nature of temporal becoming.

Let us recall that the doctrine of Eternal Recurrence, articulated on multiple occasions by Nietzsche from 1881 on, if not earlier,[99] stipulates that the universe consists in a finite sequence that repeats itself without end. Every instant that occurs has already occurred an infinite number of times and it will recur infinitely. In its most terrible form the doctrine engenders despair, as it depicts the universe as little more than a useless squandering. Yet it also holds the key for the self-overcoming of nihilism, provided that one can affirm the infinite repetition or return of every past or present state of affairs. In this manner eternity is for Nietzsche primarily a predicate of the instant viewed from the perspective of its absolute iterability, whereas it is secondarily a function of the subjective will that affirms iterability in willing the continuance of everything that bolsters its own feeling of power. For Heidegger the eternal recurrence of the same is a problematic doctrine for many reasons. Though Nietzsche sees it as the only way to combat Platonism, Heidegger suspects that in depicting a universe devoid of pure loss Nietzsche has obscured the real meaning of temporal becoming.

The debate turns on two discrete sections in Nietzsche's corpus. The first is a line from the *Nachlass* included in §617 of *The Will to Power*: "To impose upon becoming the character of being—that is the supreme will to power."[100] The second is the section entitled "On Redemption" in Part 2 of *Thus Spoke Zarathustra*, in which Nietzsche defines the essence of revenge as "the will's unwillingness toward time and time's 'it was.'"[101] In Heidegger's reading the first passage reinforces the second. Though Nietzsche may seek to purge himself of any unwillingness toward time, or more specifically toward the past as such, he nevertheless fails to overcome his abhorrence of all impermanence, his resentment against the passing of time. The act of *willing* the past, which exemplifies imposing upon becoming the character of being, is an expression of pure resentment rather than its repudiation: "The will is delivered from what is revolting in the 'it was' when it wills the constant recurrence of every 'it was.' . . . The eternal recurrence of the same is the supreme triumph of the metaphysics of the will that eternally wills its own willing."[102] Saturated with nostalgic longing, the Nietzschean will secures the duration of its own existence by willing the conditions of its emergence. As a doctrine the eternal recurrence is thus orientated primarily toward stasis and secondarily toward change and becoming. It signifies for Heidegger "the mode of permanence in which the Will-to-power wills itself and secures its own presencing as the being of becoming."[103] And to this extent it brings to completion the modern subject's search for self-certainty, summing up the metaphysical epoch that begins with Descartes's *Meditations on First Philosophy*.

Moreover, Heidegger's rejection of the Eternal Return provides the basis for his repudiation of Nietzsche's concept of truth. Far from reading Nietzsche as a thoroughgoing skeptic, Heidegger interprets Nietzschean perspectivism as shoring up the correspondence theory of truth. In a line from the *Nachlass* included in §481 of *The Will to Power*, Nietzsche famously argues that because there are no true facts, the world has countless meanings: "facts is precisely what there is not, only interpretations."[104] The assertion echoes the argument that appears in a posthumously published essay written in 1873 entitled "On Truth and Lying in a Non-Moral Sense," in which Nietzsche asserts that truth is nothing other than "a mobile army of metaphors."[105] Both texts can be read as part of Nietzsche's effort to call into question the value of truth in part by showing that truth is the sort of error that cannot be refuted. Yet for Heidegger this effort greatly amplifies the role of the willing subject in determining the meaning of beings in conformity to the values posited by it, and it implicates the concept of truth with that of justification. In "Nietzsche's Word: 'God Is Dead,'"

Heidegger examines Nietzsche's conception of justice at length, arguing that Nietzsche's notion of truth as certainty is animated by the drive toward "justification [*Rechtfertigung*] by security."[106] Though the early Nietzsche, Heidegger observes, is hardly silent on the themes of justice or righteousness (*Gerechtigkeit*) and justification (*Rechtfertigung*),[107] the real import of these terms emerges in the mid-1880s when Nietzsche adopts the Will to Power as the fundamental trait of beings. Two of Heidegger's most important proof texts come from 1883 and 1884; together they show that for Nietzsche the essence of justice is linked to that of right, and through this, to the will to domination. The 1883 text defines "right" as follows: "Right—the will to make a momentary power relation obtain eternally. To be satisfied with that power relation is the pre-condition. Everything venerable is called in to let what is right appear to be eternal."[108] Here the act of justification is bound up with a particular conception of volition as that which eternalizes, or effectively stamps becoming with the character of Being. The willing subject justifies what is right by letting it obtain eternally. The correspondence between the will, as that which eternalizes, and the momentary power relation eternalized through it, is the essence of Nietzschean truth. Inasmuch as the willing subject stipulates what is "right," Nietzsche is said to be complicit in Cartesian metaphysics, as he reduces all meaning to representation and all truth to the form of subjective certitude, as Reiner Schurmann notes.[109] Heidegger further elucidates this reduction by pointing to the 1884 *Nachlass*, in which Nietzsche writes the following: "The problem of *justice* [*Gerechtigkeit*]. The first and most powerful thing is precisely the will and strength to overpower. The ruler establishes 'justice' only afterward, which means, he measures things in accordance with his own measure."[110] If in the 1883 text the power of right is thought in terms of conservation, in the 1884 text it is thought in terms of an adjustment made in retrospect by a sovereign force. From these texts Heidegger concludes that for Nietzsche justice as *Gerechtigkeit* "is the truth of the beings that are in the mode of the will to power."[111] This sense of justice, in other words, refers to the act by which the will secures the duration of certain beings through the positing of values.

This is indeed the conclusion Heidegger reaches in the *Nietzsche* volumes. In a section entitled "Truth as Justice" (*Gerechtigkeit*),[112] Heidegger argues that the devaluation of truth in Nietzsche's metaphysics is by no means an indication that Nietzsche has discarded truth as certitude once and for all. Instead Nietzsche subjectivizes truth, making man the measure of all things. On this model, as Heidegger writes later in his *Nietzsche* lecture, "the power-based essence of truth is, according to

Nietzsche, justice [*Gerechtigkeit*.]"¹¹³ Justice as *Gerechtigkeit* is thus for Nietzsche the metaphysical name of truth as it fixes the Being of beings in terms of the Will.¹¹⁴ At the same time that Heidegger identifies *Gerechtigkeit* as the quintessentially metaphysical definition of truth without rejecting the concept out of hand, he leaves open the possibility that after Nietzsche the concept of truth can be salvaged only by re-signifying and thus retaining the concept of justification.

Here we pick up the thread of the argument that leads us back to Augustine. The centrality of justification to the criticisms Heidegger directs at Nietzsche, along with his claim that Nietzsche reinterprets the Cartesian *cogito* psychologically and thereby effectively infinitizes its drive toward self-justification, should allow us to see that Heidegger's debate with Nietzsche is an extension of the one he conducted with Descartes in 1923. The earlier debate aimed at bringing out the sense in which Descartes could be seen as articulating a theoretical Pelagianism—a system of meaning in which the subject of knowledge could save itself without divine intervention. The later debate with Nietzsche merely brings the full weight of this charge to bear upon the modern metaphysical determination of Being as Will. Though not its main focus, the theological dimensions of the charge are not absent from Heidegger's discussion, which aligns the Nietzschean conceptions of justice and justification with their Christian counterparts: "*Iustificatio* in the sense of the Reformation and Nietzsche's concept of justice as truth are the same."¹¹⁵ This claim makes sense only if we recognize that in Heidegger's eyes both conceptions, those of Luther and Nietzsche, determine justification as subjective certitude—the former in the form of absolute confidence in the alien work of God, the latter in the form of the revaluation of values.

Regardless of whether or not Heidegger is correct in grouping together Nietzsche and Luther, this coupling mobilizes the de-theologization of an alternative concept of justification drawn from the Christian-Platonist tradition. This mobilization is not entirely evident in the "Anaximander's Saying," though momentarily we shall see that it is evident in the *Nietzsche* volumes. In the *Contributions* the concept used to destroy Nietzschean justification is culled from the pages of the *Confessions* and linked to the notion of forgetting as a positive relation with the divine. It is, in short, derived from the Augustinian sources of care.

At the outset of the *Contributions*, Heidegger ceases to juxtapose faith and thinking as he does in the 1935 *Introduction to Metaphysics*.¹¹⁶ In a passage starkly opposed to the view articulated in the 1946 "Anaximander's Saying" essay, in which he maintains that "Faith has no place in thought,"[117] Heidegger here argues that those who interrogate Being itself "are the genuine *believers*, because they—by opening up the essence of truth—adhere to the ground."[118] The real import of this seemingly brief reclamation of *Glaube* becomes apparent much later in the treatise, where the concept of faith is more fully explicated as Dasein's basic comportment toward the self-withholding of Being and thus as marking the transition from philosophical inquiry to being-historical thinking. In a section of the *Contributions* entitled "Belief and Truth," Heidegger explains at length why those who question Being have true faith: "What is meant here is not its particular form as membership in a 'confession' but, instead, the essence of belief, grasped on the basis of the essence of truth."[119] The section distinguishes between two types of faith. The first type signifies holding-something-for-true, in which case faith consists primarily in affirming the truth-status of a given proposition. By contrast, the second type signifies "holding oneself [*Sichhalten*] within the presencing of truth"[120] and so does not pertain primarily to propositions but rather designates the properly ecstatic dimension of Dasein's existence.

If faith in the first sense is scarcely distinguishable from the lexical range of belief that extends from opinion to blind certainty, faith in the second sense provides Heidegger with a model for understanding how Dasein comports itself intellectually toward Being (or Beyng). Instead of being excluded from thought, the latter kind of faith serves as its dispositional ground. It is "the basic relation [*Grundbezug*] to . . . Beyng itself."[121] Heidegger suggests that those thinkers capable of enduring the withdrawal of Being exemplify this basic relation and thereby possess faith in its most authentic sense: "*Those who question* in this manner are the originary and actual believers, i.e. those who take *truth* itself—and not only what is true—seriously."[122] At the same time, he fails to indicate that the concept of faith rehabilitated in this context is not created out of thin air, but rather it is structurally analogous to the ground of Augustinian confession isolated in the 1930–1931 treatments of the term, anticipating what the *Contributions* describes as the deepest kind of questioning: "this holding-oneself, having the character of a projecting-open, is always a questioning, nay *the* originary questioning as such."[123] What matters here is that the attempt to equate faith with ontological inquiry into the self-withholding of Being shifts Heidegger's debt to the Augustinian sources of care even as it lays the groundwork for attacking the implicitly Cartesian dimensions of Nietzsche's philosophy.

The *Contributions* casts Hölderlin as one of the forerunners who set the stage for thinking after the end of philosophy, and yet the earliest conceptualization of faith as *Sichhalten* in Heidegger's corpus is evidently linked to the search for God as described in "Augustine and Neoplatonism." There Heidegger argues that Augustine's faith has nothing to do with his well-known definition of *fides* as "thinking with assent,"[124] which seems to correspond with the notion of faith rejected in the *Contributions*. Rather, faith in the context of *Confessions* Book 10 is constituted by radical concern surrounding the self-world which in turn orientates the search for divine presence. In *Confessions* 10.37 Augustine laments his susceptibility to the praise of others while rejoicing in truth. In glossing this passage, the early Heidegger underscores the fact that Augustine remains, in his words, "steadfast (keeping oneself, secure) and most certain in having the truth [*in veritate certissimus constans*]."[125] The theme of constancy-in-truth allows Heidegger to pull apart two notions of faith. Or more precisely it allows him to differentiate between the stance of remaining steadfast in truth, which is equated with the experience of worry or genuine trouble (*molestia*) and the act of holding something for true: "(1) Security, steadfastness; (2) absolute validity existing in itself, directly a being; both things do not have to go together."[126] Thus it is clear that the concept of faith rehabilitated in the *Contributions*, and equated with the question of Being, makes its first appearance in Heidegger's corpus in connection with Augustine.

The point should not be minimized or glossed over by observing that Augustine no longer serves as an explicit point of reference for Heidegger during the 1930s. Indeed, Heidegger acknowledges certain figures as heralds in the *Contributions*—Hölderlin, Rilke, and Nietzsche, among others. This belies the fact that the template for the transition he wants to enact from philosophy to thinking is indebted to his break from Christianity in ways that are never explicitly thematized in his work. In *Nietzsche* this same Augustinian concept of faith as constancy or *Sichhalten* plays a crucially polemical role. In volume 2 of the English edition, in a section entitled "The Thought of Return as a Belief," Heidegger asks why Nietzsche thinks that "the most important characterization of the thought of the eternal return of the same" is its status as a belief. Nietzsche, Heidegger notes, suggests that the doctrine itself "contains more than all religions."[127] The thought of eternal recurrence, he adds, "defines the essence of religion anew on its own terms. The thought itself is to say what kind of religion shall exist for what kind of human being in the future. The thought itself is to define the relationship to God—and to define God himself."[128] The link Heidegger espies between the Eternal Return and the Will to Power is key for understanding how the Eternal

Return redefines religion. This link depends first on Nietzsche's definition of faith, which Heidegger draws from a 1887 aphorism: "What is a belief? How does it originate? Every belief is a *holding-for-true* [*Für-wahr-halten*]."[129] Heidegger instantly ties this species of faith to representation as he does in the *Contributions*. Faith in its Nietzschean sense "means to take what is represented as true, and thus it also means to hold fast to the true and hold firm in the true."[130] Such a holding-for-true has the character of an "ought," rather than an "is," or the character of a command. It entails dictating what and how beings ought to be. The one who wills beings to return eternally grasps beings as conforming to the eternalizing affirmation or yes-saying that wills their return. To this degree the Eternal Return redefines religion on the basis of the Will to Power. If, according to Heidegger, Nietzchean belief is parasitic upon representation and if it consists in grasping firmly the particular representation of beings recurring eternally as a whole, then belief itself must exemplify the drive to secure beings as a whole in conformity with the directives issued by the willing subject. This is indeed the conclusion reached by Heidegger: "To believe in Nietzsche's sense is thus to fixate the ever-changing throng of beings we encounter in the specific guiding representations of whatever is permanent and ordered. To believe, furthermore, is to entrench oneself in this fixating relationship in the very terms of what is fixated."[131] The fact that it is impossible either to prove or to disprove the Eternal Return as a doctrine is a sign that it serves as an ontological determination of beings as a whole. The doctrine is problematic not because it cannot be refuted, but rather because it determines the way of being an entity as sheer persistence through iterability.

The fact that the notion of faith as *Sichhalten* or constancy—the constancy of one who persists in confronting the radical incertitude engendered by the absence of Being—is invoked as a corrective against Nietzsche hints at a conceptual reversal in Heidegger's corpus, one that advances an immanent criticism of *Being and Time*. This reversal becomes clear if we consider that the invocation of faith as *Sichhalten* against its Nietzschean variation must be judged not only against Heidegger's efforts during the 1930s and 1940s to bracket faith from thinking, but also against his attempts during the 1920s to distinguish radically between philosophy and theology. In March 1927, Heidegger delivered a lecture entitled "Phenomenology and Theology"[132] at Tübingen. The lecture handles theology exclusively as Christian theology, a discourse embedded solely within the drama of Christian revelation as it unfolds historically over time. Its central conceit is the difference between phenomenology and theology as scientific discourses. As the science of Being, phenomenology is first philosophy, whereas in its ideal construction theology is by contrast an ontic or regional science handling neither the Being of beings as a whole, nor Being itself, but the particular entity or *positum* that constitutes the life of faith. In its formal definition theology is a "conceptual knowing of that which first of all allows Christianity to become an originally historicasl event, a knowing of that which we call *Christianness* pure and simple."[133] And Christianness can be resolved into two major components. First, its ground is the crucified God, the entity exclusively revealed to faith and which first gives rise to the possibility of Christianness. Second, the existential context opened by the crucified God and to which this God is revealed is called faith. Faith is "a way of existence of the human (being) that . . . arises not from the human or spontaneously through him or her, but rather from that which is revealed in and with this way of existence, from what is believed."[134] The existential totality of what is disclosed by faith in its structural and dispositional specificity constitutes the *positum* for theology as an ontic science.

Now, this characterization of theology as an ontic science in 1927 is much more ambiguous than many commentators are willing to admit. Though Heidegger relegates Christian theology to the status of an ontic science, he insists that the status of its *positum* distinguishes Christian theology from all other sciences. The essential feature in every science, he states elsewhere in 1928, "is that it constitutes itself in the objectification of something already in some way unveiled, antecedently given."[135] Yet in the 1927 lecture the *positum* of Christian theology fails to meet this criterion. Both the crucified God and the totality of existence disclosed in relation to it are not antecedently given prior to adopting the stance of faith to which it is revealed. The implication is that the scientific status of theological discourse can be neither recognized nor adjudicated apart from the enactment of Christianness itself. In Heidegger's words, "faith understands itself only in believing."[136] This claim may seem to be in line with similar ones he makes about Dasein, who can understand itself only in existing. But the crucial difference is that the understanding of faith does not simply render explicit what is implicit in the structure of existence. Instead it works out something that is properly speaking extrinsic to the universal conditions of existentiality that define Dasein as factical. This explains why Heidegger offers us nothing more than an *ideal* construction of theology as a fully autonomous ontic science, without expounding further upon the structure of attestation unique to this science. The fact that the difference between philosophy and theology bears not only upon the specificity of the Christian *positum* but additionally or even primarily upon the unique structure of Christian attestation is signaled in the crucial line pitting philosophy against *faith* rather than theology: "faith, as a specific possibility of existence, is in its innermost core the mortal enemy of the *form of existence* that is an essential part of *philosophy* and that is factically ever-changing. . . . This *existentiell opposition* between faithfulness and the free appropriation of one's whole Dasein is not first brought about by the sciences of theology and philosophy but is prior to them."[137] The point here is that the relation between faith and philosophy cannot be parsed in terms of a universal structure of existential categories that embraces the two as various modalities of enactment. Faith differs in its *form* or *structure* from the very existence that is rendered explicit in hermeneutic phenomenology. Heidegger thus entertains the possibility in 1927 that faith is situated beyond the reach of rational self-interpretation.

It is precisely this possibility that Heidegger uses to his advantage in the *Contributions* and in his *Nietzsche*, without acknowledging the complex history of its relation with his own attempt to spell out the structure of factical existence. The crucial point here is that the capacity of faith to *shatter* philosophical rationality as well as the portrayal of faith as the mortal enemy of philosophy, is now shifted onto the difference between philosophy and *thinking*. It provides Heidegger with a template for describing a new beginning after Nietzsche. Indeed, we saw above that in the last lines of "Nietzsche's Word: 'God Is Dead,'" Heidegger asserts that rationality is the adversary of thinking. If we combine this assertion with the observation that Heidegger's rejection of the Eternal Return as a form of belief amounts to a rejection of Nietzsche's redefinition of religion, and moreover if we add to this the observation that the concept of faith Heidegger uses to displace the Eternal Return as a form of belief is genealogically derivable from his own critical encounters with Augustine's corpus, then we are driven to conclude that one of Heidegger's primary tools in destroying Nietzsche is a concept of faith that is structurally identical to the one he identified in 1927 as the mortal enemy of philosophy. In this manner the initial opposition in Heidegger's corpus between Descartes and Augustine is subtly re-inscribed in critical conversation with Nietzsche.

How does this conclusion bear upon the question of justification? Even as Heidegger faults Nietzsche for thinking truth in terms of justification, he still refuses to give up using the concept: "justice," Heidegger writes in "Nietzsche's Word: 'God Is Dead,'" "is the truth of beings determined by Being itself."[138] The definition, which seeks to express an ontological rather than a juridical or ethical conception of justice, seems to express what is enacted from within the dispositional stance of faith as *Sichhalten*. What, then, does the genealogical tie between this concept of faith and its Augustinian source tell us about the meaning of justice in Heidegger's later work, and about his charge that Nietzsche failed to think justice as the essence of the truth of beings?

REPENTANCE AND VIOLENCE

In his 1951–1952 lectures *What Is Called Thinking?*, Heidegger reiterates the charge that Nietzsche abhors transience, and that his pure affirmation of the past stems from a fundamental resentment against the "it was," while underscoring the need to find alternative ways of affirming the pastness of the past. In this vein Heidegger draws a brief yet evocative contrast between the doctrine of the eternal return and a generic conception of Christian repentance. The contrast bears upon two diametrically opposed ways of taking up the past. Through the "will of the eternal recurrence"[139] Nietzsche allegedly reconciles himself with becoming by willing "back" the past in its future iteration. Christian dogma, on the other hand, "knows another way in which the 'it was' may be willed back—repentance [*die Reue*]." The opposition is a curious one, as it sets Nietzsche's Cartesian manner of determining beings as a whole in terms of subjective certitude against the effects of atonement in the Christian drama of justification. "Repentance," Heidegger continues, "takes man where it is meant to take him, to the deliverance from the 'it was.'"[140] In short, the act of repentance which frees the soul from its sinful past offers an alternative form of being delivered from the "it was."

The opposition reflects the thesis stated above, namely that Heidegger's way of fending off Nietzsche is much more encoded by his critical encounters with theological texts than he is willing to admit. But the question is whether or not this opposition between Nietzschean justification and Christian repentance is reinscribed by Heidegger's own questioning of Being. On the one hand, Heidegger plainly states that Christian repentance is no less metaphysical than Nietzsche's eternal return: "Sin is the lack of faith, the revolt against God as the redeemer. If repentance, joined to the forgiveness of sin and only that way, can will the return of the past, this will of repentance, seen in the terms of thinking, is always determined metaphysically, and is possible only that way—possible only by its relation to the eternal will of the redeeming God."[141] On the other hand, Heidegger precludes himself from invoking repentance as an alternative to Nietzschean metaphysics only to the extent that repentance designates the relation with a redeeming God. If, that is, the form of relation Heidegger associates with repentance could be de-theologized—stripped of the *positum* of faith as its content, and mapped onto the question of Being—then it could provide for him the basis for conceptualizing justification as the truth of beings determined by Being itself.

This gesture—namely, the de-theologization of repentance—can be discerned in the pages of the *Contributions* at the moment when Heidegger reformulates the Nietzschean Eternal Return so as to define justification as letting-beings-be. This reformulation is the positive yield of his effort to replace the concept of care with that of restraint. Indeed the counterconcept to Christian repentance and Nietzschean justification hides in plain sight in the *Contributions*. It is foregrounded to such a degree that it is easily overlooked. At its outset Heidegger suggests somewhat cryptically that the project launched in the *Contributions* is primarily designed to carry out "the retrieval [*Wiederbringung*] of beings from out of the truth of Being."[142] The assertion takes for granted that beings as such have become disconnected from the truth of Being and must be re-grounded with respect to it. It thereby makes up for a significant oversight in Nietzsche, who, according to "Nietzsche's Word: 'God Is Dead,'" allegedly failed to think justification in a sufficiently ontological manner.

In short, what the *Contributions* calls retrieval or *Wiederbringung* is nothing other than the positive notion of justice Heidegger mentions in passing in "Nietzsche's Word: 'God Is Dead.'" In each case it is a question of re-grounding the essence of beings out of the truth of Being. And in the *Contributions*, Heidegger is particularly clear about two aspects of this dynamic—first, that Dasein is the conduit through which this re-grounding is enacted from the side of Being; second, that the re-grounding itself provides the properly ontological concept of *repetition* and thereby represents an effort to reconceptualize the Eternal Return. The sacrificial dimension of retrieving beings from out of the truth of Being is explicitly broached in the *Contributions*: "In the other beginning, all beings are sacrificed up to Beyng, and only from there do beings as such first receive their truth."[143] Through this sacrifice Dasein receives back from Being the truth of beings as a whole. The link between this sacrifice and the Nietzschean concept of the eternal return is not difficult to discern in the *Contributions*, in which Heidegger explicitly refers to Being as the eternal.[144] Moreover when Heidegger explains how the retrieval of beings is accomplished, he makes use of terms that play off the Christian themes of repentance and redemption as well as the Nietzschean Eternal Return. If Being is eternal, he asks, "then what does *eternalization* mean?"[145] Posing this question makes sense only against the background of Heidegger's charge that Nietzsche's thought falls prey to the will to rule and dominate. It matters only in light of Heidegger's sense that Nietzsche failed to describe eternalization in adequate terms, and that the theme of eternalization can be utilized in describing the self-withholding of Being. But if eternalization is not what Nietzsche took it to be—if, that is, it does not mean to impress upon becoming the character of Being—then what does it mean?

In *Contributions* §263 Heidegger employs the terminology of *Being and Time* to redefine Da-sein itself as the Eternal Return. This redefinition targets the notion of "thrown project" spelled out in the 1927 existential analytic, which is now taken up as the eternalization of beings. To show this, Heidegger begins from the side of projection: "Projection: the human being as casting oneself loose from beings and into Beyng, without beings as such having already been opened up."[146] This notion of projection is not possible from the perspective of *Being and Time*, which makes clear that in every act of understanding, the bond between entities and the understanding is unbreakable. What Heidegger calls "casting loose"[147] in 1936–1938, namely Dasein's ability to shake free of beings in order to interrogate Being directly, is scarcely surmised in 1927. A decade later, however, this free-throw becomes the defining feature of existence, coterminous with the Dasein in the human. It suggests that the understanding frees itself from every ontic foundation in its relation with Being. Indeed, it suggests that this freedom is always already achieved. This liberation from beings provides the basis for redefining the Dasein itself *as* the Eternal Return: "The human being hitherto: the one who, in casting loose, has immediately turned back [*Zurückgekehrte*], the one who in that way for the first time has traversed the *differentiation* between beings and Beyng though lacking the capacity to experience this differentiation itself, let alone ground it."[148] Here the Nietzschean Eternal Return is defined with respect to the ontological difference. Da-sein is the "one who turns back" (*Zurückkehrer*)[149] from the free-throw that projects it onto Being and free of beings, the one who holds itself toward the self-withholding of Being. The parallel with the concept of faith rehabilitated elsewhere in the *Contributions* is evident. Seen from the side of beings, Dasein is the one who comes back from Being; seen from the side of Being, Dasein is the one who holds itself toward Being, i.e. the one who has "faith." And the interplay between these two is nothing other than the "justification" of beings from out of the truth of Being—a justification that can be read as displacing the Nietzschean Eternal Return.

All lines of our argument now converge toward this curious reinterpretation of temporality in the guise of the Eternal Return. We see clearly now why Heidegger defends displacement as a kind of mantic ecstasy with respect to all existing forms of rational discourse. It is starting from the sacrificial dimension of the *Contributions* that he can diagnose, retrospectively, the *original sin* of *Being and Time*. For, what comes light within the *Contributions* is not simply a speculative effort to detach the notion of Being as standing presence or the *nunc stans* from the doctrine of the Eternal Return. It is also an effort to redefine the temporality of Dasein on this basis—to cross out its initial conceptualization in *Being and Time* as the horizon for the understanding of Being, and to lay the groundwork for the givenness of temporality starting from the side of Being itself—in a manner that relies upon the dynamic of faith as the capacity to endure the perpetual crisis[150] inaugurated by the self-withholding of Being. This capacity is what Heidegger calls the "returnership" (*Rückkehrerschaft*) of Da-sein. Included within its concept is the notion that Da-sein offers up its own Being to Being itself: "In casting loose, the human being is grounded in that which this being cannot fabricate [*machen*] but can only risk [*wagen*] as a possibility, namely, Da-*sein*. To be sure this only if one does not turn back, and never turns back, to oneself as someone who appeared in the first casting loose in the guise . . . of the natural being [*physei on*] or as animal [*zōon*]."[151] From this it is clear that the retrieval of beings enacted in Da-sein no longer turning back to itself signals a movement for Heidegger beyond the metaphysical figure of man as rational animal.

From our perspective, however, it is also clear that in this attempt to distinguish rigorously between possibility as *making* (*machen*) and possibility as *risking* (*wagen*) Heidegger reclaims the very distinction between facticity and presence-to-hand that initially motivated his very first turn to Augustine as prefiguring factical being. Although he does not describe the justificatory movement of this no-return in the *Contributions* as an act of repentance, Heidegger does describe it as akin to salvation, *Retten*.[152] In this salvation the trace of a former one, theological in character, is simultaneously effaced and retained. Da-sein paves the way for this salvation inasmuch as questioning Being is "the only way for us to come to ourselves and thereby clear a path for the original salvation [*Rettung*], i.e. the justification of the West out of its history."[153] On the one hand, it is clear that this salvation is devoid of religious significance: "Occurring here is not a deliverance or redemption."[154] On the other hand, the formal features of this "saving [*Rettung*] into Being,"[155] remain genealogically indebted to the concept of Christian faith Heidegger initially excludes, in 1927, from ontology as first philosophy, and only much later, in 1936–1938, reintroduces into the question of Being.

What results is a conception of justification that is closely related to, but equidistant from, its Nietzschean articulation and its Christian theological significance. It is precisely the difference that matters here, insofar as it allows us to reach a final conclusion regarding the way in which the later Heidegger continues to draw upon his theological heritage. What, in short, is the meaning of justification after Nietzsche? In the texts of Heidegger's middle period, what links Nietzschean justification to Platonic idealism as well as Christian conceptions of justification is the status of the eternal form as that which is truly real. As Augustine writes: "God loves us, such as we shall be, not such as we are now. As for those He so loves, He keeps them for eternity [*nos amat Deus quales futuri sumus, non quales sumus. Quales enim amat, tales in aeternum conservat*]."[156] The eternal conservation of the form or essence of the creature on the part of the creator is for Heidegger metaphysically identical to the enframing of all beings in the Nietzschean dispensation of new values. Rejecting the Nietzschean concept of justification, Heidegger is effectively trying to expunge the *rationes aeternae* from the very concept of justification.

If this is indeed the guiding impulse behind retrieving beings from out of the truth of Being, then it is evident that the *Contributions* does not abandon the initial opposition between Descartes and Augustine in Heidegger's work so much as it expounds upon this opposition in a novel, if obscure way: at the end of metaphysics, we are told in the *Contributions*, one is faced with a choice. Either one may follow "the last, definitive approach of Nietzsche, saving oneself by reducing reason . . . to life."[157] Or one can resist this movement which pushes the theoretical Pelagianism allegedly inherent in the Cartesian project to its logical conclusion by yet again building up the so-called Augustinian question concerning the relation betwen *vita* and *veritas*, life and truth, in the form of the question concerning the relation between Da-sein and the truth of Being itself.

All of this, in sum, is to suggest the following: If the role Heidegger assigns in the *Contributions* to the concepts of justification and retrieval take over the conciliatory function he associates elsewhere with Christian repentance and the Nietzschean Eternal Return, then the project announced in the *Contributions*, that of offering up or sacrificing beings to Being, can be read as the philosophical equivalent of a confession. But the project undeniably extends and radicalizes the "sin" to which it confesses, pursuing in a more resolute manner the errant question of the meaning of Being launched in *Being and Time*. The silent rejoinders Heidegger issues against the 1927 treatise involve rethinking how Dasein holds itself out toward Being in its withdrawal—a structure of transcendence which, I have tried to show, is *stamped* Augustinian. They are also tied to his effort after *Being and Time* to escalate what this treatise calls the *violence of all interpretation*: "Existential analysis, constantly has the character of doing violence [*Gewaltsamkeit*]."[158] In the 1927 treatise violence targets the everyday or fallen intepretation of existence; the authentic truth of Dasein's Being must be wrested away from it, by actively combating Dasein's tendency toward self-alienation.[159] The attempt to project Dasein upon its Being cannot avoid doing violence to it. This is because existential interpretation does violence to Dasein in its very Being, projects this Being onto an idea of existence that is merely presupposed, in order to free its phenomenal content. This is the "factical ideal of Dasein,"[160] which in *Being and Time* is anticipatory resoluteness. By contrast, the *Contributions* does violence to the factical ideal of anticipatory resoluteness itself. To this degree the treatise demands to be read not simply as analogous to a confession of praise (i.e., the offering up of beings to Being) but also as a *retraction*. It is not only the Nietzschean concept that is undermined by rejecting faith as holding-for-true; it is also the one which Heidegger himself espouses in 1927 and which he applies to anticipatory resoluteness: "To any truth, there belongs a corresponding holding-for-true."[161] Thus, to the degree that the *Contributions* portrays Da-sein as leaping past beings to interrogate Being directly, it is impossible to avoid concluding that the treatise effectively *takes back* or *retracts* the factical ideal of Dasein undergirding the ontic foundation of ontological investigation in *Being and Time*.

It does so, however, precisely by re-inscribing the structure of resoluteness in connection with retraction. Authenticity in the 1927 treatise is not simply a matter of actualizing one's potentialities or holding them for true. It also involves recognizing that because one's possibilities are grounded solely in Dasein's existential stretch, one must be ready to take back or to retract these possibilities: "The certainty of resolution signifies that one *holds oneself free* for the possibility of a *taking-back*."[162] This taking back is realized in death: "In its death, Dasein must take back simply everything."[163] For its part, the *Contributions* retains the link between retraction and death. Death is here "the highest and utmost attestation of Beyng."[164] At the same time, the project of retrieving beings from out of the truth of Being takes on the characteristics of this highest testimony. And this attestation, in its violent gesture of shaking free of beings, is nothing other than the *care of Being* or restraint. This violence marks the furthest step in Heideggerian de-theologization, which cannot take aim at Nietzsche without targeting *Being and Time*. This is the price Heidegger must pay in his confrontation with Nietzsche. It is also what allows him to take on the Nietzschean mantle.

The last section of the 1961 *Nietzsche* volumes is entitled "Nihilism as Determied by the History of Being." In it Heidegger divides Nietzschean metaphysics in two, arguing that Nietzsche thinks beings as a whole ontologically as will-to-power, whereas he treats the highest instance of Being "theologically as the eternal recurrence of the same."[165] Read by Heidegger, the Nietzschean death of God reveals the mechanism of secularization, albeit in a way that remains hidden from Nietzsche himself. The death of God does not spell the end of theology, but rather it allows Christianity to live on after its demise, giving rise to its secular descendants. The doctrine of the Eternal Return is one such descendant according to Heidegger: "Such metaphysical theology is of course a negative theology of a peculiar kind. Its negativity is revealed in the expression 'God is dead.'"[166] The production of Christianity's secular descendants occurs not via the elevation of an entity to the position occupied by divinity in classical metaphysics, but rather via the overwriting of this position by alternative forms of sovereignty—in Nietzsche's case, by the unchecked power of the will. In this sense, the statement, "God is dead," is not the confession of an atheist, but rather the confession of a metaphysician, one in which "every path toward the experience of Being itself is obliterated."[167] In light of this analysis, the violence of retraction spelled out above takes on its true significance as an act of de-theologization: the attempt to reclaim the Augustinian index of care so as to destroy the idea of existence set forth in *Being and Time* seeks to interrogate Being itself without relying upon a being par excellence, a "highest" being. It seeks to avoid regenerating metaphysical theology, even a negative one. First raised in 1926,[168] the prospect of determining Being free of beings is not achieved until the *Contributions* seeks to separate itself from all metaphysical theology: "More eminently than any being is Beyng itself. What *is* most eminently "*is*" no longer."[169] In a single move, this last line retracts the ontical ideal of *Being and Time* even as it tries to leap past Nietzschean metaphysics. De-theologizing the latter, it cannot avoid disavowing the former. This disavowal, however, coincides with the call to intensify the search for Being which first gave rise to the idea of existence Heidegger now abandons in attacking Nietzsche.

Thus, if the project of the *Contributions* is formally speaking analogous to a confession of *sin*, then it is one by which Heidegger vehemently reasserts the very thing for which he repents. In Heidegger's mode of attestation, retraction augments the violence intrinsic to existential interpretation according to *Being and Time*. This violence reaches its highest pitch in a mode of attestation that holds itself apart from metaphysical theology while reformulating "the language of beings as the language of Beyng."[170] This attestation "must retract from beings . . . must distinguish itself from them and be grasped . . . by placing itself *before* beings, as *pro*-ducing them."[171] In this manner Da-sein bears witness to Beyng, the source of the essence or truth of beings, by violently usurping "an expression that, linguistically, pertains properly to beings."[172] In other words, Da-sein names Being by violently imposing upon it the language tailored to fit beings. Heidegger sanctions this imposition without thinking the link between the form of attestation directed at Being and the religious ideal of attestation that informs it. The full complexity of Heidegger's unsteady relationship with this ideal is re-inscribed each and every time Heidegger sets out to reestablish contact with Being in its self-withholding. To this extent the remnant of Augustinian anthropology has a very specific mode of appearance in Heidegger's corpus, one that mimics Beyng itself, as it is described in the *Contributions*: "*Only what is unique is repeatable*. It alone has in itself the ground of the necessity of a reversion to it and a resumption of its incipience."[173] Like Beyng, the theological remnant carries within itself the necessity of its constant reiteration. Its limitless iterability allows Heidegger to portray his own *retraction* of care as shoring up the unity of philosophy from start to finish.

CONCLUSION

Difference and De-Theologization

"A pure illogicality."[1] That is how Heidegger first defined the philosophy of religion in the fall of 1922, and how he continued to describe it thereafter. What he left undeveloped, if not entirely unthought, is how this illogicality shifted roles in his work over time. The issue of its transformation raises the stakes of the present investigation. We saw that in 1920–1921 Heidegger described the phenomenology of religious life in paradoxical terms, as the act of comprehending the incomprehensible. When he abandoned this project, he was poised to re-signify theological terms in an effort to expunge the remains of theology from philosophy. But when *Being and Time* failed to achieve its stated goal of exhibiting the meaning of Being, he was forced to revise this strategy. Mindfully or not, he then manipulated terms he had de-theologized during the 1920s, exploiting their ambiguity from 1930 on to overhaul the question of Being. This allowed him, first, to rethink the structure of temporality; second, to reject Nietzsche's conceptions of eternity, faith, and justification; third, to shed light on the earliest trace of Being in pre-Socratic texts; and finally, to mark the transition from philosophy to post-metaphysical "thinking" by recuperating existential structures he dismissively associated with Christian theology in his early writings.

This is the narrative I have told over six chapters. But the fact that the later Heidegger's determinations of Dasein in terms of restraint, and of Being in terms of retraction, turn out to be etymologically linked to Augustine should give us pause. We saw in the foregoing chapters that Heidegger's subtle manipulations of his own de-theologized terms allowed him to undertake an immanent criticism of *Being and Time* without having to explicitly disown his early work. We also saw that rearticulating these same de-theologized terms provided Heidegger with some way of distinguishing his own thinking of Being from all existing conceptions of rationality. At the very least, then, these features of the later works suggest that the break between philosophy and religiosity or divine revelation is hardly monolithic in Heidegger, but instead that it functions differently in its different contexts. By way of conclusion, then, we must consider what the conceptual stratagems explored above tell us, finally, about how the logic of de-theologization informs the Heideggerian critique of metaphysics. Conversely we must ask what this critique reveals, ultimately, about the logic of de-theologization.

METAPHYSICS AND TRANSPOSITION

Appended to the 1961 edition of the *Nietzsche* lectures is a treatise, originally composed during 1944–1946, entitled "Nihilism as Determined by the History of Being."[2] In this treatise, Heidegger explains why he sees Nietzsche as the last metaphysician and onto-theologian par excellence. He also begins to explain why metaphysics is constituted onto-theologically. The metaphysical question of Being, the essay tells us, primarily interrogates the essence of entities rather than the truth of Being itself. This form of the question tends to neglect Being altogether, leaving it uninterrogated; metaphysics studies beings as beings by seeking out their general characteristics. It thus is onto-logy because it appeals to a common denominator or a shared essence (*essentia*) whenever it sets out to identify a being as a being. Part of this search for a common denominator, however, involves identifying one being in particular that exemplifies this shared essence. Metaphysics is thus also theo-logy, to the extent that it identifies a highest being or an entity par excellence that can be used to fix the meaning of that which truly exists (*existentia*). Invoking this entity par excellence as a standard for beings in general, metaphysics interprets this existent entity as the ground of beings as a whole.

Throughout the present study I have described de-theologization as enacting the transposition of predicates from one realm to another, the adoption and re-signification of theological terms within secular philosophical texts. The later Heidegger's diagnosis of metaphysics as onto-theology, however, requires us to revise our description of de-theologization. This is because it prevents us from adopting the division between philosophy and theology as our primary frame of reference for understanding the dynamic of transposition. Furthermore, the diagnosis has in view a radically expanded conception of metaphysics that envelops the division between philosophy and theology within a larger rubric of Being as difference. Within this rubric, Heidegger uncovers a transposition of predicates within philosophy itself. And this transposition, in turn, allows him to describe in novel terms how philosophy relates to theology in two main senses—namely, theology as a division of special metaphysics, and theology as revealed theology.

In the "Nihilism" treatise, Heidegger argues that metaphysics, whenever it asks the question of Being, inevitably appeals to the meaning of beings in general as well as to the meaning of a highest being in particular. But how are these two components of metaphysics as the question of Being related to each other? How are they brought together? "Theo-logy derives the essence [*essentia*] of the entity from ontology. Onto-logy, whether knowingly or not, transposes [*verlegt*] the entity with respect to its *existentia*, that is, as what exists, into the first ground, which theology goes on to represent."[3] Theo-logy in its search for the entity par excellence takes its lead from ontology, borrowing from it the criteria used to identify an entity par excellence. Onto-logy responds in kind by transposing this entity into the ground of beings, treating it as first ground. This latter entity is the one which theology then represents as the highest being. A double transfer, then, the first component of which is described here as a transposition, binds together onto-logy with theo-logy. This implies that each and every rational conception of the highest being, or *theos*, is essentially the product of a dynamic akin to de-theologization. This twofold process is exemplified in Nietzsche's thought. In Heidegger's view, Nietzsche interprets the essence of beings in general ontologically as the Will to Power and the existence of beings as the Eternal Recurrence of the same. The 1944–1946 "Nihilism" treatise thus claims that these two interpretations solidify metaphysics as a coherent system and that Being itself is destined to "stay away" (*ausbleiben*)[4] from this system after Nietzsche.

Heidegger would have us believe that what distinguishes his own thinking of Being from Nietzsche's completion of metaphysics is not that it avoids the transposition which locks onto-logy into place along with theo-logy, or that it circumvents this default of Being. Rather it is the ability to recognize the inevitability of the transposition itself, and on this basis, to glimpse the unthought character of Being's withdrawal. This withdrawal is thus the manner in which Being presently remains what it "is." The thinker, Heidegger writes in the "Nihilism" treatise, "follows Being in its self-withdrawal [*Sichentziehung*], follows it in the sense that it lets Being itself go."[5] Letting Being itself remain unthought is thus the primary sense in which thinking takes a "step back" after metaphysics into its history, which is reinterpreted with the unthought character of Being in mind.

From the fact that Being stays away from metaphysics, Heidegger draws the following conclusions. First, if there is presently no avoiding the default of Being, then language is necessarily suspect. All extant philosophical terms must be viewed as tainted by the transposition that constitutes metaphysics as onto-theology. Even *Being* itself is now suspect: "the name *Being*," Heidegger writes, "loses its naming power in the step back because it always unwittingly says 'presence and permanence.'"[6] In addition to employing the archaic form *Beyng* (*Seyn*), Heidegger replaces *Being* with two terms. First, the default of Being is projected temporally as an advent or a coming without arrival. To think Being in its default "means to become aware of the promise [*Versprechen*] as which promise Being itself 'is.'"[7] Being is here signified in purely futural terms as a "promise" beyond all verification. Second, because Being remains unthought, it also stands beyond all relation, as Agamben notes: "the being together of the being and Being does not have the form of relation."[8] Instead the ontological difference now has the form of what Heidegger calls use or usage or *Brauch*, a term that is linked in Heidegger, as I have shown, to Augustinian *fruitio*, signifying primarily that Being stands in need of beings while making a claim upon them.

Neither term, however, designates Being properly. The chief sign of this, Heidegger notes, is that we cannot express Being as unthought without relying upon spatial metaphors, as if the history of metaphysics were a spatial region which Being avoids like the plague: "there comes to be a relation to something like a place [*Ort*], away from which the staying away remains what it is."[9] The strong version of this proposition distinguishes two ways of relating to emplacement, two diametrically opposed topologies. The first topology resolutely employs the spatiality of objects to conceptualize the withdrawal of Being, whereas the second topology works in reverse by deriving the sense of emplacement from Being insofar as it remains unthought. This second topology heralds a shift in Heidegger's understanding of unconcealment, which is now defined as the "shelter" or "abode"[10] in which the withdrawal of Being remains what it is. In line with this, Heidegger refers to "the *Dasein* in man"[11] as the topos or place in which the forgetting of Being can be encountered as such. But neither shift assuages our sense that Heidegger, having grown suspicious that all language is necessarily metaphysical, remains unable to avoid the charges he levels against Nietzsche. Indeed, once Heidegger has delineated the mechanism of transposition at the heart of metaphysics, the prospect of finding a non-metaphysical language all but disappears.

This is precisely why Heidegger, in setting out to identify the default of Being as the ontological grounds for nihilism, is forced to confront the possibility that transcendental reflection is in fact fully determined by what is actual: "The question remains," Heidegger writes, "in fact emerges for the first time, whether the 'essence' of Being comes from entities, whether the entity, as actual, in all its concatenations, is capable of determining actuality, Being; or whether the effectuality that stems from Being itself calls forth everything actual."[12] Prompted by the twin assertions that Nietzsche completes metaphysics and that after him Being remains radically unthought, this question pushes to its logical conclusion the observation that a transposition constitutes metaphysics onto-theologically. If, that is, every meaning of beings in general results from transposing into the ground of beings the figure of an entity par excellence, then actuality is destined to be responsible for every single determination of Being. In Heidegger's terminology, this question asks if the Being of entities can render utterly inaccessible the truth of Being itself. Here in the "Nihilism" treatise, this question is embedded within a meditation on the horrors of twentieth-century politics. If it is the case that actuality has the power to render Being fully inaccessible, then from Heidegger's perspective there is no stopping the instrumentalization of the world, the destructive onslaught of modern scientific technology.

We cannot underestimate the urgency or significance of this question in the Heideggerian trajectory. As Heidegger acknowledges elsewhere, this question threatens to undercut his entire inquiry into the truth of Being: "can thinking... even be grounded on historical findings? This, objection, which threatens our entire enterprise even in its first steps—how will we get it out of the way?"[13] A genuine threat indeed: the objection noted here is not one that simply hinders Heidegger in his effort to display the truth of Being. It is rather one that threatens to cut off all access to Being at its root, including the sense of Being as self-withdrawal. But did Heidegger ever truly *confront* this possibility? Did he ever treat it as a genuine possibility, or did he simply protect his thought against this threat? In making the switch from ontology to being-historical thinking, Heidegger believes that he succeeds in getting this possibility "out of the way." The history of Being, designed to show that the history of metaphysics consists of a series of "stampings" of Being that give rise to ontological concepts, is Heidegger's attempt to interpret the actuality of the metaphysical tradition as a function of the truth of Being. This history rethinks metaphysics as the "dominion"[14] of error, a series of entanglements that fail to do justice to Being. And yet it also aims to think history starting from the epochal determinations of Being, thereby reinforcing, in its own way, the division between historical and philosophical knowledge, or rather the dependence of the former upon the latter. In this sense, Heidegger's being-historical thinking, though it never reverses the order of the sciences by reducing philosophy to mere historical knowledge, remains haunted by the suspicion that altogether avoiding this reduction is nearly impossible, and consequently that one can never fully detach the inquiry into the truth of Being from historical knowledge of beings in their Being. To this extent Heidegger's being-historical thinking is marked by an anxiety regarding the possibility of its own impossibility. Can we, however, detect any alternative ways in which Heidegger's texts deal with this unsettling threat?

BEING AND DE-THEOLOGIZATION

The threat mentioned in the "Nihilism" treatise seems to point beyond the Heideggerian domain. One could easily assume that Heidegger was either unwilling or unable to counter this threat. But this is not entirely so. The threat that the thinking of Being remains trapped in representationalist and historical modes of reflection lies at the heart of the 1957 text entitled "The Onto-theo-logical Constitution of Metaphysics." There, Heidegger's attempt to dispel it points back to the logic of de-theologization spelled out above: this text represents a last-ditch effort on his part to provide ontological grounds for the transposition internal to metaphysics, and thus to explain why theological terms are always necessarily transposed into the ontological realm.

At the outset of "The Onto-theo-logical Constitution of Metaphysics," Heidegger distinguishes his own manner of thinking from Hegelian dialectics, arguing that his inquiry targets the ontological difference as it appears in the "step back" into the history of metaphysics. This "step back" keeps in view what is unthought by the tradition. Here onto-theo-logy is defined as "the still *unthought* unity of the essential nature of metaphysics."[15] As we have said, the ontological character of metaphysics stems from the fact that, in its "free and spontaneous self-involvement with beings as such"[16] philosophy necessarily determines what beings are in general, whereas its theological character arises from the act of transposing what truly is into the ground of beings as a whole. The bond formed between onto-logy and theo-logy ensures that Being is always "previously marked as ground, while thinking—since it belongs together with Being—gathers itself toward Being as its ground."[17] The language of ground is not prioritized in the "Nihilism" treatise; by contrast, in the 1957 "Onto-theological Constitution of Metaphysics" it describes how the question of beings as a whole is answered in terms of causation. Ontology, as the inquiry into beings as beings, seeks to identify that which makes beings what they are—namely, their ground. This ground furnishes the basis for determining the entity par excellence. Theology as the inquiry into the highest being reveals the tendency of thinking to gather itself toward Being by transposing the meaning of beings in general into the figure of a highest existent par excellence, which functions as primary cause with respect to beings as a whole. As in the "Nihilism" treatise, metaphysics is here said to be constituted by means of a transposition: the meaning of Being discerned by ontology is transposed into the highest being par excellence, which in its turn completes the grounding function sought by the former. Unlike in the 1944–1946 "Nihilism" treatise, however, the question at the center of this 1957 text is how and why it is that ontology necessarily transposes the being par excellence into the ground of beings in general.

Its question, in other words, is why metaphysics takes shape as *theology* as well as onto-logy. The 1957 text, in other words, specifically interrogates theology: "the question about the onto-theological character of metaphysics is sharpened to the question: How does the deity enter into philosophy, not just modern philosophy, but philosophy as such?"[18] Heidegger quickly adds, however, that the latter question can be "sufficiently developed as a question"[19] only if we first clarify the nature of philosophy: "We can properly think through the question, How does the deity enter into philosophy?, only when that *to which* the deity is to come has become sufficiently clear: that is, philosophy itself."[20] Underpinning the essential constitution of metaphysics in its twofold nature is a crucial yet highly compact description of the ontological difference. We will quickly see that in the description of this ontological difference—or more specifically, in what conditions our understanding of it—Heidegger explains why it is that thinking Being as difference provokes the repetition and return of specifically theological language.

To see why metaphysics is theo-logy as well as onto-logy, Heidegger suggests, one must first gain insight into how Being is differentiated from beings, and thereby stands in relation to beings. It is not as though the ontological difference ever presents itself clearly and distinctly before us. In the step back into metaphysics, we are told, "Being here becomes present in the manner of a transition [*Übergang*] to beings."[21] What does "transition" mean here? We are familiar with Heidegger's assertion that Being, because it is not a being, never presents itself to us in the guise of an object or as an existent of any kind. We look around our world only to discover that we only ever encounter beings, and never Being itself. How then can Dasein glimpse this non-difference as a kind of transition?

The 1957 text suggests that we never encounter Being precisely because it is always in transit. It is always entirely taken up in the upsurge of beings before us. When we say that Being is beings, Heidegger argues, we make use of the third-person singular of Being in a transitive way: "The 'is' here speaks transitively, in transition."[22] To be clear, it does so in two ways. First, Being is said to bring beings to presence, as if thrusting them before us. Second, in this transition Being prevails over beings as a whole, but it is not in any way distinct from the arrival of beings in the realm of unconcealment: "Beings as such appear in the manner of their arrival [*Ankunft*] that keeps itself concealed in unconcealment."[23] Assigning Being this manner of appearance, Heidegger discerns its difference from beings. To the extent that it prevails over beings as a whole, Being remains radically absent from arrival as its mode of appearance or essence. The latter counts as the Being of beings, whereas the former gives itself only as a withdrawal. Being as that which "prevails" or comes over beings is not entirely identical with the Being of beings as arrival. The former is irreducible to the latter. The two are differentiated in a manner that is easily overlooked: "Being in the sense of the unconcealing coming-over [*Überkommnis*], and beings as such in the sense of arrival [*Ankunft*] that keeps itself concealed, are present, and thus differentiated."[24] Here we must cut through Heidegger's terminology in order to see how these two—the arrival of beings, and Being as prevailing over beings—stand related. In Stambaugh's translation, the decisive line is rendered as follows: "The difference of Being and beings, as the differentiation of coming-over and arrival, is the disenclosing-concealing perdurance [*entbergend-bergende Austrag*] of the two." These lines announce a new designation for the ontological difference: *Austrag* or *difference*.[25] Though one could render the term *Austrag*—Heidegger's term for the difference of Being and beings—in such a way as to suggest that Being in its transit somehow endures in its overwhelming difference from beings, one could just as easily construe the mode of its duration paradoxically as a kind of absence. In line with Agamben, that is, one could interpret this passage as indicating the discharge or self-withholding of Being from all relation, in the sense that Being and Dasein would remain together as devoid of all relation. To follow this interpretation would be to acknowledge that Being as *difference* is given precisely as the utter collapse of the ontological difference mentioned in "Anaximander's Saying."[26] It is also to interpret the figure of Being as overwhelming beings by referring it back to the self-withholding of Beyng in the *Contributions*. If we adopt this second option, then not only does the preliminary conclusion reached in the "Onto-theo-logical Constitution" text make much more sense than if we were to treat Being as perdurance, but also this option provides a firm basis for understanding the stakes of de-theologization as I have sought to delineate them throughout the present study.

Metaphysics attempts to hold Being steady as the ground of beings, but at the same time it takes hold of beings as grounded by Being as difference. When metaphysics differentiates between beings and Being in this manner, it unwittingly ensures the very collapse of the ontological difference it seeks to affirm: "The onto-theological constitution of metaphysics stems from the prevalence of that difference which keeps Being as the ground, and beings as what is grounded and what gives account, apart from and related to each other; and by this holding-apart it fully enacts the *Austrag*."[27] We see here that the very effort to distinguish between Being and beings—the effort, that is, to respect the ontological difference as such—necessarily if inadvertently brings metaphysics to completion. The metaphysical attempt at differentiating Being from beings consists in trying to account for beings by appealing to some figure of their cause. In trying to say how or what beings are in general, we necessarily look away from Being as unthought, and turn toward beings as actual.

This observation allows Heidegger to return to the guiding question of the essay as a whole, namely the question of how the deity enters philosophy. Heidegger's response to this question is well known. The deity, he maintains, enters philosophy as the *causa sui*. The *causa sui* "is the right name for the god of philosophy. Man can neither pray nor sacrifice to this god. Before the *causa sui* man can neither fall to his knees in awe nor can he play music and dance before this god."[28] The Cartesian definition of God as self-caused here represents the pure form of divinity in its onto-theological guise. Set in opposition to the god before whom one prays or sacrifices, this god is disparaged as being no more than an idol. Heidegger's explanation of how the deity enters into philosophy would seem to invite reflection upon the opposition between the god associated with the lived experience of faith—playing music and dancing—and the god of the philosophers, the mummified god derided by Nietzsche.

But in taking up this reflection, we risk falling prey to a lure. Such reflection overlooks the fact that in identifying the *causa sui* as the right name for the god of philosophy, Heidegger has not fully specified *how* the deity enters into philosophy. That is, he has not fully delineated the conditions for the possibility of its entrance into philosophy. He has merely identified *what* the deity is for philosophy. The figure of the *causa sui* tells us what the deity is for philosophy. It does not tell us how it is possible for this deity to enter philosophy to begin with. What about the entrance itself? It falls to the final paragraphs of the essay to specify how the deity can make its entrance: "The deity enters into philosophy through the difference [*Austrag*] which we at first think as the *precinct* [*Vorort*] of the essence of the difference between Being and beings. This difference constitutes the ground plan or outline in the structure of the essence of metaphysics."[29] This statement seems exceedingly obscure at first glance. If we approach it cautiously, however, its crucial significance becomes clear.

First, the statement tells us that the deity enters philosophy *through* the thought of difference, or better yet, on account of how we think Being as difference. It indicates that the entrance of the deity becomes possible precisely because we think Being as difference as the precinct or pre-place, *Vor-ort*, of the essence of the ontological difference. The term *Vorort* is admittedly obscure; it does not appear frequently in Heidegger's published writings. What he seems to have in view here is that when we "at first" think Being as difference, we necessarily think of it in spatial terms—namely, as a differentiation that somehow, somewhere takes place. According to this characterization, Being as difference can be thought only as a spatial leave-taking, an abandonment or withdrawal. Such terms certainly reflect Heidegger's own attempts to discern Being in its difference from beings in the "Nihilism" treatise described above, according to which the withdrawal of Being first determines unconcealment in its topological character as the *place* in which Being can remain what it is. Thus the only way we can make sense of the 1957 text is if it claims that we can think Being only in some minimally spatial terms, and thus through some minimal appeal to actuality. That is, in thinking Being as difference we must first establish a pre-spatial spatiality, a precinct or a *Vorort* in which we then imagine the differentiation of Being and beings as taking place by means of a withdrawal. To trace out this argument, we can say that from Heidegger's perspective this minimal resurgence of spatiality which stands at the root of all ontological concepts paves the way for the entire edifice of metaphysics that follows in its wake. Without this minimal representation of or appeal to place in its pre-spatial form (*Vo-*

rort), the outline of metaphysics could not be drawn. And without it, there would be no "place" for the deity to enter. Heidegger, in short, contends that the deity enters into philosophy precisely because we are constrained to think Being in terms of place. Each and every time we strive to think Being—or, as Heidegger might put it, each and every time we *think*—a god comes to mind. To put it otherwise, when we think Being we necessarily transpose a highest being into the ontological grounds of beings in general. If this is the case, then metaphysics is inescapable, and de-theologization is the very mechanism of thinking Being itself.

We can unpack this conclusion in two ways, both of which reflect back on the threat confronting Heidegger's thinking at this time. First, on this reading the "Onto-theo-logical Constitution" text posits that ontology is always theological for two reasons. Not only is it the case that ontological inquiry necessarily transposes the general essence of beings into their ground, portraying this ground as the highest existent. But additionally, the origins of theology as a dimension of metaphysics lie deeper than this. Prior to the theological destiny of ontology thought with respect to beings, the "fall" into beings takes place in the very attempt to think Being purified of all ontic reference. The resurgence of theological predicates is assured at the very moment we try to think Being in its difference from beings. This reading has the distinct advantage of resonating with Heidegger's interpretation of the Nietzschean death of God. In its uncanny aspect this death gives rise to new figures of divinity, not through the elevation of beings to the now-absent place that is "proper to God," which is the "region of causal effectivity and the preservation of beings as created beings,"[30] but rather through the superimposition of one realm upon another, the proliferation of functions that mask the ineffectiveness of the deity after the proclamation of its demise.[31] Second, as I have interpreted it, the term *Vorort* in the passage quoted above designates the first of all places, or better yet, the pre-place that situates all other places, akin to the Platonic figuring of *chōra*. If the deity enters philosophy precisely when we at first conjure this site as a topos before all placement, then it must be the case that thinking creates the minimal conditions for the deity either to enter or to stay away. In this sense, the deity's comings or goings would be predetermined by an infinitesimal resurgence of representational thinking, the presentiment of a locale at which the ontological difference is thought as taking place. Does the 1957 text point beyond this resurgence of representational thinking? Does it glimpse a way to construe difference that might stave off the condition for the rebirth of onto-theology?

The text ends without pointing a way forward, though this could hardly count as an oversight on Heidegger's part. The text is designed not to answer the question, but to build it up and to let it resonate as a question. The question so developed, but thus not answered, is in this case, "How does the deity enter philosophy?" From the manner in which this question is developed it is now possible to see that it leads back to the question of de-theologization, linking it with the threat that Heidegger found so unsettling: the 1957 diagnosis of metaphysics as onto-theology offers a possible explanation as to why rational reflection persists in thinking divinity in terms of *place*, while implicitly referring a wide range of concepts back to how we think difference in general.

In this regard, we can radicalize the possibility glimpsed in the conclusion to the 1957 "Onto-theo-logical Constitution" text by saying that it subtly recapitulates all modes of reflection on Being that invoke metaphors of *entrance* and *exit, distance* and *proximity, advent* and *incarnation, withdrawal* and *arrival, passing* or *remaining*. That is, it recapitulates what Heidegger takes to be *reason itself*, by showing that these metaphors signify the minimal representationalism necessary even to pose the question of Being as such. The privilege accorded to all such terms might be explained, if we stick to the strongest reading of the possibility glimpsed in the 1957 text, through an appeal to the impossibility of thinking difference otherwise than in terms of place as well as the inevitable consequence of thinking it in this manner. Both the absolute refusal of theological modes of reflection as well as the inevitability of their repetition and return are thus said to be hard-wired into our thinking by the truth of Being itself.

From our perspective this analysis signals a subtle attempt on Heidegger's part to grasp why predicates culled from theological sources seem to reappear in his own works whenever he thinks the ontological difference as such. The reclamation of theological predicates is here described as the necessary and unavoidable condition of any attempt to think Being as difference. The act of acknowledging this condition is *Heidegger's confession*. This confession pinpoints the ontological grounds for the reemergence of terms drawn from the metaphysical and theological traditions in Heidegger's work. Thus the delineation of metaphysics in its onto-theological constitution confirms at the most fundamental level the phenomenon of de-theologization, and the latter phenomenon finds its ultimate expression in the claim that the thought of Being itself remains linked to this delineation.

THE PHILOSOPHY OF RELIGION AFTER HEIDEGGER

On its own, this conclusion would be consequential for any engagement with the later Heidegger and with post-Heideggerian thought, as it undercuts a significant portion of Heidegger's postwar effort to rethink divinity, holiness, and piety—in concert with Hölderlin and pre-Socratic philosophy—while throwing off the shackles of the metaphysical tradition. As an alternative to the attempt to think divinity anew on the basis of a post-metaphysical thinking, our reading of the 1957 account of onto-theology suggests that in the subtlest of ways, this essay represents an attempt on Heidegger's part to address the possibility that threatened to topple his entire enterprise, the possibility that how we construe Being as an a priori is thoroughly determined by actuality. And yet by identifying the ontological grounds of the "transposition" that unites onto-logy with theo-logy, Heidegger still seeks to dismiss the possibility that actuality does indeed fully determine our ontological concepts.

Let us put aside Heidegger's ultimate dismissal of this possibility, as well as his anxiety that, if confirmed, it would spell the end of thinking. The evidence brought forth in the present study allows us to free this possibility from the strictures Heidegger placed upon it. If the actuality of beings were indeed to take precedence in determining the univocal sense of Being, then in Heidegger's terminology this would mean that the determination of beings in their highest actuality would provide the sole means for interrogating Being as difference. In this case, there would be no meaning of Being apart from what is dictated to us through tradition, understood as our experience of what is actual. Metaphysics would no longer be a stage in the larger drama of the history of Being, but rather it would be the origin of this drama itself. That is, the history of Being would be *fully* conditioned by the cultural and material forces that determine our encounter with beings as actual.

This possibility was never truly entertained by Heidegger, who never gave up the dream of acceding to Being directly, without a detour through beings. At best the later Heidegger acknowledged his dependence upon metaphysical language: "Thinking of Being is so decisively caught up in the metaphysical thought of the being as such that it can only grope its way with the help of a staff borrowed from metaphysics."[32] But he always maintained that this dependence was contingent rather than necessary: "At first, the overcoming of metaphysics can only be represented in terms of metaphysics itself, so to speak, in the manner of a *exaggeration* (*Über-*

hohung) of itself through itself."[33] By contrast, the work accomplished here in documenting the repetitive re-signification of theological predicates suggests that metaphysics itself has always exaggerated, and that thinking after metaphysics is nothing other than exaggeration. If now we salvage the metaphor of exaggeration while jettisoning the dream of self-liberation it is meant to support, then these lines can help us to recuperate the philosophy of religion according to the very terms that led Heidegger to repudiate it.

The philosophy of religion is thus the investigation of the historically conditioned, highly regulated set of statements that characterize modern forms of critical inquiry in their attempts to define themselves against their perceived non-critical and/or non-secular counterparts. This mode of inquiry studies the discursive formations through which reason attempts to elevate itself above its own materially conditioned history while continuing to draw upon that history in implicit and explicit ways in order to carve out new spaces of critical reflection. In approaching its objects in this manner, the philosophy of religion does not aim simply to reduce these attempts to the fundamental historical and material conditions of their emergence, but rather to chart their respective contributions to the way in which critical reflection has been configured and reconfigured over time in different philosophical and cultural settings, and with respect to various religious traditions. To this extent one may be justified in defining the philosophy of religion, with Heidegger, as an illogicality. This illogicality is a function of its method. In setting out to examine how the religious and the nonreligious have been defined over time, the philosophy of religion requires transcendental reflection upon the essences of its objects, yet it stipulates that such reflection must be seen as building upon, and thus as the product of, its historical findings. Though Heidegger dismissed the philosophy of religion on this account, its illogicality counts for us as its real strength. For it is what distinguishes the philosophy of religion from all discourses—be they philosophical, religious, or otherwise—that seek to establish themselves as foundational and feverishly protect their priority over against all interlocutors.

NOTES

INTRODUCTION

1. See Martin Heidegger, "Des hl. Augustinus Betrachtung über die Zeit: Confessiones lib. XI," in the Fiand Collection, Loyola University of Chicago Archives and Special Collections, Martin Heidegger Collection, 1918–1976, Box 1, Folder 1, Document 2, pp. 1–13 (cited here as "Fiand," followed by the page number of this archive edition). See also C. Augustìn Corti, *Zeitproblematik bei Martin Heidegger und Augustinus* (Würzburg: Verlag Königshausen & Neumann, 2006).

2. See M. Heidegger, *Augustinus, Confessiones XI (De tempore)*, in *GA* 83:39–84.

3. See M. Heidegger, *Augustinus und der Neuplatonismus*, in *GA* 60:157–302 [*Phenomenology of Religious Life*, 113–228].

4. See Heinrich Ochsner, *Das Mass der Verborgenen: Heinrich Ochsner 1891–1970 zum Gedächtnis*, ed. C. Ochwaldt and E. Tecklenborg (Hannover: Charis, 1981), 157–60, as cited in Theodore Kisiel, *The Genesis of Heidegger's Being and Time* (Berkeley: University of California Press, 1993), 72–73.

5. *GA* 62:369 [*Suppl.*, 125].

6. Martin Heidegger, "What Is Metaphysics?," in *Pathmarks*, ed. William McNeil (Cambridge: Cambridge University Press, 1998), 82–96.

7. *SZ*, 229 [*BT*, 272].

8. *GA* 9:66 [*Pathmarks*, 53].

9. Fiand, 11.

10. Fiand, 3.

11. *GA* 9:328 [*Pathmarks*, 250].

12. *GA* 65:314 [*Contributions*, 220].

13. See Hans-George Gadamer, *Heidegger's Ways*, trans. John W. Stanley (Albany: SUNY Press, 1994), 160.

14. See *GA* 12:91 [*On the Way to Language*, 10]: "Without this theological background I should never have come upon the path of thinking."

15. *GA* 66:415–16 [*Mindfulness*, 386].

16. Ibid.

17. Martin Heidegger, *Phänomenologie des religiösen Lebens*, GA 60, and the following studies: Philip Tonner, *Heidegger, Metaphysics, and the Univocity of Being* (London: Continuum, 2010); Sylvian Camilleri, *Phénoménologie de la religion et herméneutique théologique dans la pensée du jeune Heidegger: Commentaire analytique des Fondements philosophiques de la mystique médiévale (1916–1919)* (Dordrecht: Springer, 2008); Benjamin D. Crowe, *Heidegger's Phenomenology of Religion: Realism and Cultural Criticism* (Bloomington: Indiana University Press, 2008); Christian Sommer, *Heidegger, Aristote, Luther: Les sources aristotéliciennes et néo-testamentaires d'Être et Temps* (Paris: PUF, 2006); Benjamin D. Crowe, *Heidegger's Religious Origins: Destruction and Authenticity* (Bloomington: Indiana University Press, 2006); S. J. McGrath, *Heidegger and Medieval Philosophy: A Phenomenology for the Godforsaken* (Washington, DC: Catholic University Press, 2006); C. J. N. de Paulo, ed., *The Influence of Augustine on Heidegger: The Emergence of an Augustinian Phenomenology* (Lewiston, NY: Edwin Mellen Press, 2006); Frederick van Fleteren, ed., *Martin Heidegger's Interpretations of Saint Augustine: Sein und Zeit und Ewigkeit*, Collecteana Augustiniana (Lewiston, NY: Edwin Mellen Press, 2005); Jean Greisch, *L'Arbre de vie et l'Arbre du savoir: Le chemin phénoménologique de l'herméneutique heideggérienne (1919–1923)* (Paris: CERF, 2000); Sonya Sikka, *Forms of Transcendence: Heidegger and Medieval Mystical Theology* (Albany: SUNY Press, 1997); John Van Buren, *The Young Heidegger: Rumor of the Hidden King* (Bloomington: Indiana University Press, 1994); Reiner Schurmann, *Heidegger on Being and Acting: From Principles to Anarchy* (Bloomington: Indiana University Press, 1987); John D. Caputo, *The Mystical Element in Heidegger's Thought* (New York: Fordham University Press, 1986); John D. Caputo, *Heidegger and Aquinas: An Essay on the Overcoming of Metaphysics* (New York: Fordham University Press, 1982); Michael Wyschogrod, *Kierkegaard and Heidegger: The Ontology of Existence* (New York: Routledge, 1954).

18. In this manner the present study is meant to complement the work of Marlene Zarader in her book, *The Unthought Debt: Heidegger and the Hebraic Heritage*, trans. Bettina Bergo (Stanford, CA: Stanford University Press, 2006).

19. GA 17:311 [*Introduction to Phenomenological Research*, 236].

20. SZ, 199 [BT, 492]; GA 20:418 [*History*, 302].

21. GA 17:156–57 [*Introduction to Phenomenological Research*, 116].

22. Carl Schmitt, *Political Theology: Four Chapters on the Concept of Sovereignty*, trans. George Schwab (Chicago: University of Chicago Press, 1985), 36.

23. GA 17:311 [*Introduction to Phenomenological Research*, 236].

24. GA 17:123 [*Introduction to Phenomenological Research*, 89].

25. GA 23:138.

26. GA 5:106–7 [*Off the Beaten Track*, 81].

27. Ibid. See Georg Simmel, *The View of Life: Four Metaphysical Essays with Journal Aphorisms*, trans. John A. Y. Andrews and Donald N. Levine (Chicago: University of Chicago Press, 2010), 18.

28. SZ, 49 [BT, 74].

29. Ibid.

30. GA 23:103, and esp. 105–44.

31. GA 62:363 [*Suppl.*, 194, translation altered].

32. *GA* 62:348–49 [*Suppl.*, 113].
33. *SZ*, 306 [*BT*, 496].
34. Kisiel, *Genesis*, 558.
35. *SZ*, 22 [*BT*, 44].
36. Hannah Arendt, *Love and Saint Augustine*, ed. Joanna Vecchiarelli Scott and Judith Chelius Stark (Chicago: University of Chicago Press, 1998), 66.
37. Karsten Harries, "The Descent of the 'Logos': Limits of Transcendental Reflection," in *Transcendental Heidegger*, ed. Steven Crowell and Jeff Malpas (Stanford, CA: Stanford University Press, 2007) 74–92, 76.
38. On the importance of the *Contributions* in Heidegger's corpus, see for example Otto Pöggeler, *Martin Heidegger's Path of Thinking*, trans. D. Magurshak and S. Barber (Atlantic Heights, NJ: Humanities Press, 1987), 286–87. For insightful readings of this text, see Richard Polt, *The Emergency of Being: On Heidegger's Contributions to Philosophy* (Ithaca, NY: Cornell University Press, 2006); and Charles E. Scott, Susan M. Schoenbohm, Daniela Vallega-Neu, and Alejandro Vallega, eds., *Companion to Heidegger's Contributions to Philosophy* (Bloomington: Indiana University Press, 2001).
39. Martin Heidegger, "Anaximander's Saying," in *Off the Beaten Track*, ed. and trans. Julian Young and Kenneth Haynes (Cambridge: Cambridge University Press, 2002), 242–81.
40. *GA* 14:69 [*On Time and Being*, 55].
41. See the following: Jean-Francois Lyotard, *The Confessions of Augustine* (Stanford, CA: Stanford University Press, 2000); Paul Ricoeur, *Time and Narrative*, vol. 1, trans. Kathleen McLaughlin and David Pellauer (Chicago: University of Chicago Press, 1984), originally published as *Temps et Récit* (Paris: Éditions du Seuil, 1983); and Jacques Derrida's "Circumfession," in Jacques Derrida and Geoffrey Bennington, *Jacques Derrida*, trans. Geoffrey Bennington (Chicago: University of Chicago Press, 1999, originally published as *Jacques Derrida* (Paris: Éditions du Seuil, 1998). In addition to Arendt's study and to Gadamer's work, however, the earlier context of German philosophical writings on Augustine should include at the very least the following: Karl Jaspers, *Plato and Augustine*, ed. Hannah Arendt and trans. Ralph Manheim (New York: Harcourt Brace, 1966); and Hans Jonas, *Augustin und das paulinische Freiheitsproblem: ein philosophischer Beitrag zur Genesis der christlich-abendländischen Freiheitsidee* (Göttingen: Vandenbroeck & Ruprecht, 1930). See also the brief remarks of Husserl, who argued that "our modern age, so proud of its knowledge, has failed to surpass or even to match the splendid achievement of [Augustine] . . . who grappled earnestly with the problem of time." Edmund Husserl, *On the Phenomenology of the Consciousness of Internal Time (1893–1917)*, trans. John Barnett Brough, *Collected Works*, vol. 4 (Dordrecht: Kluwer, 1991), 3.
42. Jean-Luc Marion, *In the Self's Place: The Approach of Saint Augustine*, trans Jeffrey Kosky (Stanford, CA: Stanford University Press, 2012), 2.
43. Emmanuel Levinas, *God, Death and Time*, trans. Bettina Bergo (Stanford, CA: Stanford University Press, 2000), 22.
44. The list of sources examining the modern development of the philosophy of religion is too long to cite. For a comprehensive overview, see for example Jean Greisch, *Le Buisson ardent et les lumières de la raison: l'invention de la philosophie de la religion*, 3 vols. (Paris: Cerf 2002–2004).

45. The list of recently published works in this vein is long indeed; here I cite the works I take to be paradigmatic of this approach: Amy Hollywood, *Sensible Ecstasy: Mysticism, Sexual Difference, and the Demands of History* (Chicago: University of Chicago Press, 2002); Samuel Moyn, *Origins of the Other: Emmanuel Levinas between Revelation and Ethics* (Ithaca, NY: Cornell University Press, 2005); Thomas Carlson, *Indiscretion: Finitude and the Naming of God* (Chicago: University of Chicago Press, 1999); Thomas Carlson, *The Indiscrete Image: Infinitude and the Creation of the Human* (Chicago: University of Chicago Press, 2008); Benjamin Lazier, *God Interrupted: Heresy and the European Imagination between the World Wars* (Princeton, NJ: Princeton University Press, 2008); Hent de Vries, *Philosophy and the Turn to Religion* (Baltimore: Johns Hopkins University Press, 1999); Stefanos Geroulanos, *An Atheism That Is Not Humanist Emerges in French Philosophy* (Stanford, CA: Stanford University Press, 2010); Michael Allen Gillespie, *The Theological Origins of Modernity* (Chicago: University of Chicago Press, 2008); Mark C. Taylor, *After God* (Chicago: University of Chicago Press, 2007); Peter Gordon, *Rosenzweig and Heidegger: Between Judaism and German Philosophy* (Cambridge, MA: Harvard University Press, 2003); Sarah Hammerschlag, *The Figural Jew: Politics and Identity in Postwar French Thought* (Chicago: University of Chicago Press, 2010); Michael Fagenblat, *A Convenant of Creatures: Levinas' Philosophy of Judaism* (Stanford, CA: Stanford University Press, 2010); and Mary-Jane Rubenstein, *Strange Wonder: The Closure of Metaphysics and the Opening of Awe* (New York: Columbia University Press, 2010).

46. See especially Giorgio Agamben, *The Kingdom and the Glory: For a Theological Genealogy of Economy and Government*, trans. Lorenzo Chiesa with Matteo Mandarini (Stanford, CA: Stanford University Press, 2011); Slavoj Zizek, *The Puppet and the Dwarf: The Perverse Core of Christianity* (Cambridge, MA: MIT Press, 2003); Jean-Luc Nancy, *Dis-enclosure: The Deconstruction of Christianity*, trans. Bettina Bergo, Gabriel Malenfant, and Michael B. Smith (New York: Fordham University Press, 2009); Jean-Luc Nancy, *Adoration: The Deconstruction of Christianity*, vol. 2, trans. John McKeane (New York: Fordham University Press, 2013); and Simon Critchley, *Faith of the Faithless: Experiments in Political Theology* (New York: Verso, 2012).

CHAPTER I

1. *GA* 12:123 [*On the Way to Language*, 36].
2. Theodore Kisiel, *Heidegger's Ways of Thought* (London: Continuum Press, 2002), 139.
3. *GA* 12:123 [*On the Way to Language*, 36].
4. Ibid.
5. *GA* 56/57: 3-120 [*Towards the Definition of Philosophy*, 3-102].
6. Theodore Kisiel, *Genesis*, 38–58.
7. As scholars have shown, Heidegger maintained a complex and in many ways tortured relationship to the founder of phenomenology, particularly during the time when he served as Husserl's assistant. Among the many excellent studies of this topic, see especially Thomas Sheehan, ed., *Heidegger: The Man and the Thinker* (Chicago: Precedent Publishing, 1981); Steven Galt Crowell, *Heidegger, Husserl, and the Space of*

Meaning: Paths toward Transcendental Phenomenology (Evanston, IL: Northwestern University Press, 2001); B. C. Hopkins, *Intentionality in Husserl and Heidegger: The Problem of the Original Method and Phenomenon in Phenomenology* (Dordrecht: Kluwer, 1993); Søren Overgaard, *Husserl and Heidegger on Being in the World* (Dordrecht: Kluwer, 2004); Brian Elliott, *Phenomenology and Imagination in Husserl and Heidegger* (New York: Routledge, 2005), 68–69. For a reading of KNS 1919 as marking a break with Husserl, see Michael Bowler, *Heidegger and Aristotle: Philosophy as Praxis* (London: Continuum Press, 2008), 27–54.

8. GA 60:322 [*Phenomenology of Religious Life*, 244].

9. See Parvis Emad, *Heidegger and the Phenomenology of Values: His Critique of Intentionality*, foreword by W. Biemel (Glen Ellyn, IL: Torey Press, 1981), and Henri Mongis, *Heidegger et la critique de la notion de valeur* (The Hague: Martinus Nijhoff, 1976).

10. See Wilhelm Windelband, "Kulturphilosophie und transzendentaler Idealismus," in *Präludien. Aufsätze und Reden zur Philosophie und ihrer Geschichte*, 5th expanded edition (Tübingen: Mohr, 1915), vol. 2, as quoted in GA 56/57:38 [*Towards the Definition of Philosophy*, 32]. On this topic see Frederick Beiser, *The German Historicist Tradition* (Oxford: Oxford University Press, 2011), 365–92.

11. GA 56/57:48 [*Towards the Definition of Philosophy*, 40].

12. GA 56/57:46 [*Towards the Definition of Philosophy*, 38].

13. GA 56/57:59 [*Towards the Definition of Philosophy*, 50].

14. GA 56/57:73–74 [*Towards the Definition of Philosophy*, 62].

15. GA 56/57:90 [*Towards the Definition of Philosophy*, 76].

16. Ibid.

17. This topic is explored in G. Kovacs's "Philosophy as Primordial Science in Heidegger's Courses of 1919," in *Reading Heidegger from the Start: Essays in His Earliest Thought*, ed. T. Kisiel and J. Van Buren (Albany: SUNY Press, 1994), 91–110, esp. 93–100.

18. GA 56/57:61 [*Towards the Definition of Philosophy*, 51].

19. Ibid.: "I do not, through description, depart from this sphere, and when it is the sphere of primordiality so much more closely does description remain attached to it. Description does not tolerate anything that alters or re-forms the subject-matter."

20. GA 56/57:62 [*Towards the Definition of Philosophy*, 52].

21. GA 56/57:73–75 [*Towards the Definition of Philosophy*, 62–63].

22. GA 62:348–49 [*Suppl.*, 113, translation altered slightly]: "Der Gegenstand der philosophischen Forschung ist das menschlichen Dasein als von ihr befragt auf seinen Seinscharakter. Diese Grundrichtung des philosophischen Fragens ist dem befragten Gegenstand, dem faktischen Leben, nicht von außen angesetzt und aufgeschraubt, sondern ist zu verstehen als das explizite Ergreifen einer Grundbewegtheit des faktischen Lebens selbst."

23. For a discussion of this document, see David Farrell Krell, "Toward *Sein und Zeit*: Heidegger's Early Review of Jaspers's 'Psychologie der Weltanschauungen,'" *Journal of the British Society for Phenomenology* 6 (1975): 147–56.

24. GA 9:29 [*Pathmarks*, 25].

25. GA 1:401 [*Suppl.*, 63].

26. *GA* 9:30 [*Suppl.*, 92]: "When the sense of existence is investigated in terms of its origin and our genuine basic experience of it, we see that it is precisely *that* sense of being which cannot be obtained from the 'is' we use to explicate and objectify our experience in one way or another when we acquire knowledge about it."

27. Ibid.

28. *GA* 59:173 [*Phenomenology of Intuition and Expression*, 132].

29. *GA* 9:32-33 [*Suppl.*, 94]: "Having oneself arises from such *worry*, is maintained in it, and tends toward it. . . . Accordingly, the phenomenon of existence discloses itself only in a radical historical manner of actualizing our experience and striving after such actualization."

30. Edmund Husserl, *Ideen zu einer reinen Phänomenologie und phänomenologischen Philosophie*, ed. Marly Biemer, 3 vols. (The Hague: Nijhoff, 1950-1952), 1:132 [*Ideas Pertaining to a Pure Phenomenology and to a Phenomenological Philosophy, First Book*, trans. F. Kerstern (Dordrecht: Kluwer, 1983), 109].

31. Ibid.

32. Husserl, *Ideen* 1:100 [*Ideas, First Book*, 85]: "The stream of mental processes which is mine, of the one who is thinking, no matter to what extent it is not grasped, no matter how unknown it is in the areas of the stream which have run their course and which have yet to come—: as soon as I look at the flowing life in its actual present, and, while doing so, *apprehend myself* as the pure subject of this life . . . I say unqualifiedly and necessarily that I am, *this life is*, I am living: *cogito*."

33. *GA* 56/57:115 [*Towards the Definition of Philosophy*, 97].

34. Edmund Husserl, *The Idea of Phenomenology*, trans. Lee Hardy (Dordrecht: Kluwer, 1999), 46-47.

35. See Augustine, Letter 130, in *Letters* 100-155 (II/2), trans. Roland Teske, S.J., *Works of Saint Augustine for the 21st Century* (New York, New City Press, 2002), 183-200. See also Bernard McGinn, *The Growth of Mysticism: Gregory the Great through the Twelfth Century* (New York: Crossroad, 1996), 258 and 532. Husserl's formula most likely hearkens back to Cusanus's description of *speculatio* as "visio sine comprehensione," which has its roots in Augustine. See *De docta ignorantia* 1.26 in Nicholas of Cusa, *Selected Spiritual Writings*, trans. Lawrence Bond (Mahwah, NJ: Paulist Press, 1997), 85-206.

36. *GA* 56/57:117 [*Towards the Definition of Philosophy*, 99].

37. On this point see Kovacs, "Philosophy as Primordial Science," esp. 99-100.

38. For the importance of the hermeneutical intuition in destroying Husserl, see Rudolf Bernet, "Husserl and Heidegger on Intentionality and Being," *Journal of the British Society for Phenomenology* 21 (May 1990): 136-52.

39. In support of this view, see Jacques Taminiaux, *Heidegger and the Project of Fundamental Ontology*, translated by M. Gendre (Albany: SUNY Press, 1991), 1-55.

40. *GA* 56/57:110 [*Towards the Definition of Philosophy*, 92].

41. *GA* 60:54 [*Phenomenology of Religious Life*, 36].

42. On the technical use of this term in the early Heidegger see *GA* 60:62-63 [42-43]. Also see Theodore Kisiel, *Genesis*, 164-70; G. Imdahl, *Das Leben verstehen: Heideggers formal anzeigende Hermeneutik in den frühen Freiburger Vorlesungen* (Würzburg: Königshausen & Neumann, 1997); J. Greisch, *L'Arbre de vie*, 125-34; D. Kaegi,

"Die Religion in den Grenzen der blossen Existenz: Heideggers religionsphilosophische Vorlesungen von 1920/1921," *Internationale Zeitschrift für Philosophie* 1 (1996): 133–49, 141ff. See also Hent de Vries, *Philosophy and the Turn to Religion* (Baltimore: Johns Hopkins Press, 1999), esp. 158–232; and Theodore Kisiel, "Die formale Anzeige. Die methodische Geheimwaffe des frühen Heidegger," in *Heidegger—neu gelesen*, ed. M. Happel (Würzburg: Königshausen & Neumann, 1997), 22–40.

43. *GA* 60:54 [*Phenomenology of Religious Life*, 36].

44. Cf. *GA* 59:29–41, esp. 36ff., in a section entitled "Philosophy and Factical Life Experience."

45. *GA* 17:115–16 [*Introduction to Phenomenological Research*, 85–86]. For two excellent discussions of Heideggerian destruction, see Robert Bernasconi, "Repetition and Tradition: Heidegger's Destructuring of the Distinction between Essence and Existence in *Basic Problems of Phenomenology*," in *Reading Heidegger from the Start*, ed. Theodore Kisiel and John van Buren (Albany: SUNY Press, 1994), 123–36; and in the same volume, Otto Pöggeler, "Destruction and Moment," 137–56.

46. *GA* 62:362 [*Suppl.*, 120].

47. *GA* 60:54 [*Phenomenology of Religious Life*, 36].

48. Otto Pöggeler, *Martin Heidegger's Path of Thinking*, trans. Daniel Magurshak and Sigmund Barber (Atlantic Heights, NJ: Humanities Press International, 1987), 25.

49. See Sophie-Jan Arrien, "Faith's Knowledge: On Heidegger's Reading of Saint Paul," in *Gatherings: Heidegger Circle Annual* 3 (2013): 30–49; and Sophie-Jan Arrien, "Foi et indication formelle. Heidegger lecteur de saint Paul (1920–1921)," in *Le jeune Heidegger 1909–1926*, ed. S.-J. Arrien and S. Camilleri (Paris: J. Vrin, 2011).

50. *GA* 56/57:117 [*Towards the Definition of Philosophy*, 99].

51. William Wrede, *Die Echtheit des zweiten Thessalonicherbriefes untersucht* (Leipzig: J. C. Hinrichs, 1903).

52. See for example Franz Overbeck, *How Christian Is Our Present-Day Theology?*, annotated translation with an introduction by Martin Henry and foreword by David Tracy (New York: T&T Clark, 2005).

53. The central theme guiding Heidegger's commentary is thus noticeably at odds with the Nietzschean claim that the evil genius Paul was the principal corrupter of Christ's original message of glad tidings. In the *Antichrist*, Nietzsche famously argues that the history of Christianity following Jesus of Nazareth's crucifixion has been "the history of a progressively cruder misunderstanding of an *original* symbolism." See Friedrich Nietzsche, *The Anti-Christ, Ecce Homo, Twilight of the Idols, and Other Writings*, edited by Aaron Ridley and Judith Norman (Cambridge: Cambridge University Press, 2005), 33.

54. *GA* 60:104 [*Phenomenology of Religious Life*, 73].

55. *GA* 60:114 [*Phenomenology of Religious Life*, 81].

56. *GA* 60:102 [*Phenomenology of Religious Life*, 71].

57. *GA* 60:102 [*Phenomenology of Religious Life*, 71–72].

58. *GA* 60:104 [*Phenomenology of Religious Life*, 73].

59. *GA* 60:67 [*Phenomenology of Religious Life*, 47].

60. *GA* 60:131 [*Phenomenology of Religious Life*, 93].

61. *GA* 60:87 [*Phenomenology of Religious Life*, 61].

62. *GA* 60:88 [*Phenomenology of Religious Life*, 62]. On this issue see Ward Blanton, *Displacing Christian Origins: Philosophy, Secularity, and the New Testament* (Chicago: University of Chicago Press, 2007), 105–28.

63. *GA* 60:125 [*Phenomenology of Religious Life*, 89]. On this issue in the early Heidegger, see Charles Bambach, *Heidegger, Dilthey, and the Crisis of Historicism* (Ithaca, NY: Cornell University Press, 1995).

64. *GA* 60:82 [*Phenomenology of Religious Life*, 57]; see also *GA* 60:80 [*Phenomenology of Religious Life*, 55].

65. *GA* 60:65 [*Phenomenology of Religious Life*, 44].

66. 1 Thessalonians 5:1–2.

67. *GA* 60:98 [*Phenomenology of Religious Life*, 68–69].

68. 1 Thessalonians 1:6–7.

69. *GA* 60:94 [*Phenomenology of Religious Life*, 66].

70. Ibid.

71. See 1 Thessalonians 1:6. *GA* 60:94 [*Phenomenology of Religious Life*, 66].

72. *GA* 60:95 [*Phenomenology of Religious Life*, 66].

73. *GA* 60:98 [*Phenomenology of Religious Life*, 69].

74. *GA* 60:140 [*Phenomenology of Religious Life*, 99].

75. Ibid.

76. *GA* 60:153 [*Phenomenology of Religious Life*, 109].

77. *GA* 60:111 [*Phenomenology of Religious Life*, 79]. Significantly, both Origen an Augustine are said to resist this vulgarization of eschatology—a view that will shortly be reflected in *Augustine and Neoplatonism*.

78. Ibid.

79. On the concept of *Vergegenständlichung* in Husserl, refer to *Ideen* 1, §§97–100; see *The New Husserl*, edited by Donn Welton (Bloomington: Indiana University Press, 2003), 47.

80. *GA* 60:109 [*Phenomenology of Religious Life*, 77].

81. Hent de Vries recognizes the paradoxical status of knowledge in this context. In commenting upon this aspect of the Paul course, de Vries refers to the non-knowledge at play in eschatological longing as "comfort-without-comfort." See de Vries, *Philosophy and the Turn to Religion* (Baltimore: Johns Hopkins University Press, 1999), 193.

82. *GA* 60:109 [*Phenomenology of Religious Life*, 77].

83. For more on the notion of an apophatic anthropology, see Thomas Carlson, *Indiscretion: Finitude and the Naming of God*.

84. *GA* 60:112 [*Phenomenology of Religious Life*, 79].

85. 2 Thessalonians 2:1–10.

86. Paul Metzger, *Katechon: II Thess 2, 1–12 im Horizont apokalyptischen Denkens* (Berlin: Walter de Gruyter, 2005); and Ernest Best, *Black's New Testament Commentary: The First and Second Epistles to the Thessalonians* (London: Continuum Press, reprint 2003).

87. *GA* 60:113 [*Phenomenology of Religious Life*, 80, translation altered slightly].

88. *GA* 60:128 [*Phenomenology of Religious Life*, 90].

89. On this theme see Felix Ó Murchadha, *The Time of Revolution: Kairos and Chronos in Heidegger* (London: Bloomsbury, 2013).

90. *GA* 60:120 [*Phenomenology of Religious Life*, 86].

91. Ephesians 4:22-24.

92. For more on this theme see Bernard McGinn, *The Mystical Thought of Meister Eckhart: The Man from Whom God Hid Nothing* (New York: Crossroad, 2001); and on Heidegger's relation to Eckhart see John D. Caputo, *The Mystical Element in Heidegger's Thought* (New York: Fordham University Press, 2001).

93. *GA* 60:120 [*Phenomenology of Religious Life*, 86].

94. Ibid.

95. *GA* 60:121 [*Phenomenology of Religious Life*, 87].

96. *GA* 60:124 [*Phenomenology of Religious Life*, 88].

97. *GA* 60:334 [*Phenomenology of Religious Life*, 252-53].

98. *GA* 60:336 [*Phenomenology of Religious Life*, 254].

99. *GA* 60:124 [*Phenomenology of Religious Life*, 88].

100. *GA* 60:123 [*Phenomenology of Religious Life*, 88].

101. *GA* 60:114-15 [*Phenomenology of Religious Life*, 81-82].

102. *GA* 60:114 [*Phenomenology of Religious Life*, 81].

103. Metzger, *Katechon*, 25-29. For a recent version of this argument, see Allan J. McNicol, *Jesus' Directions for the Future: A Source and Redaction-History Study of the Use of the Eschatological Traditions in Paul and in the Synoptic Accounts of Jesus' Last Eschatological Discourse* (Macon, GA: Mercer University Press, 1996), 60. Compare with the reading of the *katechōn* in Paolo Virno, *Multitude between Innovation and Negation* (New York: Semiotext(e), 2008).

104. *GA* 60:114-15 [*Phenomenology of Religious Life*, 81].

105. *GA* 60:114 [*Phenomenology of Religious Life*, 81].

106. Ibid.

107. *GA* 60:107 [*Phenomenology of Religious Life*, 75].

108. Giorgio Agamben, *The Time That Remains: A Commentary on the Letter to the Romans*, trans. Patricia Daley (Stanford, CA: Stanford University Press, 2005), 111.

109. Ibid.

110. Ibid.

111. G. W. F. Hegel, *Faith and Knowledge*, trans. Walter Cerf and H. S. Harris (Albany: SUNY Press, 1977), 191.

112. *GA* 60:124 [*Phenomenology of Religious Life*, 89].

113. Ibid.

114. Ibid.

115. *SZ*, 7 [*BT*, 27].

116. *GA* 60:124 [*Phenomenology of Religious Life*, 89].

117. *GA* 62:363 [*Suppl.*, 121, and 194 note 9].

CHAPTER 2

1. This letter is cited in Kisiel, *The Genesis of Heidegger's "Being and Time,"* 554.

2. René Descartes, *The Philosophical Writings of Descartes*, trans. J. Cottingham, R. Stoothoff, and D. Murdoch, 3 vols. (Cambridge: Cambridge University Press, 1984-1991), 2:17; Adam and Tannery (AT) VII.25.

3. *SZ*, 211 [*BT*, 254].

4. *GA* 61:173 [*Phenomenological Interpretations of Aristotle*, 130]: "The *sum* is indeed the first, even for Descartes. Yet, precisely here a mistake already arises: Descartes does not dwell on the '*sum*' but already has a foreconcept of its sense of Being in the mode of mere ascertainability, or more specifically, indubitability. The fact that Descartes could deviate into epistemological questioning . . . merely expresses the more basic fact that to him the *sum*, its Being and its categorical structure, were in no way problematic." Jean-Luc Marion has already discussed the significance of this passage. See Jean-Luc Marion, *Reduction and Givenness: Investigations of Husserl, Heidegger, and Phenomenology*, trans. Thomas Carlson (Evanston, IL: Northwestern Press, 1998), 77–107.

5. This fact has been previously noted, in Greisch, *L'Arbre de vie et l'Arbre de savoir*, 222.

6. *GA* 58:57.

7. *GA* 60:298 [*Phenomenology of Religious Life*, 226, translation altered slightly].

8. The apparent similarity between Augustine and Descartes was famously raised by Arnauld in the "Fourth Set of Objections" to the *Meditations* (see AT VII.196–218), and dealt with by Descartes himself in his "Replies" (see AT VII.219ff.). There is a wealth of research on this topic. See S. Menn, *Descartes and Augustine* (New York: Cambridge University Press, 1988); E. Bermon, *Le cogito dans la pensée de saint Augustin* (Paris: Vrin, 2001); and, most recently, Jean-Luc Marion, *In the Self's Place: The Approach of Saint Augustine*, trans. Jeffrey Kosky (Stanford, CA: Stanford University Press, 2012).

9. Brian Stock, *Augustine the Reader: Meditation, Self-Knowledge, and the Ethics of Interpretation* (Cambridge, MA: Harvard University Press 1996), 260.

10. Compare *GA* 56/57:117 [*Towards the Definition of Philosophy*, 99]; *GA* 60:13 [*Phenomenology of Religious Life*, 10].

11. Descartes, *Meditationes de prima philosophia*, AT VII.25 [*Philosophical Writings* 2:17].

12. *SZ*, 211 [*BT*, 254].

13. Descartes, AT VII.20 [*Philosophical Writings*, 2:18].

14. On the early Heideggerian theme of destruction, see esp. *GA* 60:53–54 [*Phenomenology of Religious Life*, 35–37; *GA* 62:346-47; *GA* 17:115ff. [*Introduction to Phenomenological Research*, 83ff.]; and *GA* 24:26–32 [*The Basic Problems of Phenomenology*, 19–23].

15. *GA* 61:173 [*Phenomenological Interpretations of Aristotle*, 130].

16. *GA* 17:109 [*Introduction to Phenomenological Research*, 79].

17. *GA* 17:226 [*Introduction to Phenomenological Research*, 172].

18. Ibid.

19. *GA* 17:228 [*Introduction to Phenomenological Research*, 173]; compare with *GA* 23:115, in which Heidegger writes that Descartes "not only seeks a *fundamentum inconcussum simplex inconcussum* in general, but also this must likewise ensure fundamental cognition of God" (translation mine).

20. Following Descartes, even the existence of the self is illuminated by the light reflected off the purely present-at-hand, as Heidegger writes in 1924, in *GA* 64:102 [*The*

Concept of Time: The First Draft of "Being and Time," 87]: "The being of the *res cogitans* (of consciousness) means: to be there present-at-hand [*Vorhandensein*]."

21. *GA* 17:120 [*Introduction to Phenomenological Research*, 87].
22. *GA* 60:244 [*Phenomenology of Religious Life*, 183, translation slightly altered].
23. *GA* 17:239 [*Introduction to Phenomenological Research*, 183].
24. *GA* 17:235 [*Introduction to Phenomenological Research*, 178–79].
25. *GA* 17:240 [*Introduction to Phenomenological Research*, 183].
26. *GA* 17:243 [*Introduction to Phenomenological Research*, 187].
27. *GA* 17:240 [*Introduction to Phenomenological Research*, 184].
28. *GA* 23:117 [translation mine].
29. *GA* 17:248 [*Introduction to Phenomenological Research*, 191].
30. *GA* 17:249 [*Introduction to Phenomenological Research*, 193]. Some commentators have rightly pointed out that the phrase *cogito me cogitare* does not appear in Descartes's *Meditationes* and that the formula is incorrectly used by Heidegger to describe the form of the Cartesian *cogito*. Emmanuel Faye, for example, faults Heidegger for wrongly interpreting Descartes on this basis (see E. Faye, *Heidegger: The Introduction of Nazism into Philosophy*, trans. Michael B. Smith [New Haven, CT: Yale University Press, 2009], 266–67). However, Faye does not acknowledge the fact that for Heidegger the formula can be justified textually. Heidegger draws upon the description of the *res cogitans* in *Principles of Philosophy* 1.9 in order to provide such a justification. See Descartes, AT VIIIA.7 [*Philosophical Writings*, 1:195]: "By the term 'thought,' I understand everything we are aware of as happening within us, insofar as we have awareness of it." (Cogitationis nomine, intelligo illa omnia, quae nobis consciis in nobis fiunt, quatenus earum in nobis conscientia.) See also *GA* 23:117–18 for a fuller description of the *cogito* that offers evidence against the charge leveled by Faye among others.

31. *GA* 23:120.
32. *GA* 17:250 [*Introduction to Phenomenological Research*, 193].
33. *GA* 9:33 [*Pathmarks*, 27].
34. See, e.g., *GA* 9:29 [*Pathmarks*, 25] and compare with *SZ*, 41–62 [*BT*, 67–90].
35. *GA* 6.2:152 [*Nietzsche*, vol. 4, 106].
36. *GA* 17:249 [*Introduction to Phenomenological Research*, 193].
37. *GA* 61:174 [*Phenomenological Interpretations of Aristotle*, 131].
38. *GA* 61:175 [*Phenomenological Interpretations of Aristotle*, 131].
39. See *GA* 64:118 [*CT*, 16 and 16E, translation slightly altered].
40. *GA* 64:123 [*CT*, 20 and 20E].
41. *GA* 64:114 [*CT*, 9–10 and 9E–10E].
42. *GA* 64:125 [*CT*, 22 and 22E].
43. *GA* 17:249 [*Introduction to Phenomenological Research*, 193].
44. *GA* 61:106–7 [*Phenomenological Interpretations of* Aristotle, 80].
45. On the whole, the course manuscript gives one the impression that Heidegger is mired in insignificant details, that he has little invested in the course, and that he is perhaps looking forward to the end of the semester. It comes as no surprise that in August 1921 Heidegger voiced his frustrations with the seminar in a letter to Karl Jaspers. See Martin Heidegger and Karl Jaspers, *Briefwechsel, 1920–63*, ed. W. Biemel and H. Saner (Frankfurt am Main: Klostermann, 1990), letter 8 (August 5, 1921), 24:

"Das Semester war für mich im Ganzen eine Enttäuschung; es lohnt nicht die Arbeit für die, die vor einem sitzen. Der eine oder andere faßt einmal zu, um dann wieder bequemen Liebhabereien nachzugehen. Ich habe mich im vergangenen Semester oft gefragt, was wir eigentlich tun." (For me the semester was a complete disappointment; it wasn't worth all the work for those sitting there before you. Handling this one or that one so that they could pursue their comfortable hobbies. I often asked myself in the past semester, what are we really doing? [translation mine])

46. *GA* 60:235 [*Phenomenology of Religious Life*, 175]. This reconstruction remains indebted to the magisterial work of Kisiel, *Genesis*, 192–217.

47. *Confessions* 10.3.

48. *Confessions* 10.4.

49. Ibid.

50. *Confessions* 10.6.

51. See *GA* 60:176–77 [*Phenomenology of Religious Life*, 128–29].

52. See *Confessions* 10.19.

53. *GA* 60:176–77 [*Phenomenology of Religious Life*, 128–29].

54. *Confessions* 10.33.

55. On the importance of Augustine for the early Heidegger's account of selfhood, see especially Carlson, *The Indiscrete Image*, chap. 2: "'I am': Technological Modernity, Theological Tradition, and the Human in Question," 36–73.

56. See especially Augustine, *On Christian Doctrine* 1.27–40.

57. On this topic, see Jeffrey Andrew Barash, *Martin Heidegger and the Problem of Historical Meaning* (New York: Fordham University Press, 2003).

58. The clearest explanation of *Axiologisierung* can be found in *GA* 60:273–82, in which Heidegger discusses this theme in connection with *Ennarationes in Psalmos* 143.

59. Oskar Becker's notes confirm this view. See *GA* 60:272ff. [*Phenomenology of Religious Life*, 204ff.]. On this score, most commentators tend to view Heidegger as rejecting all conceptions of the *fruitio Dei* (see for example Pöggeler, *Martin Heidegger's Path of Thinking*, 29). This reading is here contested in favor of the view that Heidegger's hermeneutic destruction salvages the factical sense of *fruitio Dei* at the very end of the course.

60. *GA* 60:272 [*Phenomenology of Religious Life*, 205]: "Die *fruitio Dei* steht letzten Endes im Gegensatz zum Haben des Selsbt; beides entspringt nicht derselben Wurzel, sondern ist von außen zusammengewachsen."

61. Ibid.

62. *In Iohannis evangelium tractatus* 1.18–19.

63. Sermon 53.12: "Faciem cordis cogita. Coge cor tuum cogitare divina, compelle, urge. Quidquid simile corporis cogitanti occurrerit, abice. Nondum potes dicere: 'Hoc est': saltem dic: 'Non est hoc'. Quando enim dices: 'Hoc est Deus'? Nec cum videbis: quia ineffabile est quod videbis." English translation in *The Works of Saint Augustine: A Translation for the 21st Century*, vol. III/3, *Sermons, (51-94) on the Old Testament*, trans. Edmund Hill, O.P. (New York: New City Press, 1991), 72.

64. *GA* 60:289 [*Phenomenology of Religious Life*, 219]. This citation provides a basis for the etymological link Giorgio Agamben makes between the notion of the "face of the heart" and the concept of "facticity." See Agamben, "La passion de la facticité,"

in *Heidegger: Questions ouvertes, Cahiers du CIPH* (Paris: Osiris, 1988), 63–84. This article is reprinted as chap. 12 of *Potentialities*, trans. D. Heller-Roazen (Stanford, CA: Stanford University Press, 1999), 185–204.

65. Augustine, *In epistulam Johannis ad Parthos tractatus* (ep. Jo.) 8.5. English translation in *Augustine: Later Works*, trans. John Burnaby, Library of Christian Classics (Philadelphia: Westminster Press, 1980), 321.

66. Augustine, ep. Jo. 8.9 [*Later Works*, 322].

67. Augustine, ep. Jo. 8.5 [*Later Works*, 321]: "You may have the truest love for a happy man, on whom you have nothing to bestow.... You should want him to be your equal, that you both may be subject to the one on whom no favor can be bestowed."

68. Augustine, ep. Jo. 8.10 [*Later Works*, 323–24].

69. *GA* 60:291–92 [*Phenomenology of Religious Life*, 221]: "In this *optare* (to wish), you appropriate the possibility of genuine loving [*In dieser optare eignest du dir die Möglichkeit des echten Liebens zu*]. Authentic love has a basic tendency toward the *dilectum, ut sit.* Thus, love is the will toward the being of the loved one [*Liebe ist also Wille zum Sein des Geliebten*].... Communal-worldly love has the sense of helping the loved other toward his existence, so that he comes to himself [*so daß er zu sich selbst kommt*]. Genuine love of God has the sense of willing to make God accessible to oneself as the one who exists in an absolute sense. This is the greater difficulty of life." See See P. Birmingham, "Heidegger and Augustine: The Will and the Word," in *The Influence of Augustine on Heidegger*, ed. C. J. N. de Paulo (Lewiston, PA: Edwin Mellen Press, 2006), 115–52.

70. See *Briefe 1925 bis 1975 und andere Zeugnisse: Hannah Arendt, Martin Heidegger*, ed. Ursula Ludz (Frankfurt am Main: Vittorio Klostermann, 2002), 31; *Letters 1925–1975: Hannah Arendt and Martin Heidegger*, ed. Ursula Ludz, trans. Andrew Shields (Orlando, FL: Harcourt, 2004), 21: "And so great a day hovers over my pages and notebooks this morning, and I am reading Augustine's *de gratia et libero arbitrio.*— Thank you for your letters—for how you have accepted me into your love—beloved. Do you know that this is the most difficult thing a human is given to endure? For anything else, there are methods, aids, limits, and understanding—here alone everything means: to be *in* one's love = to be forced into one's innermost existence. *Amo* means *volo, ut sis*, Augustine once said: I love you—I want you to be what you are."

71. *GA* 66:63 [*Mindfulness*, 52]; *GA* 5:367; *GA* 81, §5: "*Amo, volo, ut sis.*" See also Hannah Arendt, *The Life of the Mind* (New York: Harcourt, 1971), esp. pt. 2: "Willing," §2: "Quaestio Mihi Factus Sum: The Discovery of the Inner Man," 55–110, 104: "There is no greater assertion of something or somebody than to love it, that is, to say: I will, that you be—*Amo, volo, ut sis.*"

72. Augustine, *On the Trinity*, 1.10.21 (translation mine).

73. Augustine, ep. Jo. 9.5 [*Augustine: Later Works*, 333]: "There are men who fear God because they fear to be cast into hell, to burn with the devil in everlasting fire. This is the fear that makes an opening for charity, but it enters only to go out again."

74. Ibid. Scholars have noted that this distinction between servile fear and chaste fear mirrors the Heideggerian distinction deployed in *Being and Time* between fear (*Furcht*) and anxiety (*Angst*). See Otto Pöggeler, *The Paths of Heidegger's Life and Thought*, trans. J. Bailiff (Atlantic Highlands, NJ: Humanities Press International,

1997), 92–93; cf. C. J. N. de Paulo, "Following Heidegger's Footnotes to Augustine on *Timor Castus* and *Servilis*," in *The Influence of Augustine on Heidegger*, 299–322.

75. *Confessions* 10.36.

76. Augustine, ep. Jo. 9.5 [*Augustine: Later Works*, 333].

77. *GA* 58:62.

78. *Confessions* 10.21.

79. Ibid.

80. *GA* 60:201 [*Phenomenology of Religious Life*, 148].

81. *Confessions* 10.23.

82. Ibid.

83. In an interview published in 1984, Emmanuel Levinas refers to the Augustinian *veritas redarguens* as an example of what he calls a "supra-ontological" notion of truth, one that breaks with the Greek tradition defining truth as manifestation. See E. Levinas and R. Kearney, "Dialogue with Emmanuel Levinas," in *Face to Face with Emmanuel Levinas*, ed. R. Cohen (Albany: SUNY Press, 1986), 13–33, 25. The original version of this dialogue may be found in R. Kearney, *Dialogues with Contemporary Continental Thinkers* (Manchester: Manchester University Press, 1984), 49–69. See also Emmanuel Levinas, "De la signifiance du sens," in *Heidegger et la question de dieu*, ed. Richard Kearney and Joseph S. O'Leary (Paris: Bernard Grasset, 1980), 240–41.

84. See Peter Brown, who mentions that for Augustine "the sheer size of the inner world was a source of anxiety." *Augustine of Hippo: A Biography*, new edition, with an epilogue (Berkeley: University of California Press, 2000), 172.

85. See *Confessions* 10.26, with respect to which Heidegger remarks: "The question *where* [*wo*] I find God has turned into a discussion of the conditions of experiencing God, and that comes to a head in the problem of what I am myself [*was ich selbst bin*], such that, in the end, the same question still stands, but in a different form of enactment" (*GA* 60:204 [*Phenomenology of Religious Life*, 150]).

86. *Ennarationes in Psalmos* 7.9; here the translation is taken from Augustine of Hippo, *Expositions of the Psalms, 1–32*, vol. III/15 of *The Works of Saint Augustine: A Translation for the 21st Century*, trans. Maria Boulding, O.S.B., ed. John E. Rotelle, O.S.A. (Hyde Park, NY: New City, 2000), 123.

87. *SZ*, 199 [*BT*, 492].

88. Augustine discusses "un-finding" God in a text that Heidegger did not have available to him. See Sermon 360B [Dolbeau 25/Mainz 61] in *Vingt-six Sermons au peuple d'Afrique*, ed. François Dolbeau (Paris: IEA, 1996), 53ff. For English translation see Augustine, *Sermons-Various (Newly Discovered)*, vol. III/11 of *The Works of Saint Augustine: A Translation for the 21st Century*, trans. Edmund Hill, O.P. (New York: New City Press, 1997), 370: "The soul must not dare to form images, as it were, of God. It must first learn to *un-find* the one it wishes to find. [*Nihil sibi anima, quasi in phantasia formare audeat de deo quem vult invenire, prius discat non-invenire.*] What's this I've just said: it must first learn to 'unfind' [*non-invenire*]? It is when, reflecting on God, and something occurs to it that it has seen, perhaps the beauty of the earth, it must clear it out of its mind [*respuat ab animo suo*]. . . . You cannot know what [God] is, unless you first learn what he is not [*non potes ergo scire quid sit, nisi didiceris ante quid non sit*]."

89. *Confessions* 10.36.
90. *Confessions* 10.39, following Heidegger's rendering of it, according to *GA* 60:238ff. [*Phenomenology of Religious Life*, 178-80].
91. *GA* 60:240 [*Phenomenology of Religious Life*, 180, translation altered slightly].
92. *GA* 60:241 [*Phenomenology of Religious Life*, 180].
93. Ibid.
94. See Marion, *In the Self's Place*, 283: "If, therefore, something like a self remains possible for me, I will never find it in my own nonplace but solely there where a place is found, even if it is not situated in my own domain. This place without me, before me, but only thus *for* me, who remains essentially outside and foreign to it, God alone is found there."
95. *GA* 60:240 [*Phenomenology of Religious Life*, 180, translation altered slightly].
96. On the notion of the creature as nothing before God, see *GA* 60:235 [*Phenomenology of Religious Life*, 175]. Compare *Confessions* 7.11; and Letter 2. See esp. Etienne Gilson, "Note sur l'être et le temps chez saint Augustin," *Recherches augustiniennes* 2 (1962): 205-23.
97. *GA* 60:240 [*Phenomenology of Religious Life*, 180].
98. See for example *GA* 23:106, in which Heidegger writes that the Cartesian subject "as *res cogitans* is conceptualized ontologically in the sense of something present-at-hand (*Das Subjekt ist als* res cogitans *ontologisch im Sinne eines Vorhandenen begriffen*)" (translation mine).
99. *GA* 17:138.
100. Hannah Arendt, *Love and Saint Augustine*, ed. Joanna Vecchiarelli Scott and Judith Chelius Stark (Chicago: University of Chicago Press, 1996), 28.
101. Ibid., 27.
102. Ibid., 91.
103. *GA* 60:245 [*Phenomenology of Religious Life*, 184].
104. *GA* 60:244 [*Phenomenology of Religious Life*, 184].
105. *GA* 12:91 [*On the Way to Language*, 10].
106. *GA* 3:291 [*Kant and the Problem of Metaphysics*, 204].
107. *GA* 61:90 [*Phenomenological Interpretations of Aristotle*, 68].
108. Ibid.
109. Ibid.
110. *GA* 61:136 [*Phenomenological Interpretations of Aristotle*, 101].
111. *GA* 61:147 [*Phenomenological Interpretations of Aristotle*, 108].
112. *GA* 61:148 [*Phenomenological Interpretations of Aristotle*, 110].
113. *GA* 61:147 [*Phenomenological Interpretations of Aristotle*, 109].
114. *GA* 61:153 [*Phenomenological Interpretations of Aristotle*, 113].
115. The concept of *Befindlichkeit* plays a prominent role for Heidegger throughout the 1920s, not only as a key feature of his rereadings of Aristotle and Kant but also as a basic feature of existence in *Being and Time*. See, e.g., *GA* 18:241-48 [*Basic Concepts of Aristotelian Philosophy*, 162-166] for the connection between *Befindlichkeit* and Aristotelian *hēdonē*, and *GA* 18:271 [*Basic Concepts of Aristotelian Philosophy*, 184] for a more general discussion: "Being-in-the-world means: having a being there that is disclosed in its look and having to do with it as disclosed. Being-in-the-world means:

having the world there in a certain way. Not only is the world had, but being-there *has itself* in disposition [*Befindlichkeit*]. Being-in-the-world is characterized by disposition. Being-there has itself: not in reflecting, as the primary mode of having-itself there is in finding-oneself [*Sichbefinden*]." On the connection between *das Sichbefinden* and Kantian moral philosophy, see, e.g., *GA* 18:57–59 [*Basic Concepts of Aristotelian Philosophy*, 41], 92–96 [64–66], 241–45 [162–64], 262–63 [176], 270–71 [184].

116. *GA* 64:18.
117. *GA* 61:107 [*Phenomenological Interpretations of Aristotle*, 80].
118. Descartes, *Principles of Philosophy* I, §52, AT VIIIA, 25 [*Selected Philosophical Writings*, 177]. Cf. *SZ*, 94 [*BT*, 127].
119. *GA* 20:236 [*History of the Concept of Time*, 176].
120. *GA* 20:237 [*History of the Concept of Time*, 176].
121. *GA* 20:403 [*History of the Concept of Time*, 291].
122. *GA* 61:176 [*Phenomenological Interpretations of Aristotle*, 132].
123. *GA* 17:290 [*Introduction to Phenomenological Research*, 221].
124. Ibid.
125. Ibid. Cf. *SZ*, 186 [*BT*, 231].
126. *GA* 17:284 [*Introduction to Phenomenological Research*, 218].
127. *GA* 17:317 [*Introduction to Phenomenological Research*, 240].
128. Ibid.

CHAPTER 3

1. *GA* 61:197–98 [*Phenomenological Interpretations of Aristotle*, 148].
2. *GA* 21:233 [*Logic*, 194].
3. See chapter 5 below.
4. Peter E. Gordon, *Continental Divide: Heidegger, Cassirer, Davos* (Cambridge, MA: Harvard University Press 2010), 30.
5. *SZ* 230 [*BT* 272]. On this point, see Karsten Harries, "The Descent of the 'Logos': Limits of Transcendental Reflection."
6. *SZ*, 199 [*BT*, 492].
7. *GA* 17:1 [*Introduction to Phenomenological Research*, 1].
8. See the very helpful section on this issue in John Van Buren, *The Young Heidegger: Rumor of the Hidden King* (Bloomington: Indiana University Press, 1994), 131–234.
9. *GA* 63:2 [*Ontology: The Hermeneutics of Facticity*, 1–2].
10. *GA* 63:2 [*Ontology: The Hermeneutics of Facticity*, 2].
11. Ibid.
12. Edmund Husserl, *Logical Investigations*, trans. J. N. Findlay (New York: Humanities Press, 1970), vol. 2, Investigation 6, pp. 780–81.
13. *GA* 63:2 [*Ontology: The Hermeneutics of Facticity*, 2].
14. Ibid.
15. *GA* 17:1 [*Introduction to Phenomenological Research*, 1].
16. *GA* 62:366 [*Suppl.*, 122].
17. *GA* 62:368 [*Suppl.*, 124].

18. *GA* 62:374 [*Suppl.*, 128].
19. *GA* 62:384 [*Suppl.*, 135].
20. In addition to Rémi Brague, *Aristote et la question du monde* (Paris: PUF, 1988); and Francisco Volpi, *"Being and Time*: A 'Translation' of the Nicomachean Ethics?" in *Reading Heidegger from the Start*, 195–212; see especially William McNeil, *The Glance of the Eye: Heidegger, Aristotle, and the Ends of Theory* (Albany: SUNY Press, 1999); Walter Brogan, *Heidegger and Aristotle: The Twofoldedness of Being* (Albany: SUNY Press, 2005); and François Raffoul and David Pettigrew, eds., *Heidegger and Practical Philosophy* (Albany: SUNY Press, 2002).
21. *GA* 62:374 [*Suppl.*, 128].
22. *GA* 62:398 [*Suppl.*, 145].
23. *GA* 62:389 [*Suppl.*, 139].
24. Ibid.
25. *GA* 62:383 [*Suppl.*, 134].
26. Ibid.
27. *GA* 62:385 [*Suppl.*, 136].
28. *GA* 62:399 [*Suppl.*, 145].
29. *GA* 62:385 [*Suppl.*, 136].
30. Ibid.
31. *GA* 62:388 [*Suppl.*, 138].
32. *GA* 62:389 [*Suppl.*, 139].
33. *GA* 61:154 [*Phenomenological Interpretations of Aristotle*, 114–15].
34. *GA* 17:159 and 311 [*Introduction to Phenomenological Research*, 117–18 and 236, respectively].
35. *GA* 62:352 [*Suppl.*, 115].
36. *GA* 62:353 [*Suppl.*, 116].
37. *GA* 62:356 [*Suppl.*, 117].
38. *Confessions* 10.35.
39. *GA* 62:357 [*Suppl.*, 117–18].
40. *GA* 62:357 [*Suppl.*, 117].
41. *GA* 62:357 [*Suppl.*, 118].
42. *GA* 61:89 [*Phenomenological Interpretations of Aristotle*, 67].
43. *GA* 61:90 [*Phenomenological Interpretations of Aristotle*, 68].
44. *GA* 61:93 [*Phenomenological Interpretations of Aristotle*, 70].
45. *GA* 61:93 [*Phenomenological Interpretations of Aristotle*, 70].
46. *GA* 61:100 [*Phenomenological Interpretations of Aristotle*, 75].
47. *GA* 61:119 [*Phenomenological Interpretations of Aristotle*, 88].
48. Ibid.
49. *GA* 61:100–101 [*Phenomenological Interpretations of Aristotle*, 76].
50. *GA* 60:295 [*Phenomenology of Religious Life*, 223].
51. *GA* 61:101 [*Phenomenological Interpretations of Aristotle*, 76].
52. *GA* 61:103 [*Phenomenological Interpretations of Aristotle*, 77].
53. *Confessions* 10.35.
54. *GA* 60:223 [*Phenomenology of Religious Life*, 166].
55. *Confessions* 10.23.

56. *GA* 60:223 [*Phenomenology of Religious Life*, 166]; see also *GA* 60:200ff. [*Phenomenology of Religious Life*, 148ff.]
57. *GA* 61:136 [*Phenomenological Interpretations of Aristotle*, 101].
58. *SZ*, 177 [*BT*, 221].
59. See, e.g., *SZ*, 348 [*BT*, 399].
60. *SZ*, 178 [*BT*, 223].
61. *GA* 20:224–25 [*History of the Concept of Time*, 166–67].
62. *SZ*, 139 [*BT*, 178].
63. *SZ*, 15 [*BT*, 36].
64. *GA* 20:224–25 [*History of the Concept of Time*, 166–67].
65. *SZ*, 54 [*BT*, 80–81].
66. *SZ*, 57 [*BT*, 83].
67. *SZ*, 56 [*BT*, 82].
68. *SZ*, 126 [*BT*, 164].
69. *SZ*, 135 [*BT*, 174].
70. *SZ*, 144 [*BT*, 184].
71. *SZ*, 175 [*BT*, 220].
72. *SZ*, 171 [*BT*, 215]. On this point, see David Farrell Krell, *Daimon Life: Heidegger and Life-Philosophy* (Bloomington: Indiana University Press, 1992), 64ff.
73. In the phenomenon of Ambiguity, for example, Dasein as lost in the theyself cannot recognize what is genuinely disclosed and what is not. Its confusion is grounded in its sociality: "Being-with-one-another in the 'they' is by no means an indifferent side-by-side-ness in which everything has been settled, but rather an intent, ambiguous watching of one another, a secret and reciprocal listening-in. Under the mask of the 'for-one-another' an 'against-one-another' is in play." (*SZ*, 174–75 [*BT*, 219]). We find here in Heideggerian ambiguity the marks of Augustine's "fellowship of like punishment" (*Confessions* 10.36), discussed in connection with worldly ambition. Idle Talk, *das Gerede*, is grounded not simply in language as expression, but rather it is co-constituted through everyday being-with-one-another as communication. Such being-with-one-another, according to Heidegger, "takes place in talking with one another and in concern with what is said-in-the-talk" (*SZ*, 168 [*BT*, 212]). Concern over "the said," or gossip, gives rise to an "average intelligibility" of entities, and this intelligibility winds up perverting the disclosive nature of language. Through such concern, disclosure reverts into an act of *"closing off"* (*Verschliessen*) access to beings, as well as to Dasein's own potentiality-for-being. Idle Talk takes off from, formalizes, and expands upon Heidegger's commentary on *ambitio saeculi*. A crucial aspect of the latter temptation is Augustine's treatment of how "human language" (*humana lingua*), the "furnace" (*fornax*) in which we are tried daily (*Confessions* 10.37) has the power to interrupt the soul's attempt to stand fast in the enjoyment of most certain truth. As we have seen, Augustine confesses that his soul is commanded to remain continent with respect to worldly praise; it can do this by "depositing" (*ponere*) its joy (*gaudium*) in God as truth. When it *de-positions* (*deponere*) its joy from truth, and subsequently repositions or *deposits* (*ponere*) it in "human fallacies" (*in fallacia hominum*), the soul succumbs to worldly ambition (*Confessions* 10.37). In "Augustine and Neoplatonism," Heidegger dwells upon the verb *ponere*, rendering it through the verb *hinverlegen*, describing how the soul

"deposits" (*hinverlegt*) its joy "in the opinions of men" (*hinverlegen in der Gesinnung der Menschen*) (*GA* 60:233 [*Phenomenology of Religious Life*, 174]). In *Being and Time* the dynamic is retained in a slightly altered form as everyday understanding, lost in idle talk, is described as "the understanding which has thus already been *deposited* in the way things have been expressed (*das so in der Ausgesprochenheit schon hinterlegte Verständnis*)" (*SZ*, 168 [*BT*, 211]).

74. *SZ*, 180 [*BT*, 224].
75. *SZ*, 176 [*BT*, 220].
76. Ibid.
77. *SZ*, 176 [*BT*, 221].
78. *SZ*, 178 [*BT*, 223].
79. *GA* 60:240 [*Phenomenology of Religious Life*, 180].
80. *SZ*, 176 [*BT*, 220].
81. *SZ*, 176 [*BT*, 221].
82. *SZ*, 179 [*BT*, 223].
83. *SZ*, 176 [*BT*, 220].
84. *SZ*, 179 [*BT*, 223].
85. *GA* 60:240 [*Phenomenology of Religious Life*, 180].
86. *GA* 61:147 [*Phenomenological Interpretations of Aristotle*, 109].
87. *GA* 61:152–53 [*Phenomenological Interpretations of Aristotle*, 113].
88. See Martin Heidegger, Elisabeth Blochmann, *Briefwechsel 1918–1969*, ed. Joachim W. Storck (Marbach am Neckar, Deutsche Schillergesellschaft, 1969), 103.
89. *SZ*, 385 [*BT*, 437].
90. *SZ*, 385–86 [*BT*, 437].
91. *GA* 64:123 [*CT*, 19 and 19E].
92. *GA* 61:198 [*Phenomenological Interpretations of Aristotle*, 148].
93. *GA* 61:197 [*Phenomenological Interpretations of Aristotle*, 148].
94. *GA* 62:363 [*Suppl.*, 194].
95. *GA* 61:198 [*Phenomenological Interpretations of Aristotle*, 148].
96. Immanuel Kant, *Religion and Rational Theology*, trans. Allen Wood and George di Giovanni (Cambridge: Cambridge University Press, 1996), 62.
97. Ibid., 61.
98. Ibid., 269.
99. Ibid.
100. *SZ*, 229 [*BT*, 272].
101. Sigmund Freud, *The Interpretation of Dreams*, trans. James Strachey (New York: Basic Books 1955), 561.
102. Freud, *Interpretation of Dreams*, 201, 205, and 563.
103. Aristotle, *Nicomachean Ethics* 6.3, 1139b15–18.
104. *GA* 62:383 [*Suppl.*, 134].
105. *GA* 62:384 [*Suppl.*, 135].
106. *GA* 18:65 [*Basic Concepts of Aristotelian Philosophy*, 46].
107. Ibid.
108. *GA* 24:242 [*Basic Problems in Phenomenology*, 170].
109. *GA* 18:72 [*Basic Concepts of Aristotelian Philosophy*, 51].

110. Ibid.
111. *GA* 18:90 [*Basic Concepts of Aristotelian Philosophy*, 62].
112. See *GA* 18:59–60 [*Basic Concepts of Aristotelian Philosophy*, 42] for a discussion of Aristotelian *proairesis*.
113. *GA* 19:49 [*Plato's Sophist*, 34].
114. *GA* 19:51 [*Plato's Sophist*, 35–36].
115. See Christopher Rickey, *Revolutionary Saints: Heidegger, National Socialism, and Antinomian Politics* (University Park: Penn State University Press, 2002), 38–39.
116. *GA* 19:49 [*Plato's Sophist*, 34].
117. Ibid.
118. *GA* 19:52 [*Plato's Sophist*, 37].
119. *GA* 18:100 [*Basic Concepts of Aristotelian Philosophy*, 69].
120. *GA* 19:56 [*Plato's Sophist*, 39].
121. *SZ*, 24 [*BT*, 45].
122. *GA* 18:95 [*Basic Concepts of Aristotelian Philosophy*, 65]. Cf. *GA* 21:220 [*Logic*, 185].
123. *GA* 24:242 [*Basic Problems of Phenomenology*, 170].
124. *GA* 24:185ff.
125. *GA* 18:267 [*Basic Concepts of Aristotelian Philosophy*, 179].
126. *GA* 24:225 [*Basic Problems of Phenomenology*, 158–59].

CHAPTER 4

1. Friedrich Nietzsche, *On the Genealogy of Morals*, trans. Walter Kaufmann and R. J. Hollingdale (New York: Vintage, 1989), 15.
2. *SZ*, 43–44 [*BT*, 69].
3. Ibid.
4. Arendt, *Love and Saint Augustine*, 80.
5. *GA* 20:307 [*History of the Concept of Time. Prolegomena*, 424].
6. *SZ*, 40 [*BT*, 65].
7. *SZ*, 5 [*BT*, 25].
8. *SZ*, 53 [*BT*, 78].
9. *SZ*, 191 [*BT*, 235].
10. *SZ*, 42 [*BT*, 68].
11. *SZ*, 113 [*BT*, 149].
12. *SZ*, 114 [*BT*, 150].
13. *SZ*, 115 [*BT*, 150].
14. *SZ*, 130 [*BT*, 168].
15. *SZ*, 136–37 [*BT*, 176].
16. *SZ*, 144 [*BT*, 184].
17. *SZ*, 146 [*BT*, 187].
18. *SZ*, 156 [*BT*, 199].
19. *SZ*, 185 [*BT*, 230].
20. *SZ*, 186 [*BT*, 231].
21. *SZ*, 188 [*BT*, 233].

22. *SZ*, 188 [*BT*, 232].
23. *SZ*, 191 [*BT*, 235].
24. *SZ*, 193 [*BT*, 238].
25. *SZ*, 372 [*BT*, 424–25].
26. *SZ*, 404 [*BT*, 456].
27. *SZ*, 196 [*BT*, 241].
28. Ibid.
29. *SZ*, 232 [*BT*, 275].
30. *SZ*, 241–42 [*BT*, 285].
31. Ibid.
32. *SZ*, 245 [*BT*, 289].
33. *SZ*, 258–59 [*BT*, 303].
34. *SZ*, 265 [*BT*, 310].
35. *GA* 20:437 [*History of the Concept of Time: Prolegomena*, 316–17]; see also *GA* 20:439 [*History of the Concept of Time*, 318], where Heidegger argues that "only in dying can I to some extent say absolutely, 'I am.'"
36. *SZ*, 266 [*BT*, 311].
37. *SZ*, 44 [*BT*, 69].
38. *SZ*, 262 [*BT*, 306].
39. *SZ*, 262 [*BT*, 306–7].
40. *SZ*, 262 [*BT*, 302].
41. *SZ*, 267 [*BT*, 312].
42. *SZ*, 77–78 [*BT*, 108].
43. *SZ*, 80 [*BT*, 111].
44. Ibid.
45. *SZ*, 82 [*BT*, 114].
46. *SZ*, 197 [*BT*, 241].
47. *SZ*, 234 [*BT*, 277, translation slightly altered].
48. See Michel Haar, *Heidegger and the Essence of Man*, trans. William McNeil (Albany: SUNY Press, 1993), 17–18.
49. *SZ*, 268 [*BT*, 313]; see Magda King, *A Guide to Heidegger's Being and Time*, ed. John Llewelyn (Albany: SUNY Press, 2001), 163–64.
50. *SZ*, 269 [*BT*, 314].
51. *SZ*, 271 [*BT*, 316].
52. On the role of expression in the analytic of conscience, see Taylor Carman, *Heidegger's Analytic: Interpretation, Discourse, and Authenticity in Being and Time* (Cambridge: Cambridge University Press, 2003), esp. 264–313.
53. *SZ*, 269–70 [*BT*, 314].
54. *SZ*, 297 [*BT*, 343].
55. *SZ*, 275 [*BT*, 319].
56. *SZ*, 273 [*BT*, 318].
57. *SZ*, 274 [*BT*, 318].
58. *SZ*, 278 [*BT*, 323].
59. *SZ*, 297 [*BT*, 343].
60. *SZ*, 280 [*BT*, 325].

61. *SZ*, 300 [*BT*, 348]: "Die Entschlossenheit aber ist nur die in der Sorge gesorgte und als Sorge mögliche Eigentlichkeit dieser selbst" (translation altered).
62. *SZ*, 193 [*BT*, 237].
63. *GA* 62:352 [*Suppl.*, 115]: "Der Grundsinn der faktischen Lebensbewegtheit ist das *Sorgen* (*curare*)." (See n. 15: "[Handschriftlicher Zusatz auf dem unteren Blattrand mit Zuordnungszeichen:] *recuratio*—das Historische! –darin die höchste Seinsverwahrung.")
64. *GA* 21:412 [*Logic: The Question of Truth*, 341, translation altered].
65. *SZ*, 311 [*BT*, 359].
66. *SZ*, 277 [*BT*, 322].
67. *SZ*, 275 [*BT*, 319].
68. *SZ*, 278 [*BT*, 323].
69. *SZ*, 239 [*BT*, 282].
70. *SZ*, 238 [*BT*, 282].
71. Ibid.
72. Ibid.
73. Ibid.
74. Ibid.
75. *SZ*, 275 [*BT*, 320].
76. See Augustine, *Confessions* 1.6.
77. A similar line of argument runs through Arendt's *Love and Saint Augustine*. Having concluded that for Augustine man can never possess his Being as a whole, Arendt's study culminates in part 3, entitled "Social Life," by arguing that individual existence finds its truth in the twofold relevance of the neighbor, and that for Augustine divine grace shifts the soul's mode of interaction with the neighbor from temptation to true community through the knowledge of humanity's common ancestry in Adam. (See *Love and Saint Augustine*, 93–112).
78. *SZ*, 294 [*BT*, 341].
79. *SZ*, 307 [*BT*, 355].
80. *SZ*, 300 [*BT*, 347].
81. *SZ*, 307 [*BT*, 355].
82. *SZ*, 306 [*BT*, 496].
83. *SZ*, 281 [*BT*, 326].
84. *SZ*, 286–87 [*BT*, 332–33].
85. *SZ*, 281 [*BT*, 326].
86. Ibid.
87. *SZ*, 282 [*BT*, 327].
88. Ibid.
89. Ibid.
90. *SZ*, 283 [*BT*, 329].
91. *SZ*, 285 [*BT*, 331].
92. On the importance of these two aspects for understanding existential guilt, see Iain Macdonald, "Ethics and Authenticity: Conscience and Non-Identity in Heidegger and Adorno, with a Glance at Hegel," in *Adorno and Heidegger: Philosophical Ques-*

tions, ed. Iain Macdonald and Krzysztof Ziarek (Stanford, CA: Stanford University Press, 2008), 6–22, esp. 13–14.

93. *SZ*, 283 [*BT*, 329].
94. Ibid.
95. *SZ*, 284 [*BT*, 329-30].
96. *SZ*, 284 [*BT*, 330].
97. Ibid.
98. *SZ*, 276 [*BT*, 321].
99. *SZ*, 22 [*BT*, 44].
100. *SZ*, 21 [*BT*, 43].
101. *SZ*, 284 [*BT*, 330].
102. William Blattner, "The Concept of Death in *Being and Time*," in *Heidegger Reexamined*, vol. 1, *Dasein, Authenticity, and Death*, ed. Hubert Dreyfus and Mark Wrathall (New York: Routledge, 2002), 307–29.
103. *SZ*, 285 [*BT*, 331].
104. Ibid.
105. *SZ*, 286 [*BT*, 332].
106. Ibid.
107. Ibid.
108. *SZ*, 288 [*BT*, 334].
109. See Thomas Aquinas, *Summa Theologica* 1a, Q. 2, Art. 1.
110. *SZ*, 323 [*BT*, 370].
111. *SZ*, 288 [*BT*, 334].
112. *GA* 17:228 [*Introduction to Phenomenological Research*, 173].
113. *SZ*, 295 [*BT*, 342].
114. *SZ*, 295 [*BT*, 342].
115. *SZ*, 333 [*BT*, 382].

CHAPTER 5

1. Martin Heidegger, Elisabeth Blochmann, *Briefwechsel, 1918–1969*, ed. Joachim W. Storck (Marbach am Necker: Deutsche Schillergesellschaft, 1989); see also Hugo Ott, *Martin Heidegger: A Political Life*, trans. Allan Blunden (New York: Basic Books, 1993), 376–77.
2. Ott, *A Political Life*, 377.
3. *GA* 9:328 [*Pathmarks*, 250].
4. *GA* 14:69 [*On Time and Being*, 55].
5. The body of literature on Heidegger's Turn is too large to cite here. For evidence that 1930 marks the beginning of the Turn, see William Richardson, *Heidegger: Through Phenomenology to Thought*, 4th ed. (New York: Fordham, 2003), 212. In addition see the excellent pages devoted to this issue by Brett W. Davis, *Heidegger and the Will: On the Way to Gelassenheit* (Evanston, IL: Northwestern University Press, 2007), 60–99; and Jeffrey Malpas, *Heidegger's Topology: Being, Place, World* (Cambridge, MA: MIT Press, 2008), 147–210. See also the work of Thomas Sheehan, Richard Capiobianco,

Parvis Emad, Lawrence Hatab, Richard Polt, Frank Schalow, and Julian Young. See also James Risser, ed., *Heidegger toward the Turn: Essays on the Work of the 1930s* (Albany: SUNY Press, 1999); and Kenneth Maly, *Heidegger's Possibility: Language, Emergence-Saying Be-ing* (Toronto: University of Toronto Press, 2008), esp. 101–37.

6. Karl Löwith, *Martin Heidegger and European Nihilism*, ed. Richard Wolin and trans. Gary Steiner (New York: Columbia University Press, 1998), 94.

7. Cf. *GA* 24:328 [*Basic Problems of Phenomenology*, 231]; and *GA* 8:105 [*What Is Called Thinking?*, 102], where Heidegger asserts that for Augustine "the essential nature of time is conceived in the light of Being and, let us note it well, of a totally specific interpretation of 'Being'—Being as being present."

8. See Fiand, 11: "Was die Confessiones nicht sind: keine Selbstbiographie, keine Selbstanalyse seelischer Erlebnisse, keine Beschreibung religiöser Erfahrungen; auch: aufzählen von anekdotischen und zeitgeschichtlichen Tatsachen, die mit religiösen Deutungen umrahmt werdern; sondern: quid est homo als Frage quid est deus. Vgl. Hegel und anders Nietzsche: Gott ist Tot–was ist der Mensch?"

9. *GA* 83:280.

10. Fiand, 3.

11. Fiand, 11. Jean-Luc Marion makes a similar assertion concerning Book 11 when he notes that "precisely because at first glance it does indeed concern time, its definition and its aporiae, it behooves us to keep this essay within the *confessio*, alone capable of securing for it a place, in the sense that Saint Augustine understands it" (*In the Self's Place: The Approach of Saint Augustine*, 191). And see also the remark a few pages later concerning the ground of confession: "And so, if one cannot, indeed if one does not want to, endorse a theological understanding of the *Confessions*, that is to say lead the *confessio* all the way to its ground and its end—creation—the best method is not to read Books XI through XIII seriously, and the chief way of doing this is to see in Book XI only a treatise on time" (195).

12. Fiand, 11.

13. Fiand, 3.

14. *Confessions* 11.7. See Augustine, *Confessions, Books I–XIII*, trans. by F. J. Sheed, intro by Peter Brown, rev. ed. (Indianapolis, IN: Hackett, 1993), 238. All references, below, to Augustine's *Confessions* are taken from the Sheed translation unless otherwise noted.

15. *Confessions* 11.15.

16. Fiand, 7.

17. *Confessions* 11.26.

18. *Confessions* 11.27.

19. In connection with this passage, Kurt Flasch has drawn a connection with Heidegger's *GA* 21:246–47 [*Logic*, 204–5]. See Kurt Flasch, *Was ist Zeit? Augustinus von Hippo. Das XI. Buch der Confessiones. Historisch-Philosophische Studie. Text-Übersetzung-Kommentar* (Frankfurt: Klostermann, 1993), 355.

20. Fiand, 7.

21. Fiand, 12, quoting Matthew 7:7.

22. Fiand, 7.

23. Fiand, 12.

24. *SZ*, 5 [*BT*, 24].

25. On this score, Heidegger's reading of *Confessions* 11 anticipates the one Ricoeur offers at the outset of *Time and Narrative*. Both thinkers agree that Book 11 progresses past the stage at which it is a purely speculative interrogation of time's essence, becoming instead a lived experience of time. What Ricoeur calls lamentation Heidegger calls prayer or petition. This dialectic fundamentally transforms the experience of distention, conveying Augustine in the direction of a time to come. Like Ricoeur, Heidegger recognizes the centrality of Genesis 1:1 as structuring the overarching argument of Book 11 from start to finish, and he insists as well that the transition from inquiry to prayer divides the book in two, marking the emergence of a concrete or lived experience of distention or what Ricoeur subsequently calls *diaspora*. The latter assertion, drawn from Ricoeur, is actually Heidegger's central point in the Beuron lecture, according to which the Augustinian concept of time as distention is opened by, and so does not stand in opposition to, the relation with eternity. See Paul Ricoeur, *Time and Narrative*, trans. Kathleen McLaughlin and David Pellauer (Chicago: University of Chicago Press 1984), 5–30.

26. Fiand, 10.

27. Ibid.

28. This confirms the views of F.-W. von Hermann in his *Augustinus und die phänomenologische Frage nach der Zeit* (Frankfurt: Klostermann 1992).

29. Fiand, 12.

30. Fiand, 13.

31. Ibid.

32. See Emmanuel Levinas, *God, Death, and Time*, trans. Bettina Bergo (Stanford, CA: Stanford University Press, 2000), esp. p. 207, where Levinas discusses time as it lends itself "to our understanding as a reference to God—as the *to God* itself—before being interpreted as a pure deficiency or as a synonym of the perishable or the noneternal. That is, what gives itself to be understood as that which is diametrically opposed to the traditional idea of God. It is as if, within temporality, there were produced a relationship with a 'term' or end (but is it properly speaking a term?) that is third to Being and nothingness—an *excluded* middle or third and, in this way alone, a God who would not be thought in an onto-theo-logical manner." The similarities here between this passage and the overarching concerns of the Beuron lecture should give us pause before the assumption, seemingly held in common by Heidegger and Levinas alike, that the notion of temporality as a relationship with a final term or end could ever stand diametrically opposed "to the traditional idea of God," or in Heidegger's case, to the traditional idea of eternity. What separates Levinas from Heidegger is the former's concern to resist interpreting this reference to God, outside of its traditional idea, in purely ontological terms, whereas the presentation of *Confessions* 11 in the Beuron lecture is prelude to its subsequent ontologization. Moreover the question of the neighbor is all but absent from Heidegger's discussion of prayer as an intensified question.

33. Arendt, *Love and Saint Augustine*, 26.

34. Fiand, 13.

35. Arendt, *Love and Saint Augustine*, 15.

36. Ibid.

37. On silence in the later Heidegger, see Emilio Brito, *Heidegger et l'hymne du sacré* (Leuven: Leuven University Press, 1999), 103–14.
38. Augustine, *Confessions* 11.29.
39. See *GA* 29/30: 397 [*Fundamental Concepts*, 274] and *GA* 35:86–88.
40. Heidegger does refer in passing to "restraint" earlier in 1930, in *GA* 29/30:397 [*Fundamental Concepts*, 274]. For the use of the term in connection with *distentio/intentio animi*, see also *GA* 83:68.
41. For the use of this term, see for example Martin Heidegger, *Mindfulness*, trans. Parvis Emad and Thomas Kalary (New York: Continuum Press, 2006), xiii.
42. *GA* 65:35 [*Contributions*, 29].
43. *GA* 65:3 [*Contributions*, 5]. On the notion that thinking must transpose Dasein into a new ground and transform its essence, see Alejandro A. Vallega, *Heidegger and the Issue of Space: Thinking on Exilic Grounds* (University Park: Pennsylvania State University Press, 2003), 166f.
44. See *GA* 9:193–202 [*Pathmarks*, 148–54].
45. See Frank Schalow and Alfred Denker, *Historical Dictionary of Heidegger's Philosophy*, 2nd ed. (Plymouth, UK: The Scarecrow Press, 2010), 33.
46. *GA* 65:17 [*Contributions*, 16]; see also *GA* 65:23 [*Contributions*, 20], where Heidegger describes *Dasein* as the "steward of the stillness of the passing by of the last god." On this topic, see the following: Paola-Ludovica Coriando, *Der letzte Gott als Anfang* (Munich: Wilhelm Fink, 1998); Jean-Françoise Courtine, "Les traces et le passage du Dieu dans les *Beiträge zur Philosophie* de Martin Heidegger," *Archivio di Filosofia* 62, 1–3 (1994): 519–38; Françoise Dastur, "Le dieu extrême de la phénoménologie: Husserl et Heidegger," *Archives de Philosophie* 63 (2000): 195–204; Henri Krop, Arie L. Molendijk, and Hent de Vries, eds., *Post-Theism: Reframing the Judeo-Christian Tradition* (Leuven: Peeters, 2000); Cristina Ionescu, "The Concept of the Last God in Heidegger's *Beiträge*: Hints towards an Understanding of the Gift of *Sein*," *Studia Phaenomenologica* 2, 1–2 (2002), 59–95; Joan Stambaugh, *The Finitude of Being* (Albany: SUNY Press 1992); and Frank Schalow, *Heidegger and the Quest for the Sacred: From Thought to the Sanctuary of Faith* (Dordrecht: Kluwer, 2001).
47. *GA* 9:306 [*Pathmarks*, 233].
48. Ibid.
49. Ibid.
50. Ibid.
51. *GA* 65:15 [*Contributions*, 14].
52. See *GA* 65:15 [*Contributions*, 14–15]; cf. *GA* 65:20 [*Contributions*, 18].
53. *GA* 65:18 [*Contributions*, 16]; cf. *GA* 65:11 [*Contributions*, 11–12] and *GA* 65:80 [*Contributions*, 64].
54. Fiand, 10.
55. *GA* 65:487 [*Contributions*, 383, translation altered slightly].
56. *GA* 65:22 [*Contributions*, 20, translation altered slightly]; see also *GA* 65:63 [*Contributions*, 50].
57. *GA* 65:119 [*Contributions*, 94].
58. *GA* 65:278 [*Contributions*, 219].
59. *GA* 65:413 [*Contributions*, 327].

60. *GA* 64:107 [*CT*, 1 and 1E].
61. *GA* 8:105 [*What Is Called Thinking?*, 102].
62. *GA* 64:107 [*CT*, 1 and 1E).
63. *GA* 23:205.
64. Jacques Derrida, *Margins of Philosophy*, trans. Alan Bass (Chicago: University of Chicago Press, 1982), 64: "It is not in closing but in interrupting *Being and Time* that Heidegger wonders whether 'primordial temporality' leads to the meaning of Being. And this is not a programmatic articulation but a question and a suspension."
65. See Françoise Dastur, *Heidegger and the Question of Time*, trans. François Raffoul and David Pettigrew (Atlantic Highlands, NJ: Humanities Press, 1998).
66. *GA* 64:110 [*CT*, 5 and 5E].
67. *GA* 64:110 [*CT*, 5 and 5E].
68. *GA* 64:123 [*CT*, 20 and 20E].
69. *SZ*, 304 [*BT*, 352].
70. *GA* 24:377 [*Basic Problems of Phenomenology*, 267].
71. *GA* 21:400 [*Logic*, 331].
72. *GA* 9:188–89 [*Pathmarks*, 144].
73. *GA* 21:400–401 [*Logic*, 331].
74. See *GA* 9:174 [*Pathmarks*, 134].
75. *GA* 3:246 [*Kant and the Problem of Metaphysics*, 172].
76. *GA* 3:280 [*Kant and the Problem of Metaphysics*, 197].
77. Ibid. For an excellent discussion of these lines in the larger context of the Davos debate, see Gordon, *Continental Divide: Heidegger, Cassirer, Davos*, 136–214.
78. *GA* 64:108 [*CT*, 2 and 2E].
79. *SZ*, 427 [*BT*, 499]. For discussions of this passage, see William D. Blattner, *Heidegger's Temporal Idealism* (Cambridge: Cambridge University Press, 199), 267.
80. See Hannah Arendt, *The Life of the Mind*, vol. 2, *Willing* (New York: Harcourt, 1978), 172–94.
81. *GA* 5:329 [*Off the Beaten Track*, 248].
82. *GA* 5:341 [*Off the Beaten Track*, 257].
83. *GA* 5:327 [*Off the Beaten Track*, 246].
84. *GA* 5:337 [*Off the Beaten Track*, 254].
85. Ibid.
86. *GA* 5:331 [*Off the Beaten Track*, 249].
87. *GA* 5:333 [*Off the Beaten Track*, 251].
88. *GA* 5:357 [*Off the Beaten Track*, 269].
89. *GA* 5:355 [*Off the Beaten Track*, 268].
90. *GA* 5:360 [*Off the Beaten Track*, 271].
91. *GA* 5:366 [*Off the Beaten Track*, 276].
92. *GA* 5:367 [*Off the Beaten Track*, 277].
93. Ibid.
94. Ibid. The citation is from Augustine's *On the Morals of the Catholic Church*, 1.3.
95. Briefly one can ask at the outset: does Heidegger misread Augustine by arguing that *fruitio* or enjoyment is a species of use? In *On Christian Doctrine*, Augustine famously juxtaposes enjoyment and use, *frui* and *uti*, as two different modes of

interacting with things. To use something is to refer it to another, an end beyond and apart from it. By contrast "to enjoy something is to cling to it in love for its own sake." Strictly speaking, only the Persons of the Trinity, along with the Godhead in its unity, are to be enjoyed. Everything else is to be used with a view toward loving God. Augustine nuances this view in his subsequent writings, tempering his initial assertion that the souls of others are objects of use properly speaking. *On Christian Doctrine* seems to controvert Heidegger's conflation of enjoyment and use. However, it is reasonable to assume that Heidegger was also aware that in at least one instance Augustine does indeed define *fruitio* as a species of *usus*. In *On the Trinity*, Augustine remarks: "To use something is to put it at the will's disposal; to enjoy something is to use it with an actual, not merely anticipated joy (*frui est autem uti cum gaudio, non adhuc spei, sed iam rei*)." In the *City of God*, Augustine cautions against reading too much into these lines, insisting that they refer only to the "common meaning of use." Heidegger's only variation on Augustine is that he identifies as the leading sense of *fruitio* a meaning which Augustine intends as no more than its common definition. See respectively Augustine *On Christian Doctrine*, 1.4; *On The Trinity*, 10.4, and finally *The City of God*, 11.25, where Augustine strongly denies that *On the Trinity*, 10.4, deals with the use and enjoyment in their strict senses: "I am well aware that 'fruit' and 'enjoyment' are properly used with reference to one who enjoys, and 'use' with reference to a user, the difference clearly being that we are said to enjoy something which gives us pleasure in itself, without reference to anything else, whereas we 'use' something when we seek it for some other purpose. . . . It was the common meaning of 'use' that I had in mind when I remarked (in *On the Trinity* 10.4) that we should look for three things in assessing a man's value: disposition (*ingenium*), learning (*doctrina*), and practice (*usus*)." See Saint Augustine, *City of God*, trans. Henry Bettenson, with an introduction by John O'Meara (New York: Penguin, 2003), 458.

96. *GA* 78:135: "Wenn wir gewöhnlich das Wort 'Brauch' hören, 'es ist der Brauch,' dann meinen wir damit 'das Übliche.' Wir bringen den 'Brauch' in die Nähe von Sitte. Brauchen verstehen wir im Sinn von 'nötig haben' bedürfen, während dürfen, darfen seinerseits bedeutet: den Gebrauch von etwas haben, z.B. der Freiheit diese genießen. Das 'genießen' in diesem ursprünglichen Sinne meint das lateinische Wort *frui* (*fruitio Dei*); dasselbe Wort ist brauchen."

97. *GA* 5:366 [*Off the Beaten Track*, 276].
98. *GA* 5:367 [*Off the Beaten Track*, 277].
99. *GA* 5:337 [*Off the Beaten Track*, 254].
100. *GA* 5:328 [*Off the Beaten Track*, 247].
101. Ibid.
102. Ibid.
103. Ibid.
104. *GA* 9:199 [*Pathmarks*, 152].
105. *GA* 5:337 [*Off the Beaten Track*, 254].
106. *GA* 5:371 [*Off the Beaten Track*, 280, translation altered].
107. Ibid.
108. *GA* 8:153 [*What Is Called Thinking?*, 149].
109. *GA* 8:192 [*What Is Called Thinking?*, 189].

110. *GA* 5:367 [*Off the Beaten Track*, 277].
111. *GA* 5:368 [*Off the Beaten Track*, 278].
112. *GA* 51:111 [*Basic Concepts*, 95]: "The first word that overtakes Being contains a saying that is a denial or an *unsaying* (*Absage*): *a-peiron*. One calls the *a-*, according to grammar, *privatum*; the *a-* expresses a 'theft,' a taking away, a lack and an absence. It could be that this 'not' has in no way the character of something negative."
113. *GA* 65:371 [*Contributions*, 293].
114. *GA* 24:463–64 [*Basic Problems*, 326]: "if Being, which has always already been understood 'earlier,' is to become an express *object*, then the objectification of this *prius*, which was forgotten, must have the character of a coming back to what was already once and already earlier understood."
115. *GA* 65:325 [*Contributions*, 257, translation altered].
116. See *GA* 65:376 [*Contributions*, 297]: "'Time' has the character of the 'I' as little as space has the character of the thing; a fortiori, neither is space 'objective' nor is time 'subjective.'"

CHAPTER 6

1. See *Rudolph Bultmann/Martin Heidegger: Briefwechsel 1925 bis 1975*, ed. Andreas Grossman and Christof Landmesser (Frankfurt: Klostermann, 2006).
2. As quoted in Hugo Ott, *Martin Heidegger: A Political Life*, trans. Allan Blunden (New York: Basic Books, 1993), 167.
3. Ott, *Martin Heidegger: A Political Life*, 168.
4. See for example *GA* 65:346 [*Contributions*, 273]. In their cautious and judicious translation of the *Beiträge*, Rojcewicz and Vallega-Neu render the term *Versagung* as "self-withholding." While mainly relying upon this edition, I simultaneously want to signal in this chapter the lexical and conceptual range of the terms *Versagung* and *Sichversagung* in this text, while emphasizing that the strong connection between Being and language in Heidegger's later works allows us to interrogate the linguistic dimensions of Being as self-withholding in terms of retraction.
5. *GA* 14:69 [*On Time and Being*, 55].
6. Augustine, *Revisions*, trans. Boniface Ramsey (Hyde Park, NY: New City Press, 2010), 23.
7. *GA* 12:79–147 [*On the Way to Language*, 1–56].
8. Jean-François Lyotard, *Heidegger and "the jews,"* trans. Andreas Michel and Mark S. Roberts (Minneapolis: University of Minnesota Press, 1990), 52. On this point, see the recent work by Emmanuel Faye, *Heidgger: The Introduction of Nazism into Philosophy in Light of the Unpublished Seminars of 1933–1935*, trans. Michael B. Smith (New Haven, CT: Yale University Press, 2009); and Christian Sommer, *Heidegger 1933: Le programme platonicien du Discours de rectorat* (Paris: Editions Hermann, 2013).
9. See *GA* 94.
10. Martin Heidegger, *Kant and the Problem of Metaphysics*, 5th edition, trans. by Richard Taft (Bloomington: Indiana University Press, 1997), xx.
11. *GA* 6.2:174 [*Nietzsche*, vol. 4, 123].
12. *GA* 17:126 [*Introduction to Phenomenological Research*, 91].

13. *GA* 83:280.

14. The perspective offered here is meant to confirm rather than to contest the basic interpretations of Heidegger's Turn put forth by Thomas Sheehan in *"Kehre and Ereignis*: A Prolegomenon to *Introduction to Metaphysics,"* in *A Companion to Heidegger's Introduction to Metaphysics*, ed. Richard Polt and Gregory Fried (New Haven, CT: Yale University Press, 2001), 3–16; and by Friedrich-Wilhelm von Hermann in *Wege ins Ereignis: Zu Heideggers Beiträgen zur Philosophie* (Frankfurt: Vittorio Klostermann, 1994), 67–68.

15. *SZ*, 360 [*BT*, 313].

16. *GA* 40:32 [*Introduction to Metaphysics*, 32].

17. *GA* 5:332 [*Off the Beaten Track*, 250].

18. Ibid. Cf. Friedrich Nietzsche, *Will to Power*, trans. Walter Kaufmann and R. J. Hollingdale (New York: Vintage Books, 1967), 330, §617: "To impose upon becoming the character of being—that is the supreme will to power."

19. *GA* 5:333 [*Off the Beaten Track*, 251].

20. *GA* 5:327 [*Off the Beaten Track*, 246].

21. *GA* 6.2:353 [*Nietzsche*, vol. 4, 214].

22. *GA* 5:327 [*Off the Beaten Track*, 246].

23. This approach is especially clear in *GA* 26:196–97 [*The Metaphysical Foundations of Logic*, 154–55].

24. *GA* 3:221 [*Kant and the Problem of Metaphysics*, 155].

25. *GA* 9:114 [*Pathmarks*, 90].

26. *GA* 9:120 [*Pathmarks*, 95].

27. On this point, see François Jaran, *Heidegger inédit 1929–1930: L'inachevable Être et Temps* (Paris: J. Vrin, 2012).

28. *GA* 36/37:3 [*Being and Truth*, 3].

29. *GA* 36/37:215 [*Being and Truth*, 163].

30. *GA* 40:1 [*Introduction to Metaphysics*, 2].

31. *GA* 40:4 [*Introduction to Metaphysics*, 5].

32. *GA* 40:5 [*Introduction to Metaphysics*, 7].

33. *GA* 9:122 [*Pathmarks*, 96].

34. *GA* 40:15 [*Introduction to Metaphysics*, 21].

35. Ibid.

36. *GA* 40:32 [*Introduction to Metaphysics*, 44].

37. *GA* 65:234 [*Contributions*, 184].

38. *GA* 71:236 [*The Event*, 205].

39. Ibid.

40. *GA* 65:170–71 [*Contributions*, 134, translation slightly altered].

41. *GA* 12:205–26 [*On the Way to Language*, 139–58].

42. *GA* 65:15 [*Contributions*, 14, translation altered slightly].

43. *GA* 9:194 [*Pathmarks*, 148].

44. *GA* 65:20 [*Contributions*, 18].

45. *GA* 65:179 [*Contributions*, 140].

46. *GA* 65:179 [*Contributions*, 125]; cf. *GA* 81:330.

47. *GA* 66:219 [*Mindfulness*, 193]: "Man can never eliminate the forgottenness of Being: even when he honors the most question-worthy by inquiring into its truth."
48. *GA* 65:234 [*Contributions*, 184].
49. *GA* 65:278 [*Contributions*, 219].
50. *SZ*, 194 [*BT*, 238].
51. Ibid.
52. *GA* 66:220 [*Mindfulness*, 194].
53. *GA* 9:343 [*Pathmarks*, 261]. For an earlier example of this formula, see *GA* 64:114 [*CT*, 9 and 9E].
54. *GA* 5:367 [*Off the Beaten Track*, 271].
55. *GA* 5:347 [*Off the Beaten Track*, 262].
56. Ibid.
57. Karl Löwith, *Martin Heidegger and European Nihilism*, 55.
58. *GA* 5:351 [*Off the Beaten Track*, 264].
59. *GA* 45:215 [*Basic Questions of Philosophy*, 181].
60. *GA* 65:25 [*Contributions*, 22].
61. *GA* 45:216 [*Basic Questions of Philosophy*, 182].
62. *GA* 5:266–67 [*Off the Beaten Track*, 199].
63. *GA* 5:266 [*Off the Beaten Track*, 198].
64. *GA* 5:221 [*Off the Beaten Track*, 165].
65. *GA* 5:237 [*Off the Beaten Track*, 177].
66. *GA* 5:255 [*Off the Beaten Track*, 190].
67. On this point, see Michael Theunissen, *Negative Theologie der Zeit* (Frankfurt am Main: Suhrkamp, 1991).
68. On this issue, see esp. Michael E. Zimmerman, *Heidegger's Confrontation with Modernity: Technology, Politics, and Art* (Bloomington: Indiana University Press, 1990), 137–38.
69. Iain D. Thomson, *Heidegger on Ontotheology: Technology and the Politics of Education* (Cambridge: Cambridge University Press, 2005), 56.
70. *GA* 5:267 [*Off the Beaten Track*, 199].
71. See Immanuel Kant, *Anthropology, History, Education*, trans. Robert B. Louden and Günter Zöller (Cambridge: Cambridge University Press, 2011), 63–78.
72. *GA* 45:215 [*Basic Questions of Philosophy*, 181]. See Michel de Beistegui, *The New Heidegger* (London: Continuum, 2005), 98; cf. Dennis Schmidt, "Ruins and Roses: Hegel and Heidegger on Sacrifice, Mourning, and Memory," in *Endings: Questions of Memory in Hegel and Heidegger*, ed. Rebeccay Comay and John McCumber (Evanston, IL: Northwestern University Press, 1999), 97–113.
73. *GA* 45:215 [*Basic Questions of Philosophy*, 181]: "The displacement of humanity . . . turns man away from himself the furthest and into a relation with Being itself."
74. *GA* 45:216 [*Basic Questions of Philosophy*, 182].
75. *GA* 65:78 [*Contributions*, 62].
76. *GA* 45:193 [*Basic Questions of Philosophy*, 167].
77. Ibid.
78. *GA* 65:28 [*Contributions*, 25].

79. *GA* 65:196 [*Contributions*, 154].
80. Martin Heidegger, *Gelassenheit* (Pfullingen: Günther Neske, 1959). [*Discourse on Thinking*, trans. John Anderson and E. Hans Freund (New York: Harper & Row, 1966), 55.]
81. *GA* 54:177 [*Parmenides*, 120].
82. *GA* 5:281 [*Off the Beaten Track*, 210].
83. *SZ*, 223 [*BT*, 298].
84. Hannah Arendt, *Life of the Mind*, 2:173.
85. Ibid., 2:181.
86. See especially Reinhard Mehring, *Heideggers Überlieferungsgeschick; Eine dionysiche Selbstinszenierung* (Würzburg: Königshausen & Neumann, 1992); Gregory Fried, *Heidegger's Polemos: From Being to Politics* (New Haven, CT: Yale University Press, 2000); Charles Bambach, *Heidegger's Roots: Nietzsche, National Socialism, and the Greeks* (Ithaca, NY: Cornell University Press, 2003), 247–325; Theodore Kisiel, "Heidegger's *Gesamtausgabe*: An International Scandal of Scholarship," *Philosophy Today* 39 (1995): 3–15; Daniel Dahlstrom, "Heidegger's Last Word," *Review of Metaphysics* 41 (1988): 589–606; Richard Wolin, *The Politics of Being* (New York: Columbia University Press, 1990); and Frank Schalow, "The *Gesamtausgabe* Nietzsche: An Exercise in Translation and Thought," *Heidegger Studies* 9 (1993): 139–52.
87. *GA* 83:310.
88. *GA* 24:463–64 [*Basic Problems of Phenomenology*, 326].
89. *GA* 66:217 [*Mindfulness*, 191].
90. Ibid.; cf. *GA* 66:219 [*Mindfulness*, 193].
91. *GA* 65:453 [*Contributions*, 357].
92. *GA* 54:184 [*Parmenides*, 124].
93. *GA* 54:106 [*Parmenides*, 72].
94. *GA* 6.2:149 [*Nietzsche*, vol. 4, 103].
95. *GA* 6.2:190 [*Nietzsche*, vol. 4, 136].
96. *GA* 6.2:149 [*Nietzsche*, vol. 4, 103].
97. *GA* 5:108 [*Off the Beaten Track*, 82].
98. On this point, see Jacques Taminiaux, *Heidegger and the Project of Fundamental Ontology*, trans. Michael Gendre (Albany: SUNY Press, 1991) 161–73.
99. On the origins of the Eternal Return in Nietzsche, see Mazzino Montinari, "Nietzsche's Philosophy as the 'Passion for Knowledge,'" in *Reading Nietzsche*, trans. Greg Whitlock (Champagne: University of Illinois Press, 2003), 57–68.
100. Nietzsche, *Will to Power*, 330.
101. Friedrich Nietzsche, *Thus Spoke Zarathustra*, trans. Adrian Del Caro (Cambridge: Cambridge University Press, 2006), 111.
102. *GA* 8:108 [*What Is Called Thinking?*, 105].
103. *GA* 5:333 [*Off the Beaten Track*, 251].
104. Nietzsche, *Will to Power*, 267.
105. Friedrich Nietzsche, *The Birth of Tragedy and Other Writings*, trans. Ronald Speirs (Cambridge: Cambridge University Press, 1999), 145.
106. *GA* 5:245 [*Off the Beaten Track*, 183].
107. *GA* 6.1:632 [*Nietzsche*, vol. 3, 137].

108. As quoted in *GA* 5:247 [*Off the Beaten Track*, 184]. For the passage as it appears in Nietzsche's works, see Friedrich Nietzsche, *Werke*, Kritische Gesamtausgabe, ed. Giorgio Colli and Mazzino Montinari (Berlin: de Gruyter, 1967–), Nachgelassene Fragmente Frühjahr-Sommer 1883 NF-1883, 7 [96].

109. Reiner Schurmann, *Heidegger on Being and Acting: From Principles to Anarchy*, trans. Christine-Marie Gros (Bloomington: Indiana University Press, 1987), 192–94.

110. *GA* 5:247 [*Off the Beaten Track*, 184–85]. See Nietzsche, *Werke*, Nachgelassene Fragmente Sommer-Herbst 1884 KGWB/NF-1884, 26 [359].

111. *GA* 5:247 [*Off the Beaten Track*, 185].

112. *GA* 6.1:632–48 [*Nietzsche*, vol. 3, 137–49].

113. *GA* 6.2:197 [*Nietzsche*, vol. 4, 144].

114. *GA* 6.1:637 [*Nietzsche*, vol. 3, 141].

115. *GA* 7:83 [*The End of Philosophy*, 97].

116. *GA* 40:9 [*Introduction to Metaphysics*, 8].

117. *GA* 5:372 [*Off the Beaten Track*, 280].

118. *GA* 65:12–13 [*Contributions*, 12].

119. *GA* 65:368 [*Contributions*, 291, translation slightly altered].

120. *GA* 65:369 [*Contributions*, 291].

121. Ibid.

122. Ibid.

123. Ibid.

124. See Augustine, *The Predestination of the Saints* 2.5, in *Answer to the Pelagians IV: To the Monks of Hadrumetum and Provence*, vol. I/26 of *The Works of Saint Augustine: A Translation for the 21st Century*, trans. Roland J. Teske, S.J., and ed. John E. Rotelle, O.S.A. (New York: New City Press, 1999), 151.

125. *GA* 60:235 [*Phenomenology of Religious Life*, 176].

126. Ibid.

127. *GA* 6.1:384 [*Nietzsche*, vol. 2, 122].

128. *GA* 6.1:385 [*Nietzsche*, vol. 2, 123].

129. *GA* 6.1:386 [*Nietzsche*, vol. 2, 124].

130. Ibid.

131. *GA* 6.1:388 [*Nietzsche*, vol. 2, 126].

132. Published in *GA* 9:45–78 [*Pathmarks*, 39–62].

133. *GA* 9:52 [*Pathmarks*, 43].

134. *GA* 9:52 [*Pathmarks*, 44].

135. *GA* 24:397–99 [*Basic Problems of Phenomenology*, 281].

136. *GA* 9:52 [*Pathmarks*, 44].

137. *GA* 9:66 [*Pathmarks*, 53].

138. *GA* 5:247 [*Off the Beaten Track*, 185].

139. Ibid.

140. Ibid.

141. *GA* 8:108 [*What Is Called Thinking?*, 105]. Cf. Nietzsche, *The Gay Science*, trans. Josefine Nauckhoff and ed. Bernard Williams (Cambridge: Cambridge University Press, 2001), §41, entitled "Against Repentance" (*Gegen die Reue*), 57.

142. *GA* 65:11 [*Contributions*, 11].

143. *GA* 65:230 [*Contributions*, 181].
144. *GA* 65:371 [*Contributions*, 292].
145. Ibid.
146. *GA* 65:452 [*Contributions*, 356].
147. Ibid.
148. *GA* 65:453 [*Contributions*, 356].
149. *GA* 65:453 [*Contributions*, 357].
150. On this topic, see Rita Casale, *L'esperienza Nietzsche di Heidegger* (Naples: Bibliopolis, 2005), esp. ch. 6; German translation by Catrin Dingler entitled *Heideggers Nietzsche: Geschichte einer Obsession* (Bielefeld: transcript Verlag, 2010).
151. *GA* 65:454 [*Contributions*, 358].
152. *GA* 65:57 and 70. [*Contributions* 46 and 56, respectively].
153. *GA* 65:54 [*Contributions*, 38].
154. *GA* 65:413 [*Contributions*, 327, translation altered].
155. *GA* 65:58 [*Contributions*, 47, translation altered].
156. Augustine, *On the Trinity*, 1.10 (21).
157. *GA* 65:440 [*Contributions*, 347, translation altered].
158. *SZ*, 311 [*BT*, 359].
159. *SZ*, 312 [*BT*, 359].
160. *SZ*, 310 [*BT*, 358].
161. *SZ*, 307 [*BT*, 355].
162. *SZ*, 307–8 [*BT*, 355].
163. *SZ*, 308 [*BT*, 356].
164. *GA* 65:285 [*Contributions*, 200].
165. *GA* 6.2:349 [*Nietzsche*, vol. 4, 210].
166. Ibid.
167. *GA* 5:258 [*Off the Beaten Track*, 193].
168. *GA* 22:329–30 [*Basic Concepts of Ancient Philosophy*, 240]: "The decisive question is how the problem of Being is necessarily impelled toward a *most genuine being*: can there at all be an ontology constructed purely, as it were, without an orientation toward a preeminent being, whether that is thought of as the first mover, the first heaven, or something else?"
169. *GA* 65:344 [*Contributions*, 272].
170. *GA* 65:78 [*Contributions*, 62].
171. *GA* 65:190 [*Contributions*, 149].
172. *GA* 65:286 [*Contributions*, 225].
173. *GA* 65:55 [*Contributions*, 45, translation altered].

CONCLUSION

1. *GA* 62:363 [*Suppl.*, 194].
2. *GA* 6.2:335 [*Nietzsche*, vol. 4, 197–98].
3. *GA* 6.2:349 [*Nietzsche*, vol. 4, 210].
4. *GA* 6.2:353 [*Nietzsche*, vol. 4, 213].

5. *GA* 6.2:368 [*Nietzsche*, vol. 4, 225]: "Only one thing is necessary, namely, that thinking, encouraged by Being itself, simply think to encounter Being in its default as such. Such thinking to encounter rests primarily on the recognition *that Being itself withdraws, but that as this withdrawal Being is precisely the relationship that claims the essence of man, as the abode of its (Being's) advent.*" A few lines later Heidegger adds: "Thinking to encounter follows Being in its withdrawal, follows it in the sense that it lets Being itself go, while for its own part it stays behind. Then where does thinking linger? No longer where it lingered as the prior, omitting thought of metaphysics. Thinking stays behind by first taking the decisive step back, back from the omission."

6. *GA* 6.2:389 [*Nietzsche*, vol. 4, 243-44].
7. *GA* 6.2:369 [*Nietzsche*, vol. 4, 226].
8. See Giorgio Agamben, *Homo Sacer*, translated by Daniel Heller-Roazen (Stanford, CA: Stanford University Press, 1998), 60.
9. *GA* 6.2:357 [*Nietzsche*, vol. 4, 217].
10. *GA* 6.2:357 [*Nietzsche*, vol. 4, 217-18].
11. *GA* 6.2:357 [*Nietzsche*, vol. 4, 217].
12. *GA* 6.2:373 [*Nietzsche*, vol. 4, 230].
13. *GA* 8:141 [*What Is Called Thinking?*, 136-137].
14. *GA* 9:197 [*Pathmarks*, 150].
15. *GA* 11:63 [*Identity and Difference*, 55].
16. *GA* 11:64 [*Identity and Difference*, 56].
17. *GA* 11:65 [*Identity and Difference*, 57].
18. *GA* 11:64 [*Identity and Difference*, 56].
19. Ibid.
20. Ibid.
21. *GA* 11:71 [*Identity and Difference*, 64].
22. Ibid.
23. Ibid.
24. Ibid.
25. See the extensive discussion of this term in John D. Caputo, *Heidegger and Aquinas: An Essay on Overcoming Metaphysics* (New York: Fordham University Press, 1982), 147-84. See also Richard Capobianco, *Engaging Heidegger* (Toronto: University of Toronto Press, 2010), 11-12.
26. *GA* 5:364 [*Off the Beaten Track*, 275]: "Being, together with its essence, its difference from the being, keeps to itself. The difference collapses. It remains forgotten. Though the two elements of the difference, that which is present and presencing, disclose themselves, they do not do so *as* different."
27. *GA* 11:76 [*Identity and Difference*, 71].
28. *GA* 11:77 [*Identity and Difference*, 72].
29. *GA* 11:77 [*Identity and Difference*, 71-72].
30. *GA* 5:255 [*Off the Beaten Track*, 190.]
31. Ibid.
32. *GA* 6.2:397 [*Nietzsche*, vol. 4, 250].
33. *GA* 7:77 [*The End of Philosophy*, 92].

SELECTED BIBLIOGRAPHY

I.I. WORKS BY MARTIN HEIDEGGER

BH   *Becoming Heidegger: On the Trail of His Early Occasional Writings, 1910–1927.* Edited by Theodore Kisiel and Thomas Sheehan. Evanston, IL: Northwestern University Press, 2007.
BT   *Being and Time.* See *SZ.*
CT   *The Concept of Time,* translated by William McNeil. See *GA* 64.
     Discourse on Thinking. See *Gelassenheit.*
Fiand   Martin Heidegger, "Des hl. Augustinus Betrachtung über die Zeit: Confessiones lib. XI." In the Fiand Collection, Loyola University of Chicago, Archives and Special Collections, Martin Heidegger Collection, ca. 1918–1976, Box 1, Folder 1, Document 2, pp. 1–13.
GA   Martin Heidegger, *Gesamtausgabe* (Collected Works) [English translation given in brackets following].
GA 1   *Frühe Schriften.* (1912–1916) Edited by Friedrich-Wilhelm von Hermann. Frankfurt am Main: Vittorio Klostermann, 1978.
GA 3   *Kant und das Problem der Metaphysik.* (1929) Edited by Friedrich-Wilhelm von Hermann. Frankfurt am Main: Vittorio Klostermann, 1991.
       [*Kant and the Problem of Metaphysics.* Translated by R. Taft. Bloomington: Indiana University Press, 1997.]
GA 5   *Holzwege.* (1935–1946) Edited by Friedrich-Wilhelm von Hermann. Frankfurt am Main: Vittorio Klostermann, 1977.
       [*Off the Beaten Track.* Edited and translated by Julian Young and Kenneth Haynes. New York: Cambridge University Press, 2002.]
GA 6.1   *Nietzsche I.* (1936–1939) Edited by Brigitte Schillbach. Frankfurt am Main: Vittorio Klostermann, 1996.
       [*Nietzsche, Volumes One and Two.* Translated by David Farrell Krell. New York: Harper & Row, 1984.]
       [*Nietzsche, Volume Three.* Translated by Joan Stambaugh, David Farrell Krell, and Frank Capuzzi. Edited by David Farrell Krell. New York: Harper & Row, 1987.]

GA 6.2 *Nietzsche II.* (1939–1946) Edited by Brigitte Schillbach. Frankfurt am Main: Vittorio Klostermann, 1997.
[*Nietzsche, Volume Four.* Translated by Frank Capuzzi. Edited by David Farrell Krell. New York: Harper & Row, 1987.]

GA 6.1/2 *Nietzsche, Zweiter Band.* Edited by Hrsg. von Brigitte Schillbach. Frankfurt am Main: Vittorio Klostermann, 1996/1997.

GA 7 *Vorträge und Aufsätze.* (1936–1953) Edited by Friedrich-Wilhelm von Hermann. Frankfurt am Main: Vittorio Klostermann, 2000.
[*The End of Philosophy.* Translated by Joan Stambaugh. Chicago: University of Chicago Press, 2003.]

GA 8 *Was Heisst Denken?* (1951–1952) Edited by Paola Ludovika Coriando. Frankfurt am Main: Vittorio Klostermann, 2002.
[*What Is Called Thinking?* Translated by J. Glenn Gray. New York: Harper & Row, 1968.]

GA 9 *Wegmarken.* (1919–1961) Edited by Friedrich-Wilhelm von Hermann. Frankfurt am Main: Vittorio Klostermann, 1996.
[*Pathmarks.* Edited by William McNeil. New York: Cambridge University Press, 1998.]

GA 11 *Identität und Differenz.* (1955–1957) Edited by Friedrich-Wilhelm von Hermann. Frankfurt am Main: Vittorio Klostermann, 2006.
[*Identity and Difference.* Translated with an introduction by Joan Stambaugh. Chicago: University of Chicago Press, 2002. (Also contains the German text.)]

GA 12 *Unterwegs zur Sprache.* (1950–1959) Edited by Friedrich-Wilhelm von Hermann. Frankfurt am Main: Vittorio Klostermann, 1985.
[*On the Way to Language.* Translated by Peter D. Hertz. New York: Harper & Row, 1971.]

GA 14 *Zur Sache des Denkens.* (1962–1964) Edited by Friedrich-Wilhelm von Hermann. Frankfurt am Main: Vittorio Klostermann, 1996.
[*On Time and Being.* Translated by Joan Stambaugh. New York: Harper & Row, 1972.]

GA 17 *Einführung in die phänomenologische Forschung.* (Winter semester 1923/1924) Edited by Friedrich-Wilhelm von Hermann. Frankfurt am Main: Vittorio Klostermann, 1994.
[*Introduction to Phenomenological Research.* Translated by Daniel Dahlstrom. Bloomington: Indiana University Press, 2005.]

GA 18 *Grundbegriffe der aristotelischen Philosophie.* (Summer semester 1924) Edited by Mark Michalski. Frankfurt am Main: Vittorio Klostermann, 2002.
[*Basic Concepts of Aristotelian Philosophy.* Translated by Robert D. Metcalf and Mark B. Tanzer. Bloomington: Indiana University Press, 2009.]

GA 19 *Platon: Sophistes.* (Winter semester 1924/1925) Edited by Ingeborg Schüßler. Frankfurt am Main: Vittorio Klostermann, 1992.
[*Plato's Sophist.* Translated by Richard Rojcewicz and André Schuwer. Bloomington: Indiana University Press, 1997.]

GA 20 *Prolegomena zur Geschichte des Zeitbegriffs.* (Summer semester 1925) Edited by Petra Jaeger. Frankfurt am Main: Vittorio Klostermann, 1979.
[*History of the Concept of Time: Prolegomena.* Translated by Theodore Kisiel. Bloomington: Indiana University Press, 1985.]

GA 21 *Logik. Die Frage nach der Wahrheit.* (Winter semester 1925/1926) Edited by Walter Biemel. Frankfurt am Main: Vittorio Klostermann, 1976.
[*Logic: The Question of Truth.* Translated by Thomas Sheehan. Bloomington: Indiana University Press, 2010.]

GA 22 *Die Gundbegriffe der Antiken Philosophie.* (Summer semester 1926) Edited by Franz-Karl Blust. Frankfurt am Main: Vittorio Klostermann, 1993.
[*Basic Concepts of Ancient Philosophy.* Translated by Richard Rojcewicz. Bloomington: Indiana University Press, 2008.]

GA 23 *Geschichte der Philosophie von Thomas von Aquin bis Kant.* (Winter semester 1926/1927) Edited by Helmuth Vetter. Frankfurt am Main: Vittorio Klostermann, 2006.

GA 24 *Die Grundprobleme der Phänomenologie (Sommersemester 1927).* Edited by Friedrich-Wilhelm von Hermann. Frankfurt am Main: Vittorio Klostermann, 1975.
[*The Basic Problems of Phenomenology.* Translated by Albert Hofstadter. Bloomington: Indiana University Press, 1981.]

GA 26 *Metaphysische Anfangsgründe der Logik im Ausgang von Leibniz.* (Summer semester 1928) Edited by Klaus Held. Frankfurt am Main: Vittorio Klostermann, 1990.
[*The Metaphysical Foundations of Logic.* Translated by Michael Heim. Bloomington: Indiana University Press, 1984.]

GA 29/30 *Die Grundbegriffe der Metaphysik. Welt-Endlichkeit-Einsamkeit.* (Winter semester 1929/1930) Edited by Friedrich-Wilhelm von Hermann. Frankfurt am Main: Vittorio Klostermann, 2004.
[*The Fundamental Concepts of Metaphysics: World, Finitude, and Solitude.* Translated by William McNeil and Nicholas Walker. Bloomington: Indiana University Press, 1995.]

GA 31 *Vom Wesen der menschlichen Freiheit. Einleitung in die Philosophie.* (Sommersemester 1930) Edited by Harmut Tietjen. 2nd edition. Frankfurt am Main: Vittorio Klostermann, 1994.
[*The Essence of Human Freedom: An Introduction to Philosophy.* Translated by Ted Sadler. London: Continuum, 2002.]

GA 34 *Vom Wesen der Wahrheit. Zu Platons Höhlengleichnis und Theätet.* (Winter semester 1931/1932) Edited by Hermann Mörchen. Frankfurt am Main: Vittorio Klostermann, 1988.
[*The Essence of Truth: On Plato's Cave and Theatetus.* Translated by Ted Sadler. London: Continuum, 2002.]

GA 35 *Der Anfang der abendländischen Philosophie: Auslegung des Anaximander und Parmenides.* (Summer semester 1932) Edited by Peter Trawny. Frankfurt am Main: Vittorio Klostermann, 2012.

GA   Sein und Wahrheit. (1933–1934) Edited by Harmut Tietjen. Frankfurt am Main:
36/37   Vittorio Klostermann, 2001.
[Being and Truth. Translated by Gregory Fried and Richard Polt. Bloomington: Indiana University Press, 2010.]

GA 40   Einführung in die Metaphysik. (Summer semester1935) Edited by Petra Jaeger. Frankfurt am Main: Vittorio Klostermann, 1983.
[Introduction to Metaphysics. Translated by Gregory Fried and Richard Polt. New Haven, CT: Yale University Press, 2000.]

GA 45   Grundfragen der Philosophie: Ausgewählte "Probleme" der "Logik." (Winter semester 1937/1938) Edited by Friedrich-Wilhelm von Hermann. 2nd edition. Frankfurt am Main: Vittorio Klostermann, 1992.
[Basic Questions of Philosophy: Selected Problems of Logic. Translated by Richard Rojcewicz and André Schuwer. Bloomington: Indiana University Press, 1994.]

GA 49   Die Metaphysik des deutschen Idealismus. Zur erneuten Auslegung von Schelling: Philosophische Untersuchungen über das Wesen der menschlichen Freiheit und die damit zusammenhängenden Gegenstände (1809). (1941) Edited by Günter Seubold. Frankfurt am Main: Vittorio Klostermann, 1991.

GA 51   Grundbegriffe. (Summer semester 1941) Edited by Petra Jaeger. Frankfurt am Main: Vittorio Klostermann, 1991.
[Basic Concepts. Translated by Gary E. Aylesworth. Bloomington: Indiana University Press, 1993.]

GA 54   Parmenides. (Winter semester 1942/1943) Edited by Manfred S. Frings. Frankfurt am Main: Vittorio Klostermann, 1982.
[Parmenides. Translated by Andre Schuwer and Richard Rojcewicz. Bloomington: *Indiana University Press*, 1998.]

GA   Zur Bestimmung der Philosophie. (1919) Edited by Bernd Heimbüchel.
56/57   2nd edition. Frankfurt am *Main*: Vittorio *Klostermann*, 1999.
[Towards the Definition of Philosophy. Translated by Ted Sadler. London: Continuum, 2002.]

GA 58   Grundprobleme der Phänomenologie. (Winter semester 1919–1920) Edited by Hans-Helmuth Gander. Frankfurt am Main: Vittorio Klostermann, 1992.

GA 59   Phänomenologie der Anschauung und des Ausdrucks. Theorie der philosophischen Begriffsbildung. (Summer semester 1920) Edited by Claudius Strube. Frankfurt am Main: Vittorio Klostermann, 1993.
[Phenomenology of Intuition and Expression. Translated by Tracy Colony. New York: Continuum, 2010.]

GA 60   Phänomenologie des religiösen Lebens: 1. Einleitung in die Phänomenologie der Religion (Winter semester 1920/1921), edited by M. Jung und T. Regehly; 2. Augustinus und der Neuplatonismus (Summer semester 1921), edited by C. Strube; 3. Die philosphischen Grundlagen der mittelalterlichen Mystik (prepared notes and introduction to an undelivered course 1918/1919), edited by C. Strube. Frankfurt am Main: Vittorio Klostermann, 1995.
[The Phenomenology of Religious Life. 1. Introduction to the Phenomenology of Religion. 2. Augustine and Neo-Platonism. 3. The Philosophical Foundations of

Medieval Mysticism. Translated by Matthias Fritsch and Jennier Anna Gosetti-Ferencei. Bloomington: Indiana University Press, 2004.]

GA 61 *Phänomenologische Interpretationen zu Aristoteles. Einfürhung in die phänomenologische Forschung.* (Winter semester 1921/1922) Edited by Walter Bröcker and Käte Bröcker-Oltmans. 2nd edition. Frankfurt am Main: *Vittorio Klostermann,* 1994.
[*Phenomenological Interpretations of Aristotle: Initiation into Phenomenological Research.* Translated by Richard Rojcewicz. Bloomington: Indiana University Press, 2001.]

GA 62 *Phänomenologische Interpretationen ausgewählter Abhandlungen des Aristoteles zu Ontologie und Logik; Anhang: Phänomenologische Interpretationen zu Aristoteles (Anzeige der hermeneutischen Situation), Ausarbeitung für die Marburger und die Göttinger Philosophische Fakultät.* (1922) Edited by Günther Neumann. Frankfurt am Main: Vittorio Klostermann, 2005.

GA 63 *Ontologie: Hermeneutik der Faktizität.* (Summer semester, 1923) Edited by Käte-Bröcker-Oltmanns. 2nd edition. Frankfurt am Main: Vittorio Klostermann, 1995.
[*Ontology: The Hermeneutics of Facticity.* Translated by John Van Buren. Bloomington: Indiana University Press, 1999.]

GA 64 *Der Begriff der Zeit.* (1924) Edited by Friedrich-Wilhem von Hermann. Frankfurt am Main: Vittorio Klostermann, 1995.
[*The Concept of Time.* (*CT*) Translated by William McNeil. Oxford: Blackwell, 1992.]
[*The Concept of Time: The First Draft of "Being and Time."* Translated by Ingo Farin with Alex Skinner. New York: Continuum, 2011.]

GA 65 *Beiträge zur Philosophie (Vom Ereignis).* (1936–1938) Edited by Friedrich-Wilhem von Hermann. 2nd edition. Frankfurt am Main: Vittorio Klostermann, 1994.
[*Contributions to Philosophy (Of the Event).* Translated by Richard Rojcewicz and Daniela Vallega-Neu. Bloomington: Indiana University Press, 2012.]

GA 66 *Besinnung.* (1938/1939) Edited by Friedrich-Wilhem von Hermann. Frankfurt am Main: *Vittorio Klostermann,* 1997.
[*Mindfulness.* Translated by Parvis Emad and Thomas Kalary. London: Continuum, 2006.]

GA 71 *Das Ereignis.* (1941/1942) Edited by Friedrich-Wilhem von Hermann. Frankfurt am Main: Vittorio Klostermann, 2009.
[*The Event.* Translated by Richard Rojcewicz. Bloomington: Indiana University Press, 2012.]

GA 77 *Feldweg-Gespräche* (1944/1945) Edited by Ingrid Schüßler. Frankfurt am Main: Vittorio Klostermann, 1995.

GA 78 *Der Spruch des Anaximander.* (1946) Edited by Ingeborg Schüßler. Frankfurt am Main: Vittorio Klostermann, 2010.

GA 81 *Gedachtes.* Edited by Paola Ludovika Coriando. Frankfurt am Main: Vittorio Klostermann, 2007.

GA 83 *Seminare: Platon-Aristoteles-Augustinus.* Edited by Mark Michalski. Frankfurt am Main: Vittorio Klostermann, 2012.

GA 94 *Überlegungen II–VI (Schwarze Hefte 1931–1938)*. Edited by Peter Trawny. Frankfurt am Main: Vittorio Klostermann, 2014.
GA 95 *Überlegungen VII–XI (Schwarze Hefte 1938/39)*. Edited by Peter Trawny. Frankfurt am Main: Vittorio Klostermann, 2014.
GA 96 *Überlegungen XII–XV (Schwarze Hefte 1939–1941)*. Edited by Peter Trawny. Frankfurt am Main: Vittorio Klostermann, 2014.
       Gelassenheit (Pfullingen: Günther Neske, 1959).
       [*Discourse on Thinking*. Translated by John Anderson and E. Hans Freund. New York: Harper & Row, 1966.]
Suppl. *Supplements: From the Earliest Essays to Being and Time and Beyond*. Edited by John Van Buren. Albany: SUNY Press, 2002.
SZ   *Sein und Zeit*. [1927] 17th edition. Tübingen: Max Niemeyer Verlag, 1993.
       [*Being and Time*. (*BT*) Translated by John Macquarrie and Edward Robinson. New York: Harper Press, 1962.]
       Zollikoner Seminare: Protokolle, Gespräche, Briefe. Edited by Medard Boss. Frankfurt am Main: Vittorio Klostermann, 1987.
       [*Zollikon Seminars: Protocols, Conversations, Letters*. Edited by Medard Boss. Translated by F. Mayr and R. Askay. Evanston, IL: Northwestern University Press, 2001.]

1.2. CORRESPONDENCE

Arendt, Hannah, and Martin Heidegger. *Briefe 1925 bis 1975 und andere Zeugnisse: Hannah Arendt, Martin Heidegger*. Edited by Ursula Ludz. Frankfurt am Main: Vittorio Klostermann, 2002.
[*Letters 1925–1975: Hannah Arendt and Martin Heidegger*. Edited by Ursula Ludz, translated by Andrew Shields. Orlando, FL: Harcourt, 2004.]
Heidegger, Martin, and Elisabeth Blochmann. *Briefwechsel, 1918–1969*. Edited by Joachim W. Storck. Marbach am Necker: Deutsche Schillergesellschaft, 1989.
Heidegger, Martin, and Karl Jaspers. *Briefwechsel, 1920–63*. Edited by W. Biemel and H. Saner. Frankfurt am Main: Klostermann, 1990.

2. WORKS BY AUGUSTINE

Augustine of Hippo, *Opera Omnia*, vols. 1–12. Migne, *Patrologia Latina*, vols. 32–46.
———. *Augustine: Later Works*. Translated by John Burnaby. Philadelphia: Westminster Press, 1955.
———. *City of God*. Translated by Henry Bettenson, with an Introduction by John O'Meara. New York: Penguin, 2003.
———. *Confessions, Books I–XIII*. Translated by F. J. Sheed. Introduction by Peter Brown. Revised edition. Indianapolis, IN: Hackett Publishing, 1993.
———. *Ennarationes in Psalmos*. Edited by D. Eligius Dekkers, O.S.B., and Johannes Fraipont. *Corpus Christianorum Series Latina* 44. Turnhout: Brepols, 1970.
———. *Vingt-Six Sermons au Peuple d'Afrique*. Edited and translated by François Dolbeau. Paris: Institut d'Études Augustiniennes, 1996.

———. *The Works of Saint Augustine: A Translation for the 21st Century*. Edited by John E. Rotelle, O.S.A., and Boniface Ramsey. Hyde Park, NY: New City Press, 1990–.

3. BIBLICAL TEXTS

Biblia Sacra: Iuxta Vulgatam Versionem. Stuttgart: Deutsche Bibelgesellschaft, 1994.
The Holy Bible: Revised Standard Version. New York: Oxford University Press, 1962.

4. OTHER WORKS

Agamben, Giorgio. *Homo Sacer*. Translated by Daniel Heller-Roazen. Stanford, CA: Stanford University Press, 1998.
———. *The Kingdom and the Glory: For a Theological Genealogy of Economy and Government*. Translated by Lorenzo Chiesa with Matteo Mandarini. Stanford, CA: Stanford University Press, 2011.
———. "La passion de la facticité." In *Heidegger: Questions ouvertes, Cahiers du CIPH*, 63–84. Paris: Osiris, 1988.
———. *Potentialities*. Translated by Daniel Heller-Roazen. Stanford, CA: Stanford University Press, 1999.
———. *The Time That Remains: A Commentary on the Letter to the Romans*. Translated by Patricia Daley. Stanford, CA: Stanford University Press, 2005.
Arendt, Hannah. *Der Liebesbegriff bei Augustin: versuch einer philosophischen Interpretation*. Berlin: Julius Springer, 1929.
———. *Love and Saint Augustine*. Edited by Joanna Vecchiarelli Scott and Judith Chelius Stark. Chicago: University of Chicago Press, 1998.
———. *The Life of the Mind*. New York: Harcourt, 1971.
Aristotle. *The Complete Works of Aristotle*. Edited by Jonathan Barnes. 2 vols. Bollingen Series 71. Princeton, NJ: Princeton University Press, 1984.
Arrien, Sophie-Jan. "Faith's Knowledge: On Heidegger's Reading of Saint Paul." *Gatherings: Heidegger Circle Annual* 3 (2013): 30–49.
———. "Foi et indication formelle. Heidegger lecteur de saint Paul (1920–1921)." In *Le jeune Heidegger 1909–1926*, edited by Sophie-Jan Arrien and Sylvain Camilleri, 155–72. Paris: J. Vrin, 2011.
Bambach, Charles. *Heidegger, Dilthey, and the Crisis of Historicism*. Ithaca, NY: Cornell University Press, 1995.
———. *Heidegger's Roots: Nietzsche, National Socialism, and the Greeks*. Ithaca, NY: Cornell University Press, 2003.
Barash, Jeffrew Andrew. *Martin Heidegger and the Problem of Historical Meaning*. Revised and expanded edition. New York: Fordham, 2003.
Beiser, Frederick. *The German Historicist Tradition*. Oxford: Oxford University Press, 2011.
Bermon, Emmanuel. *Le cogito dans la pensée de saint Augustin*. Paris: Vrin, 2001.
Bernasconi, Robert. "Repetition and Tradition: Heidegger's Destructuring of the Distinction between Essence and Existence in *Basic Problems of Phenomenology*." In

Reading Heidegger from the Start, edited by Theodore Kisiel and John van Buren, 123–36. Albany, NY: SUNY Press, 1994.

Bernet, Rudolf. "Husserl and Heidegger on Intentionality and Being." *Journal of the British Society for Phenomenology* 21 (May 1990): 136–52.

Best, Ernest. *Black's New Testament Commentary: The First and Second Epistles to the Thessalonians*. London: Continuum, reprint 2003.

Birmingham, Peg. "Heidegger and Augustine: The Will and the Word." In *The Influence of Augustine on Heidegger*, edited by Craig J. N. de Paulo, 115–52. Lewiston, PA: Edwin Mellen Press, 2006.

Blanton, Ward. *Displacing Christian Origins: Philosophy, Secularity, and the New Testament*. Chicago: University of Chicago Press, 2007.

Blattner, William. "The Concept of Death in *Being and Time*." In *Heidegger Reexamined*, vol. 1, *Dasein, Authenticity, and Death*, edited by Hubert Dreyfus and Mark Wrathall, 307–29. New York: Routledge, 2002.

Bowler, Michael. *Heidegger and Aristotle: Philosophy as Praxis*. London: Continuum, 2008.

Brague, Rémi. *Aristote et la question du monde*. Paris: PUF, 1988.

Brito, Emilio. *Heidegger et l'hymne du sacré*. Leuven: Leuven University Press, 1999.

Brogan, Walter. *Heidegger and Aristotle: The Twofoldedness of Being*. Albany: SUNY Press, 2005.

Brown, Peter. *Augustine of Hippo: A Biography*. New edition, with an epilogue. Berkeley: University of California Press, 2000.

Burdach, Konrad. "Faust und Sorge." *Deutsche Vierteljahrschrift für Literaturwissenschaft und Geistesgeschichte* 1 (1923):1–60.

Camilleri, Sylvian. *Phénoménologie de la religion et herméneutique théologique dans la pensée du jeune Heidegger: Commentaire analytique des Fondements philosophiques de la mystique médiévale (1916–1919)*. New York: Springer, 2008.

Capobianco, Richard. *Engaging Heidegger*. Toronto: University of Toronto Press, 2010.

Caputo, John D. *Heidegger and Aquinas: An Essay on the Overcoming of Metaphysics*. New York: Fordham University Press, 1982.

———. *The Mystical Element in Heidegger's Thought*. New York: Fordham University Press, 1986.

———. "*Sorge* and *Kardia*: The Hermeneutics of Factical Life and the Categories of the Heart." In *Reading Heidegger from the Start: Essays in His Earliest Thought*, edited by Theodore Kisiel and John Van Buren, 327–44. Albany: SUNY Press, 1994.

Caputo, John D., and Michael Scanlon, eds. *Augustine and Postmodernism: Confessions and Circumfession*. Bloomington: Indiana University Press, 2005.

Carlson, Thomas A. *The Indiscrete Image: Infinitude and the Creation of the Human*. Chicago: University of Chicago Press, 2008.

———. *Indiscretion: Finitude and the Naming of God*. Chicago: University of Chicago Press, 1999.

Carman, Taylor. *Heidegger's Analytic: Interpretation, Discourse, and Authenticity in "Being and Time."* Cambridge: Cambridge University Press, 2003.

Casale, Rita. *L'esperienza Nietzsche di Heidegger*. Naples: Bibliopolis, 2005.

———. *Heideggers Nietzsche: Geschichte einer Obsession*. Translated by Catrin Dingler. Bielefeld: transcript Verlag, 2010.
Coriando, Paola-Ludovica. *Der letzte Gott als Anfang*. Munich: Wilhelm Fink, 1998.
Corti, C. Augustìn. *Zeitproblematik bei Martin Heidegger und Augustinus*. Würzburg: Verlag Königshausen & Neumann, 2006.
Courtine, Jean-François. "The Preliminary Conception of Phenomenology and of the Problematic of Truth in *Being and Time*." In *Martin Heidegger: Critical Assessments*. Vol. 1, *Philosophy*, edited by Christopher Macann, 68–94. London: Routledge, 1992.
———. "Les traces et le passage du Dieu dans les Beiträge zur Philosophie de Martin Heidegger." *Archivio di Filosofia* 1–3 (1994): 519–38.
Critchley, Simon. *Faith of the Faithless: Experiments in Political Theology*. New York: Verso, 2012.
Crowe, Benjamin D. *Heidegger's Phenomenology of Religion: Realism and Cultural Criticism*. Bloomington: Indiana University Press, 2008.
———. *Heidegger's Religious Origins: Destruction and Authenticity*. Bloomington: Indiana University Press, 2006.
Crowell, Steven Galt. *Heidegger, Husserl, and the Space of Meaning: Paths toward Transcendental Phenomenology*. Evanston, IL: Northwestern University Press, 2001.
Dastur, Françoise. *Heidegger and the Question of Time*. Translated by François Raffoul and David Pettigrew. Atlantic Highlands, NJ: Humanities Press, 1998.
de Beistegui, Miguel. *The New Heidegger*. London: Continuum, 2005.
de Paulo, Craig J. N., ed. *The Influence of Augustine on Heidegger: The Emergence of an Augustinian Phenomenology*. Lewiston, NY: Edwin Mellen Press, 2006.
Derrida, Jacques. *Margins of Philosophy*. Translated by Alan Bass. Chicago: University of Chicago Press, 1982.
Derrida, Jacques, and Geoffrey Bennington. *Jacques Derrida*. Translated by Geoffrey Bennington. Chicago: University of Chicago Press, 1999.
Descartes, René. *The Philosophical Writings of Descartes*. 3 vols. Translated by John Cottingham, Robert Stoothoff, and Dugald Murdoch. Cambridge: Cambridge University Press, 1984–1991.
de Vries, Hent. *Philosophy and the Turn to Religion*. Baltimore: Johns Hopkins University Press, 1999.
Elliott, Brian. *Phenomenology and Imagination in Husserl and Heidegger*. New York: Routledge, 2005.
Emad, Parvis. *Heidegger and the Phenomenology of Values: His Critique of Intentionality*. Foreword by Walter Biemel. Glen Ellyn, IL: Torey Press, 1981.
Fagenblat, Michael. *A Convenant of Creatures: Levinas' Philosophy of Judaism*. Stanford, CA: Stanford University Press, 2010.
Faye, Emmanuel. *Heidegger: The Introduction of Nazism into Philosophy in Light of the Unpublished Seminars of 1933–1935*. Translated by Michael B. Smith. New Haven, CT: Yale University Press, 2009.
Flasch, Kurt. *Was ist Zeit? Augustinus von Hippo. Das XI. Buch der Confessiones. Historisch-Philosophische Studie. Text-Übersetzung-Kommentar*. Frankfurt: Klostermann, 1993.

Freud, Sigmund. *The Interpretation of Dreams*. Translated by James Strachey. New York: Basic Books 1955.
Fried, Gregory. *Heidegger's Polemos: From Being to Politics*. New Haven, CT: Yale University Press, 2000.
Gadamer, Hans-Georg. *Heidegger's Ways*. Translated by John W. Stanley, introduction by Dennis J. Schmidt. Albany: SUNY Press, 1994.
Geroulanos, Stefanos. *An Atheism That Is Not Humanist Emerges in French Philosophy*. Stanford, CA: Stanford University Press, 2010.
Gillespie, Michael Allen. *The Theological Origins of Modernity*. Chicago: University of Chicago Press, 2008.
Gilson, Etienne. *The Christian Philosophy of Saint Augustine*. Translated by L. E. M. Lynch. New York: Random House, 1960.
———. "Note sur l'être et le temps chez saint Augustin." *Recherches augustiniennes* 2 (1962): 205–23.
Gordon, Peter E. *Continental Divide: Heidegger, Cassirer, Davos*. Cambridge, MA: Harvard University Press 2003.
———. *Rosenzweig and Heidegger: Between Judaism and German Philosophy*. Cambridge, MA: Harvard University Press, 2005.
Greisch, Jean. *L'Arbre de vie et l'Arbre du savoir: Le chemin phénoménologique de l'herméneutique heideggérienne, 1919–1923*. Paris: Cerf, 2000.
———. *Le buisson ardent et les lumières de la raison: L'invention de la philosophie de la religion*. 3 volumes. Paris: Cerf, 2002–2004.
Grondin, Jean. "Heidegger und Augustin: Zur Hermeneutische Wahrheit." In *Die Frage nach der Wahrheit*, edited by E. Richter, 161–73. Frankfurt am Main: V. Klostermann, 1997.
———. "Stichwort: Hermeneutik. Selbstauslegung und Seinsverstehen." In *Heidegger-Handbuch: Leben—Werk—Wirkung*, edited by D. Thomä with Florian Grosser, Katrin Meyer, and Hans Bernhard Schmid, 47–51. Stuttgart: Verlag J. B. Metzler, 2003.
Haar, Michel. *Heidegger and the Essence of Man*. Translated by William McNeil. Albany: SUNY Press, 2001.
Hammerschlag, Sarah. *The Figural Jew: Politics and Identity in Postwar French Thought*. Chicago: University of Chicago Press, 2010.
Harries, Karsten. "The Descent of the 'Logos': Limits of Transcendental Reflection." In *Transcendental Heidegger*, edited by Steven Crowell and Jeff Malpas, 74–92. Stanford, CA: Stanford University Press, 2007.
Hegel, Georg Wilhelm Friedrich. *Faith and Knowledge*. Translated by Walter Cerf and H. S. Harris. Albany: SUNY Press, 1977.
Hermann, Friedrich-Wilhelm von. *Augustinus und die Phänomenologische Frage nach der Zeit*. Frankfurt am Main: Vittorio Klostermann, 1992.
———. "Die Confessiones des Heilegen Augustinus im Denken Heideggers." In *Quaestio* 1 (2001): *Heidegger e i medievali*. Turnhout: Brepols, 2001.
———. *Hermeneutische Phänomenologie des Daseins: Ein Kommentar zu Sein und Zeit*, Band 2, Erster Abschnitt: *Die vorbereitende Fundamentalanalyse des Daseins §9-§27*. Frankfurt am Main: Vittorio Klostermann, 2005.

———. *Wege ins Ereignis: Zu Heideggers Beiträgen zur Philosophie*. Frankfurt am Main: Vittorio Klostermann, 1994.

Hollywood, Amy. *Sensible Ecstasy: Mysticism, Sexual Difference, and the Demands of History*. Chicago: University of Chicago Press, 2002.

Hopkins, B. C. *Intentionality in Husserl and Heidegger: The Problem of the Original Method and Phenomenon in Phenomenology*. Dordrecht: Kluwer, 1993.

Husserl, Edmund. *The Idea of Phenomenology*. Translated by William P. Alston and George Nakhnikian. The Hague: Martinus Nijhoff, 1970.

———. *Ideas Pertaining to a Pure Phenomenology and to a Phenomenological Philosophy, First Book*. Translated by F. Kerstern. Dordrecht: Kluwer, 1983.

———. *Die Idee der Phänomenologie*. Fünf Vorlesungen, HUA 2, edited by Walter Biemel. Boston: Kluwer, 1973.

———. *Ideen zu einer reinen Phänomenologie und Phänomenologischen Philosophie*. HUA 3 Erstes Buch, edited by Karl Schuhmann. Boston: Kluwer, 1976.

———. *Ideen zu einer reinen Phänomenologie und Phänomenologischen Philosophie*. HUA 4 Zweites Buch, edited by Marly Biemel. Boston: Kluwer, 1991.

———. *Logical Investigations*. Translated by J. N. Findlay, edited by D. Moran. 2 vols. New York: Routledge, 1970.

———. *Logische Untersuchungen*, vol. 2, edited by Ursula Panzer. Boston: Kluwer, 1987.

———. *On the Phenomenology of the Consciousness of Internal Time (1893–1917)*. Vol. 4 of *Collected Works*. Translated by John Barnett Brough. Dordrecht: Kluwer, 1991.

Imdahl, Georg. *Das Leben verstehen: Heideggers formal anzeigende Hermeneutik in den frühen Freiburger Vorlesungen*. Würzburg: Königshausen & Neumann, 1997.

Ionescu, Cristina. "The Concept of the Last God in Heidegger's *Beiträge*: Hints towards an Understanding of the Gift of *Sein*." *Studia Phaenomenologica* 2, 1–2 (2002): 59–95.

Jaran, François. *Heidegger inédit 1929–1930: L'inachevable Être et Temps*. Paris: J. Vrin, 2012.

Jaspers, Karl. *Plato and Augustine*. Edited by Hannah Arendt and translated by Ralph Manheim. New York: Harcourt Brace, 1966.

Jonas, Hans. *Augustin und das paulinische Freiheitsproblem: Ein philosophischer Beitrag zur Genesis der christlich-abendländischen Freiheitsidee*. Göttingen: Vandenbroeck & Ruprecht, 1930.

Kaegi, Dominic. "Die Religion in den Grenzen der blossen Existenz: Heideggers religionsphilosophische Vorlesungen von 1920/1921." *Internationale Zeitschrift für Philosophie* 1 (1996): 133–49.

Kant, Immanuel. *Anthropology, History, Education*. Translated by Robert B. Louden and Günter Zöller. Cambridge: Cambridge University Press, 2011.

———. *Critique of Pure Reason*. Translated by Paul Guyer and Allen W. Wood. Cambridge: Cambridge University Press, 1997.

———. *Religion and Rational Theology*. Translated by Allen Wood and George di Giovanni. Cambridge: Cambridge University Press, 1996.

Kearney, Richard. *Dialogues with Contemporary Continental Thinkers*. Manchester: Manchester University Press, 1984.

———. "Heidegger, the Possible and God." In *Martin Heidegger: Critical Assessments*, vol. 4, *Reverberations*, edited by Christopher Macann, 299–324. London: Routledge, 1992.

Kierkegaard, Søren. *Fear and Trembling/Repetition*. Vol. 6 of *Kierkegaard's Writings*. Translated and edited by Howard V. Hong and Edna Hong. Princeton, NJ: Princeton University Press, 1983.

King, Magda. *A Guide to Heidegger's Being and Time*. Edited by John Llewelyn. Albany: SUNY Press, 2001.

Kisiel, Theodore. "Die formale Anzeige. Die methodische Geheimwaffe des frühen Heidegger." In *Heidegger—neu gelesen*, 22–40. Edited by Markus Happel. Würzburg: Königshausen and Neumann, 1997.

———. *The Genesis of Heidegger's Being and Time*. Berkeley: University of California Press, 1993.

———. "Heidegger's *Gesamtausgabe*: An International Scandal of Scholarship." *Philosophy Today* 39 (1995): 3–15.

———. *Heidegger's Ways of Thought*. London: Continuum, 2002.

Kovacs, George. "Philosophy as Primordial Science in Heidegger's Courses of 1919." In *Reading Heidegger from the Start: Essays in His Earliest Thought*, edited by Theodore Kisiel and John Van Buren, 91–110. Albany: SUNY Press, 1994.

Krell, David Farrell. *Daimon Life: Heidegger and Life Philosophy*. Bloomington: Indiana University Press, 1992.

———. "Toward *Sein und Zeit*: Heidegger's Early Review of Jaspers' 'Psychologie der Weltanschauungen.'" *Journal of the British Society for Phenomenology* 6 (1975): 147–56.

Krop, Henri, Arie L. Molendijk, and Hent de Vries, eds. *Post-Theism: Reframing the Judeo-Christian Tradition*. Leuven: Peeters, 2000.

La Bonnardière, Anne-Marie. *Recherches de chronologie augustinienne*. Paris: Études Augustiniennes, 1965.

Lazier, Benjamin. *God Interrupted: Heresy and the European Imagination between the World Wars*. Princeton, NJ: Princeton University Press, 2008.

Lehmann, Karl. "Christliche Geschichtserfahrung und ontologische Frage beim jungen Heidegger." In *Heidegger: Perspektiven zur Deutung seines Werkes*, edited by Otto Pöggeler, 140–68. Königstein: Athenäum, 1984.

Levinas, Emmanuel. *God, Death, and Time*. Translated by Bettina Bergo. Stanford, CA: Stanford University Press, 2000.

Levinas, Emmanuel, and Richard Kearney. "Dialogue with Emmanuel Levias." In *Face to Face with Emmanuel Levinas*, edited by Richard A. Cohen, 13–33. Albany: SUNY Press, 1986.

Löwith, Karl. *Martin Heidegger and European Nihilism*. Translated by Gary Steiner, edited by Richard Wolin. New York: Columbia University Press, 1995.

Lyotard, Jean-François. *The Confessions of Augustine*. Translated by Richard Beardsworth. Stanford, CA: Stanford University Press, 2000.

———. *Heidegger and "the jews."* Translated by Andreas Michel and Mark S. Roberts. Minneapolis: University of Minnesota Press, 1990.

Macdonald, Iain, and Krzysztof Ziarek, eds. *Adorno and Heidegger: Philosophical Questions*. Stanford, CA: Stanford University Press, 2008.
Malpas, Jeff. *Heidegger's Topology: Being, Place, World*. Cambridge, MA: MIT Press, 2008.
Maly, Kenneth. *Heidegger's Possibility: Language, Emergence-Saying Be-ing*. Toronto: University of Toronto Press, 2008.
Marion, Jean-Luc, *In the Self's Place: The Approach of Saint Augustine*. Translated by Jeffrey Kosky. Stanford, CA: Stanford University Press, 2012.
———. *Reduction and Givenness: Investigations of Husserl, Heidegger, and Phenomenology*. Translated by Thomas Carlson. Evanston, IL: Northwestern Press, 1998.
Matthews, Gareth B. *Thought's Ego in Augustine and Descartes*. Ithaca, NY: Cornell University Press, 1992.
McGinn, Bernard. *The Growth of Mysticism: Gregory the Great through the Twelfth Century*. New York: Crossroad 1996.
———. *The Mystical Thought of Meister Eckhart: The Man from Whom God Hid Nothing*. New York: Crossroad, 2001.
McGrath, S. J. *Heidegger and Medieval Philosophy: A Phenomenology for the Godforsaken*. Washington, D.C.: Catholic University Press, 2006.
McNeil, William. *The Glance of the Eye: Heidegger, Aristotle, and the Ends of Theory*. Albany: SUNY Press, 1999.
McNicol, Allan J. *Jesus' Directions for the Future: A Source and Redaction-History Study of the Use of the Eschatological Traditions in Paul and in the Synoptic Accounts of Jesus' Last Eschatological Discourse*. Macon, GA: Mercer University Press, 1996.
Mehring, Reinhard. *Heideggers Überlieferungsgeschick: Eine dionysiche Selbstinszenierung*. Würzburg: Königshausen und Neumann, 1992.
Menn, Stephen. *Descartes and Augustine*. Cambridge: Cambridge University Press, 1998.
Metzger, Paul. *Katechon: II Thess 2, 1–12 im Horizont apokalyptischen Denkens*. Berlin: Walter de Gruyter, 2005.
Mongis, Henri. *Heidegger et la critique de la notion de valeur*. The Hague: Martinus Nijhoff, 1976.
Montinari, Mazzino. *Reading Nietzsche*. Translated by Greg Whitlock. Champagne: University of Illinois Press, 2003.
Moyn, Samuel. *Origins of the Other: Emmanuel Levinas between Revelation and Ethics*. Ithaca, NY: Cornell University Press, 2005.
Nancy, Jean-Luc. *Adoration: The Deconstruction of Christianity II*. Translated by John McKeane. New York: Fordham University Press, 2013.
———. *Dis-enclosure: The Deconstruction of Christianity*. Translated by Bettina Bergo, Gabriel Malenfant, and Michael B. Smith. New York: Fordham University Press, 2009.
Nicholas of Cusa. *Selected Spiritual Writings*. Translated by Lawrence Bond. Mahwah, NJ: Paulist Press, 1997.

Nietzsche, Friedrich. *The Anti-Christ, Ecce Homo, Twilight of the Idols and Other Writings*. Edited by Aaron Ridley and Judith Norman. Cambridge: Cambridge University Press, 2005.

———. *The Birth of Tragedy and Other Writings*. Translated by Ronald Speirs. Cambridge: Cambridge University Press, 1999.

———. *On the Genealogy of Morals*. Translated by Walter Kaufmann and R. J. Hollingdale. New York: Vintage, 1989.

———. *Thus Spoke Zarathustra*. Translated by Adrian Del Caro. Cambridge: Cambridge University Press, 2006.

———. *Werke. Kritische Gesamtausgabe*, edited by Giorgio Colli and Mazzino Montinari Berlin: De Gruyter: Berlin, 1967.

———. *The Will to Power*. Translated by Walter Kaufmann and R. J. Hollingdale. New York: Vintage Books, 1967.

Nietzsche, Friedrich, and Franz Overbeck. *Briefwechsel mit Franz Overbeck*. Edited by Richard Oehler and Carl Bernoulli. Leipzig: Insel Verlag, 1916.

Ochsner, Heinrich. *Das Mass der Verborgenen: Heinrich Ochsner 1891–1970 zum Gedächtnis*. Edited by Curd Ochwaldt and Erwin Tecklenborg. Hannover: Charis, 1981.

Ó Murchadha, Felix. *The Time of Revolution: Kairos and Chronos in Heidegger*. London: Bloomsbury, 2013.

Ott, Hugo. *Martin Heidegger: A Political Life*. Translated by Allan Blunden. New York: Basic Books, 1993.

Overbeck, Franz. *How Christian Is Our Present-Day Theology?* Annotated translation with an introduction by Martin Henry, foreword by David Tracy. New York: T&T Clark, 2005.

Øverenget, Einar. *Seeing the Self: Heidegger on Subjectivity*. Dordrecht: Kluwer, 1998.

Overgaard, Søren. *Husserl and Heidegger on Being in the World*. Dordrecht: Kluwer, 2004.

Pöggeler, Otto. *Heidegger und die hermeneutische Philosophie*. Freiburg: Verlag Karl Alber, 1983.

———. "Heideggers Begegnung mit Hölderlin." *Man and World* 10, 1 (1977): 13–61.

———. *Martin Heidegger's Path of Thinking*. Translated by D. Magurshak and S. Barber. Atlantic Heights, NJ: Humanities Press International, 1987.

———. *The Paths of Heidegger's Life and Thought*. Translated by John Bailiff. Atlantic Highlands, NJ: Humanities Press International, 1997.

Polt, Richard. *The Emergency of Being: On Heidegger's Contributions to Philosophy*. Ithaca, NY: Cornell University Press, 2006.

Pöltner, Günther. "Martin Heideggers Kritik am Begriff der creatio." In *Heidegger und das Mittelalter: Wiener Tagungen zur Phänomenologie, 1997*, edited by Helmuth Vetter, 61–80. Frankfurt am Main: Peter Lang, 1999.

Raffoul, François, and David Pettigrew, eds. *Heidegger and Practical Philosophy*. Albany: SUNY Press, 2002.

Richardson, William. *Heidegger: Through Phenomenology to Thought*. 4th ed. New York: Fordham, 2003.

Rickey, Christopher. *Revolutionary Saints: Heidegger, National Socialism, and Antinomian Politics*. University Park: Pennsylvania State University Press, 2002.

Ricoeur, Paul. *Time and Narrative*. Vol. 1. Translated by Kathleen McLaughlin and David Pellauer. Chicago: University of Chicago Press, 1984.

———. "Heidegger and the Question of the Subject." In *The Conflict of Interpretations*, edited by Don Ihde, 223–35. Evanston, IL: Northwestern University Press, 1974.

Risser, James, ed. *Heidegger toward the Turn: Essays on the Work of the 1930s*. Albany: SUNY Press, 1999.

Rist, John M. *Augustine: Ancient Thought Baptized*. Cambridge: Cambridge University Press, 1994.

Rubenstein, Mary-Jane. *Strange Wonder: The Closure of Metaphysics and the Opening of Awe*. New York: Columbia University Press, 2010.

Schalow, Frank. "The *Gesamtausgabe* Nietzsche: An Exercise in Translation and Thought." *Heidegger Studies* 9 (1993): 139–52.

———. *Heidegger and the Quest for the Sacred: From Thought to the Sanctuary of Faith*. Dordrecht: Kluwer, 2001.

Schalow, Frank, and Alfred Denker. *Historical Dictionary of Heidegger's Philosophy*. 2nd ed. Plymouth, UK: Scarecrow Press, 2010.

Scheler, Max. "Liebe und Erkenntnis." In *Gesammelte Werke*, vol. 6, *Schriften zur Soziologie und Weltanschauungslehre*, edited by M. Scheler, 77–98. 2nd edition. Munich: Francke, 1963.

———. *Späte Schriften*. Edited by Manfred Frings. Munich: Francke, 1976.

Schleiermacher, Friedrich. *On Religion: Speeches to Its Cultured Despisers*. Translated and edited by Richard Crouter. Cambridge: Cambridge University Press, 1988.

Schmidt, Dennis. "Ruins and Roses: Hegel and Heidegger on Sacrifice, Mourning, and Memory." In *Endings: Questions of Memory in Hegel and Heidegger*, edited by Rebeccay Comay and John McCumber, 97–113. Evanston, IL: Northwestern University Press, 1999.

Schmitt, Carl. *Political Theology: Four Chapters on the Concept of Sovereignty*. Translated by George Schwab. Chicago: University of Chicago Press, 1985.

Schürmann, Reiner. *Heidegger on Being and Acting: From Principles to Anarchy*. Translated by C.-M. Gros. Bloomington: Indiana University Press, 1987.

Scott, Charles E., Susan M. Schoenbohm, Daniela Vallega-Neu, and Alejandro Vallega, eds. *Companion to Heidegger's Contributions to Philosophy*. Bloomington: Indiana University Press, 2001.

Severson, Richard. *The Confessions of Saint Augustine: An Annotated Bibliography of Modern Criticism, 1888–1995*. Bibliographies and Indexes in Religious Studies, no. 40. Westport, CT: Greenwood Press, 1996.

Sheehan, Thomas, ed. *Heidegger: The Man and the Thinker*. Chicago: Precedent Publishing, 1981.

———. "Heidegger's 'Introduction to the Phenomenology of Religion,' 1920–1921." In *A Companion to Martin Heidegger's "Being and Time,"* edited by Joseph J. Kockelmans, 40–62. Washington, D.C.: Center for Advanced Research in Phenomenology and University Press of America, 1986.

———. "*Kehre* and *Ereignis*: A Prolegomenon to *Introduction to Metaphysics*." In *A Companion to Heidegger's Introduction to Metaphysics*, edited by Richard Polt and Gregory Fried, 3–16. New Haven: Yale University Press, 2001.

———. "A Paradigm Shift in Heidegger Research." *Continental Philosophy Review*, 34 (2001).
Sikka, Sonia. *Forms of Transcendence: Heidegger and Mystical Theology*. Albany: SUNY Press, 1997.
Simmel, Georg. *The View of Life: Four Metaphysical Essays with Journal Aphorisms*. Translated by John A. Y. Andrews and Donald N. Levine. Chicago: University of Chicago Press, 2010.
Sommer, Christian. *Heidegger, Aristote, Luther. Les sources aristotéliciennes et néo-testamentaires d'Être et Temps*. Paris: Presses Universitaires de France, 2005.
———. *Heidegger 1933: Le programme platonicien du Discours de rectorat*. Paris: Editions Hermann, 2013.
———. "L'inquiétude de la vie facticielle: le tournant aristotélicien de Heidegger (1921–1922)." *Études philosophiques* 1 (2006): 1–28.
Stambaugh, Joan. *The Finitude of Being*. Albany: SUNY Press, 1992.
Stock, Brian. *Augustine the Reader: Meditation, Self-Knowledge, and the Ethics of Interpretation*. Cambridge, MA: Harvard University Press, 1996.
Taminiaux, Jacques. *Heidegger and the Project of Fundamental Ontology*. Translated by Michael Gendre. Albany: SUNY Press, 1991.
———. "The Interpretation of Aristotle's Notion of *Aretê* in Heidegger's First Courses." In *Heidegger and Practical Philosophy*, edited by François Raffoul and David Pettigrew, 13–28. Albany: SUNY Press, 2002.
Taylor, Mark C. *After God*. Chicago: University of Chicago Press, 2007.
Theunissen, Michel. *Negative Theologie der Zeit*. Frankfurt am Main: Suhrkamp, 1991.
Thomson, Iain D. *Heidegger on Ontotheology: Technology and the Politics of Education*. Cambridge: Cambridge University Press, 2005.
Tonner, Philip. *Heidegger, Metaphysics, and the Univocity of Being*. London: Continuum, 2010.
Troeltsch, Ernst. *Augustin, die christliche Antike und das Mittelalter. Im Anschluß an die Schrift "De Civitate Dei."* Munich: R. Oldenbourg, 1915.
Vallega, Alejandro A. *Heidegger and the Issue of Space: Thinking on Exilic Grounds*. University Park: Pennsylvania State University Press, 2003.
Van Buren, John. *The Young Heidegger: Rumor of the Hidden King*. Bloomington: Indiana University Press, 1994.
Van Fleteren, Frederick, ed. *Martin Heidegger's Interpretations of Saint Augustine: Sein und Zeit und Ewigkeit*. Lewiston, NY: Edwin Mellen Press, 2005.
Virno, Paolo. *Multitude between Innovation and Negation*. New York: Semiotext(e), 2008.
Volpi, Franco. "Being and Time: A 'Translation' of the Nicomachean Ethics?" Translated by J. Protevi. In *Reading Heidegger from the Start*, edited by Theodore Kisiel and John Van Buren, 195–212. Albany: SUNY Press, 1994.
Welton, Donn, ed. *The New Husserl*. Bloomington: Indiana University Press, 2003.
Wolin, Richard. *The Politics of Being*. New York: Columbia University Press, 1990.
Wrede, William. *Die Echtheit des zweiten Thessalonicherbriefes untersucht*. Leipzig: J. C. Hinrichs, 1903.
Wyschogrod, Michael. *Kierkegaard and Heidegger: The Ontology of Existence*. New York: Routledge, 1954.

Zarader, Marlene. *La Dette impensée: Heidegger et l'héritage hébraïque.* Paris: Seuil, 1990.

———. *The Unthought Debt: Heidegger and the Hebraic Heritage.* Translated by Bettina Bergo. Stanford, CA: Stanford University Press, 2006.

Zimmerman, Michael E. *Heidegger's Confrontation with Modernity: Technology, Politics, and Art.* Bloomington: Indiana University Press, 1990.

Zizek, Slavoj. *The Puppet and the Dwarf: The Perverse Core of Christianity.* Cambridge, MA: MIT Press, 2003.

Zum-Brunn, Emilie. *St. Augustine: Being and Nothingness.* Translated by Ruth Namad. New York: Paragon, 1988.

INDEX

Agamben, Giorgio, 48, 232, 236–37, 254–55n64
"Anaximander's Saying" (Heidegger): Being as use or usage and, 187–88; Being in Western philosophy and, 13; care in, 187, 204; dawn of history in, 185; faith and thinking in, 215–16; *fruitio* and Being and, 197; as groundbreaking postwar text, 183–84; history and, 185; justice and injustice in, 185–86; justification and, 215; ontological difference in, 237; reemergence of Augustine in, 159, 176, 184, 188, 190–91, 193; temporality and, 191–93; title of, 184; translation and, 189–90
anxiety: advancement of analysis of, 201; Augustine's, 256n84; care and, 199; conscience and, 138; Dasein's Being and, 83–85, 130–31, 202; displacement and, 205; versus fear, 130, 255–56n74; meaning of Being and, 199; nothingness and, 130–31, 172; uncanniness and, 199; unity of existence and, 132
Aquinas, Thomas. *See* Thomas Aquinas and Thomism
Arendt, Hannah: on community in Augustine, 264n77; Heidegger criticized by, 12; on Heidegger's "Anaximander's Saying," 183–84; on Heidegger's condemnation of modern metaphysics, 209–10; on love and Augustine, 77, 125; temporality in Augustine and, 160, 168–69
Aristotle and Aristotelian thought: versus Augustine in Heidegger's thought, 11; Being and, 91–92; conception of time in, 160–61; critical retrieval of, 89–94; definition of the now and, 180; dianoetic virtues and, 116; disposition and, 257–58n115; divine intellection and, 92; *entelechy* in, 121; existence as unified action in, 120; facticity and, 93–94; the good and the limit of action and, 118; having and being-finished in, 91; Heidegger's destruction of, 117; Heidegger's early courses on, 87–88; hermeneutics and, 88, 93; movement and movedness and, 91, 92, 94; Natorp Report and, 90–91; *Nicomachaean Ethics* by, 91, 93; ontology of, 88–94, 119, 155; origins of Cartesian thought and, 7; *ousia* and property in, 91–92; *Physics* by, 162; pragmatics and, 116–17, 120–21; prudence and, 92–93; self-possession in, 122; *telos* of action in, 119–20; transposition of categories and, 94–95
Arnauld, Antoine, 252n8
Augustine and Augustinianism: aesthetic concept of truth and, 74; ambiguity and, 103–4, 260–61n73; anthropology of in Heidegger's corpus, 228; anxiety of, 256n84; versus Aristotle in Heidegger's thought, 11; Aristotle's conception of time and, 160; Augustinian quarrel and, 14; Being and, 6, 13, 64–65; Being-in and, 101–2; on benevolence, 67; care and, 72, 88, 98, 197, 215, 216, 227; carelessness and, 209; Cartesian doubt and, 57; Christian religiosity and, 53; *City of God* by, 269–70n95; *cogito* out-of-reach and,

297

Augustine and Augustinianism (continued) 121; community and, 264n77; curiosity and, 99, 103–4, 260–61n73; Dasein's Being and, 139–40; versus Descartes and Cartesian metaphysics, 14, 54, 61–62, 161, 196, 220, 225, 252n8; destruction of, 65; de-theologization and, 4–5, 7–9, 88, 94–101, 104–5, 121–23; dialectic of self-opacity and self-revelation and, 134; dispersal and gathering of the soul in, 165; *distentio animi* in, 176, 178; effect of on Husserl, 10, 18; enjoyment of God and, 269–70n95; on eschatology, 250n77; eternal conservation of the creature and, 225; on face of the heart, 66; facticity and, 224; faith and thinking and, 216–17; on fear, 68, 255n73; forgetting as a mode of retention and, 211; forgetting of Being and, 160; four types of private excellence and, 73–74; *fruitio* and Being and, 188–92, 197; Hannah Arendt on, 77; on hate, 101; having-a-self and, 62, 77; Heidegger's appropriation of Augustinian terms and, 4, 260–61n73; Heidegger's changing portrayal of concepts of, 2–3; in Heidegger's debate with Nietzsche, 198, 208; Heidegger's departure from, 87–88; Heidegger's lack of explicit post-1931 engagement with, 158; Heidegger's linking of Descartes and Nietzsche and, 211; Heidegger's philosophical categories and, 9–10; Heidegger's reconsideration of, 157–58, 159–60; Heidegger's rethinking of temporality and, 184; Heidegger's shifting debt to, 196; Helleno-Christian anthropology and, 88; idle talk and, 103–4, 260–61n73; intellectual context of, 64; justice and justification and, 221; love and, 67, 77, 101–2, 125, 255n67, 255n70; Nietzsche and, 14, 210–21; nothingness and, 55, 62; notion of self and, 55; origins of Dasein and, 176; origins of thought of, 7; as out of place in Heidegger's lineup, 2; Pelagianism and, 57; prayer and, 165, 166–67; predecessors to everydayness and, 114; proximity to and distance from God and, 78–79, 133; on proximity to ourselves, 124; questioning versus cognizant seeking in, 166; reemergence of in Heidegger's 1946 work, 159, 176; relation between life and truth and, 60; representational thinking and, 114; restraint and, 169–70; retraction and, 194, 195–96; ruinance and, 81; Scholastic ontology and, 56; on seeing God, 66–67; seeing without understanding and, 248n35; self-affection and, 129; on self as a whole, 125; on self-certainty, 54; self-consciousness and, 53, 57; self-denial and, 78; selfhood and, 61; self-idolatry and, 75, 76, 153; self-occultation and, 85; self-possession and, 73; self-reflexivity and, 75–76; self-renunciation and, 62, 76–77, 85, 122, 134, 140; self-representation and, 62, 73–76, 140, 153; soul and, 62, 78; subjective certitude of, 6; supra-ontological notion of truth and, 256n83; temporality as tripartite ecstatic structure and, 173–74; tension in Heidegger's early writings and, 4, 5; Thomas Aquinas and Thomism and, 5–6, 7, 9, 56–57; time in light of Being and, 266n7; on Trinity, 67; truth and existence for, 57; turning from God and, 100; Turn in Heidegger's thought and, 12–13; two senses of world in, 12; uncanniness and, 86; unfinding God and, 256n88; worldly ambition and, 71–74, 260–61n73. *See also* "Augustine and Neoplatonism" (Heidegger lecture); *Confessions* (Augustine)

"Augustine and Neoplatonism" (Heidegger lecture): Augustinian concepts dismissed in, 65; versus Beuron lecture, 159; categories to express existence in, 112–13; *cogito* out-of-reach in, 78, 82, 85; commentary on *Confessions* in, 62–63; content of, 54–55; disposition in, 82; enjoyment of God in, 79, 81–82; facticity in, 79–80; falling tendencies and, 96; *fruitio* in, 188–90; grace in, 79; having-oneself and, 57; Heidegger's debate with Descartes in, 85; Heidegger's frustrations with, 253–54n45; hermeneutic destruction in, 65; intuition in, 66; joy in, 69–70, 260–61n73; love in, 67; manuscript materials for, 62; Nietzsche and, 185; nothingness in, 78, 79–80, 81, 106; proximity to and distance from God in, 78–79; rest and restlessness in, 66; results generated by, 61; reversal of *cogito* and, 77, 79; ruinance in, 81–82; search for God in, 153, 217; self-interrogation in, 62, 81–82; self-representation in, 79; servile and chaste fear in, 68; similar texts to, 160; structure of Dasein's Being and, 94–95; temptation and sin in, 71–72, 95, 96

Beatitudes, 66
Being: absence of, 218; actuality and, 233, 241; anamnesis and, 210–11; anxiety and, 83–85, 172, 202; Aristotelian view of, 91–92; assignment of value and, 64–65; becoming a Christian and, 30; Being-in and, 101; as being-produced, 116; beings and, 191, 201, 206, 222, 227, 232, 235–36, 241, 277n26; being-there and, 8–9, 82; Being-towards-death and, 104, 121, 125–26, 132–34, 136, 138, 150, 177, 179; *Beyng* and, 171–76, 183, 192, 195, 202–3, 208, 222, 226, 228, 232, 237; care grounded in relation to, 204; Cartesian doubt and, 58; categories structuring, 94–95; Christianity's present, past, and future and, 42; Christian theological investigations of, 7; *cogito sum* and, 59, 252n4; of consciousness versus as presence-at-hand, 121–22; correspondence with and detachment from Dasein and, 203; Dasein and clearing of, 173; Dasein and truth of, 225; Dasein letting go of and retaining, 174–75; Dasein's interrogation of, 223; Dasein's transcendence toward, 200; Dasein's way of, 101; death of God and, 227; definition of Dasein's, 127; definition of the "I" and, 59; denial and, 271n112; de-theologization and, 122, 234–41; versus de-vivified meaning of object, 22; as difference, 230–31, 238–40, 241; distance from ourselves and, 124–25; ecstatic stretching of Dasein's, 173–74, 177, 179; ego as thinking thing and, 55–56; ego's ability to access, 84; of an entity, 83; eschatology of, 198; as the *eschaton*, 198; as the eternal, 222–23; European nihilism and, 212; existence as threat to itself and, 84–85; facticity and, 23, 27, 83; faith and, 216, 217, 224–25; finitude and infinitude and, 12, 182, 189, 191–92, 198; forfeiture of, 106; forgetting of, 6, 158–60, 173, 198, 203, 210–11, 232; *fruitio* and, 188–92, 197–98, 232; genuine being and, 276n168; Greek approach to, 90; ground and, 235; ground of Dasein's, 181; as having become, 35; Heidegger's critique of Descartes and, 6; Heidegger's 1930 turn on question of, 2; Heidegger's overhaul of, 158; Heidegger's questioning of, 221–22; Heidegger's theological roots and, 159; historical traces of, 13, 184–85, 190–91, 196, 229, 233–34, 241; holding-oneself-out toward, 199; of the inquirer, 127; insecurity of, 80; integrity of Dasein's, 131; language and, 271n4; letting-beings-be and, 181; lived experience and, 21; loss of in death, 141; meaning of, 63, 170, 177; metaphysical question of, 91, 230–31, 232; mineness and, 127–28; new questioning of, 203; nihilism and, 233; nonessence versus essence of, 171; not-Being and, 104, 105–6; as no thing, 90; nothingness and, 74, 199, 201, 210; objectification of, 271n114; objectivity and, 80, 92, 190; obstruction of Dasein's, 107–8; offering up beings to, 225, 226; onto-theology versus, 240; overhauling the question of, 229; in Pauline epistles, 36; phenomenology as science of, 219; place and, 238–39; politicization of, 199–200; possibilities for, 108, 144, 174–75; presencing of, 186–87, 188–89, 197–98, 204; the present-at-hand and, 57; primordial context of, 12, 127; reconceptualization of Dasein's, 170; as representation, 211–12; restraint and, 174; retraction and, 195, 229; reversal of *cogito* and, 56; right mode of, 119; at risk, 117–18; science of, 4; of the self, 77; self-consciousness and, 57; self-deception and, 28; from self not God, 74; self-reflexivity and, 26–27; self-representation and, 155; self-scrutiny and, 23–25; self-veiling of, 198; as self-withdrawal, 233; self-withholding of, 201–2, 206, 208–9, 211, 216, 223–24, 228, 237; source of essence of, 233; structure of Dasein's, 88, 134, 147, 155–56; *telos* of action and, 118, 119–20; temporality and, 60–61, 169, 178, 184, 191–92, 269n64; terms replacing, 232; thinkers and thinking and, 204, 207–8, 231–32, 234–36, 239, 277n5; threat to Heidegger's

Being (continued)
inquiry into, 233–35; time as unhinged and, 186; time in light of, 266n7; transformation in Dasein's way of, 160; in transit, 236; translation and, 186–87; truth of, 225, 233–34, 240; turning away from Dasein, 158; as unified whole, 125; as unthought, 231–32, 233; as use or usage, 187–88, 189; violence and, 190, 226; why-question and, 200–201; as Will, 196, 197–98, 215; withdrawal of, 171–73, 190, 196, 202, 216, 226, 231–32, 277n5; in-the-world, 127–28

Being and Time (Heidegger): anticipatory resoluteness in, 175–76; anxiety in, 83–84, 130–32, 172, 255–56n74; Augustine in Heidegger's changing philosophy and, 1–2, 105, 185–86; Augustine's Confessions and, 140, 158; Being as unified whole and, 125; Being-in in, 101–2; care in, 128, 139–40, 145, 197, 202, 203, 209; categories to express existence in, 112–13; circularity in, 50–51, 127; cognizant seeking in, 166, 170; conscience in, 137–38, 143, 145; criticism of, 159, 195, 218, 229; Dasein's facticity in, 105; Dasein's relation to its past in, 175; de-theologization in, 7, 139–40; ecstatic temporality in, 42–43, 176–78; endless revisions stimulated by, 17; engagement with historical past in, 107–8; Eternal Return in, 223; eternity in, 177–78, 182–83; everyday life in, 124; everyday understanding in, 260–61n73; existence in, 227; existential categories in, 9; falling in, 103, 106–7, 115, 122; figures of irretrievability in, 154; finitude in, 132–33, 148, 198; forsakenness and, 141–43; fruitio and, 189; fundamental standpoint of, 158–59; genealogical origins of, 188; guilt in, 10, 144–45, 152–54; Heidegger's "Anaximander's Saying" and, 184; Heidegger's attack on Nietzsche and, 226–27; inauthenticity in, 95–96, 209; incompleteness of existential analytic in, 131, 134; indwelling Spirit and, 126; integrity of Dasein's Being in, 131; Kant faulted in, 120–21; meaning of Being in, 63, 192, 225, 229; meaning of entities in, 171; 1919 War Emergency Semester and, 19; nothingness in, 104; original sin of, 224; origins of Heidegger's categories in, 4; Pelagianism and, 154; projection and, 223; questioning of Being in, 203; reference and assignment in, 155; reversal of cogito and, 53–54, 55, 79; securing the whole of Dasein in, 126–27; signs in, 135–37; structural cohesiveness of existence in, 127; temporality in, 49, 179; temptation in, 100–101; tension in Heidegger's early writings and, 4; testimony in, 134–37; thrownness in, 106, 149; Turn in Heidegger's thought and, 159, 161; unity of existence and, 155–56; use of testimony in, 11; violent interpretation and, 197, 226, 228

being-there. See Dasein

Benedictine Archabbey (Beuron, Germany), 1, 2, 157. See also Beuron lecture

Bernard of Clairvaux, 45

Best, Ernest, 41

Beuron lecture: versus "Augustine and Neoplatonism" (Heidegger lecture), 159; Augustine as foil for metaphysical tradition in, 161; changes in Heidegger's language and, 192–93; cogito and, 165; cognizant seeking in, 166; dark night of the soul in, 168; distentio versus intentio in, 174; Heidegger's Contributions to Philosophy and, 173; Heidegger's developing philosophy and, 1–2; lived experience of distention in, 267n25; originality of, 165; past, present, and future in, 167–68; prayer as questioning in, 165, 166–67, 171; restraint in, 170; temporality in, 170, 174, 183, 267n32; time and eternity in, 161–66, 168–69; Turn in Heidegger's thought and, 159–60, 166

Blochmann, Elisabeth, 157
Brown, Peter, 256n84
Bultmann, Rudolph, 194–95

call and the caller, 137–44
care: alienation and, 97; anxiety and, 199; Augustinian sources of, 215, 216; being-ness and, 203–4; versus carelessness, 208–9; care-structure and, 197, 198, 201, 203–5, 208; categories of, 98–100; as concern and solicitude, 128; Dasein as, 5; Dasein's factical situations and, 131; definitions of, 203; destruction of, 206–7, 208–10; ego and, 72; existence and, 127,

130, 169; facticity and, 80, 96; finitude of, 189; *fruitio* and, 198; futural aspect of, 126; grounded in relation to Being, 204; guilt and, 145; letting-be and, 208, 209–10; limits of, 202; movement or movedness and, 98; nullity and, 150, 156; phenomenological groundwork for, 130; presencing of beings and, 186–87; privative mode of, 203; reclamation of Augustinian index of, 227; restraint as ground of, 169–70, 173, 174; restraint versus, 158, 201–4, 222, 226; retraction and destruction of, 197–209; self-care and, 139; as *Sorge*, 187, 189, 201, 204, 209; structural manifoldness of, 132; structure of, 97–98, 100; structure of Being of, 95; suppression of, 99–100; *telos* of, 117; temporality as meaning of, 133, 156; theological origins of, 202; unity of, 127, 134–40, 145; unity of existence and, 125; unrest and, 98

Cassirer, Ernst, 79, 88, 182

Christianity: becoming a Christian and, 30, 34–36, 38, 45–46; borrowed categories in, 94; brokenness versus unity of time in, 43–44; Cistercian spirituality and, 45; corruption of Christ's message and, 249n53; cross and crucifixion in, 49; death of God and, 227; eschatological problem in, 31; existential brokenness and, 120; existential structures associated with, 229; faith versus philosophy and, 220; fractured character of Christian life and, 44; grief and affliction in, 35–36, 38–40, 42, 46–49; guilt in, 152; Heidegger's abhorrence of, 157; Heidegger's break from, 217; Heidegger's changing position on, 1–2, 3; Heidegger's idealized portrait of, 10; Heidegger's philosophical ends and, 3–4; in Heidegger's training, 3, 4; hope in, 35, 36, 38, 39; "I am" in, 152; isolation of Christian life and, 44; joy in, 35, 46; versus Judaism, 30–31; justice and justification and, 215, 221, 225; liberation from the Church and, 6–7; lived experience of religiosity and, 33; mission of Christians and, 36–37; Nietzschean critique of, 206; Nietzsche's doctrine of Eternal Return and, 227; novel idiomatic contexts for theological sources and, 158; ontological foundation of, 110; ontology versus revealed theology and, 4; origin of time and, 49; versus phenomenology, 218–19, 220; proximity to and distance from God and, 78–79; reason and, 111, 112; religiosity and, 50–52, 55; repentance in, 221–22; representational modes and, 112; temporality in, 49; transcendence and, 7

cogito: Beuron lecture and, 165; as bulwark against skepticism, 211; *cogito me cogitare* and, 75, 84, 121, 253n30; *cogito sum* and, 53–54, 252n4; Dasein and, 122; ego and, 24, 58–59, 61, 248n32; emergence of, 57; facticity and, 59; as foundation of universal science, 56–57; Heidegger's description of, 253n30; Nietzsche's reinterpretation of, 212, 215; out-of-reach, 78–79, 82, 85, 120–21, 126, 134, 140, 152–53, 164, 188, 197; reversal of, 53–61, 73, 77, 79, 165

confession: difference and, 240; facticity and, 65; fruit of, 63; ground of, 266n11; Heidegger's confession and, 240; Heidegger's *Contributions to Philosophy* and, 227–28; in Heidegger's postwar work, 195; offering up beings to Being and, 225, 226; of past versus present, 63; purpose of, 81–82; tripartite structure of, 64. See also *Confessions* (Augustine)

Confessions (Augustine): *Being and Time* (Heidegger) and, 140, 158; care in, 98–99, 170, 171, 215; circular logic and, 52; confessions of past versus present and, 63; creation in, 162; curiosity in, 96, 103–4; dangers of worldy ambition in, 72–73; disposition in, 82; enjoyment of God in, 65–66, 68–69, 76–77, 81–82, 189, 254n59, 260–61n73; falling in, 96, 103, 106; ground of confession in, 266n11; happiness and joy in, 69–70; hardening of hearts in, 99; hatred of the truth in, 100; Heidegger on importance of, 162; Heidegger on independent value of, 54; Heidegger's dismissal of eternity and, 177–78; Heidegger's 1921 seminar on, 1, 54–55; Heidegger's 1930–1931 work on, 1, 2, 158, 192–93; hermeneutic destruction and, 64–65, 254n59; intention of mind toward eternity in, 158; justification in, 215; loss of Being in, 106; memory in, 63;

Confessions (Augustine) *(continued)*
    mental representations in, 69; Neoplatonic metaphors in, 168; nihilism and, 210; ontology and, 267n32; past, present, and future in, 167; prayer in, 267n25; questionability in, 173; radical insecurity in, 69; religious core of, 62; rest and restlessness in, 66; reversed *cogito* in, 55, 73, 77; search for God in, 63–66, 68–69, 70–71, 77, 141, 160, 217, 256n85; self-interpretation and self-renunciation in, 55; self-interrogation in, 63, 70; self-possession in, 77–78; temporality in, 160, 161–66, 168–69, 210, 266n11, 267n25; temptation and sin in, 71, 72–73, 95, 96–97, 105; Turn in Heidegger's thought and, 160; unrest and, 98; vanity in, 106; what the *Confessions* are not and, 161. *See also* confession
conscience, 137–44, 151, 154
Contributions to Philosophy (Heidegger): Augustinian *distentio animi* in, 176; Being as that which retracts and, 195; Being versus beings in, 201, 206, 222; Beuron lecture and, 173; *Beyng* in, 228, 237; changes in Heidegger's language and, 193; confession of sin and, 227–28; Dasein in, 13, 203, 208; derangement of temporal becoming and, 186; Descartes versus Augustine in, 225; de-theologization of repentance in, 222; Eternal Return in, 223–24, 225; faith and thinking in, 215–17; faith versus philosophy and, 220; figures recognized in, 217; Heidegger's 1930–1931 reading of Augustine and, 159; justice and justification in, 215, 222, 225; last god in, 175; meaning of entities in, 171; metaphysical theology and, 227; renunciation in, 180, 202; repentance in, 225; restraint in, 170, 202, 203; retraction in, 199; retrieval in, 222, 225; temporality in, 174–77, 183–84, 191–93; violence to ideal of resoluteness in, 226
Cusanus, 248n35

Dasein: anxiety and, 83–84, 130–31, 138, 172, 199, 202; Aristotelian pragmatics and, 117; Augustinian origins of, 4, 11; authentic selfhood of, 133; being-gone and, 119; Being interrogated by, 223; Being-in-the-world and, 104, 142, 143; as Being-in-the-world versus innerworldly entities, 128, 129–30; as being-limited, 118–19; Being of an entity and, 83; Being of as far from itself, 139–40; Being turning away from, 158; Being versus beingness and, 204; Being versus beings and, 235–36; being-with-one-another and, 260–61n73; *Beyng* and, 192, 228; as caller, called, and content of the called, 140–41, 143; care and, 5, 158, 169, 170, 173, 199; categorical determination of, 120; in Christian and Heideggerian texts, 5; circularity and, 50–51; clearing of Being and, 173; *cogito* and, 122, 153; conscience and, 137–38, 142–43, 144; correspondence with and detachment from Being and, 203; *Da-* of, 161; death as end of, 132–33; death as outmost possibility of, 119; death of God and, 226; deceased, 143; definition of, 60–61, 121; definition of Being of, 127; destruction of Augustinian origins of, 176; de-theologization and, 122; displacement and, 13, 205, 207–8; disposition and, 82, 257–58n115; distance from ourselves and, 124–25; distancing and, 102; ecstatic dimensions of, 216; ecstatic stretching of Being of, 173–74, 177, 179; enjoyment of God and, 269–70n95; equiprimordial characteristics of, 129–30; Eternal Return and, 223–24; everydayness and, 103–4, 260–61n73; existence as threat to itself and, 84–85; existential constitution of, 104–5, 106, 115; facticity and, 29, 60, 63, 74–75, 90, 102, 131, 219, 226; faith and, 216, 223; falling and, 103–5, 106–7, 147, 260–61n73; as far from itself, 144; finitude and, 12, 60–61, 121–23, 182, 190; forfeiture of Being of, 106; forgetting and, 175, 210–11; forsakenness and, 140–41, 142–43; free appropriation of, 220; *fruitio* and, 189–90, 198; the good and, 117–18; grace and, 82; ground of Being of, 181; as guilty, 145–46, 150, 151, 152–53, 155; having-a-self and, 63–64, 74–75; Heidegger's construction of, 19–20; Heidegger's overhaul of, 158; Heidegger's reevaluation of Descartes and, 53–54; history of metaphysics and, 175; indwelling Spirit and, 82; intentionality and, 117; in and for itself, 23; last god and, 175; letting go of and retaining Being and, 174–75; lived experience and, 23; madness and, 205, 206–8; in man, 232; mineness and, 127–28; mood and, 129; negation and, 149–50, 203, 207, 209; new beginning of philosophy after Nietzsche and, 208; new questioning of Being and, 203; non-uniformity of, 129; not-Being and, 104, 105–6; nothingness and, 79, 83, 210; as object of philosophical research, 8; obstruction of Being of, 107–8; as one who turns back, 223–24; as outside of itself, 128; potentiality-for-Being and, 108, 134–37, 144, 148–49, 152, 156, 175; the present-at-hand and, 101–2, 135–38, 148–49; primordial ontology of, 156; primordial truth and, 138–39; reason for existence of, 120–21; reconceptualization of Being of, 170; refiguring of, 196–97; repetition of the past and, 108; restraint and, 13, 171, 174, 229; right mode of Being of, 119; ruinance and, 81; salvation and, 224; as a self, 128; self-deception and, 28–29; self-denial and, 202; self-distortion and, 90; self-reflexivity and, 75–76, 82; self-renunciation and, 195, 201; self-representation and, 155; self-showing of, 9; self-understanding of, 63, 219; self-veiling of Being and, 198; self-withholding of Being and, 202, 216; *Seyn* and, 195; signs and testimony and, 135–37; silent approach to, 208; sociality and, 129, 146; specificity of, 179; as steward of stillness, 268n46; structure of Being of, 88, 94–95, 147, 155–56; *telos* of action and, 118, 119–20; temporality and, 174, 176, 191–92; temptation and, 101; thrownness and, 105, 147–50, 151, 154; time as, 178–79; together with Being, 237; transcendence of toward Being, 200; truth of Being and, 225; truth of beings as a whole and, 222; uncanniness and, 86, 131, 138–39, 141; as unified whole, 125–26; unity of, 60–61, 144, 155; unity of existence and, 140; violence to Being of, 226; violent presentation of, 197; way of Being of, 101, 160; the whole of, 126–27, 130–31, 136, 139, 140; "who" of, 128–30; withdrawal of Being and, 226; as in-the-world, 101–3, 118; world as component of, 96–97

Davos debate, 182
death: anticipation of, 133–34; Being-towards-death and, 104, 121, 125–26, 132–34, 136, 138, 150, 177, 179; dead as species of the living and, 142; as end of Dasein, 132–33; forsakenness and, 141–42; guilt and, 152; loss-of-Being and, 141–42; mourning and, 142–44; versus totality of existence, 132
Deissmann, Paul, 30
Derrida, Jacques, 177, 269n64
Descartes, René, and Cartesianism: as *alter ego* of Cartesian subject, 154; Augustine and, 161, 196, 220, 225, 252n8; Being of an entity and, 83; certainty and, 221; Dasein as *alter ego* of Cartesian subject and, 154; destruction of the *res cogitans* and, 59; doubt and, 57–58; ego and, 83; fundamental cognition of God and, 252n19; God as self-caused and, 237; having-a-self and, 62; Heidegger's analysis of, 6; Heidegger's linking of Nietzsche to, 211, 220, 221; Heidegger's misinterpretation of, 253n30; Heidegger's reevaluation of, 53–61, 84; Heidegger's strenuous attacks on, 122; irruption of ego and, 165; Nietzsche and, 215–16; Pelagianism and, 76, 120, 154, 196, 215, 225; present-at-hand ego and, 252–53n20; *regula generalis* and, 154; respectiveness and, 59; search for certainty and, 71; self-certainty and, 211–12, 213–14; self-consciousness and, 75, 85; subjectivity and, 196, 197; substantialist accounts of the self and, 114; truth and certitude and, 153. See also *cogito*; *res cogitans*
de-theologization: anticipation of death and, 134; Augustine and, 12–14, 158; Augustinian terms and, 99, 101, 104–5, 121–22, 158, 193; Being and, 234–41; borrowing of theological categories and, 115; confirmation of, 240–41; conscience and, 144; continuity in process of, 108–9; creation of central categories in, 95, 113, 114–15; deity in philosophy in, 240; by Descartes, 4–5; destruction of religious texts and, 112–13; facticity and, 113; framework of, 120; *fruitio* and, 189; Heidegger's lack of reflection on, 110; Heidegger's later work and, 158, 159;

de-theologization (continued)
    Heidegger's motivation for, 107; Heidegger's politics and, 195; Heidegger's Turn and, 156; holding-oneself-out toward Being and, 199; inauthenticity and, 95–96; incompleteness of existential analytic and, 131; justification and, 215; language of, 9–10; logic of, 107–15, 172, 229, 234; manipulation of de-theologized terms and, 229–30; meaning of Being and, 170; metaphysical theology and, 227; metaphysics as accomplice to, 6; nothingness and, 104; philosophy of religion and, 15; refiguring of Dasein and, 197; of repentance, 221–22; repetition and retrieval and, 108–9; stakes of, 110, 118, 237; temporality and, 18, 184; as term, 7–8; transposition and, 230; twofold enigma of, 107; unity of care and, 139–40; violence and, 226–27
de Vries, Hent, 250n77
Dilthey, Wilhelm, 19, 62

Eckhart, Meister, 44, 87, 191, 208, 209–10
ego. *See* self
eschatology: Antichrist and, 46; awaiting the parousia and, 30–32, 34–42, 45–47, 68, 78, 250n81; delay of the parousia and, 35, 37, 40–41, 46–49; eschatological longing and, 250n81; eschatological problem and, 27–34; guilt and, 79, 134, 152; kairos and, 42–43; *katechon* and, 40–41, 46; nothingness and, 152; as problem in Christianity, 37–38; representational ideation and, 38, 250n77; self-occultation and, 39; temporality and, 29, 33–34, 41–43, 47; timing of Second Coming and, 31
everydayness, 103–4, 106, 114, 128–30, 260–61n73
experience. *See* lived experience

facticity: anticipatory resoluteness and, 226; Aristotle and Aristotelian thought and, 93–94; Being and, 23, 27; the caller and, 143; care and, 80, 96; categories of everydayness and, 114; circumspection and, 96; *cogito* and, 59; confession and, 65; conscience and, 143, 144; curiosity and, 96; Dasein and, 29, 60, 63, 90, 102, 131, 219; destruction of religious texts and Western categories and, 112–13; de-theologization and, 113; distancing and, 101; enjoyment of God and, 254n59; face of the heart and, 254–55n64; falling and, 96–97, 105; guilt and, 147; having-a-self and, 71, 74–75; hermeneutics of, 91; "I" and, 83; internal and external world and, 99; lived experience and, 23, 28, 29, 33; nothingness and, 78, 79–83, 86, 106; obfuscation of in Greek metaphysics, 90–91; objectivity and, 80; ontology and, 59; practical truth and, 116–17; the present-at-hand and, 224; questioning of, 82; self and, 59–60, 62; structure of factical existence and, 220; thrownness and, 105, 148, 149; uncanniness and, 85; whole of, 129; worldly content of, 101
faith: Heidegger's exclusion then reintroduction of, 224–25; holding-for-true and, 226; Nietzsche's definition of, 218; thinking and, 215–16. *See also* Christianity; religion
falling: in *Being and Time* (Heidegger), 106–7, 115, 122; Dasein and, 103–5, 106–7, 147, 260–61n73; facticity and, 96–97, 105; guilt and, 147; temptation and sin and, 103–4, 105, 260–61n73
Faye, Emmanuel, 253n30
fear: versus anxiety, 130, 255–56n74; chaste versus servile, 67, 255–56n74; enjoyment of God and, 68; love and, 67; worldly ambition and, 72–73
Fichte, Johann Gottlieb, 111
Freud, Sigmund, 104, 113–15

George, Stefan, 201–2
German Idealist tradition, 111–12
Gordon, Peter, 88
grace, 45–46, 67, 79, 81, 82
guilt: care and, 145; conscience and, 151; Dasein as guilty and, 12–13, 145–46, 150, 151, 155; death and, 152; definition of, 146–47; eschatology and, 79, 134, 152; inexpiable, 152; the irretrievable and, 144–54; latency of, 151; negation and, 146–47, 150–51; nothingness and, 146, 152; Paul's, 37–38; Pelagianism and, 154; philosophy versus religiosity and, 10; as predicate of the "I am," 152–53; temporality and, 40, 49, 50; truncated meaning of, 153; unity of existence and, 155

Harnack, Adolph, 62
Harries, Karsten, 12

INDEX

Hegel, G. W. F., and Hegelian dialectics: on Christianity and reason, 111; crucifixion and, 49; Descartes's subjective certitude and, 6; end of philosophy and, 89; God and man and, 161; Heidegger's distancing from, 234; history's possibilities and, 185; religion and representational modes and, 112
Heidegger, Martin: acknowledgment of Christian theological sources and, 158–59; Augustine in developing philosophy of, 1–2; being-historical treatises of, 170; "Black Notebooks" of, 195; Christianity in training of, 3, 4, 243n14; confession in postwar work of, 195; confrontation of with Christianity, 1–2, 3; continuity and discontinuity of corpus of, 228; continuity with theological sources and, 113; disturbance in regress of, 115–22; dream of acceding to Being directly and, 241–42; on dying and "I am," 263n35; Edmund Husserl's relationship with, 246–47n7; German *Volk* and, 199–200; hermeneutical presuppositions of, 95; hermeneutical regress toward Aristotle and, 115; on irretrievability of human existence, 12; versus Kant on religion and reason, 110–13; as lodestar of hermeneutic phenomenology, 122; medieval Christian texts abandoned by, 87; Nazi politics and, 194, 195, 209; near-dismissal of from University of Freiburg, 194; 1919 War Emergency Semester course of, 19–27, 29, 33–34, 39, 44–45, 50, 54, 75; ontological foundation of, 110; phenomenology of religious life and, 5; philosophical goal of, 109–10; philosophy of as disguised theology, 107; political implications of philosophy of, 194–95; *religion* as term for, 8; religious vocabulary of, 95, 97–98; rethinking of divinity, holiness, and piety by, 241; self-assessment of, 13–14, 17; as self-styled spiritual revolutionary, 157; spiritual and intellectual development of, 157; tension in early writings of, 4; *theology* as term for, 8. *See also* Turn in Heidegger's thought; *and Heidegger's major works*
hermeneutics: Aristotelian versus phenomenological, 93; of facticity, 91; generation of hermeneutic categories and, 114; Heidegger as lodestar of hermeneutic phenomenology and, 122; Heidegger's nascent hermeneutic method and, 55; Heidegger's presuppositions and, 95; hermeneutic circle and, 50; hermeneutic destruction and, 11–12, 28–29, 45, 64–65, 88, 90–91, 93, 149, 195, 203, 254n59; intuition and, 19–27, 30, 33, 248n38; negation of Dasein and, 209; phenomenology as, 20; precondition of ontological inquiry and, 50; religiosity versus, 10; self-interpretation as, 25; as self-interpretation of Dasein, 63; theologemes and, 120
history: as becoming-in-time, 33; as highest object of religion, 20; object-historical versus absolute-historical, 38–39; philosophy of religion and, 50; temporality and, 28
Hölderlin, Friedrich, 172, 191, 207, 216–17, 241
Holy Spirit, 35, 36, 47, 48
Homer, 204–5
Husserl, Edmund: on Augustine and temporality, 161–62; on Being, 90; Being of an entity and, 83; Cartesian metaphysics and, 10, 18; *cogito* and, 24–25, 248n32; on ego, 39; end of philosophy and, 89; generalization versus formalization and, 25; on Heidegger and Christianity, 1–2; Heidegger's relationship with, 246–47n7; hermeneutic intuition and, 248n38; intentionality and, 117; on phenomenological reduction, 20; phenomenology of, 89–90; praise for Augustine by, 245n41; on seeing without understanding, 26, 248n35; on self-givenness of essences, 26; shortcomings of phenomenology of, 18; study of research and, 89; transcendental reduction and, 24, 26; on truth, 27

Introduction to Phenomenological Research (Heidegger): Augustinian question in, 87; Cartesian doubt in, 57–58; destruction of the *res cogitans* and, 60, 61; Heidegger's reevaluation of Descartes and, 84, 153; philosophy's demise and, 89; pre-question of Being in, 200, 202; rupture in, 200
"Introduction to the Phenomenology of Religion" (Heidegger): circular logic of, 50; guilt of Christians and, 79; Heidegger's phenomenological method and, 27–28;

"Introduction to the Phenomenology of Religion" (Heidegger) (continued)
Heidegger's reevaluation of Descartes and, 54; hermeneutic destruction and, 29; 1 and 2 Thessalonians in, 30, 31–32, 79; phenomenological gaze and, 32–33; religiosity in, 50; spirituality in, 44–45; temporality in, 49
intuition: hermeneutics and, 26–27, 30, 33, 248n38; restlessness and, 66; seeing without understanding and, 26, 248n35

Jaspers, Karl, 23, 253–54n45
joy and happiness: despair versus, 46, 48–49; Holy Spirit and, 35; mental representations and, 69; in truth, 69–70, 260–61n73

Kant, Immanuel, and Kantianism: Being of an entity and, 83; Being-towards-death and, 121; on *cogito*, 24; *Critique of Pure Reason* by, 162; Dasein and, 120–21; definition of the "I" and, 59; displacement and, 208; disposition and, 257–58n115; ego and, 83; human as end-in-itself and, 121; human infinitude and, 182; on madness, 207; on philosophy and biblical theology, 110–11, 112; reason and revelation and, 15; time as self-affection and, 179–81; transcendental and empirical ego and, 59–60
Kierkegaard, Søren, 207
Kisiel, Theodore, 19

Leibniz, Gottfried, 200
Levinas, Emmanuel, 14, 168, 256n83, 267n32
lived experience: actualization of, 248n29; of Christian religiosity, 33; concreteness of, 21–22; of distention, 267n25; facticity and, 23, 28, 29, 33; founding interconnections of, 22–23; generalization versus formalization and, 25–26; happy life and, 69–70; internal and external world and, 99; intuition and, 66; objectification of, 248n26; pre-theoretical level and, 22–23, 26, 54; primordial bearing of, 27; the psychic and, 22; self-understanding and, 26–27; unity of, 19; worry and, 24
love, 66–67, 70, 72–73, 77, 255nn69–71
Löwith, Karl, 53, 160, 204
Luther, Martin, 215

Marburg Theological Society, 163–64, 177
Marion, Jean-Luc, 14, 257n94, 266n11
metaphysics: absence of divinities in, 171; Augustine and, 62, 64–65; correspondence between Dasein and Being and, 203; determination of a human's being and, 56; de-theologization and, 7, 172, 230; exiting, 110; forgetting of Being and, 198; ground of beings and, 230; Heidegger's attempts to overcome, 15; Heidegger's destruction of, 84; Heidegger's distancing from, 13, 241; history of, 171, 175, 196, 233–34; history of Being and, 241; liberation of time from, 176–77; metaphysical theology and, 227–28; Nietzsche on critique of, 207; as nihilistic pursuit of power, 209; objectivity and, 190; ontological source of notness and, 151; onto-theology and, 230–36, 240; origins of Heidegger's criticism of, 91; origins of theology and, 239; overcoming of, 242; Pelagianism and, 57; Plotinian, 64; as question of Being, 230–31; resignification in Heidegger's critique of, 159; reversing ill effects of, 11; rudiments of Heidegger's critique of, 6; self-certainty and, 211–12, 213–14; transposition and, 230–34; truth and, 215; why-question and, 200–201; worldview and, 20. *See also* Descartes, René, and Cartesianism
Metzger, Paul, 41, 47
morality and moral perfection, 110–12
mysticism, 45
Myth of Er, 209

Natorp Report: Aristotelian thought and, 90–94; categories of care in, 96–98
Neoplatonism. *See* "Augustine and Neoplatonism" (Heidegger lecture)
Nietzsche, Friedrich: Augustine and, 198, 208, 210–21; Being as Will and, 196, 197–98, 215; Christian Platonism and, 197; contemplation of Being and, 207; critique of Christianity by, 206; the dead and the living and, 142; death of God and, 7, 161, 205–6, 213–14, 227, 239; definition of faith and, 218; Descartes and, 6, 14, 215–16; de-theologization and, 227; end of philosophy and, 89; essence of modern scientific technology and, 207, 212, 233; on eternalization, 223;

Eternal Recurrence or Return and, 212–13, 217–18, 220–25, 227, 231; force and, 211; Heidegger's attack on thought of, 185, 196, 220, 226–27; Heidegger's debate with, 193; Heidegger's invocation of faith against, 218; Heidegger's linking of Descartes to, 211, 220, 221; Heidegger's rejection of, 229; history of metaphysics and, 196; history's possibilities and, 185; justice and justification and, 215, 220–22, 225; as last metaphysician, 14, 230, 233; madman of, 205–6; Martin Luther and, 215; metaphysics and, 207, 227; on mummified god, 238; nihilism and, 205–6, 207, 211, 212, 227; as onto-theologian, 230; Overman and, 206; on Paul, 249n53; reason reduced to life and, 225; redefinition of religion by, 220; on revenge, 213; on strangers to ourselves, 124; temporal becoming and, 186; on truth, 213–15; value and values and, 205, 206, 207, 211, 225; Will to Power and, 197–98, 206–7, 211–14, 217–18, 223, 227, 231

nothingness: anxiety and, 130–31, 172; Augustine and, 55, 62; Being and, 74, 198, 199, 201, 210; Cartesian doubt and, 58; creature before God and, 78; of Dasein, 79, 83; everydayness and, 106; facticity and, 78, 79–83, 86, 106; guilt and, 146, 152; manifestations of, 104; ontology and, 164, 198–99; ruinance and, 80–81; self-nullification and, 80–81; of soul before God, 76; thrownness and, 106; uncanniness and, 84–85

ontology: Aristotelian, 88–94; Being of the self and, 77; of Dasein, 156; Descartes and, 56; dismantling of history of, 115; distance from ourselves and, 124; facticity and, 59; faith excluded from, 224–25; foundation of Christianity and Heidegger's thought, 110; the good and, 120; Heidegger's destructive regress toward, 89, 90; homogeneity versus non-homogeneity and, 130; negation and, 150–51; nothingness and, 198–99; notness and, 156; ontological poverty and, 164; preeminent being and, 276n168; reference and assignment and, 155; regress to Aristotle and, 122; reopening of inquiry into, 54; repetition and retrieval and, 222; retraction and, 195; stakes of de-theologization and, 118; supra-ontological notion of truth and, 256n83; theological origins of Heidegger's, 158; theology and, 234–35, 239–40, 241; thrownness and, 154–55; transposition and, 241; turned against itself, 86; understanding of God and, 267n32

Origen, 250n77
Ott, Hugo, 157, 194–95
Overbeck, Franz, 30

parousia. *See* eschatology
Pascal, Blaise, 87, 98, 101, 129, 209
Paul and Paul's epistles: apostolic life in, 45; authenticity of 2 Thessalonians and, 47; authorship disputes and, 30; Being in, 36; despair versus joy in, 46, 48–49; de-theologization and, 122–23; divine guidance and, 79; eschatology in, 27–30, 33–40, 47–48, 78, 134, 152; faith as dying with Christ in, 41–42, 43; guilt and, 134, 152; Heidegger's motivation for reading, 29–30; Heidegger's philosophical categories and, 12; hermeneutic destruction and, 28; Judaism and, 30–31; kairos in, 42–44; *katechon* in, 40–41, 43, 46–47, 48, 153; life's dominant structure in, 29; man of lawlessness, or Antichrist, in, 40–41; mind of Christ in, 32; nature of proclamation and, 34; Nietzsche on Paul and, 249n53; Paul as type for crucified Christ and, 49; Pauline "I" and, 40–49; Paul's guilt in, 37–38; Paul's worry in, 40; phenomenological understanding of, 33; proximity to and distance from God and, 78; recent philosophical treatment of, 48; religiosity versus hermeneutics and, 10; restraint in, 169; self-consciousness and, 19; self-renunciation and, 76–77, 122; spirit and spirituality in, 44–46, 48–49, 82; standing firm in, 42; temporality and, 18–19, 61; tension in Heidegger's early writings and, 4–5; uncanniness and, 86; unity of Christian belief and practice and, 28. *See also* Christianity

Pelagianism: Cartesian metaphysics and, 57, 154; of Descartes, 76, 120, 154, 196, 215, 225; guilt and, 154; theoretical knowing and, 56 phenomenology: Aristotelian versus phenomenological hermeneutics and, 93; Being and, 90; care in, 130; versus Christian theology, 218–19, 220; critique of representational modes and, 112; as descriptive science of consciousness, 114; emergence of research and, 89; Heidegger as lodestar of hermeneutic phenomenology and, 122; as hermeneutics, 20; Husserlian, 89–90; intentionality and, 117; nature of phenomenological description and, 32; of nullity, 156; objectivity of the object and, 89; phenomenological destruction and, 28–29; of religion, 17–19, 27–28; religiosity versus hermeneutics and, 10; of religious life, 229; as science of Being, 219; as science of the historical, 20; theologemes and, 115; uncanniness and, 86; understanding of religiosity and, 32

philosophy: as antagonistic with religion, 109; asceticism of, 109, 110; being-historical thinking and, 216, 234; borrowings from biblical theology in, 110–11; *causa sui* in, 237–38; deity's entrance into, 237–40; destructive historical research and, 11; earliest traces of Being in, 13; end of, 89, 110, 216–17; faith excluded from, 224–25; as hermeneutics, 8; introspection in, 129; main task of, 198; new beginning of after Nietzsche, 208; as primordial science, 21; of religion, 8–10, 14–15, 18, 50–51, 229, 241–42; religiosity and, 50; residues of Christian theology and, 113; secularized theological concepts in, 6; self-obstruction in, 28–29; theology expunged from, 88, 229; versus theology for Heidegger, 12, 218, 220; transposition and, 230–31; worldview in, 20

Plato and Platonism: anamnesis and, 210–11; Augustine and, 64; Heidegger and Nietzsche's rejection of, 197; justice and justification and, 215, 225; Nietzsche's doctrine of Eternal Recurrence and, 212; origins of Cartesian thought and, 7; place in, 239

Plotinianism, 64, 66–67
Pöggeler, Otto, 29
pragmatics, 117, 120–21

prayer, 165, 167–69, 171, 267n25
primordial sphere, 21, 27, 247n19
psychic sphere, 22, 247n19

questioning: Being versus beings as such and, 201; as cognizant seeking, 166; definition of the question and, 166; new questioning of Being and, 203; prayer as, 165; pre-question of Being and, 200, 202; why-question and, 200–201

reason: Being at risk and, 117–18; conscience and, 119–20; morality and, 111; ontotheology versus, 240; rationality versus thinking and, 220; reduced to life, 225; religion and representational modes and, 110–13; revelation and, 15; structure of rational inquiry and, 166; *telos* of action and, 117, 120

religion: borrowings from in philosophy, 111; guilt and, 152; Heidegger's portrayal of religious life and, 152–53; Nietzsche's doctrine of Eternal Return and, 217–18, 220; as penultimate stage in progression toward self-knowing, 112; phenomenology of religious life and, 229; philosophy of, 8–12, 14–15, 18, 50–51, 229, 241–42; reason and, 111; representational modes and, 112; as term, 8. *See also* Christianity; faith; theology

res cogitans: *cogito me cogitare* and, 121, 253n30; destruction of, 59–60, 61; present-at-hand ego and, 54, 77, 257n98

restraint: absence of Being and, 172–73; care versus, 158, 201, 202, 203–4, 222, 226; determinations of Dasein and, 229; displacement and, 202, 204; double function of, 171–72; as ground of care, 169–70, 173; madness and, 204–5; self-renunciation and, 202; Turn in Heidegger's thought and, 173, 193

retraction: Augustine's, 194–96; destruction of care and, 197–209; determinations of Being and, 229; Heidegger's thematization of, 195–96, 199; Rudolph Bultmann's challenge to Heidegger and, 194–95

Ricoeur, Paul, 267n25
Rilke, Rainer Maria, 209
Rojcewicz, Richard, 271n4
ruinance, 80–81, 84, 86

Schelling, Friedrich Wilhelm Joseph, 111
Schiller, Friedrich, 207
Schmitt, Carl, 6, 41, 48
Schurmann, Reiner, 214
self: ability of to access Being, 84; Augustine's lack of term for, 55; authenticity and, 129; Being of, 77; being-questionable and, 61, 78; care and, 72; *cogito* and, 24, 58–59, 61, 248n32; consciousness unified by the ego and, 39; Dasein as, 128; Dasein's authentic selfhood and, 133; dialectic of self-opacity and self-revelation and, 134; distance from ourselves and, 124; ego as thinking thing and, 55–56; endangerment and, 78–79; facticity and, 59–60, 62, 71, 74–75, 83; fractured, 125–26; having-a-self and, 59, 61–64, 71–72, 74–75, 77; having-oneself-with-oneself and, 121; Husserlian phenomenology and, 89–90; irruption of ego and, 165; objectivization of, 75; out-for-something and, 58–59; place of, 257n94; presence-to-self and, 179; present-at-hand ego and, 54, 252–53n20; resonance and, 25, 26; reversal of *cogito* and, 56; search for God and, 63; seeing God and, 67; self-affection and, 58–59, 129–30, 179–81; self-care and, 139; self-certainty and, 211–12, 213–14; self-consciousness and, 59–60, 85; self-dispossession and, 39; self-doubt and, 58, 60; self-idolatry and, 75, 76, 153; self-interrogation and, 62, 81–82, 84, 85; self-legislation and, 6–7; self-nullification and, 80–81; self-occultation and, 39, 85; self-possession and, 122; self-reflection and, 74–75; self-reflexivity and, 39–40, 75–76, 82; self-renunciation and, 62, 76–77, 85, 122, 134, 140, 188–89, 195, 197, 201–2; self-representation and, 59, 62, 75–76, 140, 153, 155; self-understanding of life and, 26–27; self-withholding and, 195, 271n4; self-world and, 74; temptation and sin and, 71; transcendental and empirical ego and, 59–60; uncanny, 139; as unified whole, 125; worldly ambition and, 72–73, 74
Simmel, Georg, 7
sin. *See* temptation and sin
Stambaugh, Joan, 236

Stock, Brian, 55
Stoicism, 64

temporality and time: Augustine and, 160, 161–66, 168–69, 178; becoming and, 49–50; Being of, 178; of Christian spiritual life, 49; confession and, 266n11; constancy and, 180–81, 183; cruciform, 49; dark night of the soul and, 168; Dasein as time and, 178–79; Dasein's being and, 127; definition of Dasein and, 60–61; definition of the now and, 180, 181; derangement of temporal becoming and, 186; desire to know time and, 165; ecstatic stretching and, 176–78, 182, 186; eschatology and, 29, 33–34, 41–43, 47; Eternal Recurrence or Return and, 212–13, 224; eternity and, 167, 176–78, 182–83, 222–23; finitude and infinitude and, 169, 175–76, 183; forgetting and, 210; *fruitio* and, 191–92; guilt and, 40, 49, 50; in Heidegger's being-historical treatises, 170; Heidegger's 1924 lecture on, 60–61; history and, 28; "I am" and, 50; *lectio divina* and, 168; liberation of from metaphysics, 176–77; as meaning of care, 133, 156; measurement of passage of time and, 178; nothingness and, 152; origins of time and, 49; past, present, and future and, 167, 177; in Paul's epistles, 18–19, 61; presence-to-self and, 179; primordial, 177–78, 183, 191, 269n64; primordial ontology of Dasein and, 156; renunciation and, 180; restraint and, 169; rethinking of in Heidegger's middle period, 176; silent questioning and, 168; structure of, 229; subjectivity of time and, 271n116; as theological question, 182–83; time as *distentio* and, 163, 166–67; time as prayer and, 168; time as self affection and, 179–81; time as the *to-god* and, 168; time in light of Being and, 266n7; as tripartite ecstatic structure, 173–74, 177; understanding of God and, 267n32; without duration, 192
temptation and sin: falling and, 96–97, 103–4, 105, 260–61n73; having-a-self and, 71; Heidegger's religious vocabulary and, 95, 97; translation of temptation and, 100–104

Tertullian, 41
testimony, 134–39
theology: apophatic, 39–40; Kant on, 110–11, 112; metaphysics and, 227–28, 231, 239; as ontic science, 219–20; ontology and, 234–35, 239–40, 241; onto-theology and, 230–31; origins of, 239; phenomenology versus, 218–19, 220; philosophy and, 12, 107, 110–11, 113, 218, 220; revealed, 230–31; as term, 8. *See also* Christianity; de-theologization; religion
Theophrastus, 185
Thomas Aquinas and Thomism, 5–6, 7, 9, 56–57, 152
Thomson, Iain, 207
thrownness: conscience and, 151, 154; Dasein and, 105, 147–50, 151, 154, 223; facticity and, 105, 148, 149; guilt and, 147–48; Heidegger's invalidation of, 148–49, 155–56; irretrievability and, 154; negation and, 149–50; nothingness and, 106; versus possibility, 130; precursors to, 35; self-occultation and, 154–55
Trakl, Georg, 191
Troeltsch, Ernst, 62
truth: aesthetic concept of, 74; of Being, 225, 233–34, 240; of beings as a whole, 222, 228; correspondence theory of, 213; existence and, 56–57; experience and, 20; forgetting of, 6; holding-for-true and, 226; joy in, 69–70, 260–61n73; justice and justification and, 214–15, 220–22, 223; life and, 225; love of, 70; objectivity and, 27; primordial, 138–39; steadfastness in, 217; supra-ontological notion of, 256n83; unity of existence and, 140
Turn in Heidegger's thought: author's unorthodox approach to, 159; Beuron lecture and, 159–60, 166; confirmation of earlier interpretations of, 272n14; Heidegger's self-description of, 173; Heidegger's theological roots and, 159; hermeneutic destruction and, 195; relativization of, 197; renunciation in, 193; restraint in, 173, 193; retraction and, 194–95; return to Augustine and, 12–13, 158; temporality and, 160; texts documenting, 159–61; timing of, 171

Vallega-Neu, Daniela, 271n4
van Gogh, Vincent, 207

Windelband, Wilhelm, 20
Wrede, William, 30